"Here is a sweet backward glance at those who worshiped in a unique Christian fellowship. Perry Cotham's portraits of these church folk include accounts of stern sermons and sometimes sour singing, but of pure and hopeful hearts as well. He makes us laugh at the eccentricities of some, yet wish we could have sat in the pews beside others. In an age of sophisticated congregations and mega-churches, this book is pleasantly nostalgic. It is also wickedly funny. My favorite chapter is the one focusing on the *a capella* efforts and adventures of congregational singing. If your church heritage is not at all similar to the church Perry describes, you might find yourself a bit relieved, yet wishing it were."

--**James W. Thomas,** Professor of English, Pepperdine University, author of *Repotting Harry Potter*

"Dr. Perry Cotham's latest book on life among the saints in the Church of Christ is sure to warm hearts and bring laughter to all who love the body of Christ. He recalls his days from early childhood in the church and through his many years of service among us, bringing a healthy perspective on our strengths and our foibles as we walk together toward eternity. With the perspective of years, he helps us laugh at ourselves and be grateful all over again for grace that covers a multitude of sins. With respect and humor, he shows us that we stand on the shoulders of giants who, like us, had feet of clay. By all means, read this book!"

--**Nan Gurley,** Singer, Writer, Actor, Author of three published children's books

"The ability to laugh at our foibles and not take ourselves too seriously is one of the most important attributes we can possess to get us through life with minimum stress. God must have a sense of humor and appreciates those in his creation who have one. Many of our most revered leaders, both in government and in the church, maintained a healthy sense of humor. Perry Cotham is a master at identifying the humor in what we sometimes take too seriously. I can imagine St. Peter greeting Perry at the Pearly Gates by saying, "'Welcome. By the way, God loved your book on Church of Christ humor.'"

--**Fletcher Srygley,** retired Professor of Physics, Lipscomb University

"In reading some of the early chapters in *Please Don't Revive Us Again*, I felt that Perry had written my own autobiography as a young aspiring preacher—the influence of wonderful Christian men at David Lipscomb College, our anxieties as young preachers, and the descriptions of small rural churches we served. Perry narrates numerous funny events that happened in churches, some embarrassing, some seemingly irreverent, and even some sad and sobering ones, too. Yet one senses he respects those men and women of his church family whom he felt privileged to serve. Additionally, he offers much sound advice for young preachers, following the model of those who influenced him in his own youth."

-- **Sam McFarland,** Professor Emeritus, Department of Psychology, Western Kentucky University.

"Dr. Perry Cotham has the unique and refreshing, though paradoxical, ability to be "in" the Church of Christ (in the sense of an open, inclusive, and seekers' fellowship) but not "of" it (in the sense of a narrow, exclusive, sectarian group of believers). He honors and delights in its many faithful followers, while also appreciating both their creative gospel interpretations and the important truths of the Scriptures to which they so faithfully adhere. Perry can laugh and call out idiosyncrasies without being critical or judgmental. He narrates story after story with humor and understanding, mixed with a bit of perplexity. He clearly is a lover of Christ and his church and the brothers and sisters who compose it. This book will bring to mind many memories and incidents that both unite and delight. Hopefully, it will soften the hearts of those who have never understood the Church of Christ tradition while making those in that fellowship feel justifiably proud. Thank you, Perry, for making what is all too often a source of debate and division, and turning it on its head to bring light and laughter and the true Spirit of Christ. Religious communities need books such as this one to make the journey towards our home a little easier to walk together."

--**Stacy Clayton,** Teacher/Therapist, Nashville, Tennessee

To Denny, with so much respect and appreciation for your long career in both Christian higher education and church ministry. You are a big part of my memories of faculty at OLC in the 70s. I'm glad you are still teaching adults. Much continued blessings wished for you,

Perry

Enjoy!.   Feb. 10, 2020

PLEASE DON'T REVIVE US AGAIN!

The Human Side of the Church of Christ

PERRY C. COTHAM

Archway Publishing books may be ordered through booksellers or by contacting:

Archway Publishing
1663 Liberty Drive
Bloomington, IN 47403
www.archwaypublishing.com
1 (888) 242-5904

Scripture taken from the King James Version of the Bible.

ISBN: 978-1-4808-8597-4 (sc)
ISBN: 978-1-4808-8598-1 (e)

Library of Congress Control Number: 2019920194

Print information available on the last page.

Archway Publishing rev. date: 12/20/2019

Contents

Honoring the Memory of

Larry W. Locke (April 5, 1942 – April 29, 2018)

Roommate, classmate, colleague in pulpit ministry, teacher, supporter/encourager, and friend

and

Don Haymes (December 3, 1940 – June 1, 2019)

Student, scholar, researcher/writer/editor, theological archivist/librarian, community organizer, social justice advocate, and friend.

These two friends died when each had more years to live and more servant-ministry to give unselfishly to others. Larry would have been the first to say that at least two or three of the stories in this book should never have been reported, and Don would have vigorously insisted that two or three of his own wild and crazy stories should have been included.

and

Carolyn Taylor Wilson (June 10, 1936 – October 12, 2019)

Librarian, University Library Director, teacher, officer in professional organizations, consultant, and my long-time respected friend. Carolyn always unselfishly gave not only support and encouragement to me personally, but also much practical counsel to so many friends and colleagues about the business of book writing, publishing, and marketing. Carolyn died following a brief illness after the first submission of this manuscript to the publisher. She always encouraged me by stating the writing of church satire and church humor was almost a lost art, but that such writing served a healthy purpose.

Something Old and Something New

The Owen Chapel Church of Christ was founded in 1859 and this chapel was constructed in the early to mid-1860s. The building originally was a one-room chapel and had no baptistery. While it is not quite the oldest congregation of the Church of Christ, the actual church building is likely the oldest one in continuous use since its construction. All around this old chapel, the city of Brentwood in affluent Williamson County, the city itself only fifty years old, has grown in population as a thriving suburb of Nashville. (Credit: Owen Chapel Church.)

The Osman Fountain which includes the Jones Baptistery was constructed through the generosity of the Osman and Jones families. It is located at Bison Square in the middle of the Lipscomb University campus, between the Collins-Alumni Auditorium and a modern student center. The Fountain and Baptistery were dedicated in 2013. (Credit: Kristi Jones, Lipscomb University Photographic Services.)

Foreword

"The Christian life is essentially serious. This is a vale of tears," wrote Edward J. Poole-Connor a good number of years ago when I first contemplated writing this book. The quote was published in one of America's leading religious periodicals. "Humor has no place in the pulpit or the Sunday School," this minister concluded (*Christianity Today*, June 24, 1991).

True enough, most Christians do not think of church worship assemblies as places for mirth and levity. A half century or so ago, advocates for social justice claimed that 11:00 A. M. on Sunday was the most segregated daylight hour of the week. One might have also claimed that time slot was the dourest hour of the week. You could generally have heard more laughter in the urologist's waiting room than you could hear in many Christian assemblies. And that observation may be just as valid, or almost so, in many of today's worship assemblies. Encouragingly, however, in an increasing number of Christian assemblies today there exist occasions of hearty laughter and frequent smiles.

If you concur with Poole-Connor's statement above, even though this material is neither devotional nor pulpit literature, please pass on reading this book. If you think that humor and satire are heresies of the Christian faith or that the humor and hyperbole of Jesus were atypical of his teaching strategy, then this book is not for you. Some students of Scripture have pointed out that nowhere in the gospel narratives is Jesus depicted as laughing or even smiling, much less telling a joke.

If, on the other hand, you believe that most of life is neither a poetic Hallmark card nor a colorful Thomas Kincaide painting and that the True Church contains a delightful mixture of the good, the bad, and the ugly, then please proceed. In the first chapter I'll explain something of my purpose in writing this book.

THE MAIN POINT TO REMEMBER

The main point I wish my readers to remember is that the Church of Christ heritage and those men and women who composed it are viewed with a healthy measure of respect and appreciation—not with personal disdain, regret, or impugning either their commitment or sincerity! They lived in conformity with the light they saw and the knowledge they attained. Those in my generation are seeing already how our adult children are finding joyfulness in lampooning some of our own thinking, traditions, and habits.

The stories in this book are only a sample of the ones available. By far, most of the dramatic events which have impacted the lives of ministers have been sad rather than humorous. Only the passage of years and the gaining of wise perspective can transform a truly sad event into a recollection that just might produce a smile or laughter.

Additionally, these stories are not the funniest events I've experienced or been told. My best personal stories should not, indeed cannot, be told. Well, maybe I could tell them to my family and some of my closest friends. Even still, some readers will likely hit their sensitivity ceiling on some stories herein and ask, "How dare he tell that?" or "Surely that did not happen!!!"

I assure readers all my stories are true. Nothing has been embellished. The stories of my friends in church ministry are faithfully reported as told to me and I believe them also to be true. I have kept a diary for over a half century and, with only a few exceptions, have written a page (sometimes several pages) on each day's occurrences for some fifty-three years and counting. A few times I have consulted that diary to double-check a name or detail. As for sharing longer stories that were told to me, in contrast to longer stories in which I personally played a role, I not only had verbal permission to re-tell and publish these stories, but I have secured written confirmation from the sources or their next of kin to share these stories.

Readers will note that most of the time I will report names of people and places, but there are a few events that I deemed wise not to call specific names in some of these stories, especially the tragic or the most embarrassing stories. Sometimes a minister-friend would instruct me as such: "You can tell my story in your book, but omit or be vague with the names of people and congregations involved." As I tell these stories, I have felt free to invent a new word or two that may not be found in the dictionary or come up with a special abbreviation—such can be the liberty and pleasure in writing memoirs with a humorous and satirical bent.

BACKGROUND FOR THIS BOOK

Much of this book was written back in the late 80s and early 90s. There were times when, in social situations with preachers and teachers I respected, I would simply ask them about the funniest events that happened to them in preaching and teaching. The reader will find lots of stories that have come from Carroll Ellis as he had been both my college teacher and also my faculty chairman; I spent many hours with him in all kinds of situations. I would frequently encounter Jim Bill McInteer walking on the Lipscomb track (near the Lipscomb high school football stadium) at the same time I was there, and we would walk together, exchange stories, and laugh together. I recall visiting with Willard Collins both in his office and even while he worked in his front yard on Lealand Lane, considering myself one of those "rare birds" outside his own family to see this man in casual attire.

For personal reasons in 1992, I just put this project aside. The document rested electronically on my first personal computer, a MacIntosh SE. (As an aside, I paid far more for that computer than for any computer or electronic device purchased since that time.) Upon retirement from university teaching in May 2018, after finally getting the chapters transferred from that old Mac SE to Microsoft Word (thanks so much for the kind, professional assistance of Professor Al Austelle of Lipscomb University, who succeeded in making the electronic transfer where others I consulted at "help desks" did not even know what a "floppy disk" was), I returned to this material. Obviously, I have collected a number of new stories since 1992.

I cannot say when I first made attempts to stir laughter or at least bring a smile to people's faces. As a high school student and then during college undergraduate days, I presented after-dinner speeches for congregational adult banquets and special dinners. I learned that people laugh harder if you attach the name of an actual person at the dinner, and laugh even harder if there is a major component of truth in your joke. I did write some humorous and satirical material in high school. As minister at McMinnville's Westwood church, I began writing religious satire under the pen name "Harry Tick" for the weekly church bulletin that was distributed by U. S. postal services. Non-Westwood members would often contact the office and request to be added to the mail list. There were avid readers who often complimented those columns and, of course, everyone knew who wrote them.

I brought Brother Harry Tick (a thinly veiled reference to "heretic") with me to Nashville's Otter Creek Church in 1982, thinking the brothers and sisters there would be even more appreciative of Tick's satirical commentaries and reflections on church life. I soon learned such was not the case. The elders asked me to retire Brother Harry Tick or at least move his writing to the back page of the bulletin and label it clearly as satire. The complication was that Otter Creek distributed bulletins and the worship program by placing them in the pews on Sunday morning, and the elders deemed worshipers so distracted and so amused (and, at times, so distraught) that they could not, in Church of Christ parlance, "prepare their minds for the worship." I retired Brother Tick and decided not to replace him with the writings of Harold O. Truth, another fun pen name. I just simply placed church news and serious comments on the first page under the title "Otterances."

The gift of humor is not cited in New Testament Scripture as one of the gifts of the Holy Spirit, thus I cannot claim humor and laughter to be a church ministry. However, I thank God for people who have—through their life experiences, their anecdotes, their satire—evoked hearty laughter from me and others. Humor can lighten a load and deepen a connection of fellowship. A generation ago, many of us laughed heartily at the monthly satirical installment of "Balaam's Friend" as written unashamedly by Gary Freeman for *Mission Journal*, as well as laughed in reading two small books he authored: *A Funny Thing Happened on the Way to Heaven* and *Are You Going to Church More and Enjoying It Less?* (The latter was an adaptation of a commercial jingle for Winston cigarettes: "Are you smoking more, but enjoying it less?") I also enjoyed a little volume by Methodist clergyman Charles Merrill Smith, *How to Be a Bishop Without Being Religious*. And, then, the *Wittenberg Door* always contained such a delightful blend of satire and seriousness.

PARTNERS IN THE "HERESY" OF RELIGIOUS HUMOR

Then there are those friends whose insights into stark reality could be couched in rich satire and facetiousness. I think of the many hours that James (Buddy) Thomas (English professor), Patrick Deese (Political Science professor), as well as one or two others of kindred mind, and I would sit at a lunch table in the Lipscomb faculty lounge and facetiously "review" the latest political events of the 70s or the latest issue of *Gospel Advocate* (in those days, professors were given a complimentary subscription and issues were placed in faculty mail boxes). There are times I used those faculty mailboxes to play a few practical jokes, most of which I am not at this point ready to confess.

Our little group of "heretics" pretended such seriousness when reading the many religious articles that lavishly praised the current editor or dealt with topics I might list in the "Legalism Hall of Fame." (I vividly recall one article entitled, "Is Humming During a Hymn Considered Scriptural Worship?" The author contended humming during a hymn to be "false worship" because one cannot obey the apostolic command to "speak to one another in psalms, hymns, and spiritual songs" by humming.) There will be a number of stories in this book that also qualify for the Legalism Hall of Fame.

Names of many others come to mind, Christian brothers and sisters who could laugh heartily at the foibles and absurdities of the True Church tradition, all the while maintaining humility and respect. The list of former Lipscomb students in my classroom would be too long, but those who stirred and encouraged such hearty classroom laughter would certainly include Charles Ottinger, Jay Shappley, David Shepherd, Gary Pearson, David Sampson, Jim Jenkins, Randy Goodman, Dan Dozier, and Russ Corley. And then Woodmont Hills gave me Wesley Paine, Leland Dugger, and Jerry Jennings. Owen Chapel friendships include Jo-David Keith and Lester McNatt.

At Westwood in McMinnville I was "encouraged" by Harold and Judith Roney, and Harold's law partner, Harry Camp, and by the intelligent facetiousness and wit of Glenn and Lynn Davis and by Bob and Mary Winton; at Franklin's Fourth Avenue by the wonderfully zany Daniel and Stacy Clayton, Kent and Elizabeth Sweatt, John and Kim Walker, Kyle Bills, Josh Brown, Clay Stafford, Kent Cleaver, Judy Tamble, and Deena Trimble.

Otter Creek Church has been a hotbed of humor-loving souls and that would include, most especially, Fletcher and Gail Srygley, Jerry and Sandra Collins, Ed and Janey Gleaves, Ed Cullum, Bob and Barbara Enkema, Wayne and Nan Gurley, Brad Forrister, and Carolyn Wilson.

Finally, in more recent years, my facetious nature in discussing either "church life" or national politics has been fostered by Keith Crow and Sandy, his late wife, and now Brenda Crow. So many others could be named.

In the past few years I have been blessed to know Richard T. Hughes not simply as a scholar and a colleague in teaching but as genuine friend. And a very fun friend at that! Richard's definitive study *Reviving the Ancient Faith: The Story of Churches of Christ in America* (Eerdman's, 1996) and his revised edition of *Myths America Lives By: White Supremacy and the Stories that Give Us Meaning* (University of Illinois Press, 2018) remain simply outstanding examples of research and writing, and both books are filled with important and abiding stories. Richard's collection of his own stories of being raised in the True Church, appropriately entitled *75 Years in Fantasyland*, nudged me gently to move ahead with telling my own stories and in feeling free to use "True Church" and "the Lord's Church" in a respectful yet facetious way.

HUMBLING AND SAD REALITY

A humbling and sad reality has been how many of my older friends and professors whom I had known and interviewed have died since 1992. For example, Will Campbell had a printout of an earlier edition of this book and was planning to write an introduction for it at the time of his passing. I felt Will to be the ideal person to write an introduction, not simply due to his stature as writer, preacher, and social activist, but because of his unique combination of commitment to racial and economic justice and his counter-balancing sense of humor and wit.

I hope to speak respectfully of all these people in my life, though I plan to avoid using the expression "the late ..." as a prefix before the names of those who have passed; I will simply use an appropriate past tense or present tense on the verbs.

While I have pursued more than one career path in my lifetime, most of the stories to follow are told from the perspective of church ministry, beginning with collegiate training for that ministry. I have been blessed to serve churches in a rural setting, a large urban setting, and a small town setting. Each setting possessed its own culture and challenges. All along since this book's inception, when I was "between jobs"—a nice euphemism for being unemployed full-time—I considered this to be a fun project.

This book can be fairly criticized for being too much of a genre-mix: personal stories and anecdotes; stories told me by others, mainly by other preachers and evangelists; a little church history; a large number of personal memoirs; and a few serious remarks, tinged even with some theology, and bits of advice to others in ministry.

Some friendly critics have stated they sometimes see a quick shift from an absolute absurdity to the heavily serious observation, seeing these shifts as a puzzling distraction. There are so many names and personal memories embedded in the text that I seriously considered adding the word "memoirs" to the sub-title. Actually, chapter two is totally devoted to Lipscomb memoirs and not at all to satire or humor. I have attempted to conclude almost every chapter on a note that is both serious and positive. And yes, there are times when subject matter overlaps into more than one chapter.

I am so fully aware that any possible readers who do not share a Church of Christ background will not understand or appreciate many of these stories and observations. For that matter, even current Church of Christ members who were born after 1990 are likely not to understand or appreciate the complexities, dilemmas, concerns, and absurdities of earlier generations. These younger Christians are likely busy creating their own occasions for joy and laughter.

This book has been a joyful experience. After having written a number of books that required major research and a careful writing style that respects sources and gives proper attribution, it is so much fun just to sit behind a keyboard and the only research is from the recesses of one's mind. As such, any errors are those of memory, not careless research.

The chapters to follow, then, are not a slice of some divine pie in the sky, but, instead, a slice of human reality. Most senior True Church saints should be able to relate to most of these narratives. Hopefully, all will enjoy them.

Perry C. Cotham
January, 2020

1

"Woe Is Me if I Preach Not!"

"And what do you plan to major in, young man?" the female teller asked, making polite conversation.

The moment was a rather awkward one. Here I was at eighteen years of age and on the verge of commencing my college career. My father had patronizingly accompanied me to a local bank to open my very first checking account and deposit eight hundred dollars to cover tuition and living expenses for the fall quarter. I would soon be heading some seven hundred miles northeast to Nashville, Tennessee, to attend David Lipscomb College.

Most people in the Dallas-Fort Worth area had never heard of this college, so I usually took pains to tell well-wishers its location and approximate student body size. But I honestly had no idea what I wanted to major in. I nonchalantly informed the bank teller as much.

The moment we exited the bank my dad stopped on the sidewalk and almost literally pinned me against the wall of the building. "Son," he implored earnestly, "don't be ashamed to tell people that you're going to major in Bible and that you plan to preach the gospel!"

Sure, I had given thought to being a minister. I had been arm carried, led by hand, and/or driven to church services three times a week—Sunday morning, Sunday night, and Wednesday night—since I was a few days old. There are summers I must have attended evangelistic and revival services half to three-fourths of all weeknights.

Besides my father, one grandfather was a preacher as was one uncle. Several cousins became preachers or married preachers. Truly, all male members of my family must have been on the Lord's party line when the call went forth to "preach the Word." Or perhaps there existed some "call to preach" gene running through every male in my family. My dad wanted—and expected—every male Cotham to be a minister or missionary and every female Cotham to marry a minister. How could I possibly have entertained a thought that I was destined to be anything else? A lost world remained to be saved!

My earliest childhood memories include my mother reading Bible stories at the end of my day from *Hurlbut's Story of the Bible*—the classic book by Jesse Lyman Hurlbut (a Methodist-Episcopal clergyman who served several churches in New Jersey during his career), with 168 stories from both the Old Testament and the New Testament that combine to form a continuous narrative, originally written in 1904. I thrilled to the color illustrations in the *Hurlbut* storybook, but I was not allowed to read the Sunday color comics before attending Sunday School and church services. The thought of visiting one of the two or three local movie theaters in Wewoka, Oklahoma, or Paris, Texas, where I spent the first dozen years of my life, seldom entered my mind. And I never considered the idea of attending a movie on a Sunday, the Lord's Day, to be appropriate or justified.

I recall sitting in the Sunday School class taught by my spinster Aunt Laurel (dubbed "Toady" by my grandfather) at the historic Pearl and Bryan (downtown) Church of Christ in Dallas, where my grandfather, Coleman Overby, ministered the last years of his life. The major *dramatis personae* of the Bible were represented by colored paper cutouts poked gingerly into the sand in a big flat box; a piece of cut glass was wedged into the sand to represent a body of water such as the Sea of Galilee or the Dead Sea.

In other classes the ubiquitous tilted flannel board on a thin-wood pedestal was the surface on which the likes of Abraham, Isaac, and Jacob (though usually neither the hairy Esau nor Rahab the harlot) adhered for pedagogical purposes. ("See Jesus hang on the cross where he died for—oops! Jesus just fell from the cross" were dismaying commentaries on the weakened felt surfaces in those pre-hi-tech Sunday School days.)

Sometimes there were color picture-illustrated workbooks that began with the first story in the Bible depicting the garden of Eden, Adam and Eve standing around casually with innocent smiles or smirks on their faces and strategically placed shrubbery, foliage, or long hair in Eve's case, that concealed private anatomical parts. No one then would have imagined the use of a video or DVD to teach a Bible lesson—we knew precious little even about black-and-white screen television in those days!

With the aid of these simple, inexpensive, but creative visuals, biblical characters of both testaments came to life. Except for Jesus, the most interesting characters were in the Old Testament. I learned the name of all twelve apostles as well as the names of all twenty-seven books of the New Testament before I could begin to spell or even read all those names. The pedagogical method of Bible name recognition occurred when my mom taught me two children's songs that began "Jesus called them one by one: Peter, Andrew, James, and John," and then the more challenging children's song that started "Matthew, Mark, Luke, and John, Acts, and the letter to the Romans." I came to know the road from Jerusalem to Jericho and what happened along it as well as I knew the road from Paris, Texas, to Dallas where my mom's closest relatives lived. Jesus loved me, this I knew, for the Bible told me as much—at least as this heartwarming message was passed along by my saintly teachers and family.

LIVING IN "PERILOUS TIMES"

Interesting developments were occurring in the fall of 1960. Most Americans were fearful of Soviet Premier Nikita Khrushchev, who, in a shoe-pounding tantrum on a United Nations podium, had warned our nation that "we [Communists] will bury you." The Cold War, already in progress for a decade or longer, was heating up. The oldest man to serve as president was soon leaving the White House, and there was a heated contest to determine his successor. I had already heard a number of sermons in both Texas and Tennessee pulpits forecasting the perilous times awaiting the USA if we Americans thoughtlessly elected a Roman Catholic as president.

I was, unfortunately, too young in 1960 to vote for Richard Nixon, but given the chance, I certainly would have—not out of political principle, mind you (I had neither political convictions nor substantial knowledge of political history in those days, much less any party affiliation), but out of fears the Roman Catholics and "Commies" would conspire to take over the land of the free and the home of the brave. I had signed up in my Lipscomb Bible class at the beginning of the fall quarter to lead prayer in chapel, and as it turned out, my assignment fell on the Wednesday after Election Day. Feeling a huge sense of doom that might soon befall the liberties and freedoms of this nation with this newly elected Catholic president, I really did not know what to say in a prayer in front of the entire college community. I wrote out my prayer early that morning when Kennedy was finally declared the winner and just simply beseeched the Almighty that the United States, as we now know it, would survive as a free nation in the years ahead.

We were living in "perilous times," or so we were often told by the college president, Athens Clay Pullias, and that sentiment was echoed by other Bible instructors (discussed in the next chapter). The imperative to go out on Sundays and preach seemed even more crucial. Being enthralled by all that I was learning in the Dean's Bible classes, I certainly wanted to take that material, rework it, and present it to any church or churches who were willing to engage me to proclaim it.

So much of the sermon content of my first year as a student minister was drawn from Dean Mack Wayne Craig's daily Bible classes, augmented by two books tailor-made for a novice preacher: Leroy Brownlow's *100 Sermons You Can Preach*, which contained some clever acrostic sermons, and his *Why I Am a Member of the Church of Christ,* the latter book seeming a veritable official creed book of the True Church. The book gave twenty-five stock arguments as to why our church was right and all others were wrong, buttressed by so many scriptures lifted out of context. At the time, Brownlow was a long-time preacher in Fort Worth, Texas, and a family friend.

THE FREDONIAN CALL

My wait to enter pulpit ministry was not a long one. The following January, Willard Collins, vice president of the college and long-time family friend, called me into his office. In his deep, emphatic tone of voice, Brother Collins informed me that he was dispatching me to a rural church of nearly eighty-five members near Manchester, Tennessee. Without further theological education, without ordination, without even an automobile (my old, gray '52 Chevy coupe from high school days had been semi-retired and left in Texas). I, like the apostle Paul, was "equipped" and ready to "preach the Word, being instant in season and out of season" and ready to "rebuke and exhort." I was as ready and desirous to share the "milk of the word" as an unmilked cow at high noon.

This rural church was named Fredonia. Just as the apostle Paul received his Macedonian call in a vision ("Come over and help us"), I proudly told some classmates that I had received the Fredonian call. For a month of Sundays I hitched a ride from my roommate to the old Nashville airport (Berry Field) and rented a new 1960 Ford Falcon (the car offered at the lowest daily rate) to drive to the site of my fledgling homiletic efforts. By the time I had put a few "ones" into the collection plate and then later on Sunday evenings turned my car in to the leasing agency and paid my lease fee, most of my weekly twenty-five-dollar salary had evaporated.

I had been called to preach, nonetheless. I reasoned, again with the apostle Paul, "Woe is me if I preach not the gospel of Christ." My family's dreams about me began to be fulfilled and, praise the Lord, my dad soon arranged for me to take delivery of a brand new white '61 Chevrolet sedan. He thus made good on his promise to purchase an automobile for me if I took a regular preaching position. Though disappointed the new vehicle was a Bel Air six cylinder, four door sedan (instead of an Impala V-8 sport coupe), with a "stick shift" for three speeds ("three on the tree"), for four years this car became the vehicle for carrying the good news all over Middle Tennessee, Southern Kentucky, and even into the further most parts of West Texas as I inflicted my novice skills and sound doctrine on any church willing to be subjected to them.

My own pulpit odyssey, as well as my spiritual pilgrimage in general, has led me through some interesting experiences in a variety of places. I have served pulpits in rural churches, inner city churches, and suburban churches. I experienced mission work overseas in three different nations (Great Britain, Russia, and Guatemala) for a few months. Through many dangers, toils, and snares I've already come and I just might be facing a few more. But I've also experienced some unusual and interesting incidents, some funny and some embarrassing, and my life's been blessed by meeting and sharing experiences with some truly wonderful and fascinating people within this fellowship called the Church of Christ.

A LOVER'S QUARREL

Borrowing a metaphor from Robert Frost, my years in church ministry have led me to the conclusion that many well-trained preachers develop a life-long "lovers quarrel" with the church. Some of the most endearing, most encouraging, most loving, most supportive moments in my life have been experienced within this church. That's not to say that the quarrel is angry and vindictive, as it may be humble, conciliatory, and loving. There are times in which sweet moments of love, worship, or fellowship seemed to lift me into the presence of the Almighty and motivate me against all odds to be the best person, both spiritually and morally, I know how to be.

On the other hand, some of the most discouraging, most disappointing, most alienating moments in life, as well as the worst power plays and worst betrayals, have been experienced within this same church fellowship. Those are moments when the church provides no motivating forces to be the best one can be. So painful have been these experiences that I have felt the force of the old saying: "Organized religion is the devil's sandbox."

What a paradox! And what irony! The church is called to be saints, yet it is filled with active sinners of every stripe and color. Called to be holy, at times it is anything but separate and sanctified. The church is divided, yet united. Bearing a message of transformation, the church at times needs reform as much as any other institution. Called to be separate from worldly mindset and values, it has too often served as an agent for conformity, accommodation, and the cultural status quo. Rather than being Christians who happen to be Americans, the church has often seemed composed of Americans who happen to be Christians.

Enough serious analysis. This book is about some experiences that have emerged from the ministry of a preacher. Preacher stories are, of course, a dime a dozen, and every preacher worth his salt has committed a nice repertoire to memory. And how easily the authentic stories get embellished with apocryphal details through the passing of years! My only standard for including a story of human interest, apart from general appeal, is that it be true. For that reason, I have chosen to include as many names of people and places and as many dates as possible. In some rare cases, it seemed prudent either to change a name or delete names altogether to protect privacy or spare embarrassment.

THE ONE TRUE CHURCH

Ask the mainstream Church of Christ preacher when his particular church was established and his answer would be "A. D. 33 in Jerusalem," an inscription often found on the cornerstone of many of our church buildings. There would be no doubt in his mind that the Church of Christ on Main Street in White Bluff, Tennessee, or on 14th and Main Streets in Big Spring, Texas, is the same church in all details that really matter—and there are a lot of details that really matter—as the Jerusalem church of the first century A. D.

Although there are many religious bodies in the United States (exact count varies from preacher to preacher in making the claim, typically ranging from 250 to 300), there is only *one* true church. That "true church" is the Church of Christ. It must not to be confused with the United Church of Christ, a group from which we are as different theologically as Lady Gaga from Amy Grant.

So, within this "one true church" I was raised. This church is often called "the Lord's church" or "the Lord's people." How comforting to know that one is in the "true church" or the one "right church!" How reassuring to know that I could be correct when others were so wrong, could be more virtuous in my conduct when members of other religious bodies were more permissive in their social recreation or private morality! And I could feel sadness and regret for friends who were sincere members of other churches, known as "the denominations," but feel incredibly fortunate and blessed I was raised in the "right" church and not in some "denomination."

Yet, as friend and distinguished church historian Richard Hughes has pointed out, "There is no such thing as 'one true church.'" Richard has related a wide range of his own experiences being raised in the "one true church" that "sometimes seemed like Fantasyland." It is "Fantasyland," Richard states, because the idea of "one true church thrives in the minds of believers, but never in objective reality. It suggests a perfection and innocence impossible to achieve."

A UNIQUE HERITAGE

To recapitulate: The True Church does not consider itself to be a denomination. Most members see their church as an outgrowth of American frontier evangelism and, in particular, of the Restoration Movement. Restoration leaders, especially Thomas and Alexander Campbell of West Virginia and Barton Stone of Kentucky, were convinced that the division and fighting among the various Protestant religious groups were self-defeating and an offense to the cause of Christ. After all, Jesus prayed earnestly that his disciples might "be one."

Because historically there have been other restoration movements in other centuries, the Stone-Campbell Movement is a better name for this frontier, revivalistic phenomenon. Unity of all believers is based on the New Testament alone. Therefore, humanly-composed creeds are quite unnecessary, thus these creeds could and should be dispensed with. A favorite scripture for many in my church, conveniently brief enough for a modern day bumper sticker, is found in Romans 16: 16—"The Churches of Christ salute you." (I have also seen another bumper sticker: "Join the Church of Christ's choice—Romans 16: 16").

In more recent times, writers and editors in our movement refused to use upper case "C" when referencing the Church of Christ, consequently rendering "church of Christ" or "churches of Christ." The point intended by the lower case "c" was a subtle cue that the True Church is not a denomination and therefore does not have a proper name. Those compiling directories and Yellow Pages did not seem to buy into that dubious semantic.

Unfortunately, nowadays, the modern Stone-Campbell Restoration movement has been just as divided as the Protestant world of two centuries ago. The divisions were factors in three larger groups emerging: the Church of Christ, the Christian Church, and Disciples of Christ. Within these larger groups many subgroups have developed, each making exclusive claims. The subgroups are called by different names and sometimes by nicknames, such as "the anti's" or "the one-cuppers." (As a boy, I would often hear the older "brethren" talk about the "anti's" as though they were the worst enemy in civilization, and I wondered silently, "Who on earth are the 'anti's'"?)

Major denominations somehow survive in much the same way with theological infighting and subsequent divisions into smaller groups maintaining "purity." Divisions deepen through internecine warfare that is often conducted in open debate or church publications. Each little sect thinks all other groups are terribly wrong on certain doctrinal points, in some cases so wrong that adherents will one day lamentably find themselves in the "lake of fire and brimstone." And too often those petty differences are not only infused with major importance, but are often aired before the general public.

COMMUNICATION WITH MEMBERS OF OTHER CHURCHES

Communication with other religious groups has always been a challenge for some Church of Christ members. Two reasons: One, apart from telling denominationalists to "obey the gospel first and we'll talk later," our preachers have not typically brought much to the table. And second, we haven't always talked the same language as leaders of other religious groups. We've typically assumed that everyone else meant the same things by terms such as "inspiration," "inerrancy," and "sound doctrine" as we mean by them.

In order to promote better communication between other religious groups and ourselves, I offer a listing of safe, acceptable words which should be used copiously in sermons, class lessons, conversation, and dialogue (see the left column).

In the right column I offer another listing of words which our well-meaning religious neighbors should either avoid altogether or use sparingly when talking to us. The words in the right column are not bad or inappropriate, but they may be infrequently used by life-time Church of Christ members. Just perusing the generalized, simplified list should provide additional insights into our doctrine and practice.

GOOD WORDS	WORDS OF ILL REPUTE
The True Church	Denomination
The Truth	The understanding
The Bible (and back to it)	biblical manuscripts
Contribution	Offertory
Song books	hymnals
Christian college	seminary
Singing only	organ, piano
Scripture schedule	lectionary
Brother/brethren	laymen; laity
Preacher/minister	Reverend (as title)/pastor
Offer the invitation	altar call
Bible scholar	theologian/seminarian
preacher's home	parsonage
inspiration	modern criticism
conservative	liberal
baptism	sacrament
gospel meeting	conference
Bible major	Religious Studies major
preaching	dialogue
Christmas	advent
Chorus	choir
Revelation	Epiphany
Opening prayer	invocation
Closing prayer	benediction

HOLIDAYS AND HOLY DAYS

Growing up in the True Church, from infancy into adulthood, the vast majority of our members did not possess the foggiest notion of the stories behind certain religious festivals or the meanings of certain terms. We certainly were given no understanding of how Christian rites and festivals were sometimes blended with ancient Roman rites and festivals in the early centuries of church history or how they had changed over the course of other centuries. We were not taught, and usually did not bother to learn, the meaning of several words and terms in the right column above. For example, we were not taught the meaning of advent, Eucharist, epiphany, invocation, and benediction.

So many terms were confusing and/or irrelevant to our church experience. If we ever heard or read them, we had to guess the meaning. Some believed a lectionary must be akin in some way to a dictionary. "Epiphany" may have been some practice connected to a symphony or symphonic performance. Maundy Thursday may have seemed as though some hybrid combination of an abbreviated work week. To outdoorsmen, Hanukkah could have been a Tennessee hunter's duck call. As a youngster who loved baseball in the 50s and 60s, all I knew about Yom Kippur was that it served as explanation for Sandy Koufax's refusal to pitch on certain days for the Dodgers in the World Series against the Yankees.

We had, indeed, heard of Passover, even if we never would have known all the elements of the story and meanings behind certain rituals and foods at that special table. And while at one level we knew that Jesus of Nazareth was a Jew, the idea that he lived and practiced Orthodox Judaism his entire life and died as a Jew was not deeply ingrained in our mindset. Somehow it seemed easier to think of Jesus with a second name of "Christ," as the one who had visited earth for the express purpose of teaching totally new commandments and establishing a new world religion. In time, of course, we learned about circumcision, even if we were not quite certain what it was, and through the story of Samson had heard about the Nazarite vow.

Knowledge about Pentecost was limited to several big facts: It was on a specific "Day of Pentecost" the Apostle Peter delivered a keynote address to the large, diverse gathering of celebrants in Jerusalem; the speaker's theme was that the recently-crucified Jesus was truly the Son of God; his sermon was interrupted by cries of desperate sinners demanding to know how to obtain forgiveness; some three thousand souls repented and were baptized (we are not informed the location of the mass baptisms, who performed all the baptisms, how much time was required, and whether the figure was an exact amount or rounded off); and this momentous event was the official start-up date for the True Church. Origins and original meanings of the Pentecost festival, as well as other Jewish festivals, were not taught.

Staunch True Church preachers and members contended for an enigmatic and paradoxical approach to the religious holidays they did understand— Christmas and Easter! On the one hand, they indeed proclaim the birth of Jesus and his resurrection, especially, are crucially important in "God's scheme of redemption." On the other hand, they insist: (1) We are never commanded to celebrate the birth of Jesus, thus such celebrations are either unnecessary or even divinely disapproved; (2) we can't know the exact dates of Jesus' birth and resurrection anyway; and (3) we don't celebrate the resurrection because, in the communion service, the resurrection is celebrated *every* Sunday and not just one Sunday a year.

Growing up in the True Church, then, Good Friday often meant the start of a fun and possibly longer weekend. Easter was a Sunday in which all of us young kids would take our little baskets with fake green grass and hunt for the colorful eggs our moms had boiled and decorated and our dads had ingenuously hidden for us enthusiastically to seek and joyfully discover. The Easter church service was a Sunday assembly in which we might wear some light-weight colorful new clothes. We would sit in the church assembly and notice a larger attendance. We just might or might not hear a sermon and hymn selections on Jesus' res-urrection, and the preacher might well have made a judgmental complaint, if not outright condemnation, of "those who never darken the church house doors except for this one Sunday of the year."

Higher education, intelligence, and giftedness do not always trump seemingly indefensible theological thinking. One personal example remains unforgettable.

The year was 1999 or 2000. Easter Sunday was a few days away and our worship minister/song director at Franklin's Fourth Avenue church informed me he would be out of state with his family for that weekend, but that he had already arranged for another song director to handle his worship directing assignment for all Sunday services. In fact, it seemed terrific news that our guest song director had built a great reputation in church music, came from a family of song directors, had directed singing in large congregations, and had been the choral director in two or three Christian schools and colleges.

A few days before that Easter Sunday, this guest song leader called me and asked what my sermon theme would be so that he could make appropriate hymn selections. "I'm sure you're kidding me when you ask that question," I replied. "Being Easter Sunday, you just know I am going to preach on the theme of resurrection. There are several selections you can consider, from the traditional 'Up From the Grave, He Arose,' 'Christ the Lord is Risen Today,' and 'I Know that My Redeemer Lives,' to the Gaither hymn 'Because He Lives,' and there are others you might have in mind."

There was a long, almost "deafening" pause after I made that statement and offered my recommendations. I wondered if I had said something wrong or if possibly we had lost phone connection. I followed up: "We should have eight hundred or more in our assembly, hopefully even more than that, and fill up our auditorium, so this is a great time for you to be our guest song director. People will get to know and hear you for the first time and I trust this will be a good experience for you."

"Are you serious that you are going to preach on the resurrection?" he asked after a few more moments of silence.

"Of course," I replied immediately. "Are you serious about this being an issue?" Given his long pauses I was fairly certain he was not joking around with me.

"I'm as serious as sin," he replied, "and I am guessing you will not change your topic, so therefore I cannot in good conscience come this Sunday and you will need to find another song director."

Then I was the one who paused. This seemed incredulous. And patently ridiculous. "Well, then, we both know resurrection is a biblical theme. We teach Jesus was resurrected on the third day and that the Apostle Paul cites that event as providing evidence of our own resurrection, then why shouldn't I preach on that topic? No one in attendance should be surprised by a sermon on this theme."

His reply was unforgettable: "You are just like all the denominationalists. That is what they do on Easter Sunday. In the Lord's church, we don't do what's done in the denominations and so I won't be a party to this travesty. You'll just have to find another song director for this Sunday."

Considering this person to be a good gentleman and gifted song director, I thanked him for his forthrightness, and we hung up. I sat quietly for a few moments behind my desk in disbelief. Despite his giftedness and intelligence, his system of logic remained astoundingly incredulous to me. We contacted another person to lead singing for that Easter Sunday.

REMAINING IN THAT CHURCH FAMILY

Like all other churches of any size, the Church of Christ has been the home of many divergent elements and characteristics. The Christian church today is, and always has been, both sublime and ridiculous; relevant and petty; alive and dead (or perhaps in a functional coma). This church's members are highly literate and somewhat illiterate; educated and uneducated; well-informed in current events and almost totally clueless; diligent and lazy; tolerant, accepting and prejudiced, non-inclusive; spirit-filled and spirit-dead (or spirit faintly flickering).

Some fellowship members are winsome and others repulsive. Some enjoy Garth Brooks and Carrie Underwood; others (perhaps very few) enjoy Isaac Stern and the Italian tenors. Some enjoy the Grand Ole Opry; others (probably not many) enjoy Italian opera and string quintets. Some fellowship members who look, talk, and dress in a certain style are open to enjoying other members who look, talk, and dress in a different style; they all feel they can learn from each other. On the other hand, there are some church members who see Christians who look, speak, dress, or enjoy activities, foods, and enjoy recreation totally different from their preferences, and they cannot possibly imagine spending an entire eternity in heaven with these members who are "so different." Some members you would gladly take along on a weekend camping trip; others you would want to see only on the other end of your twenty-foot pew for one hour a week.

Polar extremes also exist for our preachers and the sermons they deliver. Some worship services draw us closer to God; some drive us further away. Some sermons inspire us; others insult our intelligence. Some sermons command our attention; others put us to sleep. Some services make us laugh, when we don't intend to laugh, and others make us cry, also unintentionally. Admittedly, the same generalizations could be uttered about any regular church assembly in any denomination.

With that heritage I still gladly identify—a heritage which has placed great emphasis on the study of the Word and on the importance of proper conduct and personal discipline. Some elders and fellow preachers have attempted, however, to disown me as one of their brothers; however, I can no more leave my spiritual family than I could leave my human family. This is the church which has given me indoctrination and insight, nurture and direction, love and support, relationships and role models. When functioning at its best, it is no less than "a foretaste of glory divine." Indeed, "what a fellowship, what a joy divine!"

WHY THIS BOOK?

Purposes for a book that recounts selected historical events and anecdotes vary. One is to invite people to smile, at times even to laugh, but always reflect on some of their own personal memories of their early church life. So many memories here are rooted in the early to mid-twentieth century, and I feel quite certain that current Millennials and GenXers will have trouble relating to many of these stories.

Another purpose is to play a small role in preserving a valuable part of one church's heritage. Much like the human side of Jesus, the human side of his body, the church, gets lost in our formal histories and recollections on special days. One certainly gets the impression there were sobering fights and divisions in the first century church, but does this mean the early Christians totally lived lives of dead seriousness?

The question is valid. There are no Scriptures telling us about early disciples sitting around and telling jokes and stories, enjoying fun and laughter, or having a hearty laugh at some unexpected event such as a botched healing or some young man going to sleep in church and falling out of his window perch? Could they have mentioned the Old Testament narrative of Balaam's talking donkey without a little smile on their faces? And why do we not have a single narrative telling us about Jesus laughing or even smiling? Can we imagine Jesus playfully blowing a kiss or winking at someone?

These questions merit serious consideration. An untenable stereotype of first century Christians just might exist, similar to stereotypes of Colonial New England Puritans. Surely there were numerous developments and events the earliest of Christian saints could laugh about, perhaps even months and years after they occurred. Who knows? Some of the disciples of Galatian congregations might have poked fun at the Apostle Paul for quoting so many Old Testament scriptures in his epistles. Some may have light-heartedly complained his epistle to the Romans was too long and too difficult to understand. Years after Cornelius's conversion, some disciples may have teased Peter about having once harbored such deep ethnic prejudice. Some Gentile Christians may have felt they heard too much about circumcision from Paul.

Did Jesus ever experience joy and laughter? The answer is surely affirmative. The Master performed his first miracle at a wedding feast so that the host would feel no shame and embarrassment over exhausting the wine supplies. Can we imagine anyone going to a wedding reception and not enjoying the moment with laughter and smiles? Would one meet and congratulate the new bride and groom with a glum frown on one's face or with a look of total boredom? Then surely Jesus felt and expressed joy and happiness on certain occasions. On what basis would critics accuse Jesus of being "a glutton and a drunkard"? A number of Bible scholars, Elton Trueblood especially, have pointed out that so many of Jesus' original sayings contained both wit and irony.

So, then, Jesus surely uttered some great one-liners. They might not have fallen into the L.O.L. category, but those sayings in various situations demonstrate the Master could be witty and light-hearted. We may have missed much of the wit and humor because we read these sayings in our own modern English language. God has given human beings the gift of laughter. I wholeheartedly agree with the late Archbishop Fulton Sheen, who once declared: "The only time laughter is wicked is when it is turned against him who gave it!"

FINDING HUMOR IN BENIGN INCONGRUITY

Throughout life, situations and events occur that invite us to laugh. At times that laughter is both unavoidable and irrepressible. Truly, one of the most defining characteristics of being human is that sense of humor. Possessing that sense of humor is not really a character or personality weakness, psychologists inform us, but rather a highly positive personality trait that builds relationships and enables personal sanity.

Most psychologists also concur that humor involves the recognition of incongruity—the ability to laugh or even the inability to refrain from laughing at the huge, gaping chasm between what we profess to be and what we actually are; between what we intend to do and what we actually accomplish; between what we think we certainly know and what we actually know; and between what we are certain we can accomplish and what in reality we are able to achieve. That gap between the noblest ideals and the starkest realities can often, though not always, be hilarious. True enough, at other times the gap brings a bitter, even tragic, sadness.

There are also times in the most solemn and sanctified moments of life experience a patently absurd and unexpected intrusion may occur. The more you try to control yourself and stifle the laughter, the more uncontrollable it seems. Rather than feel shame and embarrassment, perhaps the smiles and laughter are reminders that we have values and priorities from which we fall short.

So let's laugh at ourselves and laugh with others. My desire here is to be both loving and nonjudgmental of the people discussed or mentioned. Admittedly, being human and with my own values and principles, there are times when some judgment has seeped into my thinking and writing. Nonetheless, I have long and consistently taught that we must think more highly of others than of ourselves and that ultimate judgment belongs only to God.

SATIRE AND SARCASM—ANY DIFFERENCE?

Sarcasm can be mocking disrespect of another human being, to view another person as something less than human. In the ancient Mount Carmel showdown of deities, the prophet Elijah definitely engaged sarcasm and mockery when challenging the 350 Baal prophets to call down fire from heaven. (As we know, Baal's prophets came up short on the challenge and later met a doom far worse than getting an earful of biting sarcasm from a true prophet!) Making light of people through malice is, of course, a contemptuous exercise in judgment and is inexcusable. Sarcasm is more than condescending in nature—it is hugely disrespectful!

To write with satire and to speak facetiously, on the other hand, is to acknowledge the humanity of others while seeing a gap between professed ideals and actual performance. That gap can be, at least at certain times, quite humorous! Facetiousness can be playful fun. Poking fun at people whom we basically respect, and then being open to their poking fun back at us, enhances dignity and serves to usher us back into the reality of mortal existence.

Would an admission of the frail humanity of flesh and blood Christians expose us to the scorn of the ungodly? Surely not! That vast alumni of the church (*i.e.,* those who have left our ranks) know we're not perfect. The non-Christian world knows we're sinners also, a conviction so strongly held that the accusation of being "filled with hypocrites" is often unfairly leveled at the church.

Rather than sanctimoniously sweep our foibles and failures under the ecclesiastical rug, how much healthier to take them seriously, confess them, overcome them, and then poke fun at them! Even though we may conceive of moral perfection, the redeemed will always be imperfect. Though we may somehow conceive of omniscience, there are always questions even the best and brightest among us cannot answer. Despite that perennial quest for truth, what philosopher or theologian even came close to attaining it?

Why can't we admit who we are and what we are? And then why not have a few honest-to-God smiles, chuckles, maybe even roars of laughter, when our stories of admission appropriately call for them? As Minister Charles Merrill Smith once said, "More devils can be routed by a little laughter than by a carload of humorless piety."

While tearing down the false idols outside our churches, we need to tear down the high pedestals we have built within our churches. Yes, we preachers sometimes enjoy the pedestals on which we are occasionally placed by those who appreciate and respect the ministry we perform. Satire and humor may serve as valuable hammers and chisels in this essential operation of tethering us to reality and humility.

Many Christians have an Eleventh Commandment, some bit of practical instruction that keeps them sane and spiritual but that somehow did not make the cut for the "Big Ten" that were etched in stone on Mount Sinai so many centuries ago.

I hereby offer my Eleventh Commandment—one that I have seldom kept perfectly, but in those moments when I have obeyed it my mind and my heart have been served well and I have experienced emotional liberation: "Thou shalt not take thyself seriously."

2

David Lipscomb College and Learning from the Masters

October 5, 1891—a date that surely every graduating class at Lipscomb over a dozen decades has been reminded of numerous times! On this day three teachers met classes in a rented house with only nine male students, but each wanted training in biblical studies in order to "preach the gospel." Thus, the initial step in a dream for a new school by co-founders David Lipscomb and James Harding had been realized.

The school began without even a name. Called unpretentiously and simply "Bible School," Harding later added "Nashville" to give the academic project an official name. Before the session concluded, thirty-two students had enrolled in what was known as Nashville Bible School. And, while this school was very much like our generation's "schools of preaching," this was the humble beginning of today's Lipscomb University.

The founders realized that if the school were to grow it needed permanent facilities. They speculated that some campus site would entice a hundred or more students to enroll. In the first decade, Nashville Bible School moved to an acreage on what is now Eighth Avenue, saw enrollment increase to 120, offered a variety of courses even out of the field of Bible training (such as Greek, Latin, French, English, elocution, art, and natural science), and had three hundred volumes in the school library. In 1897 there were twelve teachers on the faculty and ninety-four males and forty-three females enrolled coming from a dozen or so states. By 1898 there were eighteen faculty members.

Harding disagreed with the decision to charter Nashville Bible School, thus he resigned and moved to Bowling Green, Kentucky, to found Potter Bible School. Harding was later acknowledged by a new college being formed in Arkansas in 1924, eventually relocating in Searcy and named in his honor.

With 118 students enrolled in 1902 there was a stronger desire for larger quarters and room to grow. On August 22, 1902, David and Margaret Lipscomb donated sixty acres of their farm on Granny White Pike for a new campus. Construction followed: Harding Hall, a classroom building; Avalon, the Lipscomb family home which also housed young women; and Lindsay Hall, a residence hall for young men.

By 1913 David Lipscomb had become enfeebled enough to relinquish his teaching on the campus. His health became so poor that in November 1917 he died. After debate among board members, the board bestowed an honor well deserved—it renamed the school David Lipscomb College.

A WISTFUL REFLECTION

During the senior years of our lives, we may reflect wistfully on our past association with a college campus, especially if we have lived three to four years on that campus. Those college years were so formative to the man or woman we became.

For most decades of Lipscomb history, the institution was relatively small. And alumni who reflect on their college experience, like alumni of any college or university, harbor a range of feelings about having attended Lipscomb—from believing they received an inferior education and regret attending, at one end of the spectrum, to believing their educational experience was excellent and being on campus was akin to "heaven on earth," at the other end of the spectrum. I have always believed more Lipscomb alumni have positive feelings than negative ones.

I have often thought of a brief statement by a young attorney named Daniel Webster, who was honored to argue on behalf of his alma mater, Dartmouth College, before the Supreme Court in 1818. Webster made a direct appeal to

Chief Justice John Marshall: "It is a small college, Sir, but there are those who love it." Plenty of Lipscomb alumni would have uttered the same sentiment about their own alma mater.

In retrospect, I have either attended or taught classes at eight different colleges and universities, most of which are located in Middle Tennessee. My connection with Lipscomb is far deeper and more extensive than my connection with any other college or university. I attended two years in the elementary school (sixth and seventh grades); four years of college curriculum and graduating with a B. A. in Bible; four years as faculty member on leave for graduate studies; seven years in full-time teaching in both the Speech Department and the History and Political Science Department; and some ten to fifteen years as adjunct professor in the Bible, History and Political Science, and Communication Departments. Currently, I am teaching classes in the Lipscomb Lifelong Learning program.

Memories remain so diverse. As with experience in full-time church life, at Lipscomb I have experienced the "highest of highs" and the "lowest of lows." I can only share a few reflections on people and events on this campus in South Nashville, a campus that is still growing, that impacted my life. In preparing to enter ministry I considered these administrators and professors not only mentors, but also "masters" of the various arts and skills of the preaching ministry. I knew there was much to be learned from them and other professors and I accorded them immense respect.

1. A BELEAGUERED PRESIDENT

As a high school senior already committed to attending David Lipscomb College, I first met and visited with President Athens Clay Pullias. He had been invited to present an evening lecture at the fledgling Fort Worth Christian College in early 1960. My family agreed to meet "Brother Pullias," as we called him, at the airport, treat him to supper, then deliver him to his lecture appointment. I remember him sitting in the front passenger seat of our family Olds 88 sedan and our asking questions about how the current school year was going and anything else he wanted to discuss. He came to our city on the heels of a most unfortunate campus accident wherein a male student was killed by an empty coke bottle that was carelessly thrown by another male in Elam Hall, the "boys dorm" as it was called then. In somber tones he discussed the inexcusable tragedy and how it impacted the entire Lipscomb community.

While decades have passed, I still have a strong memory of that night. There was a turnout of several hundred church members in the Fort Worth meeting hall. Brother Pullias had been assigned the topic "The Character of Jesus," and he based his lecture on certain passages in the Sermon on the Mount. I still remember some points and illustrations he offered. I was so impressed. The speaker seemed direct and conversational in style, his content was strong, and he was highly interesting throughout the address. He was so well received. Little wonder this administrator-educator-preacher was later invited to speak at a Fort Worth city-wide meeting at the large city auditorium.

As students in the early 60s, President Pullias had an imposing and distinctive presence. A large man, bald, he had two fingers that had been severed from one hand in a childhood accident. He did not look physically fit. He usually taught one senior level Bible class for one quarter term during the school year. I do not recall his regularly attending daily chapel except on the days he had requested to speak.

Though Pullias' speech content could be much stronger than credited by most students, the students seemed to dread his appearance on stage. When he was present in the group of worship leaders who emerged on stage from behind the curtain, carrying in hand his speech folder, there was a collective and audible groan from the student body. We all felt we would be enduring a much longer chapel talk and most likely on one of the President's favorite themes: why we students are required to have both a Bible class and chapel service every school day (one major theme); the nature of authority that begins with the biblical authority, and then moves to the administrators' authority, and then trickles down to the instructors' authority on down to us lowly students (another theme); and why it is totally scriptural for congregations to make financial contributions directly to a Christian college (a third theme). These speech themes seemed so self-serving, or, perhaps, more fairly stated as institution-serving.

IMPETUS FOR RACIAL INTEGRATION

President Pullias often spoke of how "the winds of change" were blowing and how Lipscomb needed to keep up with the times—ironic because in issues of race relations and social justice the Lipscomb board and administration had ignored or resisted the "winds of change." In fact, it was pretty much an "open secret" that Pullias maintained racial segregation at Lipscomb as long as he could. Racial desegregation in admissions was the stipulation an institution of higher learning that required compliance in order for that institution to receive federal funding under the Higher Education Act for construction of new facilities. Thus, in a faculty meeting in the mid-60s, Pullias informed all college faculty that Lipscomb needed a new science building, that federal funding for higher education was available for racially desegregated institutions, and that "since sooner or later we are going to have to de-segregate and admit Negros to the college, we might as well go ahead and integrate now and take advantage of the funding."

Most of our faculty who discussed this decision, and that was nearly everyone, felt that Pullias made the decision with regretful reluctance. I heard him say in several faculty meetings how the British colonial settlers made a huge mistake in bringing Africans to the colonies for the purposes of slavery, that these colonial governors had myopically sown the wind and the nation now is "reaping the whirlwind."

Thankfully and providentially, racial integration at Lipscomb finally happened. Still, President Pullias attempted to minimize its impact, substantiated by so much evidence. One friend who interviewed for the varsity men's basketball coaching position was then invited to Pullias' office for the final interview. He reported to me that the President told him he did not want more than two black players on the squad and that he did not want more than one black player on the court at any time during the game. Another faculty member informed a group of us colleagues that Pullias was "raging mad" after the 1972 homecoming ceremonies when Bruce Bowers (Lipscomb star basketball player who happened to be African-American) kissed homecoming queen Andrea Boyce on the forehead during half-time coronation ceremonies. The President declared, in his own words, "that little act will cost the school a lot of money." He also instructed the faculty sponsor for the *Backlog* not to include "too many Negros" in the annual.

Even in my first year of full-time Lipscomb professorship, I was amazed at the low morale of what seemed as though the entire faculty experienced. So often, at tables in the faculty dining room (closed to students), professors despondently commiserated over the huge "disconnect" and disaffection with the President. In one of my journal entries (November 9, 1972), I recorded my experience of sitting at a table with two English professors and a Political Science professor, and how I was shocked that they anticipated the President's demise as the only hope for positive change. One of the English professors (who also preached regularly for a Nashville congregation) declared soberly and simply: "We need the help of the Lord."

Of course, our huddled discussions were not all doom and gloom as we could see humor in statements and requests that surprised us, such as the time Pullias called John Hutcheson, Art Department Chairman, reported he bought a new dog house for his son's dog and asked if John could come to his home and paint the new dog house. (As an aside, John told us he wondered if that is what the President thought art teachers do; nonetheless, he bought the paint and got his brushes, drove to the Pullias residence on Graybar Lane and respectfully honored that unusual request.)

The one redeeming application that President Pullias made most of his pet "winds of change" metaphor was the reality of year-round college education, namely to promote Lipscomb's summer quarter enrollment. The big "plus" there, he kept reminding us, is that students could complete a bachelor's degree in three calendar years instead of four. There was also the guarantee that we professors with an earned doctorate would have full-time summer employment.

CAMPUS ENVIRONMENT OF THE SEVENTIES

As a faculty member in the 1970s, there was much more personal interaction with President Pullias than as a student. At the start of the school year we could have a day and a half of faculty meetings, each meeting beginning with a fifteen-minute devotional with various male faculty being assigned to lead some hymns, read a Scripture, make a devotional address, and lead prayers. Female faculty could just relax for the devotional period knowing they would never be called on to take a lead. President Pullias spoke earnestly of his philosophy and concerns at each faculty meeting.

In the early 70s the President continually drove home certain points: One, no civil disturbance, and not even a campus protest demonstration, would be permitted on the Lipscomb campus. He reminded us that he kept the phone number of civil authorities in his billfold and could easily adduce it to summon local police or even the National Guard if necessary to quell any campus disturbance. At the time, having spent several years on the campus of a large urban university, this warning seemed totally untethered to reality. While I had attended both civil rights demonstrations and anti-war rallies at Wayne State University, I knew that such a political demonstration on the campus of Lipscomb was as likely to happen as Tom Hayden or Jane Fonda being invited to speak in the Lipscomb lecture series or Joan Baez or Bob Dylan being invited to sing in the guest artist program series.

A second point of concern: A strict code of student dress and grooming must be enforced by all means. As for the young men, even though long hair and beards were typical at public and most private universities, no Lipscomb male was permitted to wear long hair. And "long hair" was defined as hair that grows below the back and side collar of the shirt. Also, sideburns were required to be of moderate length and neither too low nor "flared" at the base of the sideburn. A number of students made an appeal for cancelling the rule on beards by referencing a portrait of David Lipscomb next to the clock in the entry foyer to Burton Administration building. Alas, to no avail. For a Christian male living around the turn of the century to have a beard was very much in vogue, Pullias and other administrators contended, and no one would have interpreted a long beard in 1900 as a "sign of rebellion against authority."

As for the young women, they were to be adorned with a dress or long skirt at all times on campus outside their dorm. Naturally, bare shoulders, bare midriffs, or even one or two millimeters of cleavage or tight shirts or tight sweaters were unthinkable. Bison cheerleaders and the Bisonettes (a cheer squad that marched around the floor and then sat in the stands and cheered on cue during the game) were required to wear knee-length skirts. Shorts were permitted, of course, for athletic activity. Some co-eds told me that when they wanted to wear shorts off campus on a warm day they would wear a raincoat over the shorts while walking on campus and then remove it once getting in a car. One told me she preferred carrying an old tennis racket while wearing shorts on campus and that would project the nonverbal message she was headed to the tennis court.

FACULTY CONCERNS

During my first year of full-time teaching (1970-71), I learned a lot more about Lipscomb from the vantage point of a professor. Of course, I knew salaries for everyone on campus were low. My first year salary, even with a Ph. D., was $8500, but with the doctorate I was contractually guaranteed another $2,000 if I taught in the summer. I understood that all Lipscomb employees were expected to make a monthly contribution back to the college as well as to increase that contribution each year. Clearly, male professors were expected, though not required, to preach regularly at some Nashville area congregation in order to represent the institution but also to augment their regular salary. Some male faculty were actually excellent preachers. And some male faculty were constitutionally opposed to regular Sunday preaching.

Each year non-tenured faculty signed a new contract that contained a list of stipulations. Active membership in an area congregation of the Church of Christ was required, of course, as well a requirement to abstain from any and all alcoholic beverages and tobacco products. Generally, my perception was that most faculty were in compliance with all the rules, though there were some notable exceptions regarding some rules.

Academic freedom was a major concern. Knowing I would never teach a textual interpretation that I did not believe, I felt I would rapidly be in big trouble if I were ever assigned a Bible class. One of my administrators informed me that I should no longer submit articles for publication in two religious periodicals, one was named *Integrity* and the other *Mission Journal*. I felt stifled and sad at this directive, believing it the antithesis of academic freedom.

At the end of that first year as professor, a dozen or so among my most respected faculty colleagues were leaving Lipscomb for other positions. This group included Bible professors John Willis, John McRay, George Howard, and Don Finto. Don, whom I knew well and respected for his inner city ministry and reaching out to "disaffected youth" (some derisively called them "hippies"), was leaving under major duress, to say the least. The President "forgave" his substantial financial debt (Vanderbilt graduate tuition and half salary for several years on leave) if he agreed to leave the college quietly. My friends David Martin and Hal Wilson were also departing the faculty ranks that same year for professorships at Tennessee State University and Middle Tennessee State University respectively.

A PRIVATE CONFERENCE WITH THE PRESIDENT

While so many on the faculty felt major discouragement and complained among themselves yet failed to express concerns to the President directly, I decided I would express my concerns and ask questions. I felt this would be more honest and direct face-to-face communication. I thus made an appointment with President Pullias. I confessed to him I was concerned about academic freedom, especially in matters of religious faith and doctrine. I informed him that faculty morale was quite low. I told him I had been prohibited from submitting articles to certain religious publications and that I felt censorship was wrong. I talked candidly and shared details, but with as much humility, deference, and respect that I could genuinely muster.

President Pullias did not discuss the dozen or so professors who were leaving. He told me there was a biblical pattern of authority, that people should obey those in authority—citizens were in subjection to the branches of the federal government, Lipscomb professors must obey their chairmen (most, if not all, chairs were male); chairmen were to obey him as president, and he, as president, was expected to obey the Board of Directors. He stated that he personally did not object to periodicals in which I had been published, but if my chairman objected then I must obey his directive. He then stated that in every decision he makes that he asks: "Is this in the best interest for the growth of David Lipscomb College?"

I then pondered if this was why the administration had maintained racial segregation for so many decades? (I had already had direct conversations on the topic of Lipscomb race relations with the Dean, the Bible Department chairman, and my own chairman, and thus felt a need to raise the issue cautiously and diplomatically with the President then. Also, I had represented a group of African-American students who selected me to go to the administration and attempt to convince the administrators to curtail the frequency of the college band playing "Dixie" so many times during a basketball game. One administrator flatly told me that the black students' request was "ridiculous.") Turns out, the President apparently preferred not to discuss this topic.

President Pullias then gave a clear and emphatic directive. He looked me in the eye and patted the front of his desk right in front of me. "If you do not like the way that I am running this college," he instructed emphatically, "then lay your resignation letter right now on this desk and you may quietly leave." He kept looking at me and patting the front of his desk right in front of me. I truly felt he was asking for my resignation. At that point, I attempted to reassure him most calmly and respectfully that I had not come to judge and criticize unfairly but only to gain understanding and insight from his perspective.

A couple of side notes on the lighter side. One, my conference with Pullias was on the day before the June 1971 graduation. There was a big reception for graduates and their families the following day; all faculty were expected to attend. We would wind our way through the Frances Pullias Room and then through the reception line. Actually, food served at the reception was quite delicious, always including country ham biscuits, fresh fruit, and other tasty delicacies served, of course, with fruit punch or spice tea. At this reception, after word of my conference with Pullias had widely circulated among faculty, I was in "big demand" and "called aside" by other professors who wanted to talk to me and hear first-hand what was exchanged by the President and me. Several colleagues gave commendation for my "courageous act" and/or my "honesty and candor" in the conference. Seemingly, I had gained a new and higher level of respect from these colleagues.

Second, at another conference in the President's office about two years later, I was asked to do some fund-raising work for the college in lieu of not having a full load of class assignments in the summer quarter. Pullias was instructing me on what to say when asking for contributions. The conference was most congenial and pleasant. Then, Pullias paused a few moments, looked at me earnestly, and stated: "Perry, let me ask you to do something. You need to raise your sideburns by at least a quarter-inch or so and take out the flare at the bottom of the sideburns. We are trying to teach moderation on this campus, and someone like you with this radical look about you will 'undo' all the good things we try to teach and model." That was a surprise. "Unreal, simply unreal!" I said to myself at the time, but I did not express my surprise aloud.

While my professional colleagues' appreciation and respect meant so much, I figure that the first conference cost me several thousand dollars. In the ensuing years, my raises were minimal or non-existent and I was never promoted from Assistant Professor to Associate Professor. In 1976-77 I was interim pulpit minister for the Westwood Church of Christ in McMinnville. The elders there kept offering a full-time position. When they gave my family a "walk-through" in the spacious brick church parsonage, located on eight to ten acres of land with abundant trees and varied nursery stock all around (Warren County claims to be "the nursery capital of the world"), and I had already known of the tennis court and basketball goals and picnic tables on the adjacent church grounds, and then the elders offered about $7,000 more in annual salary than Lipscomb was providing, I could only exclaim: "Oh, Lord, I just know you have called me to return to the ministry!!"

Of all the coincidental ironies, within a few days after my family had moved to McMinnville to return to full-time ministry, it was announced that President Pullias was stepping down from Lipscomb. While I know much of the story of that summer that led to his sudden departure, perhaps it is best untold here. Suffice to say, sadly, the President retained so very little support among board, faculty, and students to remain in that highest administrative position. Much faculty and staff disaffection was related to low salaries across the entire campus, including elementary and secondary school teachers, combined with the President's decisions to spend large sums on refurbishing Alumni Auditorium and other seeming cosmetic projects that had no connection to quality education or faculty morale. Many faculty and staff members stated that the generous tuition discount (up to 75 percent for themselves or other family members including children while minors at home) was a major factor in remaining in the college's employ.

Pullias, who began teaching at Lipscomb in 1934 in various subject areas, agreed to a financial settlement and stepped down from the presidency in the summer of 1977. Soon thereafter he disassociated himself from the Church of Christ. As it turned out, Pullias was far more liberal and open in his theological thinking than most people realized. I recall that on every social occasion, he praised his wife, whom he called "Miz Pullias," for her steadfast support; he even had a large room with an attached entrance way in the new student center named "Frances Pullias Room" and it hosted graduation and other receptions. Starbucks leases that floor space now. Today, one sees little if any public evidence on campus that Pullias was ever a campus figure—no monument, building, or other facility named in his honor despite his many years of service.

Charitably, I would return to my earliest memories of President Pullias as a speaker and preacher. He was even one of a dozen speakers featured in a series of twelve books of sermons, *Great Preachers of Today*, published by Biblical Research Press. I prefer to think of his administrative leadership as a time in which Lipscomb moved from junior college to senior college status, a time when the enrollment increased, a time when additional properties were acquired and new buildings were constructed. Of course, many U. S. colleges and universities expanded and thrived during those decades and it might have been hard for a college president to fail. Nonetheless, Athens Clay Pullias' dreams and plans laid groundwork for what Lipscomb has become today.

2. THE "PEOPLE PERSON"

One or two people exerted the greatest influence on my young professional life. Willard Collins was one of them. My first memory of him was his coming to the Lamar Avenue congregation in Paris, Texas, when I was a student in elementary school, and "holding a meeting."

The week my family moved from Paris to Nashville in 1954, my dad left town for some gospel meeting and left my mom, brother, sister and me alone in a new residence and new city. We had never owned a television set. So Brother Collins ventured to some local store, bought a big table top General Electric television set with some gift money our family had been given, and delivered it to our house. Bulky and heavy, both he and I were needed to carry the TV up the stairs to the second floor, set it up with a rabbit ears antenna, turn it on, and make certain it could draw signals from Nashville's three stations: WSM, WLAC, and WSIX.

Thrillingly, the set gave us nightly entertainment for the next decade or so and enabled us to know Lucille Ball, Milton Berle, Gale Storm, newsman John Cameron Swayze and a host of others. Brother Collins' simple, unselfish act of courtesy occurred over sixty-five years ago, yet it remains unforgettable. Perhaps at that point as a young boy, though I did not think much about it at the time, I realized that Brother Collins genuinely loved and cared about people and that he was unselfish with his time and other resources. He was glad to have our family in Nashville, for us to live on Rosemont Avenue just two doors north of the Lipscomb campus, and to have my sister and me enroll in the campus school (at that time tuition was around $150 per semester).

Brother Collins held a meeting at the old Lindsley Avenue church building where my dad was minister. Naturally, we attended every night. I can't recall any single sermon topic, but I do recall a trait that always remained a strong memory about Brother Collins—his speaking style, especially his preaching style, best known for a deep, forceful, and dynamic voice and physical manner.

Indeed, the voice was unforgettable, but the facial expressions, combined with pregnant pauses, were also part and parcel of this dynamic delivery. Brother Collins was Vice President of Lipscomb during my early years of student enrollment, but he was first and foremost this dynamic preacher. His style was inimitable, yet, interestingly, there were plenty of "preacher boys" who had fun trying to imitate him. My classmate Steve Kepley and I both liked to stand out on campus and imitate Brother Collins; perhaps the best imitation was offered by a preacher named Jim Mankin, though there were surely scores of preachers, young and old, who had fun performing their best imitation.

All ironic, in a sense, because few of us could remember Willard Collins' sermon topics and themes. His lessons were always quite simple. He saw most issues as black or white. Clearly he loved both the Church of Christ and he loved Lipscomb. Over his preaching career he must have conducted hundreds upon hundreds of gospel meetings. His simple lessons were presented in most states in the Union and even in a Far East lectureship. His voice was heard almost every day in chapel as he opened and closed each service with introductions and then with closing announcements that ended with the simple words "and that is all."

Of course, the one announcement that was the most popular, emphatically announced once each fall quarter, was: "This is a beautiful day. No more classes for today. All of us may gather in Warner Park for a picnic lunch with games and activities." Quite understandably, Brother Collins was requested over the decades for more than his share of wedding officiating and funeral eulogies.

Brother Collins possessed genuine affection for all kinds of people. He has been called a "people person." Everyone liked him. Even if you disagreed with him, you still liked him. He was so approachable. He had a simple manner and a loving and caring heart. He seemed to see the best in people, faculty and students alike. Seemingly, it pained him when he felt no choice but to render strong discipline to students who had broken college rules.

FROM STUDENT BODY PRESIDENT TO COLLEGE PRESIDENT

Willard Collins came to David Lipscomb College from Lewisburg, Tennessee, in 1934. As a student, he became involved in all kinds of speech activities, appearing in plays, leading the debate team, preaching frequently for area churches, winning student body presidency, and winning the Founders Day Oratorical

Contest. Being so effective in raising money for the school, he was named vice president when Lipscomb became a four-year college in 1946.

Fast forward to 1977. A cloud of scandal hovered over the Lipscomb administration. For a number of reasons, including a financial crisis, an abrupt change in presidential leadership was essential. And while numerous candidates might have been interviewed for Lipscomb president, there was one person right there on campus, already both loved and trusted and with the highest possible credibility, who was humbly willing to step in and serve the institution he loved and to which he had devoted heart and soul.

Brother Collins was the students' president. He was so approachable. His face was seen and voice was heard in almost every daily chapel service. On Bison Day he was willing to be "fall man" for student stunts. In chapel announcements he could seem naïve when students laughed at some mistake in his reading those announcements. He seemed to enjoy "playing dumb" when students laughed at his comments; when they laughed, he could make impromptu comments that brought more laughter. Then, when at a pretended or actual loss for words, he could grimace that unique face and nod his head as though to say, "I can't believe your response" or "I am at a loss for words." At times students chuckled at his wardrobe, for example, when wearing light-colored socks with a dark suit.

Brother Collins was the right man at the right place in 1977. He was replaced by Harold Hazelip, a scholar and theologian who also possessed gifts of administration and personality. The Board of Directors created the position of chancellor for this "people person" and, as Jim Turner has rightly named him, "A man for all seasons."

Stories about Willard Collins are legion. Though he could make people laugh through his reaction to situations or to his own naiveté when making conversation, he failed at times to see the humor. I recall once just visiting with him on a warm day when he was working in his Lealand Avenue front yard. I asked if he had some funny stories in church life he could share. He thought a while and then said seriously, "Perry, I can't think of any." And I do not recall him telling a joke or deploying planned humor in any way in any sermon.

ONE-NIGHT PREACHING GIGS

Brother Collins had one-night speaking appointments quite frequently, and often they were in a city of some distance from Nashville. While he did travel to "preach the gospel," seemed his real purpose was serving as ambassador for DLC. I served as driver for him during some of my student days. I recall his owning a white 1960 Oldsmobile 88 four-door sedan. As we would drive to a city, Brother Collins would talk to me as a friend, one on one. I loved those moments and sacrificed study time on campus for my own "driving Miss Daisy" assignment.

On every occasion, Brother Collins would talk as a father to a son: "Perry, you can be a great preacher in the brotherhood. When you leave Lipscomb, earn your Masters and then go for the Ph.D. in some field," he advised. "Then you can return to Lipscomb, teach Bible classes, and preach every Sunday at a large congregation. Then, when you retire, write a book of memoirs and tell everyone how the Lord has used you at Lipscomb and throughout the brotherhood." I never forgot that advice though even then I thought his plan for my life was a bit unrealistic.

On one occasion, Brother Collins asked me to drive on a school day down to Bremen, Georgia. On the way to Bremen he sat beside me in the front seat and we chatted as I drove. Upon arrival we were invited into a nice residence of a devoted and hospitable Christian family and were sumptuously fed a great Southern supper prior to church meeting time. Brother Collins sat at the end of the dining table as the person of honor and almost all questions were sent his way. As conversationalist, he could make everyone feel good by taking genuine interest in each life. We then sat and visited a few minutes in the living room till time to go to the church house and greet the brethren and sisters with hand-shakes and name exchanges.

There might have been 300 to 400 people in attendance, surely the local audience was augmented by visitors from area congregations. As with all sermons, Brother Collins began remarks by graciously thanking anyone who had done him or Lipscomb the least favor. He thanked the host and hostess in the home where we had just enjoyed supper. He acknowledged some youth from the congregation who had attended Lipscomb. "I want to thank my young brother

Perry Cotham, who is my chauffeur for the round trip from Nashville," he then declared. "His dad and granddad, Brother Perry B. and Brother Coleman Overby, have been great preachers in the brotherhood and young Perry is following in their steps." Then he transitioned to his sermon theme, a variation of his sermons I had often heard.

A side note: Willard Collins never used notes while preaching. He would simply hold a Bible in hand or lay it on the pulpit.

Around 9:00 to 9:15, we said our "good-byes" and prepared for the drive back to Nashville. This was a weeknight and Brother Collins needed his rest as he planned to be back in his office (or at least at chapel) the next morning, so he took off his coat and loosened his tie and got in the backseat with a small pillow. Once we got out of town, he informed me he planned to sleep on the return trip. I recall that we were going through northern Alabama (no interstate) and the speed limit was posted as sixty for daytime and fifty for the dark hours. There was very little traffic on the highway. Carelessly, my speed crept up to around eighty to eighty-five mph sometime between 11:00 P.M. and midnight. I passed a patrol car parked perpendicularly on the side of the highway, my heart began racing, and though I slowed down immediately I saw the flashing blue lights coming toward me.

As I slowed down and began to pull over to the shoulder, I spoke up loudly enough to awaken my passenger: "Brother Collins, I've got a problem. I am being pulled over by the Alabama highway patrol and I know I was speeding." My passenger may have grunted or groaned just a little, but did not say anything at that point.

After my stopping and rolling down the window, the officer said, "Young man, may I see your license please?" So I pulled out my Texas driver's license and handed it to the officer.

At that moment, Brother Collins raised up from the back seat and in his deep, thunderous voice he explained: "Officer, I'm Willard Collins, Vice President of David Lipscomb College in Nashville, and I have been on a preaching appointment tonight. And the driver is Perry Cotham, one of our young preacher students at Lipscomb. He drives so that I am able to rest and sleep on the return home."

The patrolman looked at my license and then had a long pause. I sat behind the wheel with both embarrassment and shame. There was nothing I could say. After a few more seconds the officer handed back the license and said, "Given the circumstances, I am not giving you a ticket. The speed limit is fifty in this state at night, so just hold it close to fifty as you drive the rest of the way in Alabama."

"Yes, sir, and thank you so much," I humbly uttered. As we drove away, very slowly of course, meekly I said, "Brother Collins, I sure am sorry. I was going nearly eighty-five. There's almost no traffic on this highway, so I thought I was being safe. I can't believe I was not given a ticket and a hefty fine. I surely deserved a ticket."

"That's alright, Perry, don't worry about it," Brother Collins said. "You might feel better to know that has happened several times before to some other drivers I have had. When I raise up and tell them who I am and that I had been to preach the gospel and to please give my driver understanding, then, Perry, I can tell you that my driver has never been issued a ticket. It works every time."

The last statement surprised me a bit: "It works every time." Therein I saw the humanity of the man as never before. And I had to smile. The totally renovated and modernized Alumni Auditorium at Lipscomb is now known as Collins-Alumni Auditorium—the venue in which brother Collins unforgettably reached the most people on an ongoing basis. Brother Collins is truly a Lipscomb legend.

3. THE LEAN DEAN

It was near supper time one warm afternoon in the third week of September. A group of incoming students were visiting on the lawn near the paved circle which connected the Sewell and Elam residence halls (called dormitories in those days). Freshman orientation lasted several days, upperclassmen had not arrived, and classes had not begun. Having traveled some seven hundred miles to attend Lipscomb and knowing it would not be until Christmas break that I would return to visit my family, I was already in the throes of anticipatory homesickness.

Circling the drive was a lone motorist. He pulled up to our group and got out of his car. We all recognized him instantly, in fact had already begun to make references to him by his widely circulated "lean dean" nickname. "If any of you students would like to eat a home-cooked meal instead of school cafeteria food tonight, just get in the car," he beckoned. "I'll come back and pick up another load if you want to invite any of your friends."

One by one we piled into the Dean's light blue, '60 Ford Fairlane station wagon. Once at his home on nearby Scenic Drive, we all introduced ourselves, enjoyed our first home-cooked meal since arriving on campus, spent a delightful evening visiting together, and were transported back to campus. For those of us who had casually visited on campus a few hours earlier, the occasion was a most unexpected, but unforgettable sharing of warmth and graciousness.

What seemed like a rare and fortuitous experience for a few students that evening was, I soon learned, commonplace for this young administrator and single father of three young children. (Sadly, his wife, Dottie, had died of cancer a few months earlier.) Students were always welcomed in his home. His doors were seldom if ever locked. And on many a holiday, students who lived at too great distances to travel home were invited into his home to sit at his table. The Lipscomb family of students was genuinely his family. In the summer of 1962, the Dean invited me to live in an apartment behind his large residence on Graybar Lane.

Mack Wayne Craig, born in Obion, Tennessee, was raised in Jacksonville, Florida. In January 1943 he traveled to Nashville to enroll in David Lipscomb College, thus beginning a relationship with the institution which would traverse five decades. When J. P. Sanders, highly respected Dean and professor, resigned in 1957 from the Deanship for a position at Pepperdine College, President Pullias passed over one or two others considered to be strong candidates to head the school's academic program and looked across the campus to a young man in whom he had the highest confidence—Mack Wayne Craig was named Acting Dean. His doctoral dissertation at George Peabody College, now a division of Vanderbilt University, was entitled "The Deanship of Church-Related Colleges." He served in that position for twenty-one years and then was named a Vice President for Institutional Planning and Director of the National Development Board.

If one were to list three or four Lipscomb people who have directly and personally impacted the highest number of students, alumni, and the Nashville community at large, Mack Craig must surely be on that list. And perhaps no one in the school's history has wielded a greater influence on the institution's academic program than this tall and lanky administrator whose body bore no signs of having joined heartily in countless church "pot lucks" and "dinners on the ground." This man who seemed to have four first names—when called by his administrative title—must have been blessed by great genes or raging, non-stop metabolism.

In my case, the ole career windmill was already tilting toward the preaching ministry, but the final and telling gust of godly influence was blown my way in the fall of 1960 by "the lean dean." He was also my first college Bible teacher. He liked me as a student, invited me to speak as a guest at his home congregation, Charlotte Avenue Church of Christ, and he alone made a decision to invite me to return to Lipscomb to give my life to Christian education. He offered a contract that provided a very small salary while I was in graduate studies and paid my tuition and fees. His influence on my early life was incalculable.

The greatest moments of that first term as a homesick freshman were sitting at the feet, as it were, of Dean Craig with about eighty or ninety others in a required daily Bible class. As an early mentor as well as a role model, there was nothing in the whole gamut of church ministry he could not do well—preaching, song leading, public praying, you name it. He must have known four hundred hymns, and all stanzas except those marked with an asterisk (our hymnals informed worshipers that these asterisked stanzas could be skipped over without damaging the thematic structure of the hymn), by heart.

When we students would see Dean Craig sitting on the stage during a period of chapel singing, his countenance was one of such spiritual ecstasy that to gaze upon him seemed like an invasion of privacy. At other times, while sitting on the stage or pulpit during messages of even moderate length by guest speakers, the lean dean appeared to be drifting peacefully off into dreamland. Fortunately, perhaps even providentially, he always slowly returned to the world of the conscious in time for the speaker's conclusion.

THE DEAN'S PEDAGOGICAL STYLE

In college Bible classes the Dean's impact was felt most deeply. When I came to Lipscomb in the fall of '60, I brought along an extensive indoctrination of Bible facts and narratives, rooted in eighteen years of regular Sunday School and Wednesday class attendance and having been exposed to innumerable sermons delivered by my father, grandfather, one uncle, and a variety of other preachers. Freshman Bible would surely be little more than glorified Sunday School. I already had enjoyed daily Bible study at home and had the classic texts of the King James Version of the Bible, such as the Twenty-third Psalm, 1 Corinthians 13, John 3: 16, and most of the Sermon on the Mount, already memorized. Fortunately, some adviser placed me in the Dean's class and, from day one, I felt blessed indeed.

Dean Craig's theology was as simple as mine at the time, but he possessed a unique gift for effectively recounting stories in early Hebrew history I had heard all my life. No one could narrate a Bible story, personal story, or even a Civil War story with more dramatic flair. Each class was a self-contained sermon, complete with humor, exposition, and an emotional conclusion which summoned us to appropriate action. Most important, in all the Bible narratives, this instructor could draw practical applications I had never considered. Soon, a burning desire welled up within me to find a church—any church—in which I could recycle this same material and emotion on a regular basis.

In that fall quarter, stories of Adam and Eve, Cain and Abel, Noah and his family, and, most of all, Moses, came to life as never before. The quarter ended with the story of Moses on the mountain, viewing the Promised Land, but being informed by God he would not be crossing Jordan and entering. That story was problematic for me, then and now, but the Dean told us that God had something even better prepared for Moses than some real estate property in Canaan. The explanation seemed convincing at the time.

In the winter quarter, the Dean brought new, insightful perspectives on the life of Jesus and the same was true for the apostles in the early life of the primitive church in the spring quarter class. The Dean's pedagogical method was to present biblical characters as real people and then make practical applications to everyday life. He taught with a flair for the dramatic (so many times you could have heard the proverbial pin drop), his lectures had a vitally clear beginning and a dramatic ending (he surely disdained the old "let's stop at this verse and pick up at the next one tomorrow" approach), and his main points were often poignantly illustrated by narratives drawn from personal life, ancient history, the antebellum South, and, most especially, the Civil War. In that freshman year, the nation was commemorating the hundredth anniversary of the beginning of the Civil War.

The Dean always maintained a sense of humor and wit in his classes and consistently cleared his throat with a certain resonance as a cue to class laughter, or at least slight chuckling, when a statement was meant to be funny. If a student took the Dean for more than one class, that student would hear several of his stories a second and third time.

The one biblical theme most associated with Craig was "the Cross of Christ," a class which compelled students to identify with at least one or more of the passion characters. Still another of his popular Bible classes was "Marriage and the Christian Home," a pleasant and pleasurable tour of several biblical narratives as well as the rich mine of the instructor's anecdotal material and personal experiences as husband and father. In retrospect, I concluded that many of the Dean's recommendations for resolving marital conflict were overly-simplistic and impractical, even if entertaining and unforgettable. Little wonder the Dean was in heavy demand among students for officiating at wedding ceremonies.

A UNIQUE ENDURING MEMORY

Mack Craig made another enduring contribution to the Lipscomb legacy. How fascinating that literally hundreds of former students would rank a weekly, fifteen-minute, late night, outdoors devotional as among the most memorable highlights of their campus days! This campus tradition had a most inauspicious beginning. "When I was on the Abilene Christian campus in February of '60 to speak in their lectureship, I attended a wonderful devotional at night on their campus," the Dean recalled to me. "Upon returning to Nashville, I proposed that we start one on our campus, and I told the administration 'if you don't object I'll take the lead in it myself.'"

As the clock moved toward 10:00 each Tuesday evening of the school calendar, scores of students put down their books or ended their activities and emerged from their residence halls and the library, a few even drove to campus, for a spontaneous songfest. Usually from the beginning, Dean Craig accepted requests from the assembly and led all songs from memory. One rule he followed was beginning the devotional promptly at 10:00 and ending promptly at 10:15. The melodious *a cappella* music could be heard from steps of nearby residence halls and other campus buildings.

The devotional was conducted in all kinds of weather. If rain was coming down we moved up the steps and huddled under the high roof above the columns of "Alumni." If the temperature seemed freezing or below zero we bundled up. The Dean often wore a long trench coat. Students would shout out a title for a song they wanted sung. "My God and I" was one favorite; that hymn concluded with a little humming and poetic recitation. The Dean loved "Peace, Perfect Peace." At times a less-familiar hymn title was thrown out and the Dean would say, "We'd better pass on that hymn tonight as it is not so familiar to many of us." I smiled inside on those moments, my theory being the Dean himself was probably unfamiliar with the lyrics but could never in that spiritual moment admit it.

THE COLLINS-CRAIG MEETING

In the 60s it seemed all the rage for cities in the Bible Belt to conduct gospel meetings in spacious city auditoriums or arenas. Such meetings demonstrated "importance" and "bigness," and gathered attention and free publicity. The first one I attended was in my hometown of Dallas, Texas, in 1958. The Dallas Municipal Auditorium was fairly new. Naturally, planners realized there must be participants who draw people outside the fellowship so the Dallas church leaders selected Pat Boone to lead singing, Bobby Morrow, 1956 two-time Olympic Gold Medalist who ran track at Abilene Christian College, to make a brief opening talk, and George Bailey, outstanding orator and evangelist, also from Abilene, to deliver the keynote address.

Leaders in the city of Nashville had long considered the need for a municipal auditorium that could host more diverse events, as well as seat more people, than the War Memorial Auditorium, home of Nashville Symphony concerts and other special programs.

So the new $5,000,000 Nashville Municipal Auditorium was completed in 1962 under the leadership of Mayor Ben West, and the very first event in the new facility was a week-long gospel meeting sponsored by area Churches of Christ. This seemed a Lipscomb event all the way—Mack Wayne Craig led all the singing and Willard Collins did all the preaching, and local preachers did all the praying. Little wonder the event was promoted as "The Collins-Craig Meeting." At the time I felt some level of discomfort at the name for the meeting, focusing on two men (albeit well-known and godly men) on the marquee rather than on Jesus, but the meeting seemed a model for other Bible Belt urban areas in the 60s.

The opening service was conducted on October 7, 1962. The attendance for that night was 15,500, with an estimated 5,000 being turned away. Of course, the audience that night had been mobilized by as many as a hundred or so congregations dismissing their Sunday evening services with worshipers being urged to go downtown for the meeting. I had to stand toward the back for this service, but I attended on all subsequent nights, sometimes bringing a date, and there seemed ample seating available.

Despite the drop off in attendance on subsequent nights, morale was still high. The Dean led the old hymns of Zion that many, if not most of us, knew by heart. And Brother Collins was still Brother Collins, speaking with that powerful voice, sincere facial expression, earnest appeal, and delivering a simple message of grace and hope from Holy Scripture. I don't recall many "visible responses," nor did I see any studies on how many non-Church of Christ visitors attended. Nonetheless, the closing service was October 14 and total attendance was announced as 90,467— the event was deemed a successful one "crowned by the Lord with success."

As an aside, David Lipscomb College hosted the first athletic event conducted in this same Municipal Auditorium when a few weeks later the Bisons met the Western Kentucky Hilltoppers in a varsity basketball game. Western had a special ceremony and award planned for Ed Diddle, long-time coach, at the end of this game they expected to win easily. WKU has enjoyed a rich basketball tradition. The Lipscomb student body showed up in major support for the Bisons. We made our way into that large new venue that made McQuiddy Gym look puny by contrast. What a close and exciting game! Many of us yelled and screamed like crazy as our Bisons took the lead and worked to hold it. And Lipscomb Bisons shocked Western Kentucky by upsetting the heavily favored Hilltoppers 75-68. The ceremony for the legendary Diddle and his milestone win was put on hold till the Hilltoppers' next game.

4. ACADEMIC ADVISER, MODEL FOR STUDENT PREACHERS, AND FRIEND

What would be required for someone to be properly labeled or described as a "master" in the art of some skill, in this case the art of public proclamation of spiritual truth? Would not that person have specific training and a well-rounded educational background that prepared oneself for the art? Would not the person know the theory of homiletics and oral proclamation and, more importantly, model the exercise of that art? Would not the person need wide-ranging and diverse experiences in the practice of that art? Would not the practitioner of that art be able to analyze one's audience and adapt to each audience with a strategy to maximize effectiveness? Most of all, would not the master in proclamation be someone whose motives were clearly honest and transparent and whose passion was so manifestly obvious? (Incidentally, such an orator fits the model of the effective orator/rhetor as described by ancient theorists and rhetoricians Aristotle, Cicero, and Quintilian.)

Batsell Barrett Baxter was an unforgettable mentor who met all those standards. Additionally, I have been honored that we had the experience of being both friends and colleagues despite a generation of age difference. As a boy, I had often heard his name, his first name seeming a bit unusual at the time, then the alliteration of the entire name tempted some to reference him as "Triple B" or simply "BBB." The vast majority of colleagues and students harbored far too much respect for the man to call him, or even reference him, by some flippant nickname. Though he had earned a doctorate in speech communication from the University of Southern California, many students and members of Hillsboro Church of Christ called him simply "Brother Baxter."

Baxter was born into a family with deep roots in both ministry and Christian education. His dad, also Batsell Baxter, began serving as Lipscomb's president in 1932. The younger Baxter went to Abilene Christian College and was extensively involved in extracurricular activities. The older Baxter was appointed as the founding president of George Pepperdine College in Los Angeles in 1937, and a newly married Batsell Barrett and his young bride also moved to L.A. and immersed himself in a range of important commitments: teaching speech at Pepperdine, coaching debate at Pepperdine, preaching at L.A.-area congregations, and, on top of all these engagements, pursuing graduate studies at USC.

With his doctorate completed, Baxter returned to the Lipscomb faculty. As one of very few professors with an earned doctorate, he taught both speech and Bible classes and chaired the Speech Department. The senior Baxter died in 1956 and in that same year the younger Baxter, having completed a Bachelor of Divinity at Vanderbilt University, was named the new chair of the Bible Department. Altogether, Baxter served Lipscomb for almost forty years.

In the summer of 1960, while making preparations to head to Nashville for my college experience, I received a letter from the admissions office informing me that I had been assigned to Batsell Baxter as my academic advisor. He remained my advisor in more ways than one the next four years. Most who knew him well think of his serving, in addition to heading Lipscomb Bible Department, as regular pulpit minister of the Hillsboro Church of Christ and then as the featured speaker on the national radio and television program "Herald of Truth," a ministry headquartered in Abilene, Texas.

SOURCES OF EFFECTIVENESS

During his generation, probably most Church of Christ members, especially the church historians and other observers, if asked to name the one most effective and best-known preacher and evangelist in this fellowship, there would be near consensus on one person: Batsell Barrett Baxter. Some considered him the Church of Christ answer to Billy Graham though their sermon delivery styles were quite different. While his name and some stories involving him are found in other chapters, I propose now to offer my personal perspective on his effectiveness and his influence on my life.

First and foremost, Brother Baxter possessed the highest dimension of *ethos*, what Aristotle and other Greeks called "source credibility". Undoubtedly, the most valuable classes for me and other aspiring ministers were the junior level course "Preparation and Delivery of Sermons" along with the follow-up course "Practical Aspects of Preaching." Very early in the class, Brother Baxter spoke of a godly moral life as the most important element in the equipping of a person to be a preacher.

Baxter, to illustrate this point, held up a white sheet of paper. The paper was perfectly usable except for one small ink blotch right in the middle of the sheet. He asked us, "When I hold this up, what do you see?" "A big black spot" or "An ink spot," answered some classmates. Then the instructor reminded us that no student had said, "I see a single piece of paper." We were all focused on the spot or blemish in the middle. His point: If there is an obvious, glaring sin or other shortcoming in one's life as a minister, a congregation and community will notice and comment on the one glaring blotch or stain and not on the overall respectable life.

Brother Baxter lived that kind of life—a living example of the lessons he taught. He preached goodness and holiness and seemed always to embody those and other fruit of the Spirit. One of his classic sermons was entitled "The Beauty of Holiness" and one of his favorite hymns was entitled "More Holiness Give Me." Culturally a very conservative man, also largely apolitical, he modeled a good and blameless life—his succumbing to a huge moral failure or scandal seemed wholly unimaginable to any who knew him or heard him preach. He taught us that moral credibility was the most important trait that led a minister to be requested to perform a family funeral or wedding, not necessarily the preacher who is best educated or the most eloquent or most handsome.

Second, Brother Baxter modeled effective pulpit delivery. Having studied rhetoric and public address for most of my life, I know that styles of delivery have changed. Before the days of public address systems, a loud and bombastic, an almost "acting" performance with exaggerated gestures, seemed the most effective way to hold a large audience. William Jennings Bryan, who actually did religious speaking toward the end of his life, might have been the best model of this bombastic oratorical style. Professors of public speaking now teach students the "conversational manner" of delivery wherein speakers have "enlarged conversation" with an audience—taking the best traits of lively conversation (naturalness, sincerity, liveliness, empathy, genuineness, attention to feedback, etc.) and deploying them in the delivery of speeches.

When Brother Baxter preached or taught, his style was not some unnatural and exaggerated use of voice and body. He would stand behind a podium and then "converse" with an audience. Sometimes he would hold an open Bible in one hand and gesture with the other. On other occasions, he would simply fold one hand on top of the other, tilt his head just a little, employ modest facial expressiveness (often lifting his eyebrows), and then speak in conversational, genuine tones. His eye contact was always excellent; he was not tied to a manuscript; and he knew how to make pregnant pauses to allow listeners a moment to reflect.

Little wonder that Brother Baxter was engaged as the main speaker for the radio and television ministry *Herald of Truth*. Few preachers who stand each week behind a podium can adapt effectively to simply sitting behind a desk or in a comfortable chair and just conversing with the unseen audience—all the while avoiding distracting mannerisms. Baxter possessed those skills and in many ways he was ahead of his time in sermon delivery.

As an aside, it was understandable that in our homiletics class we aspiring pulpit speakers would present original sermons in our class. What was unforgettable are the times we were requested to come to the Hillsboro church auditorium, stand in that pulpit, and present our sermons with only one person sitting a third of the way back at the end of a pew with a notepad and pen in hand. A private conference with our professor for commendation and suggestions would follow each sermonic presentation.

Third, the influence of Brother Baxter, especially on young ministers in training, is simply immeasurable. Challenging enough would be any calculation of how many people he reached with gospel messages through the various churches he served, through the national radio and television ministry, through the Bible classes that he taught, and through the various meetings he held. Yet just imagine how many were influenced by his biblical exposition and teaching homiletics to gifted young men who, in turn over their own life-time of preaching, reached thousands upon thousands of people.

Harold Hazelip, a learned theologian and highly skilled preacher who has enjoyed immense influence in many roles, was once asked who had exerted the greatest influence on his life and thinking. His answer came without hesitation: "I would say Dr. Batsell Baxter." Surely there are scores and scores of preachers of all ages who have been influenced by this same godly man. This professor seemed to take a special sense of pride in the achievements of a number of his former students. I have heard him frequently mention preachers and missionaries that he felt privileged to have influenced as his student majors, evangelists such as Philip Slate, Philip Morrison, Prentice Meador, and too many others to name here. The author of Hebrews once made a brief statement about Abel that applies here to Brother Baxter: "Having died, yet still speaking."

UNFORGETTABLE PERSONAL MEMORIES

There are personal memories, of course. At times Brother Baxter and I would sit in his office and converse. He invited me to be a guest teacher for his large Bible class at Hillsboro on Wednesday night when he was scheduled to speak elsewhere. Occasionally, I would do some errands at his request, such as picking up a HAM radio in Dallas for his son Scott and bringing it back to Nashville. Scott became quite proficient in electronics technology.

My respected friend Philip Morrison enjoyed so many interactions with Brother Baxter, especially when both were in pulpit ministry and connected with Herald of Truth. Philip was bedside with Brother Baxter during his last days of critical illness and volunteered to sit for those last several days outside the hospital room and politely inform well-meaning visitors that it was not in the patient's best interests to have any company.

Brother Baxter and Philip enjoyed a warm, mutually respectful friendship that had roots in the latter's David Lipscomb College student days. Dr. Baxter had been the Lipscomb debate coach in the early 50s and Philip, along with Robert McGowan, who later became an attorney, composed the college's best debate team even as freshmen. Baxter accompanied them to the state debate tournament at then Memphis State University, and, as tournaments are conducted, the coach would be a judge for various rounds of debates involving other teams.

As the state tourney proceeded, Dr. Baxter pulled Philip and Robert aside and confided that in an upcoming round he [Baxter] had been assigned as judge. This was most irregular—a debate coach judging a round in which one's own team competes. Perhaps the tourney had one judge *in absentia* or perhaps one judge became ill and had to leave his or her assignment. Regardless, the Lipscomb coach viewed his ethical responsibility clearly.

"No matter how well you fellows [Philip and Robert] perform in the next round, I must give the decision to the opposing team. That way there is not going to be any accusation of bias or favoritism," Dr. Baxter informed them. Philip and Robert did not relish the thought of an automatic defeat of a round of debate and questioned their coach's personal fairness to them. "This irritated the fool out of me at the time," Philip recalled.

Dr. Baxter gave an immediate reply: "I understand your sense of fairness. But consider that we represent a Christian college, and we must leave no room for any criticism that we might have been unethically biased in awarding one team victory over another team." Thus, after that round of debate, Dr. Baxter marked on his ballot a victory for the other college team. This being a double-elimination tournament, Philip and Robert, both freshmen, won the remaining rounds and were awarded the Tennessee state college debating championship. And they won the state championship tournament two other years as well—thus three out of four years winning the state tournament.

"I loved this man," Philip told me. "He changed my life because he changed my outlook."

My own most impactful memory was Brother Baxter's inviting me to join a group that spent several weeks in England as part of two long gospel crusades, the first in Aylesbury, an hour or so out of London, and the other in the Wembley section of London. A smaller contingent of us left early for Aylesbury, and this was my first time to visit New York City and fly on a jet (a Boeing 707/Pan American flight) across the Atlantic; then, another group joined us for the Wembley campaign for the congregation Philip Slate served as missionary. This was an opportunity to learn and experience so much!

In the spring quarter of 1964, the Bible majors were required to complete a senior-level "Bible Comprehensive" course as directed by our chairman. Having taken almost every Bible course in the curriculum, I felt I knew biblical Scripture and narratives fairly well. I had at this point, in fact, perhaps more than half of the New Testament memorized in the KJV. However, under the Lipscomb rule of each student being required to complete a Bible class and attend chapel every day, I was required to repeat a Bible course I had already taken simply to fulfill that inflexible rule (I did this both in winter and spring quarters)—legalism won another victory.

The disappointing news at the beginning of that spring quarter was learning Brother Baxter would be incapacitated for several weeks due to undergoing surgery and treatment for cancer. However, he was permitted to meet with just one class—our Bible comprehensive class. At the outset of the term, he gave us a long list of challenging questions and instructed us to do research and give thorough answers to the questions, compiling these responses into a big notebook. So I splurged on a complete set of *International Standard Bible Encyclopedia* to augment my library and personal sources, girded the loins of my trusty, green and metallic Royal portable typewriter, and prepared in elite typescript a workbook with more than 125 pages. He gave the workbook an A.

One memory of a heartwarming experience: After Brother Baxter was in recovery from surgery, though unable to leave his home, he invited our small class over to his home on Mayfair Avenue, behind the Lipscomb campus. The professor, wearing a robe over pajamas and house shoes, sat in a comfortable chair and we students sat in a big circle around him and discussed the answers to his research questions. (I still have that notebook.)

Upon returning to campus to teach as a professor with graduate degrees completed, Brother Baxter then became my colleague. At times I would sit in his paneled office and we would chat briefly. I was always conscious that he was in demand by students and other professors on campus, but also by so many in the "brotherhood" at large. I tried not to impose on his free time. I was disappointed at times that Brother Baxter felt I had drifted into a liberal way of thinking, and he sometimes expressed concern about the direction of my thinking. His concerns were based mainly on articles that I had published in *Mission Journal* and other periodicals. I lobbied extensively with him for the Bible Department to offer a course in Christian ethics. He then asked me to draft a prospectus for such a course. The proposal I submitted encompassed thirty or more pages of course objectives, topics, and bibliography. My strong passion being in issues of social justice, especially race relations and anti-war, such that I used every line of reasoning I could devise in attempting to get such an ethics course added to the Bible curriculum.

Brother Baxter fought an eighteen-year battle with cancer. He had several surgeries and several rounds of radiation and chemotherapy. The amazing reality is that this minister/professor completed some of his most important and impactful ministry during the medical treatments. Never once did I hear him complain, either in his messages or private conversations. His earthly sojourn ended on March 31, 1982. I did not think so much about it at the time, but Brother Baxter was not really an old man when he left us.

Brother Baxter's funeral was conducted in the Hillsboro church building a few days after his passing. Some old hymns about obedience and holiness were sung by the congregation. There were readings and prayers. Several made brief comments. The main eulogy was delivered meaningfully by Harold Hazelip. Though years have passed I still remember what Harold told the packed house after making only a few personal comments: "Brother Baxter did not want his funeral service to be so much about him but to be more about the gospel story he attempted to preach, thus I now read a New Testament text and offer exposition."

On a lighter note, Brother Baxter typically did not tell jokes or attempt to be funny in classes or sermons. I do remember only one juvenile joke that he offered at the beginning of a college Bible lesson in front of a fairly large class. "Do you know how you can identify a happy motorcyclist?" he asked. Then there was the pause. No one in our class knew the answer. "Well, when he smiles, there are bugs wedged all in his front teeth." Most of us chuckled at such a corny joke mainly because he even dared to be funny.

On September 29, 2016, on the occasion of the one hundredth anniversary of Baxter's birth, a special memorial dinner was held in Lipscomb's Ezell Center. The program was filled speakers who had known and interacted with this great person who spent so many years of service on that campus, though I am certain almost all of the almost two hundred people present could have shared one or more interesting stories or special memories.

5. PROFESSOR, CHAIRMAN, DEBATE COACH, AND FRIEND

The Lipscomb Speech department of the 1950s, 60s, and early 70s gained well-deserved attention and recognition for training some outstanding orators. In the 50s, Batsell Baxter, Ira North, and Carroll Ellis were the main professors in the department. The three professors were also preachers. I would contend they loved preaching and teaching Bible classes more than teaching speech, but speech provided a most complementary discipline to their first love. Furthermore, it was much easier and deemed "safer" in those days to pursue a doctorate in speech communication than in religious studies. Therefore, some majors in speech became ministers.

Dr. Carroll Brooks Ellis, diminutively standing a few inches over five feet with big jaws and thick black hair that encircled a bald spot in the back of his head, greatly influenced my life. He was a congenial person who was typically smiling when conversing with others. He possessed a sense of humor about his Zaccheus-like stature and sometimes quipped that it was nearly impossible for pranksters to frustrate him by "short-sheeting" his bed. Dr. Ellis was my teacher in Bible and Speech in the 60s, my collegiate debate coach, and my department chairman in the 70s. Most of all, he was my friend though we each intensely tested the friendship of the other on a number of occasions.

Restoration Movement history, more specifically the history of the Stone-Campbell movement, was the first academic love of Carroll Ellis. His doctoral program in speech from LSU, especially his doctoral dissertation on argument and controversy in the movement, prepared him to teach a year-long, upper-division course labeled "Restoration Preaching." As Bible and preaching majors, we were required to know Alexander Campbell's major debates and write a special rhetorical and biblical analysis of one of them. Ellis also taught a number of Bible courses that lasted one quarter, for example, "The Parables of Jesus."

Ellis' Bible classes were fairly simple, and their effectiveness was rooted in the sincerity and goodness of the instructor rather than depth exegesis. Each lesson contained a listing that summed up the main points and each listing was composed of alliterative points—each beginning with the same letter of the alphabet. Preparing for one of his exams was largely a matter of memorizing those listings and being prepared to regurgitate them on exam sheets that his secretary could later grade and then record the scores in the gradebook.

With that good sense of humor, Dr. Ellis seemed to enjoy some students poking good-natured fun at him, even imitating him. At times, his thought process seemed a bit slower than his words and in every class, especially when asked a question, he would begin his answer: "Oooooooooh, I think this …" Quite immaturely during a class or two, I joined two or three other fellows in a contest guessing the actual number of times Dr. Ellis would use this long verbal pause on that class day. We would keep count as the 50-minute class proceeded, and the winner almost jumped for joy at the end of class. Estimates were offered in the range of twenty to thirty elongated verbal pauses for most classes. Our instructor had this puzzled look as to what we might be celebrating at the end of a class session.

Because of his sincerity and love for others, Dr. Ellis possessed a tender heart. On several occasions I have seen tears come to his eyes and begin rolling down his face. Once in an early morning Bible class, Dr. Ellis soberly began by saying, "We can't have a regular Bible lesson this morning, because I need to tell you about something tragically sad that happened only two or three hours ago."

Our instructor then proceeded to tell how his neighbor, a Mr. Traughber who headed Lipscomb's cafeteria and food services, had a teenage son who was delivering the *Nashville Tennessean* in the early morning darkness and was struck and killed by a hit-and-run driver. Dr. Ellis spent the entire period weeping and discussing lessons that could be drawn from such a tragedy. We listened with rapt attention and total, respectful silence. Dr. Ellis was teaching another Bible class in November 22, 1963, when someone entered the classroom and interrupted the lesson and announced that John F. Kennedy had been assassinated in Dallas. This sensitive professor immediately ended his lesson and soberly led a prayer for the nation and the Kennedy family before dismissing the class. Such class sessions are never forgotten.

CLASHING ON ISSUES AND A LIPSCOMB "TEACH-IN"

As colleagues, Dr. Ellis and I often clashed on political and cultural issues. On occasion he would call me into his office, quietly shut the door, and then express his concern about statements I had made in publications about social justice and American race relations or in opposition to the U. S. participation in the Vietnam War. His convictions and emotions were deeply felt. He believed my stated political positions to be detrimental and possibly fatal to my remaining on the faculty at Lipscomb and he made that transparently clear to me. Those conversations were deeply sobering and concerning.

In the 1972 national election, Senator George McGovern, a Democrat who opposed the war in Vietnam and advocated immediate troop withdrawal, had been nominated to oppose incumbent Republican Richard Nixon. Dr. Ellis was a passionate supporter of Nixon. A faculty debate was organized and there were three or four faculty speakers for each major candidate. This faculty debate, announced in chapel as Lipscomb's version of the "teach-in," was conducted in

McFarland Hall on Monday, November 6, and was open to faculty and students. Several teachers strongly encouraged their students to attend.

When I began my carefully-prepared remarks, I joked that the speakers on the other side of the podium *represented* the Republican faculty members, and that the three or four of us on my side actually *were* the Democratic faculty members (meaning there were no other faculty voting for McGovern). Joining me on the Democratic side were my colleagues Patrick Deese, Cynthia Dilgard, and John Dawson.

Dr. Ellis presented his speech on behalf of Richard Nixon. Then next on the program, my speech was the hardest hitting and most emotional speech of the afternoon, an opinion expressed by others. I closed with some strong questions regarding Nixon's failed "secret plan" to end the war in Vietnam and more questions about evasion and possible deceit about Watergate, a potential scandal that was currently unfolding.

To my surprise and disappointment, my political speech deeply vexed Dr. Ellis, who was sitting behind me as I spoke. When I finished my remarks and appeal, he stood up and announced to the audience: "I did not think this debate would turn to political harangue, but it has and therefore it can continue without me because I am leaving right now." Other faculty on his side immediately rose and gently patted his back and urged him to stay, simply reassuring him this debate was totally an academic exercise to educate our students and, as such, should not be taken as any kind of a personal attack. Dr. Ellis thought a moment, quietly sat back down, but clearly he was displeased and added no comments during the open discussion period. His being my chairman, then I was especially embarrassed. In retrospect, I should have been more cognizant of how intensely people hold their political views and more respectful toward their convictions and sensitive to their feelings.

Another issue that Dr. Ellis and I saw differently surfaced about three years later: the proposed Equal Rights Amendment. By that time, I was teaching more political science classes than speech classes. I felt the ERA could be a symbolic victory for women, and that it had taken too long for the nation even to guarantee women's suffrage rights, much less equal pay and opportunity for women. On the other hand, Dr. Ellis's devoted wife Tottie, herself a strong and confident orator, became known as a strong opponent of the ERA. Tottie traveled to various audiences in the Bible Belt and gave rousing anti-ERA orations warning her listeners of what terrible social and cultural consequences would follow ERA ratification (*e.g.s.*, young women in military combat, homosexual marriages, males and females using the same public restrooms, etc.) An article I wrote in support of ERA goals was published in a major conservative church periodical (much to my surprise as I had submitted the piece almost as a joke), one for which Dr. Ellis had been a staff writer, and that published article produced the highest level of tension between us.

Fortunately, the values that Dr. Ellis and I shared in common were greater than the controversial justice and cultural issues we did not see alike. Dr. Ellis was passionate about preaching. He took special pride in some of his former students who had become effective preachers, students such as Dr. Marlin Connelly, who joined the Lipscomb Speech Department three years before I arrived. Other Lipscomb speech majors who pursued doctorates in that field include Bill Banowsky, Prentice Meador, Mike Adams, Ken Durham, and Russ Corley. When Marlin and I arrived, Dr. Ellis basically ended coaching the debate team, but always took special pride in debaters who won trophies for Lipscomb. Understandably, he would be the one to appear in chapel and hold up any tournament trophy won by one or more of our debate teams.

A LESSON LEARNED ON BOURBON STREET

One practical reason Dr. Ellis remained connected to the Lipscomb debate program, in addition to released time from classroom instruction, seemed to be the respite and pleasure he enjoyed when accompanying one or two debate teams to New Orleans each year and also in attending the national conference of the Speech Association of America, always conducted in a large U. S. city. With his ties to LSU, which granted his doctorate, and the church in southern Louisiana, it remained such a pleasure for him to return and visit the old sites and relish the memories. These visits always included the French Quarter and Bourbon Street along with at least one or two visits to an exquisite restaurant for fine dining.

One evening after tournament rounds were completed, Dr. Ellis led his four top male debaters down Bourbon Street, perhaps a first-time visit for these collegians. Live jazz music was easily heard and enjoyed by all. There were revelers in the street, some of whom, in addition to Dr. Ellis and the debaters, may have been totally sober. This Lipscomb entourage passed the entrance of three or four adult entertainment venues. There was always a male head usher at the entrance beckoning new customers to enter to see strippers on stage and purchase drinks. At each adult strip club, the male usher would swing open the door so the potential customers could get a tantalizing peek at some attractive young woman performing her act on stage. He would then shout out an invitation to come on in and enjoy the show. After six or seven seconds, the usher would then close the door and once more beckon the men on the sidewalk to buy their "cover charge" tickets, march in, and take a seat.

Perhaps being aware he was faculty chaperone for a Christian college and/ or perhaps possessing truly a deep spirituality by having "set his mind on those things which are above," Dr. Ellis could stand in the doorway of the strip club but would not for one second turn his eyes and look inside toward the stage. The young Lipscomb debaters showed no such restraint and their quick glances of an attractive stage dancer/stripper likely served as education for one or more of them in the "ways of the world." Their coach just maintained unflinching, face to face, eye contact with the usher, politely turning down the usher's invitation and beckoning to enter, and never turning or lifting his head to look inside toward the stage.

When the little Lipscomb group walked away and had taken a few more steps down Bourbon Street, Dr. Ellis motioned for them to huddle next to a building because he wanted to seize a teachable moment. "Boys, you see what goes on down here. There's the good and there's the bad. I don't believe in supporting those kind of places," he moralized. "Besides, those men who go in those strip places, some are old and some are young, they are not really having fun—they just *think* they are having fun!"

Almost instantly after their coach had made that opinionated statement, one of the debaters asked, "Dr. Ellis, how can you know whether those guys are having fun or they just think they are having fun? And what's more, does it really matter if they are actually having fun or they just think they are?"

There was a long pause. "Ohhhhhh, you young fellows!" Dr. Ellis replied with a long guttural groan in his voice and a half-smiling grimace on his face. "What am I ever going to do with you?" The questions from the college debaters seemed valid at the time. The coach's answer, or in this case his non-answer, was unforgettable.

LEAVING THE LIPSCOMB SPEECH DEPARTMENT

When I resigned from Lipscomb to re-enter full-time ministry, the Speech Department hosted a little farewell dinner party in a private room at the Loveless Café. There were speeches that shared memories of funny events in that department and speeches of farewell. When Dr. Ellis stood to close the occasion and offer his own farewell speech to my family and me, he became so choked up with tears that he could hardly complete his remarks. At that point, I, too, became so tearful, but also deeply grateful for how much he had meant in my life.

After leaving Lipscomb, Dr. Ellis and I enjoyed several occasions to be together. On one occasion, he and Tottie came to McMinnville for her to appear at an area women's event wherein she was a keynote speaker; again, her topic was the biblical role for women and the insidious dangers posed by the proposed Equal Rights Amendment. Dr. Ellis stayed at our house during the event and we kicked back and enjoyed a nice visit. Several of his preacher stories that I heard from him first-hand emerged from our various personal visits and are found elsewhere in this book. My former chairman supported Tottie's "political" career and took special pride in achievements of their beloved and gifted children Mufti, Brooks, and Bernie.

As an aside, it is almost ironic that that Dr. Ellis served as pulpit minister at Otter Creek in the 70s and I served in the same position in the 80s. Before accepting that position, I went to his Lipscomb office, sat down with him as

I had so many times in previous years, and sought his counsel in making the decision. I well recall his concerns that, stating himself as exception, most if not all Otter Creek preachers left the ministry after leaving the Otter Creek pulpit position. Our mutual pulpit experiences gave us much more in common to share.

6. GREEK AND GRACE

What is wrong with this picture? Most mornings, except for rain or ice and snow descending, a young man who is wearing a suit, dress shirt, and tie, is riding an old bicycle off Belmont Avenue onto campus. Actually, this old bike is the only bicycle on the campus. The bike is never locked down against a rack or railing. At times it is simply laid down on the grass in front of a side entrance to the Burton administration building. Apparently, the bike owner did not feel anyone would be tempted to steal his means of transportation.

In many ways, we might argue with a smile, Harvey Floyd was ahead of his time. By riding his old bike to campus on most days, he was able to save gas, find a convenient place to "park," and get some aerobic exercise. Manifestly, he did not care about his image on campus. For that matter, his style of teaching was a bit unorthodox, too.

Harvey Floyd developed in all Bible and preaching majors a keen awareness of the importance of serious, scholarly study of the Holy Scriptures. Of course, his passion for a depth understanding of the Bible was communicated to serious students of all major fields. Brother Floyd's style of teaching was unique. In the classroom I never saw him sit in a chair or on a stool though he often would lean on the podium. At times he would pace in front of the classroom and stare off in space as though that brilliant mind was considering what was imperative to utter next. To emphasize an important point, he could quickly jerk off his glasses and then his voice and gestures would explode with emotion, sometimes repeating words or phrases. He could also use that voice and body to communicate irony and satire. In vocal expression he knew how to employ the pregnant pause. Put succinctly, as a professor Brother Floyd was unforgettable. Clearly, the college classroom was not "just another job" for him—it was life's divine calling!

Harvey Floyd was a Lipscomb product all the way. As a student with a strong academic record he was elected Bachelor of Ugliness in 1953, his senior year. Though he had received theological training at Harding Graduate School it was only after I was a Lipscomb student that he pursued a doctorate in classical and comparative literature from Vanderbilt University, thus I always addressed him as "Brother Floyd" as an instructor and later as "Brother Harvey" as a fellow colleague on the faculty.

Floyd was culturally conservative. For example, I remember seeing him sitting in the Burton Administration third level hallway floor leaning against a wall, just outside his office, and telling a few students who were standing around him that he had seen "Godfather." The movie had a brief nude scene, he reported in somber tones, "and that scene was so unnecessary to the plot." No student dared to take issue. "I don't know why they put that scene in there," he despondently uttered with a pained expression on his face.

One time in a class, dating and romance were raised as a topic and Brother Floyd was asked if serious couples should engage in romantic kissing. The instructor gave a long pause and then said, "I think romantic kissing is so morally inappropriate. Some activities need to be saved for marriage." Once again, no student took issue with this pronouncement. We knew he held that conviction so deeply. It's possible, perhaps even likely, that no students in the class concurred with him.

GREEK, GRACE, AND THE HOLY SPIRIT: THREE GREAT PASSIONS

Harvey Floyd was Lipscomb's Greek teacher. In my sophomore year I sat in his class of "Introduction to New Testament Greek" with about twenty-five aspiring preachers and one female, Linda Redmon. The class met for one hour five days each week. Greek was not easy for most of us, but Brother Floyd put energy and enthusiasm into its study, and he gave special tutoring to those who struggled. I doubt he failed anyone who was truly making a valiant effort to pass the class, even if such a student struggled to recognize the difference between an alpha and an omega.

By the end of the third quarter, all students were expected to memorize and write out in Greek from memory the prologue to John's gospel (1:1-18). At the end of the quarter, I asked this instructor if he felt I should continue with a second year of Greek and should have guessed his response: "By all means." Thus, I registered for the second year of New Testament Greek; it was even more challenging. His position was that no serious Bible teacher or preacher should take an easy by-pass on the study of New Testament Greek—it was inarguably indispensable!

Brother Floyd taught several New Testament courses, instructing us without notes of any kind on the podium. The only book in his hands was the Greek New Testament and he translated "on the fly," that is, as he read the text aloud to the class. This was truly a "living translation." For us Bible majors he taught courses we truly needed, such as "Introduction to the New Testament" and "Text and Canon," if we aspired to be serious students and expounders of the Word. Those courses significantly influenced the way I understood the New Testament.

Two courses truly stand out: "Romans and Galatians" being one outstanding class and "The Holy Spirit" being the other. In the former, Brother Floyd led students to understand the grace-faith-works inter-connection as the vast majority likely never understood it. In the latter, his insights on the Holy Spirit were well-considered and most helpful to students who would have previously viewed the topic as mysterious and unfathomable. His analysis and insights were recorded in his book, *Is the Holy Spirit for Me?*

Sad to say, there were some students who contended that Brother Floyd was teaching doctrinal error and thus lobbied with the college administration for his removal from teaching these crucially important courses. Those complaints were deeply wounding to this good man. The students who loved and appreciated him most were fearful that he might resign and depart from Lipscomb, but Brother Floyd reassured them he was like an old hound dog that had only lived on the porch of one farm house—neither could be run off from the only home it knew.

Brother Floyd always seemed a simple man with a loving and humble attitude—the kind of person who could make no enemies. True, his teachings and lines of analysis did alarm a handful of listeners who felt they knew more about grace than did he. Yet the light he brought to students with his insights, and the passion he stirred in their hearts, created for this professor an almost cult following.

Brother Floyd was in demand as a speaker at various workshops and retreats and, like other Bible professors, received his share of invitations to officiate at weddings. For some fifty-five years Brother Floyd taught at the college he loved, even if he slowed down on riding his bike to campus. Many Lipscomb students have looked retrospectively on his classes as being the most memorable Bible classes in their entire college years. Little wonder that several times he was granted "outstanding teacher awards." And then, for forty years, he taught the international Bible class at the Harpeth Hills church, a class that included Japanese citizens who had migrated to Middle Tennessee to live and work. With these special students, a special bond was created.

McMinnville's Westwood congregation conducted an annual retreat for all adults at Fall Creek Falls State Park. One memorable component of the retreat was a Bible class under some highly capable guest instructor. One year, some of our members who were Lipscomb alumni commissioned me to invite Harvey Floyd to be our guest instructor. My role as minister was to make contact with him, offer a teaching invitation, give directions to the park, and then promote the retreat.

Ordinarily, there could be seventy-five to one hundred adults attending this retreat. This year, for some reason, only thirty or forty adults had signed up to attend. So I "primed the pump," making public appeals from the pulpit and church bulletin, saying great things about our guest resource person, and declaring the overall retreat experience would be fantastic. Even still, it seemed our attendance was far below average and I felt embarrassed and disappointed. Incidentally, these are times a minister can feel like a personal failure.

After calling and setting up an evening visit with Brother Harvey at his home near the campus, I drove to Nashville and was welcomed into his living room and sat with him and his wife. "Brother Harvey," I said. "We have been so honored you are willing to come teach in our retreat and we might have expected a hundred or more adults in your sessions, but there may be only thirty to forty in attendance, and I am hoping you won't be disappointed." Actually I was giving him opportunity to back out of the assignment and avoid the 100-mile drive to Fall Creek Falls State Park.

"Perry," he softly replied after this long pause and earnest look on his face, "it doesn't really matter how many attend my classes. Your congregation has given me an opportunity to teach the Word and I have set aside that time to be with your group, and, honestly, I don't need a big audience," he explained. "If there were only three or four to attend, and if they really wanted to study and learn, then I would be happy to come and teach." Consequently, Brother Harvey came to the resort and taught three or four sessions as assigned. Those who attended felt truly blessed.

Those minutes in the living room of the Floyd residence that evening reinforced lessons on the virtues of goodness, humility, and kindness. That time, as well as classroom learning experiences, and the man himself—all unforgettable!

A NEW DAY

A generation ago, General Motors ran television ads for one of their automobiles with the slogan, "This is not your father's Oldsmobile." The Oldsmobile was one of the first U. S.-manufactured automobiles, thus one might imagine all kinds of changes in that brand over the decades. (Of course, the biggest change is that the Oldsmobile brand is no longer manufactured.)

Walking onto the current Lipscomb campus and seeing staff and students in all kinds of casual dress and grooming styles, I think of something I could say to them: "This is not your father's David Lipscomb College." The campus has been expanded with several new, modern, high-tech buildings. All old buildings, especially the Burton Administration building and Collins Auditorium, have been renovated and modernized. A spacious Beaman Library has been constructed. The sidewalks have been widened and the colorful beauty of campus landscaping is obvious. Professors and instructors may dress more casually and comfortably. Male professors may wear jeans and sport shirts in the classroom, as well as grow a beard and long hair if that's "their thing."

Additionally, the traditional and time-honored daily Bible class and daily chapel requirements have been relaxed. Seemingly, those sacred cows have been sacrificed in the names of reality and relevance in reaching a modern, fast-paced, highly-competitive, high-tech youth culture. Oh, yes, I might note that moderate consumption of alcoholic beverages at faculty social gatherings is hardly a big deal. As we know, smoking and other tobacco use have long been banned on campus, but my generation remembers when male students could smoke tobacco in any form in Elam Hall rooms, automobiles on campus, and in the lower and third floor restrooms of the Burton building.

More importantly, academics have grown stronger. President Harold Hazelip deserves much credit for upgrading standards for new faculty as well as for students graduating from what is no longer simply a college but now a university with new fields for majors and graduate study. As a theologian as well as educator, Dr. Hazelip took measures to build a first-rate program in Bible and Ministry, thus achieving accreditation for a Master's in that field. This humble and plain-spoken administrator seemed to take more personal satisfaction in the construction and design of the new Beaman Library during his tenure than any other construction or renovation project.

Today, under the leadership of President Randy Lowry, the University has advanced to new academic heights and developed a community outreach and an identity in the competitive Nashville area as a quality institution of higher learning.

My generation of Lipscomb alumni has been surprised and amazed at new modern facilities on the expanded campus. In the 1960s and even 1970s, I am not sure we could have envisioned the antiquated McQuiddy gym replaced by the modern Allen Arena that hosts musical concerts, special events, and graduations as well as men's and women's Bison basketball games. Modern baseball and softball fields and stadiums have been built as well as two parking garages. Even still, adequate campus automobile parking remains a huge challenge.

Our generation might have imagined a classroom and office building such as Ezell, but one may doubt we could have imagined the James D. Hughes Center, the Hutcheson Art Gallery, the Shamblin Theater, or the George Shinn Event Center, just to cite a few examples. We may remember dramatic productions of *Abe Lincoln in Illinois*, *The Miracle Worker*, and *1776*, but we could not have imagined professional musical-dramatic productions of *Les Miserables* and *Godspell* on the stage of Collins-Alumni Auditorium.

As for the Bible Department, well, so much has changed. During my undergraduate days, I felt all my Bible instructors were good men and some were effective evangelists; however, many of those instructors had no graduate training in religion and Bible. Their approach to the text seemed more devotional than exegetical and critical. There were some class meetings wherein I felt a Bible instructor had taken one of his thirty-minute sermons and stretched it with personal stories and anecdotes to fill fifty minutes of class time. And the curriculum and instruction in those years might have appeared an unmistakable invitation to sectarianism—there were courses actually entitled "Errors of Roman Catholicism" and "Errors of Denominationalism."

Now this department is called "Bible and Ministry Department" and is headed by Dr. Leonard Allen, one of the brightest scholars and best writers/editors in the broader Stone-Campbell movement. Leonard is a humble, soft-spoken scholar, one who carefully prepares every class lesson, every departmental meeting, every official statement, and even every public prayer. And that department is blessed indeed with a number of well-trained, highly effective and productive scholar-professors who have earned higher degrees in biblical languages and religious studies.

And what has brought Lipscomb University more national publicity than its academics? Quite possibly it's the basketball program of 2018 and 2019 that has garnered immeasurable national attention. The 2018 Bison team won the Atlantic Sun Tournament that earned an automatic bid to its first NCAA tournament seeding with a game in the "Big Dance" against the storied North Carolina Tarheels. The 2019 Bison team convincingly competed against some excellent teams, including Davidson, NC-Greensboro, North Carolina State, and Wichita State, before losing to the mighty Texas Longhorns in the National

Invitation Tournament championship game in Manhattan's storied Madison Square Garden. Most of these tournament games were broadcast on national television. The Bison basketball teams of this generation have proven they can competitively stay on the court with any NCAA basketball team.

My purpose here has been to share a portrait of those men at Lipscomb who influenced my own thinking and practice as a pulpit minister. I stand in debt to these and others I did not allot space to discuss. Their evaluation and opinions I deemed important. I can only conclude that these professors and administrators who so influenced me would have, eventually at least, come to esteem highly those administrators and professors who followed in their steps as well as respect and appreciate their research, writing, and academic achievements.

3

"Ready to Suffer"—Preparing the Congregation for a Student Preacher

A preacher's first full length pulpit performance is very much like any man's first intimate romantic experience.

Every preacher who ever lived, this side of senile dementia, remembers his first experience (in the pulpit, of course). He remembers when it happened, where it happened, how he felt before and during the experience, and how he felt the morning after. Unlike many first-time romantic experiences, the memory of that first sermon can be haunting indeed for many preachers.

My first sermon was delivered a few days before my seventeenth birthday. The scene of the incident was at the Lakeview Church of Christ in the Dallas-Ft. Worth area, a congregation of less than a hundred people. I have never been in that church building since that time, but the congregation seems to have survived my first-time preaching experience.

Here's the context of how the homiletic event happened: Seems strange now, as I reflect on the attitudes of many teenagers I have observed today, but as a teenager I enjoyed going to church. I listened carefully to whomever was preaching. I enjoyed my Bible classes. At my home church I had delivered a number of successful "talks," which translated means that I had somehow haltingly completed a brief presentation on some unimposing occasion (*e.g.,* Wednesday night devotional) which I had plagiarized from some source, and someone suggested that I might be an adequate summer replacement at some church where little sermonic damage could be inflicted.

When, upon ample notice, I was invited to fill the pulpit one Sunday at Lakeview, I was ready and willing, if only somewhat able to assume this assignment. I spent hours preparing the lesson, one I had assimilated verbatim from one of the Fogarty brothers in a Memphis tent revival. My rehearsal *modus operandi* involved propping a TV tray on a bed, standing behind it as though it were a podium, and speaking to an empty bedroom; a propped-up watch enabled me to time the oration during each dry run. To further prepare myself I attended a service at Lakeview the Sunday before my speaking appointment, thus giving me the opportunity to case the place out and to judge the quality of the regular homiletic fare with which I expected to be compared.

Invariably, some unusual, unexpected turn of events develops in a novice preacher's maiden pulpit voyage. For me it was the sudden, unexpected appearance of the regular preacher, whom I was mistakenly informed would be away on vacation. I don't remember his name, but I can see him now as he casually strolled into the building right before the service was scheduled to begin.

"This is your church. I'll gladly sit down so you can preach," I implored him, quite willing to allow all my preparation time and anxiety go for nought. "I'll try to use this lesson another time."

"Oh no," he replied, "I didn't come to speak. I came to hear you."

Of course, what I wanted to say was, "I'm willing to preach for you, especially if it pays some cash, but I'm asking you to leave so that I can do it without you as a listener and critic."

He stayed. I stayed. I had to speak. He chose to listen. After service, he offered the obligatory compliment as did others.

TWO BIG DIFFICULTIES

The two most common difficulties encountered by first-time preachers are surely stage fright and sudden loss of memory. The two are, of course, linked. One preacher friend spent many hours planning his first sermon on the parable of the prodigal son—always a good topic for a first sermon. His early rehearsals of the sermon required twenty-five to thirty minutes. "When the time came that I was actually delivering the sermon before the live audience," he confessed, "I had the poor prodigal out of the far country and trudging the road home after only twelve to fifteen minutes."

Few if any preachers in his era of the True Church seemed more confident in the pulpit than did Ira North, long-time pulpit minister of the Madison Church of Christ, the largest congregation of its fellowship in the 60s and 70s, and speaker on the "Amazing Grace" television show. Ira became so well known throughout Middle Tennessee that on one occasion, while leisurely riding his big Harley into the western part of the state, he stopped randomly at some general store along the highway to buy a cold soft drink. "Why, there's ole 'I-ree,'" the store owner shouted when he walked in and took off his helmet. What is generally unknown is that a twelve-year-old Ira competed in the state oratorical contest for his age group and, while declaiming, fainted and fell on his face. Young Ira was given attention and revived, according to son Steve, and stood on his feet and completed the speech. He won first place that day. Maybe he benefited from the sympathy of the judge(s).

How well I remember the time that my parents delivered me from Dallas to Nashville to enroll in college. We had loaded up that '55 two-tone, green Oldsmobile 88, equipped with a push button AM radio which took a few seconds to warm up, an electric clock that never ran, and an "add-on" (after manufacturing production) air conditioning system with the unit and controls bracketed under the middle section of the dash.

One memory stands out about that last leg of our journey from Memphis to Nashville alternating on Highway 100 and Highway 70—the large number of church buildings that dotted the highway route. Most of the church buildings were small, many of them wood frame. Most of them, it seemed, had signs in the front churchyard declaring "Church of Christ." I knew that I was seeing only the tip of the steeple, so to speak, and that there were many more of these church houses on other highways, the paved secondary roads, and even the unpaved back roads.

TENNESSEE AND KENTUCKY RURAL CHURCHES

These small churches, typically ranging in size from twenty-five to 125 members, constituted the training camps for the young recruits in the Lord's army who were being trained at Freed-Hardeman College and David Lipscomb College. Few of these churches could afford, or even desired, a full-time preacher. But hungry sheep cry out for feeding, and most were willing to accept a student speaker as a regular preacher, knowing full well that his tenure would last, in most cases, only a few months.

These churches were mostly composed of virtuous, hard-working people who earned their living by the sweat of their brow. In the early '60s their lives were simple with all their days beginning with sunrise and ending just after sunset. Many of the farm houses were just beginning to be equipped with television sets. A tall, exterior, rotating antenna would be necessary to receive the best picture on those black and white sets, although most picture tubes provided as much snow as a winter's day in Anchorage.

Many of the churches had been long established. Most were tied together more by family relationships than by religious creed, although most members would aver that they were all members of the "one true church." Everyone in the church seemed to be kin to nearly everyone else, thus it especially ill-behooved any young preacher to avoid speaking disparagingly of any one person in his own congregation.

Sometimes there were two major family clans, such as the Hatfields and McCoys, which comprised the rural church. In times of conflict each clan leader would seek to recruit the support of the young, perhaps naive, preacher for its side. Generally speaking, there was no real conflict in these rural churches, so long as the churches did not attempt to do anything big, such as grow numerically, explore new ideas, seek diversity, or begin a new ministry. The rural congregation's chief mission was simply to exist and to maintain a church house and grounds for worship assemblies, for funerals, and for weddings. A good number of these rural churches maintained a graveyard on their grounds, although increasingly this tradition was being abandoned.

NAMING A CONGREGATION

There were two ways that a rural congregation could be named. First, the congregation could be named after the community in which it was located, such as Thompson Station Church of Christ, or after the road or highway on which the building was located. Sometimes the name of a nearby river, lake, or creek might be used as part of the name. There have been some humorous names for congregations, such as the Only Church of Christ (in Only, Tennessee). Interestingly, there is a Hell, Michigan. One day while reading the *Detroit News* I noticed and clipped out and saved a headline for a brief story which read "First Baptist Church in Hell Burns," a reference to a calamity of fire faced by a small Baptist church in that community.

A second source of church names was, of course, the Bible—Bible towns and places, definitely not Bible personalities. Old Testament names could be appropriate, but were not used as frequently as the New Testament names. Among the biblical names used as a prefix to "Church of Christ" have been the following: Bethany, Bethel, Berea, Bethlehem, Corinth, Mars Hill, Philippi, Antioch, Ephesus, Smyrna, Philadelphia, Zion, and Berea (I don't recall Thessalonica, Thyatira, Pergamum, Sardis, Iconium, Phrygia, or Laodicea being used as names for congregations). Biblical themes such as Hope, Harmony and Providence have been used in naming churches; the prefix "New" can be added to all these theme names. Salem could be used as a church name but definitely not Jerusalem. Many church names included "chapel" in the title, usually following a family name as in Owen Chapel, Berry Chapel, or Mead Chapel.

Quite a few congregations incorporate some kind of wood into the name of the church, such as Walnut Hill, Pinewood, Oak Grove, Sycamore View, Pecan Plains, Mulberry Grove, or Hickory Valley, to name just a few. I have not seen Catalpa, Mimosa, Mesquite, Hackberry, Weeping Willow, Thorn, Pineapple, Coconut, or the biblical Gopher Wood used in congregational names. Fruit, nuts, milk and cheese products, and vegetable plants are not used in naming congregations, presumably because they do not connote strength or longevity; such a shame because they do provide vitamins and minerals. Admittedly, a little difficult to imagine a "Cheddar Church of Christ" or "Swiss Cheese Church of

Christ," and definitely not a "Cottage Cheese Church of Christ" or "Smoothie Church of Christ"!

As an aside, churches in larger towns and cities are frequently named for the neighborhood, street, road, or highway on which their building is located, such as 10th and Cedar Church of Christ or Highway 100 Church of Christ. If there are no more than four congregations in a city, each congregation could be named for the side of town in which the church house is located. From 1955 to 1957 my dad was minister in Duncan, Oklahoma, at the Northside Church of Christ, but there were also an Eastside Church of Christ and a Westside Church of Christ—indeed, the mission field was ripe for a Southside Church of Christ. In the Nashville area, "Hills" seems quite popular in congregational naming even if the church facilities sit on a flat acreage. Thus we have Woodmont Hills, Harpeth Hills, Nolensville Hills, Maury Hills, Southern Hills, Western Hills, Woodland Hills, and Brentwood Hills, to name a few.

Just looking at some of those church names might bring a range of images. For example, the Golf Course Road Church of Christ in Midland, Texas, might inform worshipers and visitors that a golf course is nearby, and White Station Church of Christ in Memphis would remind everyone that Jim Crow was once alive and well in Tennessee's Bluff City.

Seemingly, only a minority of the rural churches had officially appointed elders and deacons. But all churches had at least one, usually two, unofficially recognized "leaders." The status of these one, two, or three men had been enhanced by longstanding faithful membership, being the patriarch of a large family within the church, and/or landing a prestigious job in a nearby city. Sometimes it is one of these patriarchal leaders who makes announcements at every Sunday morning assembly; his commentary on the announcements is regarded as official if not inerrant.

"TRYING OUT" AND "ASKING OFF"

Invariably, the process for hiring any preacher, whether a student preacher or an older one, involves a "try out" sermon. The aspiring preacher might be recommended by an outside party or have a contact within the congregation, but he is given a date in which one or two "try out" sermons must be presented. He may also be expected to teach an adult class.

If the leaders are impressed by the young preacher's knowledge, personality, and delivery skills, he might be offered the regular position on the "try out" Sunday. It always helpful to have an attractive girl friend who traveled with the student preacher, and a fiancé would be even more impressive. In rare cases the "try out" speaker might already be married.

If the student preacher falls a bit short of expectations, the leaders might inform him they have an interest in his availability but would like to "try out" other speakers. Some leaders might even spiritualize the "try out" experience, thus they inform the candidate there are others desiring the position and they want to pray and seek the Lord's will in making a final decision. In the decade of the 60s, the pay range for regular preaching in rural churches generally ranged from twenty-five dollars to seventy-five dollars a week, depending on the size of the congregation and weekly contribution.

If a young preacher needed to "ask off" for a Sunday or had a question about some policy of the church, he would be instructed to "go talk with the leader(s)," which usually meant a brief huddle away from the rest of the congregation, perhaps under a tree or, in the winter, in a corner of the church house. The leaders knew full well the traditions of the church and could be depended upon to maintain them. Generally, the leaders were quite congenial and understanding; communication with them was easy.

Visitors to these rural churches are almost invariably welcomed with a "down home" hospitality. Since members of the church family have worshiped together all their lives, they instantly spot any visitor entering the HOW and extend the right hand of fellowship. In larger city congregations, by contrast, many members might look around in the assembly and not be able to distinguish "regular members" from visitors.

In the 60s, unlike more recent times, adults freely giving one another hugs was not commonly practiced. Handshakes were the most typical form of greeting. One handshake I'll never forget. This handshake was offered twice each

Sunday by a Brother Thomas at Fredonia. Though I was only eighteen at that time and he was thirty to forty years my senior, he always greeted and referred to me as "Brother Cotham," which seemed a bit awkward to me as a teenager. Then, bracing my right wrist with his left hand, he grabbed my right hand with his right hand and proceeded to squeeze every bit of life out of it. Though he was a wonderfully kind gentleman, my right hand quivered when I saw Brother Thomas coming. I had to wonder how many dairy cows he had milked in his lifetime and how many cows had made their way from the barn possibly maimed or "udderly" injured after his daily milking rigor.

Male visitors known for certain to have been baptized are ideal candidates to be drafted for some role in the service, such as leading a prayer or waiting on the communion table. A guest prayer leader was always a refreshing break for the rural churches because, otherwise, the people would bow their heads for a standard recitation which they had heard scores of times previously from one of few men willing to lead a public prayer.

Quite a number of very small churches always needed fresh male blood to discharge the worship functions. The experience of Hoy Ledbetter as a young man is typical of other rural churches. Hoy lived in a little community in Arkansas where an evangelist conducted a gospel meeting and a handful of Christians then started the Drake's Creek congregation. At the first regular Sunday service, there was no male present who was willing to lead the prayer. "A father and son were present, and the son called the father 'Brother Dad,'" Hoy informed me, "but neither was willing to pray publicly."

A man named Will walked in later. As soon as he entered, Will was asked if he would lead the prayer. "Naw, I can't lead anything," Will quickly replied.

The male in charge of the service announced, "I guess there won't be a prayer today." Some women in attendance were greatly distraught. "During the week my aunt wrote out an absolutely beautifully-worded prayer and gave it to me," Hoy recalled. "When it came time for prayer on the second Sunday, I read aloud her prayer. And that's how the first prayer got offered in this new church."

"AMEN CORNERS," OUTHOUSES, AND SMOKE BREAKS

The church houses in Middle Tennessee and Southern and Western Kentucky, just like almost countless other rural church houses throughout the Bible Belt, were generally simple in design. Many were T-shaped, with one classroom toward the front on each side of the building. Many buildings had "amen corners" on each side of the pulpit. Seldom were there more than two or three classrooms available for Sunday School. Cars pulled up around the building and parked in the same spots where wagons were parked and bridled horses hitched to posts in generations past.

A few buildings, such as Sycamore Flat in Stewart County, Tennessee, were designed as "one room." When the Sunday School hour rolled around at 10:00 each Lord's Day, the small congregation divided into four groups for study— men at left front, women at right front, children at right rear, and junior and senior high students at left rear. A constant, dull cacophony of sounds could be heard from any point in the building during the Bible study hour. Distractions were easy. The grounds had the convenience of a gravel drive which circled the building and there was mounted a large, single unit window air conditioner which labored noisily to bring slight comfort to the gathered saints on hot summer Sundays.

Most typically, the Sunday School hour began at 10:00 A. M. and "church" at 11:00 A. M. At 10:00 o'clock, all who came for the Bible class would gather in the auditorium for a few songs, the reading of that Sunday's scripture text, and the memory verse (or Golden Text) from the *Gospel Advocate* standardized "quarterlies," and a prayer. Then we heard those six words: "Classes may now take their places."

The *Gospel Advocate* curriculum was designed to walk students of all ages through the Bible in a few years. What I recall most about the adult "quarterlies," however, is the standardized, "preachery" tone in which they were all written (a style I would label "King James pedantic") and the difficulty of teaching those remotely-known narratives in later Hebrew history—it was ever so challenging to draw Christian principles for everyday life, especially for teens, from the stories of conspiracy, plundering, rape, dismemberment and mass murder (even genocide), especially those narrated in later Hebrew history! Some teachers and parents would require school-age children to memorize that Golden Text. The main application of each lesson, no matter how problematic the text, was the importance of obedience to God.

A little bell which always remained perched on the pulpit podium was jingled four or five times when class time had ended, signaling a break before the regular church service. In many cases, that little jingling bell brought a sigh of relief to both instructors and class members. Teenagers and women then rose and formed their separate groups for visiting, young mothers with babies changed diapers, and men of all ages went outside into a huddle to light up an unfiltered Camel or Lucky Strike cigarette. There was not sufficient time to enjoy a king size Pall Mall or Chesterfield product, and, as I recall, the brands of Winston, Salem, and Marlboro had not as yet appeared on the market.

As time for the service arrived, there were a number of folks arriving who never came for Sunday School. Everyone knew who these congregants were as they never attended Sunday School and they were seldom, if ever, chided for waiving this learning opportunity. Most of the smoking brothers would hastily and deeply inhale one last puff, purse lips heavenward and audibly exhale, then either flick the butt a few feet away (ideally to a parking lot or other paved surface) or drop it vertically to the ground or sidewalk and extinguish it under the suffocating force of one grinding shoe. It was not unusual to see a line-up of men serving communion and most having packs of cigarettes in their shirt pocket and, quite often when they wore a light-colored shirt, the brand enjoyed by each communion-server could be easily identified.

Often, the line-up card for prayer and communion table was drafted outdoors among these dairy, corn, and tobacco farmers. Sometimes the song leader would sit on the front pew between the Sunday School and "regular worship" composing his list of the hymns he planned to lead, much like a baseball manager would compose his starting line-up for a baseball game. The number of hymns for the service, just like the number of players in a starting baseball line-up, never changed.

At the top of the hour, the song leader then would stand and announce the first number, and the men would trudge in and seek out the end spot on the family pew. The fact that these men, some being older teen youngsters, reeked of cigarette smoke was neither surprise nor concern or offense to anyone.

These old country churches were built before the era of modern plumbing. In some churches, a member would be charged with the responsibility of bringing a pitcher of ice water and a glass, placing each on the pulpit stand. There was no running water and, therefore, neither baptisteries nor water fountains. The idea of a church kitchen and fellowship hall would be impossible, sometimes opposed, and often unimaginable. Those preachers who really got hot and steamy in the sweatbox sanctuaries denouncing the sins of the modern world could only pause and pour a drink. The luxury of bottled water was two generations away.

The lack of plumbing presented a far greater personal need for me than the lack of a water fountain. By the time I got near the church building, after an earlier breakfast and one or two hours on the highway, I sorely needed the convenience of a rest room. Fredonia, like so many other country churches, maintained a crude, outdoor facility of convenience. This was a simple wooden, unisex (hence, politically correct before its time), air-ventilated structure, but a two-seater at that. As an aside, while I often did view a young mom or dad take a small child inside the outhouse, I could never feature two adult parishioners being in that cramped facility at the same time. In those days, no one seemed to give serious thought to personal hygiene, thus no pans of water with soap nor any other strategies were provided for sanitizing one's hands.

This structure of convenience at Fredonia was located on the north side of the church yard and to the left and a few yards away from the front entrance. This facility was in plain view of the whole house of Israel, at least so it seemed. I attempted valiantly never to use that facility, lest some of the assembled saints conclude that I had a few biological needs common to the entire human family. Somewhat regrettably, Sycamore Flat had neither rest room nor outhouse. In the case of urinary or other emergency, one sought permission of the husband of the household next door to get a key and enter his residence to use the bathroom. It could be embarrassing, but it prevented a much larger embarrassment.

Finding seclusion for that pause that refreshes is crucial, as learned by two student preachers who eventually continued their higher education to complete doctorates in their separate fields and assume professorial rank in college teaching at Lipscomb. Traveling to perform song leading and preaching at a country church, the pair stopped their automobile within reasonable distance of the building. The two ambled to the side of the road and, while in the act of finding bladder relief, a family automobile suddenly appeared. Dad, mom, and the young kids in the back seat all gave the two young ministers a quirky, amused stare. As the pair arrived at the building a few minutes later, already embarrassed, who was there to give the first greeting? Answer: This same family which had passed them standing on the roadside where the dust was much more settled than it had been before their stop!

A GRACIOUS HOSPITALITY

In small town and rural congregations, true community developed naturally due not only to multi-generational families that attended, but also due simply to the basic goodness of these Christian people. In the middle decades of the twentieth century, there was no published church bulletin that was mailed to members' households. Telephone service eventually was installed and many members were connected on a party line and either openly or surreptitiously could keep up with some news of other families. As for the basic statistical information about the congregation, there were wooden informational boards mounted on the front wall of the meetinghouse in which the following statistical information could be posted: Attendance; Sunday School Attendance; Attendance Last Sunday; Contribution Today; Contribution Year to Date. Another board for the wall on the other side of the pulpit provided lines on which the song leader could list by number (in the song book) and by sequence the hymns he planned to lead that Sunday.

A gracious hospitality permeated the entire typical country church. Since the student preacher did not have time to travel home or back to campus between the Sunday AM and PM services, he spent Sunday afternoons in the home of one of the church families. Many churches posted a calendar or a listing of

Sundays in which hosting families could sign up for this hosting privilege. The young evangelist could check the list for future bookings. In time, the student preacher developed favorite homes to visit and could predict with great accuracy the menu for many of the dinner tables.

Because the food was scrumptious at nearly all family tables—laden with fresh garden vegetables, fruit cobblers, homemade cakes and pies, fried chicken, fresh beef and/or country ham—at times I found myself short of wind for the Sunday night presentation (indeed, the same food had been placed again on the table for supper before the evening sermon and it was almost as tasty the second time around). No matter, for the quality of my evening sermon was not crucial to my employment security anyway as most of the parishioners seemed to drift more or less into slumber. The pews were not cushioned or padded, most pews gave no lumbar support, yet such discomforting inconveniences in no way impeded the saintly drowsiness or slumber.

Some might not admit it, but all preachers develop preferences for favorite homes in which to visit from the start of their preaching career. At my first pulpit assignment, I preferred the homes which provided a TV set (in those days a black and white, "snowy" picture where the signals were drawn by some kind of exterior antenna), especially during the NFL and NBA seasons, and a room air-conditioner for the summer Sundays. I would also request a private room to rest or study. I preferred also to visit families which enjoyed conversing about their lives, showing me around the farm, and displaying a sense of humor about ordinary occurrences. There always seemed to be a lot to learn and appreciate from these farming families.

THE GOOD NEWS AT SYCAMORE FLAT

Most of all, I preferred to spend a Sunday afternoon with a family which included an attractive young lady. So much so that, in the middle of my sophomore year at Lipscomb, I resigned at Fredonia and began preaching for the Sycamore Flat church in Stewart County, Tennessee. Sycamore Flat was a smaller church and further from Nashville, but it was the home church of one of my best college buddies,

Bailey Heflin, whose older sister was one of the most beautiful, blonde-headed, young women I had ever seen. Their dad, Bailey Sr., was an amiable, hard-toiling farmer and the song leader for this little congregation of fifty or so members.

I was paid thirty dollars each for Sunday to travel the 160-mile round trip from Nashville to Stewart County to deliver morning and evening homilies with Brenda Heflin accompanying me each way nearly every Sunday. As I came to know her better, I realized she was such a sweet person with high moral character. The overall enjoyment was so gratifying that I would have, like the Apostle Paul, proclaimed the Word without any remuneration.

Each Sunday afternoon, no matter in which home I enjoyed Sunday dinner, I drove to the Heflin residence. These were afternoons for motoring around the countryside, singing around the old piano (not gospel hymns, of course), hand-cranking the old ice cream freezer and immediately consuming its cholesterolic delights, playing Rook, or playing croquet.

As an aside, croquet is an ideal game for any preacher and any of his church brothers and sisters. Croquet requires little or no skill to compete, is non-contact for either gender, does not quicken the pulse rate for those whose cardio-vascular system cannot tolerate over-excitement, does not require one to know the history of great croquet competitors of the past, allows polite conversation while being played, and no one gives a royal flip who wins or loses. I recommend croquet for such tame fellowship situations, but also recommend a game called "corn hole" that also meets all the above criteria.

Brenda liked me. Her parents liked me. I liked her and I liked them. We spent many hours eating and visiting together. I even volunteered some summer days to labor in the tobacco patch and corn fields, enduring the sweaty curse of Adam and Eve without salary, just to be around this family.

My ministry at Sycamore Flat lasted two years. The church financially assisted me on a mission campaign to England in the summer of 1963. My senior year in college I began serving a much larger church, the city church in downtown Franklin, Tennessee, which had some seven hundred members, as an interim pulpit minister. I felt like I had been called up to the major leagues from the Class D farm club. Oh, what a feeling! After graduation I got married, took my first full time job (a pulpit position in the Detroit area), and later entered graduate school. Meantime, Brenda became homecoming queen at Lipscomb. She eventually married a preacher.

FINDING SERMON MATERIAL

The sources of homiletic material for student preachers were rather limited and the perils and distractions of presentation were many. Most novice preachers knew little about crafting a sermon by scholarly exegesis of a text and then drawing practical applications through the use of history, great literature, and current events. We did well to re-hash our Bible teacher's best lessons or, in my case, find some clever outlining scheme from sermon outline books, such as Leroy Brownlow's *One Hundred Sermons You Can Preach*.

I never spoke for a rural church which offered nursery services for the little ones, thus often the sounds and behavior of children too young to attend an adult assembly could be persistent distractions. Steve North learned as a young man that even young mothers could become a distraction. "As a teenager speaking at a country church, there was a young woman with a little baby who found a space to sit on the front row right in front of the pulpit," Steve remembers. "Right in the middle of what I thought was some heavy theological point, this woman pulls out an ample breast and starts nursing her baby. Yes, it was distracting. I'll tell you, it was hard for me at that time to 'set my affections on those things which are above.'"

Truth is, the quality of preaching by college students at these country churches was too often lamentably low. Sometimes there would be a totally inexperienced college youth who wanted to earn a fast twenty-five or thirty bucks and was willing to fill the pulpit for a friend. The best that could be said for some of these preaching efforts was that, like Jacqueline Susann or E. L. James novels, they aimed low and missed. At one of the churches, the song director quite often led the song "Ready to Suffer" right before the student preacher mounted the pulpit to speak. What an appropriate sentiment for the entire church!

If a student preacher received considerable compliments, he could easily become infatuated with his own homiletic prowess and spiritual wisdom, not knowing how limited and deficient he was in each category at that early stage in his adult life.

While delivering a sermon in my first year of study in New Testament Greek, I turned around to the chalk board and wrote in large Greek letters the two Greek words for "burden" in Galatians chapter six to make my point. It mattered little to me that no one in this innocent and unsuspecting audience knew their alpha from their omega (I guess one could say "they cared not one iota"). What mattered most to me was my less than subtle but benign demonstration of new found erudition in the Greek language! My hope was that all listeners would be impressed.

The lesson I had yet to learn: Arrogance and ignorance make a deadly combination. Ignorance born consciously as a burden is no vice. Unconscious ignorance paraded as virtue breeds self-righteousness.

PARTNERS AND BROTHERLY COMPETITORS IN MINISTRY

My college roommate for three years, Larry Locke, also studied for the ministry, as did Julian Goodpaster, an appropriately named chap (sounding like "good pastor") with whom I roomed during my senior year. (As an aside, I always felt sorry for an older preaching brother that I knew named Holland Boring, but I always smiled a bit when hearing the names of Goebel Music, Mid McKnight, Creed Spurgeon, Hunt Zumwalt, and a few others.) Both Larry and Julian served a number of rural churches in their college days. Both were in our wedding; Larry was our "best man" as I was given the same role for his wedding the previous year. Both steadfastly continued in the pulpit ministry since those days. Coincidentally, both Julian and I later wound up being full-time pulpit ministers in McMinnville, Tennessee, during the same time period.

Larry and I enjoyed taking Bible classes and traveling to hear "big name" preachers who visited the Middle Tennessee area, a bonding force for the two of us. Each Sunday night, we would visit in our old Elam Hall room and share experiences at our respective rural assignments and rehearse what great things, if any, God had done through us that Lord's Day. Then we would share evenly whatever food some good sister may have packaged for one or the other for the journey to the Lipscomb campus, quite often some homemade cake or pie or a batch of homemade cookies.

One lesson many student preachers do not learn easily is that there is a difference between commitment to the ministry as a profession and a commitment and passion for people. There seemed to be a friendly competition between Larry and me as to which of us as college student preachers could garner the most "firsts"—the first to speak in a full length gospel meeting, the first baptism, the first wedding, the first funeral, the first to "land" a bigger congregation and a larger salary, and so forth. These were careers on the move.

Larry baptized his first sinner before I immersed mine. I witnessed this event and was proud for Larry even though he was one milestone ahead of me. I think the baptism "stuck," but Larry committed a technical error in this leased city baptistery (in Shelbyville, Tennessee)—he faced the back wall rather than his audience during the baptism. I enjoyed teasing him about this technical lapse in baptismal ritual. My first response for baptism, Connie Heflin, came at the time of my first gospel meeting. Likewise using a borrowed baptistery, this one in Dover, Tennessee, I experienced the thrill of assisting in a new birth in Christ. Oh, what a feeling! My meeting week had been made!

That night I experienced some other feelings, too, such as putting on a baptistery wading suit for the first time (I was never a wading fisherman) and stepping into the tank, feeling a strange sensation as the water gripped my ankles and legs. As a novice baptizer, I had not learned the importance of lacing up the top of my suit. As I brought my arms together and plunged Connie as deeply into the water as my arms could reach, water flooded rapidly into the open wading suit and drenched all my clothes. Little matter. Joy had flooded all our souls.

DISASTROUS ORDEALS CAN HAPPEN

Not every student preacher found it easy to survive emotionally the ordeals and tribulations of rural ministry. Fletcher Srygley, long-time esteemed friend and colleague on the Lipscomb faculty, once learned that even the most earnest beckoning of the lost and erring sinners can be undermined by either carelessness, big feet, slippery steps, or all of the above.

During their college years in the late '50s, seems that Fletcher was "filling in" the pulpit for Larry Connelly, who held a position at the Santa Fe church in rural Maury County, Tennessee. Fletcher had delivered his sermon commendably and "offered the invitation." Stepping to the main floor to assume the pastoral readiness and earnestly beckoning posture, Fletcher realized he had exited the pulpit on the same side as the song director who was leading the hymn.

Nature abhors both a vacuum and logistical imbalance, so Fletcher decided to move to the other side of the pulpit area. With no bone of rudeness in his body, the student preacher, himself a descendant of several great Tennessee pioneer evangelists, chose not to move in front of his song leader, but to traverse the area via a step which adjoined the pulpit.

Midway to his chosen position, Fletcher did the very thing that a "big name" preacher would never do. He slipped and fell! Not just landing anywhere, but landing squarely across the yet-to-be-served communion table. Collection plates, unleavened bread plates, glass communion cups crashed loudly to the floor. Unleavened bread and grape juice were mixed flat on the floor with glass and trays.

The service was halted while, providentially, a general store operated by one of the church members was opened for a special procurement of communion supplies and rushed back to the HOW. How "unleavened" the communion bread actually was that was purchased spur-of-the-moment is not known.

Fortunately, Fletcher did not receive a request for baptism or special public prayer on that day.

Over sixty years have passed since that incident in a rural Tennessee church. Fletcher eventually earned a doctorate in physics from Duke University, served as a professor at Lipscomb, and later served as an elder at the Otter Creek congregation where his wife Gail had effectively administered the kindergarten program. Given his Bible knowledge as well as his compassion and understanding of people, Fletcher has the requisite characteristics for success in the ministry.

He remains active and, to use a tired expression, is present every time the doors are open—a stark contrast to those who never "darken the doors." I know of no person who does pastoral ministry more effectively, yet quietly and humbly—he is a genuine and devoted pastor!

Fletcher has never preached a full-length sermon since the Santa Fe incident.

POSTSCRIPT FOR THE TWENTY-FIRST CENTURY

The blessing of worshiping in a rural congregation in the Bible Belt does not happen often for me anymore. However, I have enjoyed a few visits in the past few years.

By contrast to the old days, some changes have been made: Almost always central heating and air conditioning units have been installed; better flooring or carpeting may have been installed; a brick veneer may have been added to a wood frame church house; sometimes a new church building has been constructed; a parking lot may have been paved and marked off; new, more up-to-date hymnals are utilized; new classrooms and perhaps a fellowship area have been added; maybe a new podium has been built for the old pulpit. When one visits these rural congregations one might see late model, well-equipped pickup trucks and luxury sedans in abundance around a paved parking lot.

During the service, much to my surprise, some preachers for these rural churches have actually set up a projector and screen and employ PowerPoint sermon presentation aids. And the song leader might even inject a few songs that were composed after 1970 to complement the old standards such as "Trust and Obey."

What does not seem to have changed in these rural churches? Answer: The "down home" basic goodness, sincerity, and hospitality of hard-working people, whether farmers or people employed in city jobs, who maintain these congregations because of family ties that span two or three generations. These are the people who, if you experienced a dire need, would do anything in the world for you they possibly could. These "brothers and sisters in Christ" are truly what Jesus described as "the salt of the earth" and "light of the world."

4

Please *Don't* Revive Us Again— Some Memories and Reflections on Gospel Meetings Past and Present

The scene was a picture of massive incongruity.

Jogging and walking with some friends in Nashville's Green Hills area late one afternoon several years ago, we passed the Granny White church building, so named because of the avenue on which the meetinghouse is located. As an aside, in 2018 the congregation changed its name that had been part of its identity for several decades to The Church of Christ in Green Hills because, as argued by change advocates, the new name would attract younger people who otherwise would be "put off" by any name with "Granny" in it. Older members there persist in calling the church Granny White, however.

The Granny White/Green Hills church building is a large, imposing brick structure with a high ceiling and an assembly hall that accommodates several hundred souls. This is a venue in which I have heard a number of distinguished preachers: Clay Pullias, Willard Collins, Batsell Baxter, Carroll Ellis, Paul Rogers, Alonzo Welch, Norvel Young, Charles Chumley, Dennis Loyd, Dwain Evans, and many more. In the small church yard in front of this large, impressive structure was posted a small, crude wooden sign with amateurish, paint lettering which made an announcement for the entire community—"Gospel Meeting. Hear Jim Mankin preach. Each night at 7:30."

Hundreds of private vehicles and scores of city buses pass that sign each day,

"But," I wondered aloud to a friend as a few stray cars pulled into the parking lot two to three minutes before services were set to begin, "how many people will attend even a single service of this series based on having read that anemic sign?" My educated guess, buttressed by much experience, was that not one lost soul attended the meeting based solely on seeing this *ad hoc* outdoor advertising. Seeing only a few automobiles in the parking lot within a couple of minutes of start time, alas, it appeared as though the church would be fortunate if it secured the presence of one-fourth to a third of its own membership and perhaps one or two visitors.

"The gospel meeting in the Church of Christ is such an outdated notion and nearly dead practice. It looks like we should stop singing 'Revive Us Again' and start singing 'Please *Don't* Revive Us Again,'" I commented once to Jerry Masterson, a friend and fellow preacher alumnus.

"I couldn't agree more," Jerry concurred. "'Please *don't* revive us again'" because we don't want to be revived to the same style of legalism and irrelevance we're finally pulling away from. Please don't send us back."

THE "MOTHER OF ALL REVIVALS"

The gospel meeting has long enjoyed a long and venerable position in the life and traditions of the True Church. As a matter of fact, the entire Disciples movement owes much of its origin, according to Vanderbilt church historian Paul Conklin, to a big revival meeting conducted at Cane Ridge, Kentucky, the week of August 6-13, 1801.

This "mother of all revivals," called by some "the American Pentecost," was, according to Conklin, "arguably the most important religious gathering in all of American history." (See Conklin's interesting and valuable study, *American Originals: Homemade Varieties of Christianity,* University of North Carolina Press, 1997, especially chapter 1.) When the dust at Cane Ridge had settled, the camp meeting inspired revivals across the region and gave rise to new denominations, including the Cumberland Presbyterians and Christian Church (Disciples of Christ).

Response to Cane Ridge preaching and singing was largely spontaneous and uninhibited, to say the least. Barton W. Stone believed that the frontier audience was experiencing a mighty movement of the Holy Spirit. In the midst of dramatic gospel preaching, those listeners least moved by the Spirit experienced weakened knees or a dizzy head.

Hundreds of other lay people responded more emotionally—some fell prostrate on the ground as though "slain in the Spirit" or victimized by grand mal seizure or another type of hysteria. Now grounded, they unleashed holy groaning and holy laughter. Women fell in scandalously unladylike postures with previously clothed epidermis being exposed and men occasionally fell off horses; a few others, doubtless due to spiritual intensity, lost bladder control.

THE EVOLUTION OF THE GOSPEL MEETING

Today's typical Church of Christ congregation has assiduously avoided that kind of ecstatic expression. Far from embracing it, the church has largely shunned intense emotional expression and many of its preachers have sarcastically ridiculed the ecstatic emotionalism of American Pentecostal churches and charismatics in general.

If one were to attend a typical gospel meeting (remember that we have almost never employed "revival" to label these special efforts at saving the lost), she or he might find by contrast a church building half-filled with lifeless, inert, working class men and women and a few children who are struggling to stay awake while some contracted guest preacher offers his tired, worn-out recital of the party platform. Little wonder we are not revived!

The history of the gospel meeting in the Church of Christ is one of evolution from assemblies in brush arbors, under tents in open fields, in rural and small town meetinghouses, to meetings in luxurious church buildings and finally to cavernous, rented municipal auditoriums and civic centers where evangelistic extravaganzas were staged before hundreds if not thousands in a single evening. I would estimate that between one and two million gospel meetings have been conducted by Churches of Christ alone since that Cane Ridge revival. Any estimate of gospel sermons preached in meetings during that same period must range widely from seven to eight million to fifteen million.

The gospel meeting is a virtual corpse in many congregations and it displays weakened vital signs in other congregations. "The gospel meeting is the evangelistic arm of the local congregation," Willard Collins once told me. Collins, whose first meeting was held in 1936 in Prairie Hill near Duncan, Oklahoma, became undeniably one of the most powerful and effective guest evangelists in the Church of Christ. His deep, profound voice was an instrument which reached hundreds of thousands and evoked almost seven thousand baptisms and nearly as many restorations within a half century. "Sadly," Collins stated to me personally, "the gospel meeting has been dying since the mid-70s."

Weekend meetings, special seminars, workshops, and retreats have replaced the two or three week marathons of the early to mid-twentieth century. Usually these "seminars" and "lectureships" represent genuine efforts to bring fresh insights on issues of the Christian's everyday life; sometimes, however, they are new names for the same old themes and stock arguments.

The hearing of these old themes and arguments was the final impetus for thousands of women and men to "obey the gospel." Chances are that fully a fourth to one half of today's middle-age and older-age members of the Church of Christ "responded to the invitation" during a gospel meeting. During the childhood and most of the adulthood of these generations, the gospel meeting was considered the most important weapon for "winning the battle for the minds of men." The meeting was also the highlight of the year on each church calendar. Some congregations sponsored two meetings a year, one in the spring and the other in the fall. And sometimes there were both morning and evening services each meeting day.

Throughout my college Bible training years I could hardly wait until some church invited me to "hold a meeting." Much like an unattractive woman dropping hints to available men that she'd like to go out with them, I "flirted" with several rural and small community churches by letting them know of my availability for the plying of my biblical knowledge and evangelistic skills. I had attended meetings all my life both at home and with my father on the road in any one of several states from the Gulf of Mexico to the Great Lakes; my dad took pride in claiming he had preached in all the forty-eight states (making this claim before Hawaii and Alaska were admitted to the Union).

At last, in the July before my senior year in college, I conducted my first gospel meeting and my first baptism at Sycamore Flat, a rural church between Dover and Clarksville, Tennessee. There were more to follow.

A VISITING KING IN A HUMBLE ABODE

Gospel meetings in the rural and small town congregations presented the visiting evangelist with glorious occasions for rest and relaxation as well as generous nourishment for both body and ego. The guest preacher would visit each evening in a different home an hour or two before the gathering of the elect. In these humble abodes he would be treated like a veritable king from a foreign empire. In rural areas the guest evangelist was shown around the farm where he could offer mundane comments on the health of cash crops or vegetable gardens. He might be escorted to the barn where he might need to step circumspectly amidst the "meadow muffins" while learning about the latest milking machines, the newest tractor and other farm equipment, or the cost of feed.

To sit as guest evangelist at the dinner table of some good family in the congregation was considered a distinct honor for the host and hostess. For the guest preacher, entering the dining room seemed like entering an elaborate cathedral of cholesterol with an altar laden with fried chicken ("the gospel bird"), country ham, roast, home-made rolls and/or biscuits, gravy, and home garden-fresh tomatoes, corn, green beans, okra, squash, cucumbers, peas, potatoes, and baked apples. For dessert the guest of honor usually enjoyed a choice of several home-baked cakes and pies served with ice cream. Most likely, the guest would call for a sampling of each dessert, much to the delight of the cook who graciously labored long hours in a hot kitchen to produce such scrumptiousness.

Having sat for well-scrubbed chit-chat with the preacher while his wife and daughters prepared the meal and set the table, the head of the household usu-ally uttered a standard comment to the guest of honor as the abundant table is approached. Pointing at the table laid out like a newly completed zig saw puzzle with its variety of dish size, shape, and color of food, the host would offer a mock apology: "Preacher, I'm glad you could be here with us for supper tonight, because I just wanted you to see the kind of cooking I have to put up with every night of the week."

Alas, the poor homemaker who labored and perspired all day to prepare this feast of gustatory delights undoubtedly anticipated the quip and managed a smile; after all, she had heard her husband make that mock complaint intended for humor on previous such occasions. However, her worth and motives, as well as her talents, would soon be validated by the first happy sighing and words of praise from the guest preacher ("Um, um delicious!"). Incidentally, sometimes the church's regular preacher might also "luck out" and be invited to the same supper occasion.

The guest evangelist, sitting at the head of the table, is usually called on to "say grace" before the first meat platter is passed to him. All heads are then bowed, sometimes hands are joined (but not always, especially in the old days). "Our Father, we thank thee for this home and for this good fam-ily and please bless our gospel meeting in progress," the prayer begins, "and thank thee for this food and bless it to the nourishment of our bodies and us to thy service. In Jesus name. Amen." The children of the host family know that they will likely be the last to receive the chicken platter, perhaps last to receive the other dishes, and their role is to be seen and not heard until called on to answer a friendly, innocuous question such as "how's school going for you this year?"

The ultimate compliment was offered when the preacher took second and third "helpings" of several of the dishes, and few and far between were gospel meeting veterans who did not indulge to the full limits of stomach and intes-tinal capacity. Indeed, a preacher could gain five or six pounds in a one-week meeting. Little wonder there were so many hefty evangelists on the full-time meeting circuit. Delivering a soul-stirring oration with much passion was often an exercise in hyperventilation—an exercise that usually began less than one hour after such a waist-expanding ritual—and the evangelist who could convert a potentially sonic-sounding burp at either major orifice into a sanctimonious sound or plosive consonant was gifted indeed!

One thing is certain as night following day: Of all the sins of the flesh assailed during the meeting, gluttony was conspicuously absent from the list. To this day it remains the forgotten entry on the historic "seven deadly sins" list. The unspoken motto of the guest evangelist: "Preach the Word. Eat the bird."

A SECOND-STORY CHALET WITH DOWNSTAIRS PRIVILEGES

In the old days the guest evangelist typically stayed in a private home of one of the church families. Though considered a much cherished honor by the hosting family, for the guest preacher the experience could be one of life's wondrous serendipities or it could be one of life's most grueling challenges. During several rural meetings I was assigned an upstairs bedroom, often a converted attic space, with no bathroom—a situation retired preacher Cecil Hook called "accommodations in the upstairs chalet with downstairs privileges."

In many older farm houses there was only one bathroom and the stairway from the upper bedroom descended directly into the master bedroom. If the evangelist was a "late night person," as I am, he must choose between tiptoeing down the dimly lit stairs into the privacy of the slumbering, snoring saintly couple en route to the only bathroom or, on the other hand, finding a less conventional or even unmentionable means of meeting basic physiological needs. I preferred the latter.

Many meetings included both morning (usually at 10:00 A. M. but sometimes as early at 7:00 A.M.) and evening services and, until recent years, most meetings began on a Sunday morning and were protracted (sometimes called "betracted") daily until the following Sunday evening or even through a second Wednesday evening or a third Sunday evening. Of course, in previous generations there was no television with which evangelists were required to compete.

The evening service was the main event, of course, and typically the local congregants assembled, sang the songs of Zion, listened to a visiting area preacher lead a prayer, sat patiently and stirred a personal breeze with cardboard fans (each with a colorful religious scene on one side and a printed advertisement for the local funeral home on the other side), and waited through another gospel presentation which blended some of the most precious words and truths and insights of all time with a threadbare rehearsal and defense of the party platform.

Since the pew was at least half-way comfortable to people staying up perilously close to their bedtime and the sermon and stock arguments were more than half-way predictable, little wonder so much weariness of the flesh manifested itself in the evening service. One recalls the irreverent Clarence Darrow's cryptic comment that if you laid all the people who went to sleep at church end to end they'd be a lot more comfortable.

Mothers of small children in evangelistic assemblies possessed a special advantage, according to minister and English professor Robert Meyers, because they could find blessed relief by tuning out the preacher and demonstrating solicitous concern about their children's immediate needs. If a child became too fussy or fretful, then who could but respect, perhaps even envy, the maternal care which rendered it necessary to remove the precious little one from the assembly? The widely-held speculation that mothers intentionally pinched a baby to induce crying so that they could justifiably retreat to home or nursery lacks quantitative research foundation.

SEVEN MAJOR MEETING THEMES

Most "big name" gospel preachers—those wise, highly-regarded, and experienced keepers and expounders of our tradition—expended their homiletic and pulpit energies in gospel meetings on some standard themes deemed crucially important. Here, we will simply note the rhetorical argument and strategy or paraphrase the essence of their basic message on each topic (and using revivalists' actual phrasing when possible).

1. Errors of Denominations

All churches except the Church of Christ are merely denominations and all denominations are in error on a wide range of doctrinal issues ranging from the proper title for preaching brethren (one would not call a preacher "pastor" and definitely not "reverend") to the "plan of salvation." Many preachers denounced other churches by name, often lacing their remarks with sarcasm and scorn. True enough, some of these denominations come close to the truth, but they still remain in error on some points and thus remain counterfeits of the True Church.

The Roman Catholic Church presented a veritable Pandora's Box of doctrinal errors and practices to inveigh against. Denominationalists erred by adding human doctrine and human interpretations to the pure Word, beginning with the adoption of human names such as "Methodist" and "Baptist" ("The Churches of Christ salute you," Romans 16: 16, gives us the proper name for the True Church and may be quoted often in sermons and placed on bumper stickers.)

2. The Restoration of the True Church

The crucial task of every generation is to restore the True Church of the New Testament, because "the church is only one generation away from apostasy." One or more lessons in a gospel meeting were usually presented on the identity of the New Testament church—its origin, founder, prerequisites for entrance, work, worship, mission, and proper organization.

The New Testament contains a pattern or architect's plan for building the True Church; it is also a map to guide us to heaven. The game of baseball provided a stock analogy: Suppose baseball were not played for over one thousand years. Then some boys, looking for a new form of recreation, discover and begin to read and follow an old baseball rule book. This rule book they fortuitously discovered laid out diagram and dimensions for the home plate, bases, and pitcher's mound. The boys then respected the specifications and implemented the rules of the game (such as "three strikes and you're out" and "a ball hit over the fence is a "home run" and "nine innings in each game and each inning has three outs"—in essence these boys have restored the game which all along existed in "seed form" in the baseball rule book—a great analogy here!

3. The Necessity of Full Obedience and the Impertinence of Sincerity

Salvation comes only when the total plan is obeyed. "Incomplete obedience is precisely wherein our good Baptist friends have erred," one preacher proclaimed. "By always placing salvation *before* baptism, they have gotten the heaven-bound cart before the horse."

I vividly recall one True Church preacher telling a group of preachers at the monthly ministerial luncheon, a meeting that was held just prior to an upcoming Billy Graham crusade in our urban area: "I tell my listeners they should go hear Billy Graham so he can lead them to Jesus, then come to our gospel meeting in order to learn how to obey the gospel and be saved."

The Old Testament character Naaman provides an example of an individual who might have anxiously checked his skin condition after each of his first six immersive dips in the Jordan River, but whose leprosy did not vanish until completing his seventh plunge. Ole Naaman was not too enthralled by having to perform the full dipping in a river he deemed too dirty for such medical remedy and unsuccessfully pleaded for cleaner rivers closer to his home. Suppose Noah had used a few oak or hickory planks in constructing the ark. Then that boat would have never risen with the flood waters nor stayed afloat—the earth would have been totally uninhabited by any animal or human life (fish and other aquatic life being possible exceptions)!

Sincerity is an admirable trait, but it counts for nothing if the sinner does not manifest true obedience. Even the best intentions are not enough. Had aforementioned Naaman become distracted by witnesses on the river bank and only taken five or six dips, though fully intending seven immersions, he would have remained a frustrated, ostracized leper.

The New Testament is a road map to heaven. There's only one road to heaven and that way is straight and narrow and few there be who find it. You might have missed an exit ramp and thought you were on the highway to St. Louis, but then actually be traveling the road to Chicago—it doesn't matter where you think you're going or where you want to go! True Christians will want to study the map (the New Testament) and will persistently reject the false doctrine that "it doesn't matter what road you take to heaven as long as you sincerely strive to please God."

4. Baptism

All Christian groups practice something called water baptism, but the many errors surrounding this doctrine provided the basis for many gospel meeting sermons (see chapter 9). Actually, regardless of the topic, each sermon emphasized the importance of baptism and ended with a call for the non-baptized to "obey the gospel."

5. False Doctrine and False Teachers in the True Church

In more recent times it has not been sufficient simply to reproach and convict the evildoers outside the walls of the household of faith, but a need has arisen to ferret out the false teachers from within. Some of these straying brethren are dangerous not because they openly espouse "the doctrine of Baal" or "speak the language of Ashdod," but because they give off "an uncertain sound." These "troublemakers in the church" become even more spiritually dangerous by using modern Bible versions that erroneously translate several key texts.

In the 1970s, for example, some preachers began to talk about the Holy Spirit as though he had actually emerged from some 1900 years of retirement and was now was operating "separate and apart from the written word." Other preachers "compromised the truth" by associating with "denominationalists" or by permitting innovation and spontaneity in their worship assemblies. Entire meetings, sometimes called lectureships, have been devoted to the theme of "Modernism in the True Church." Not only were these trends to be condemned in the True Church, but it seemed permissible to call names of several proponent preachers and teachers who espoused these "human doctrines and innovations."

6. Worldliness

"Be not conformed to the world" and "Come ye out from among them and be ye separate, saith the Lord" has been the Scriptural foundation for a standard theme of many a gospel sermon. In many meetings the sermons on worldliness wielded the greatest impact. Then, decades later, these emotional messages have been recalled the most vividly of all sermon themes proclaimed, especially by tender-hearted youth who almost incessantly felt they had encountered the devil in the form of cinematic and internet stimulation, hyperactive glands, and raging hormones.

Historically, the litany of worldly ways, those "pleasures of sin that last but for a season," was seemingly almost endless—playing cards (except for Rook or Uno; "42" with dominos is a safe alternative); gambling; sexually explicit movies; dancing; wearing shorts, tight skirts, halter tops, bikinis and other immodest clothing (men rarely if ever received censure on clothing issues); social drinking; profanity ("taking God's name in vain"); general cussing; parking (or "necking"), petting, and fornication; foolish jesting and dirty joking—on and on the list of worldly sins continued. Only on the rarest of occasions did tobacco use take a violent rhetorical hit because rural congregations in the Bible Belt often were composed of tobacco farmers; and, for all practical purposes, preacher salaries were often paid with contributions from market tobacco sales.

Some evangelists encountered timid squeamishness when speaking explicitly about sexual impropriety. Consequently, with such discomfort in publicly speaking of matters related to sex, these evangelists found it convenient to lump several scandalously pleasurable misbehaviors under the categories of "fornication," "promiscuity," "carnality," "lasciviousness," or "concupiscence." As younger teenagers, we listeners often wondered what on earth some of those four-syllable and five-syllable words meant. All we knew is that the words were surely in the King James Version of the New Testament and they likely stood for some kind of sinful sexual behavior.

For preachers less enamored with puzzling King James Version parlance, vague phrases such as "this, that, and the other" or "things like that" served as convenient catchall expressions. For example, the revivalist might say: "Evil companionships corrupt good morals, so you young people stay away from classmates who use bad language, smoke, drink, dance, and do this, that, and the other." More than once I have heard a preacher warn young people that "the praying knee and the dancing leg don't grow on the same person."

Other evangelists may have said more than they intended. The kind and gentlemanly H. A. Dixon, during his tenure as president of Freed Hardeman College, once was preaching a sermon in Henderson, Tennessee on worldliness. After citing and lamenting several manifestations of the flesh at work in contemporary society, according to FHC professor Porter King, Dixon then declared: "Yes, there are many signs of moral decay in our world. Some things have been bad for a long time. But now sinful society has come along with that mini-skirt. Brethren, we've just about reached the bottom!" Porter reports that many in the audience began looking at each other and grinning. Later when he conveyed to Dixon what he had said, the esteemed preacher counseled, "Now, Porter, you've put the wrong interpretation on that statement."

7. The Bliss of Heaven and the Horror of Hell

The last few services in a gospel meeting were occasions for touching the heart-strings of the listeners. Some gospel evangelists used imagination to describe how the Second Coming might impact the average working person in the middle of the day and the sheer terror of being swept up unprepared into the great judgment hall of God.

Providing some scary sense of the duration of eternity in perdition was a special challenge to homiletic ingenuity. "Imagine with me, if you will, that the earth of some 26,000 miles in circumference is a solid steel ball," I heard more than one meeting preacher offer, "and imagine also that a lowly ant is dispatched to walk around this giant terrestrial ball enough times until a one-inch rut is worn into that massive steel ball. Brothers and sisters, once that rut has been made, that will just be the first second of the first minute of the first hour in the first day of eternity."

The guest preacher was free, of course, to select any other theme to present in a meeting series. Many preachers developed narrow one-issue interests, phenomena labeled "hobbies" by brethren and sisters who did not share a common zeal for the "hobby-rider's" issue. Consequently, a lot of time and energy was squandered on irrelevant, pet issues. Alas, sometimes there was precious little "gospel" in a gospel sermon.

OLD-FASHIONED VISUALS

Evangelists of previous generations frequently used a large chart as a visual aid for their sermons. My dad owned scores of these charts. He could submit the content and desired Scriptures to some "professional" who would provide the lettering and simple sketches, such as of the cross or the ark with abbreviated Scripture references sprinkled around the sketches.

Sometimes made of a canvas or linen material, more typically the chart was a bed sheet with diagrams and bright lettering which hung by thumb tacks above the baptistery curtain or on the back wall. The chart could also be draped over a chalk board and unveiled during the early minutes of the sermon. Such an unveiling often removed any remaining vestige of audience curiosity about the topic and content of the preacher's message.

Chart sermons presented a good news/bad news scenario for most listeners. On the positive side, preachers who incorporated charts were ahead of their time in understanding a concept some of their successors have not realized—listeners' interest remains focused and retention is enhanced by a speaker's use of visual aids. Additionally, a preacher using charts should not need extra notes placed on the podium. Truth is, veterans of the meeting and revival circuit had much earlier memorized the basic content of these stump messages and thus needed no notes.

The downside of chart sermons was felt by listeners who realized that after twenty to twenty-five minutes the preacher was still pointing to lettering toward the top left corner, then it would still be considerable time until the shadow of the pointer would be falling on the lettering in the lower right corner. Yet this was the most practical way to estimate length of the gospel sermon.

THE POWER OF "INVITATION SONGS"

The term "invitation songs" is not found in the New Testament, of course, but all members of the True Church know its meaning and significance. When the powerful evangelist concludes by imploring alien sinners and straying disciples with the dramatic, pre-set words: "Won't you come? Right now, as together we stand and sing!"—then it's quaking time for the devil and his angels. The devil and his conniving host must surely know there is more holy horsepower packed into a few poignant invitation songs sung softly and tenderly than an entire volume of gospel sermons hot off a vanity press.

Whatever the hymnal, each typically has a compilation of at least twenty-five to fifty selections which may be categorized as invitation songs. Many of these songs rhapsodize about the sinner's wretched condition and his or her horrific fate, or they are songs projecting a special plea and exhortation to the sinner. Some songs sound an upbeat note of joyous glad tidings such as in "Sinners Jesus will receive: Sound this word of grace to all." Others take the lower road of stirring negative emotions such as "There's a sad day coming when the sinner shall hear his doom" (from the third stanza of "There's a Great Day Coming").

Many invitation songs begin by asking the sinner a question: "Why do you wait, dear brother?" "Who will follow Jesus?" "Why keep Jesus waiting?" "Have you been to Jesus?" "Who at the door is standing?" or "Are you coming to Jesus tonight?" (The last number is one that technically could be sung at a morning service, the idea being the sinner has all afternoon to think about the answer.) The greatest invitation song query is, of course, "O why not tonight?" This classic also asks in everyday conversational speech, "And wilt thou thus his love requite?"

THE TWO GREATEST INVITATION SONGS OF ALL TIME

What song has brought more heavy-laden sinners down the aisle and into the fold of safety than any other? For all evangelistic purposes, two hymns have virtually tied for that honor. One is "Almost Persuaded," P. P. Bliss' poignant lament of the unredeemed soul who was so close yet so far from the path of penitence and salvation ("Harvest is past … doom comes at last! 'Almost' cannot avail. 'Almost' is but to fail. Sad, sad that bitter wail—'Almost, but lost'").

The other power-packed invitation song is Charlotte Elliott's classic, six-stanza hymn "Just As I Am." Each stanza begins with the words "Just as I am" and ends with the declaration "O Lamb of God, I come! I come!" so that a complete thought is concentrated into each stanza. Both of these classic invitation songs are sung with dirge-like sobriety and earnestness.

The successful evangelist will guide the selection of invitation songs just as he manages sermon topics. And the more powerful invitation hymns are harnessed with powerful sermons to be unleashed in the last services of the meeting. During the invitation singing—always, always performed with the entire congregation standing—the guest preacher still possesses the tools of crowd psychology and the power of suggestion. Among his options:

1. Interrupting a song between stanzas and making another appeal.
2. Walking several rows up the aisle with one hand raised (two hands raised would seem charismatic and should be avoided).
3. Shouting exhortations while the congregation is singing, in essence a major voice-over strategy.
4. Calling for a repeat of one or more stanzas after a "visible response." Veteran evangelists will never allow an invitation song to end on the stanza in which someone has walked forward. On the other hand, when the responses seemed to have ended it is appropriate to offer a statement which gives warning to remaining holdouts and relief to the redeemed: "We're going to sing just one more stanza and if no one else responds to the Lord's invitation then our service will be over for tonight."
5. Asking the local preacher, who certainly knows the exact pew location of the vilest offenders and staunchest hold-outs, to make a personal appeal. Some of these supplementary appeals are virtual sermonettes and usually contain the most emotionally-charged content of the meeting.

In larger churches there are typically one to five veteran "hold-outs" who have persistently and doggedly resisted for many years rendering obedience to the commands of repentance, confession, and baptism. Yet, almost as gluttons for punishment, these obstinate rebels faithfully attend the services, sing heartily the songs of praise, listen to the sermon, and then stand on cue for the invitation song while family members earnestly urge them to respond; at times the preacher walks up the aisle and almost takes the obstinate sinner by the arm and leads him to the front.

Such is the battle between the forces of good and the forces of evil. This battle is often precluded by pre-meeting strategy huddles between the guest speaker and concerned souls. The high-powered sermon and heart-wrenching hymn-singing seem like the intense shaking of a limb to dislodge that coveted but well-attached fruit. Even when the fruit does not fall, the locals seem to appreciate the evangelist who can give the tree one unrelentingly horrific shaking.

HARVEST TIME IN THE MOTOR CITY

The most vivid recollection for me as a young minister of a meeting's harvest time occurred during an area-wide series conducted in 1966 in Detroit's spacious and modern Cobo Hall, in those years the home court of the NBA's Detroit Pistons. With main floor seating, this hall could accommodate up to 20,000 people. Congregations within a hundred-mile radius of Detroit dispatched busloads of church members each evening for a week to hear Jimmy Allen of Searcy, Arkansas, preach the gospel.

I had no doubt that Jimmy was the most intense, the most persuasive, evangelist for audiences of any size I had ever heard. I first heard him in a Dallas area-wide meeting in 1964 which lasted two weeks. Vividly picturesque sermons on themes such as "What is Hell Like?" helped fill the Dallas Memorial Auditorium nightly for two weeks. Years later the two of us enjoyed opportunities to work and visit together in two local meetings in McMinnville, Tennessee, and I was easily convinced that Jimmy's passion emanated from his convictions, humility, and sincerity as much as from his manifest rhetorical skills and emotional appeals.

As an aside, during those meetings I learned first-hand that Jimmy was in terrific physical shape and liked to play tough pick-up basketball with younger men. More importantly, I learned he is truly a Christian gentleman who remains deeply concerned about worldliness and secularism making inroads into church membership. Humbly arriving in his small Ford Escort that he drove from Searcy, an unimpressive vehicle that he dubbed the "Ford Excuse," Jimmy was the only basketball player in our group wearing slacks instead of shorts on a hot, summer Sunday afternoon.

What happened the last night of that Cobo Hall meeting began to stir serious questions in a young preacher's mind about the ethics of traditional evangelistic strategy. Earlier that day Jimmy had informed our group of area ministers that he was aiming for a record response "when the invitation is offered." His sermon was powerful enough, for sure, depicting the horrors of hell and subsequent personal "lostness" and separation. When the invitation was offered, the audience then stood for forty-five to sixty minutes as we sang intermittently "Just As I Am" and "Almost Persuaded." No other hymns were sung at invitation time. All stanzas were sung several times. Gradually, the number of people walking forward began to multiply and the longer we sang the more precious souls were harvested.

One hundred or so men and women, boys and girls, ambled their way to the front of the assembly. A wide range of emotions was expressed—many were openly weeping and a few looked as calm and collected as "Cool Hand Luke," the name of a Paul Newman movie running at that time. Stanza by stanza, the front rows of people were motioned by hand gestures to relinquish their seats so that the heavy-laden and contrite souls could sit down and fill out a response card. Two portable baptisteries had been installed, one each side of the pulpit, and the immersions alternated between the two tanks, thus speeding up the obedience process.

Most respondents who walked to the front, however, were "confessions" or "restorations." Some respondents I recognized easily because they were members in my own home congregation and had been "repeat customers" of my preaching, having walked down the aisle at the conclusion of a few of my own evangelistic sermons. At that time, I facetiously wondered about the feasibility of granting some kind of golden response card where enough punches for "going forward" would merit some kind of gift or recognition. My serious hope was that these lives were being changed for the better and the change would last a lifetime.

THE QUINTESSENCE OF EFFECTIVE EVANGELISM

Once it was a sawdust trail which led to the front row of seats where one or more earnest evangelists stood waiting to extend the warm hand of acceptance to the penitent. Then it was a wooden floor, later linoleum. Now it is more likely to be a cushioned carpet with color to match the decor. No matter the walking surface or color of the aisle, however long or short the distance to the front pew, and whether there are side aisles or only a center aisle, the success of the evangelist is measured by his ability to get people to walk down some aisle at the conclusion of his message. Nothing else matters as much.

Is there a man who ideally epitomizes these principles of effective assembly evangelism? I've thought often of the evangelists in my own fellowship that I have been privileged to hear and observe in gospel meetings. There's no doubt that Willard Collins, with his thunderous voice and sincere manner, has been one of the best. Jack Evans and the late Marshall Keeble demonstrated effectiveness before either black or white audiences. Jimmy Allen and George Bailey remained two of the best.

I've also had the opportunity to hear in gospel meetings such stalwarts as Gus Nichols, Batsell Barrett Baxter, Reuel Lemmons, Marlin Connelly, Johnny Thompson, Burton Coffman, Guy N. Woods, "Firey Ira" North, Norvel Young, James Bales, B. C. Goodpasture, Marshall Keeble, my own dad, and John Allen Chalk before he attended law school. Of course, I'm sure there are scores of excellent speakers in our fellowship I have not been blessed to hear.

Perhaps no one exemplified the power and the effectiveness of the gospel meeting better than the late W. A. ("Willie") Bradfield, truly, in the words of Claude Gardner, "not just an ordinary soldier, but one of God's generals, one of his mighty generals, a prince of a man." It would have been impossible to over-hype W. A. Bradfield as a meeting speaker. He was so persuasive as a pulpiteer that he could have sold hams and sausage in the foyer of a synagogue.

Born in 1910, Bradfield was for twenty-three years associated with Freed-Hardeman College as a Bible teacher and public relations representative. He was a big man, both in physical size and in reputation as an evangelist throughout Tennessee, Kentucky, and Alabama. By the time of his death on March 4, 1972, he had already joined that elite "10K club," having over 10,000 people respond to the invitation call under the sound of his booming voice.

Bradfield distributed some nine million copies of twenty-six tracts. A man in Dallas picked one tract, entitled "The Way to Heaven," out of a gutter, stud-ied it, obeyed the commands he read about in the tract, and wrote Bradfield to tell about it. Another person, a woman who found a Bradfield tract wrapped around a pound of bacon, studied it and then became a member of the Church of Christ—amazing providence or terrific folklore!

Bradfield practiced all of the principles of effective evangelism. First, he knew the technique of finding a brief, catchy title for his messages. Among his more popular titles were: "Five Great Questions," "From Paradise to Paradise," "Four Types of Sinners," "A Prayer Meeting in Hell," "Things that Hinder," "Marriage and the Home," and "Scenes at Judgment."

Bradfield was an equal opportunity hell-raiser, easily frightening young and old and male and female alike during his evangelistic efforts. Guilt and fear seemed his main emotional appeals according to many who recall vividly those powerful rhetorical arguments. "Young mother, you're out of Christ. You love those little children you have in your arms. Do you want to say good-bye to them for eternity and never hold them tenderly again?" Bradfield would plead. On other occasions he would inject a statement such as "Sir, you remember you stole that ham when you were a boy. Did you ever make it right? Don't you need to come forward and repent and confess?"

When the invitation song was sung after a Bradfield sermon, young and old alike made their way to the front. One friend, Harold Duncan, a long-time family counselor in Dallas, recalls having heard many Bradfield sermons:

Brother Bradfield could scare the wits out of everybody. Even if you had already been baptized, after a Bradfield sermon you had the feeling that one baptism was not enough. You wanted to come forward again. He would shout and pound the pulpit. Young children were especially frightened when he described the searing flames of hell.

And during the invitation song, Bradfield was almost irresistible. He'd walk several rows up the aisle and during the singing of the invitation song he'd be repeating "No hope. No hope. No hope. Without God. Without God. Without God." At times he would call out the names of the people he would want to come forward. This evangelist would appeal to different age groups: "You husbands who get baptized and become Christians, you will please your wives and be a blessing to your children" or "You children who come forward will bring joy to your parents as well as to the angels in heaven." "Oh, won't you come? Only a few steps. One day it will be too late! Won't you come as we sing?"

All the while Brother Bradfield uttered these sober and scary appeals, he would be using that one chopping or slicing gesture—a gesture that was a precursor of the "tomahawk chop" made famous by Atlanta Braves fans during the World Series. Oh man, I've never heard anybody like him.

An English professor and Freed-Hardeman alumnus, Porter King, also remembers the Bradfield style vividly. He felt Bradfield exploited guilt as much as any evangelist he had ever heard. Most listeners remember Bradfield naming the specific sins he felt must have been committed by people in his audience. Porter vividly recalls what might be labeled a Bradfield "slip of tongue" when the veteran evangelist made this appeal: "Oh fathers, why won't you come? Oh young boy or young girl, why oh why won't you come? Why won't you come, oh why in the hell won't you come?"

The language seemed shocking for a veteran evangelist. Porter later asked

Brother Bradfield about that statement, if he had realized what he had uttered in the passion of the moment. "Yes, I know what I said, Porter," he replied, "and that's exactly what I meant to say—that they'd be in hell and crying out in hell if they didn't respond the invitation and obey the gospel!" A rapid re-interpretation of unintentional verbiage or slip of tongue is a very present help in time of need!

A NOTE OF SERIOUS APPRECIATION

In modern times, gospel meetings seem almost a relic of the by-gone days, at least with more progressive congregations. Those congregations that retain the meeting strategy, owing to the competition of television and busy lifestyles, have abandoned a two-week or one-week meeting for the weekend gospel meeting. There is practical, sensible consensus that focused workshops, seminars, and spiritual retreats for specialized groups may not only be more effective teaching strategies but will also succeed in fostering ties of fellowship.

Gospel meetings are still very much alive with conservative and mainstream congregations, however. To conclude on a note of seriousness, it was during the days of special evangelism and revival that many of us learned or had reinforced some of the great narratives of Scripture, the importance of proper obedience to God, and the summons to righteous living.

Others of us may bear the marks of excessive emotionalism and the unhealthy guilt we internalized during the teenage years, the most difficult life stage to negotiate. Succumbing to emotional appeals and the influence of peer pressure in a social situation, many youth were likely baptized prematurely. Encouragingly, some listeners received the essential message that salvation is rooted in God's grace and not in human performance; unfortunately, however, many missed that message in the emotionalism of meetings they attended and the trivialities of some messages they heard.

Regardless, how immeasurably impoverished our movement and our heritage would have been had the dedicated preachers named in this chapter, as well as countless others who used the meeting series to teach and exhort, never preached in a gospel meeting!

5

Whether Expounding, Evangelizing, or Reviving—How to Be Impressive in the Pulpit

"Don't preach at me!" You may have heard those words if you've ever attempted to offer verbal correction or advice. Does anyone like to be preached to? Sadly, the word "preaching" has fallen into much disrepute. Not the profession necessarily, but the word.

No doubt all of us have been part of a captive audience within the walls of a church house when the gospel did not seem "good news" to all listeners. Regrettably, there have been occasions wherein the whole church was subjected to absolutely abominable sermons—sermons delivered by men who spent little time in reading, research and reflection, whose premises and assumptions about biblical interpretation were faulty; who demonstrated poor or non-existent exegetical skills; who made little real life application; whose word choice or English grammar would have offended Eliza Doolittle before she met Professor Higgins, and whose delivery skills were virtually non-existent. In essence, a preacher caught somewhere on a continuum between inept and inert.

"Some sermons are like the rumbling of thunder and the flashing of lightning among the clouds high in the heavens," noted one critic. "Lovely to behold, giving forth a promise! But little rain falls on the thirsty soil." Did not William Barclay once poetically observe, "The hungry sheep look to the shepherd and they are not fed"?

On the other hand, sometimes the preacher is well-educated, loves the Lord, is motivated by a desire to educate and inspire his listeners, and is seriously prepared for the Sunday event—and still somehow fails to connect with his audience and seems to do no one in the pews any good. So sad! So regrettable!

The following strategies are recommended for successful preaching and a long career of preaching ministry in the True Church. With the previous chapter discussing the "gospel meeting" or revival, the following suggestions provide sure-fire successful strategy for revivalists and meeting-holders, but most of these strategies will also work wonders for effective "regular" preaching by the "local preacher," as he is usually called.

PROFILE OF A SUCCESSFUL EVANGELIST: TEN RECOMMENDATIONS

Consider: The guest evangelist is always invited to "hold a meeting" for a congregation for one reason and one reason alone—his distinctive personality and persuasive style. Successful evangelists build a national reputation and it is not based on their appearances or their nurturing, pastoring, or counseling skills but solely on pulpit persuasiveness. The good news: A "located preacher" might lack dynamic preaching skills but still achieve a long local tenure with compensating pastoral and social skills.

Aspiring evangelists can learn much from studying the techniques employed by the masters and veterans of gospel meetings. Ten recommendations for preachers are hereby offered:

1. The first rule for the popular preacher is to remember that a sermon must be labeled with a catchy title. The best titles are clever puns or phrases with alliteration. For example: A sermon on the giddy worldliness of Noah's day and the shock of sudden flooding conditions could be entitled "When Giggling Turned to Gargling." Memphis Baptist evangelist Robert Lee's most famous sermon, based on the story of Ahab and Jezebel, was memorably titled: "Payday Someday!" Carroll Ellis once preached a sermon on Naaman cleverly entitled "Seven Ducks in a Dirty River."

A good title for a sermon will stir immediate if not enduring attention. I have taught speech students that a title's connection to the thesis and content of the message should be simple: "half-revealed/half-concealed."

One day at the Westwood church office, I received a phone call from Frances Meeker, religion editor at the *Nashville Banner*. Ms. Meeker was on our bulletin mailing list and had read my title in my sermon series on Acts for the coming Sunday, "A Message to a Guilty Governor." "I'm planning to drive to McMinnville, hear your sermon and then report on it in a *Banner* feature news story," she informed me.

The sermon was scheduled to be preached in the late 70s amidst of heightened interest in the scandals of the current Tennessee governor Ray Blanton. "It's both courageous and a little risky to address a sermon to Governor Blanton, so I believe it merits state-wide coverage," Meeker offered. I felt flattered the religion beat-journalist would drive 170 miles round trip to cover my sermon. The better part of me decided to save her the drive, thus I informed her the title referred to Paul's sermon to Governor Felix in Acts 24. Alas, Ms. Meeker did not visit Westwood that Sunday but I found her to be a most gracious and friendly professional reporter.

Not a few preachers strategize each sermon by developing three main points that follow the introduction to their message, thus: a clever and perhaps humorous introduction, a body with three main points, and a tear-jerking story for conclusion. And many preachers deploy alliteration with each of the three main points beginning with the same letter; sometimes even sub-points are alliterative. Carroll Ellis could be a master of homiletic alliteration. Several current Otter Creek members recall one of Ellis' sermons—and who knows the title, though one can guess some of his content—that developed three memorable points: (1) the Roller-coaster of recklessness; (2) the Rocket-ship of reason; and (3) the Runway of redemption.

As you explain your title and develop your central idea (thesis), remember that all listeners love an old-fashioned acrostic even when they don't know it's an acrostic they're admiring. Suspense builds as the speaker allows each letter of some word to represent another word beginning with the same letter. For example, you could do a sermon on CROSS: C for Church; R for Redemption; O for Observance (here you would discuss the Lord's Supper); S for Salvation; and the other S for Separation (here you would talk about separating from worldliness, referencing "Come ye out from among them and be ye separate"). The value to audience memory is the payoff here. The strategy of cleverness might keep some listeners awake and focused as they wonder what the next letter in the same word will stand for.

Great acrostic sermons can always be built using the words "gospel," "church," "Christ," and "mother." Do not select words such as "insubordination," "ecclesiasticism," "transubstantiation" or "pre-millennialism" for acrostics—this would frighten the people in the pews as to how lengthy the sermon might be.

Here is opportunity to be creative. Sure, every acrostic may have at least one letter (such as "x") that you will have to strain to find an acceptable word to parallel it, but your audience will anticipate your difficulty and appreciate your cleverness. Strive for creativity, but no True Church preacher or teacher could possibly surpass Presbyterian use of the word TULIP to state succinctly the essence of Calvinist theology (look for the meaning later in this chapter).

2. Always say something nice about one or more people early in your sermon before any listeners begin to drift off into dreamland or fantasy. Be careful that when you call a name and praise your fellow brother or sister in the Lord that you do not omit naming someone else or others just as praiseworthy. Consider that, except for the precious few on the church staff, all others in the assembly volunteer for the work that gets done in the congregation. Those who volunteer their time, if nothing more than their attendance and financial contributions at the services, compose the heart of the congregation. Brag on the ones you can commend in all honesty, but never despise or neglect others who need encouragement. Remember that excessive commendation of the elders can be interpreted as "brown-nosing" for job security or a raise.

The successful meeting-holder will offer generous praise for the local preacher and his elders. Such praise is simply good "p. r." Additionally, the local congregation has already had sufficient time to learn that the local preacher is another frail human and he likely needs a salary raise or an ego boost.

Such an ego boost was given me once in the opening meeting salvo by Marlin Connelly at a congregation I was serving in the 70s. His words provide a model of diplomacy and ambiguity, two traits that serve any minister well. "Do you as a church know how fortunate and how blessed you are to have Perry Cotham as your preacher?" he began. "Why, I know the city of Nashville pretty well," he continued as my interest quickened and pride swelled from the front row, "and I'll tell you that Perry Cotham could preach in any pulpit in the city of Nashville!"

Connelly was right, of course. I could preach in any pulpit in Nashville, but the issue was "How *well* could Perry preach in any pulpit and how long would Perry last in any pulpit in Nashville?" Do you think that I saw to it that Marlin was invited to return years later for another meeting? After such a lavish compliment you can bet your eternal life he was invited for a return engagement. (Of course, I had previously lavished well-deserved high praise on Marlin as a person and a preacher. My parents often used a folksy saying: "I'll scratch your back if you'll scratch mine," a less sophisticated way of saying *quid pro quo*.)

3. Develop the skills to make your audience experience both laughter and tears. The faster you can move them from one feeling to another, the more skilled you become at making the audience feel it's enjoying an emotional roller coaster.

What kind of laughter does the preacher seek? Even the best of preachers seldom receive the side-splitting, uncontrollable belly-laughs evoked by night-club comedians whose audiences are half-drunk to totally inebriated. Some collective chuckles or even a number of wide grins will allow the preacher to know that some people in the audience at least understood the joke and felt it possessed some wholesome merriment.

Every preacher should collect a wide range of appropriately clean jokes and stories to share with an audience, preferably quite early in the sermon. There are books which have jokes and stories; newspapers and magazines contain articles with humorous material. Buy the books. Clip and file articles for future reference. Use any of the stories whenever "you take a notion." Work on transitions such as "Now this reminds me of the story …" That a story does not in any way fit the thesis or key points of your lesson does not matter in the least—any speaker with an ounce of creativity can make some kind of link between an anecdote and some point in the lesson even if no one remembers the link and no one cares.

The best stories are narrated in the first person so, when you hear a good story that brings laughter for one speaker, then re-tell the story to your next audience as though the interesting and bizarre story happened to you. Let's be realistic: No audience is likely to laugh when you say, "A funny thing happened to Brother Elrod when he was on vacation at the Grand Canyon …" Never mind that several in your audience might suspect that the story did not happen to you—most preachers seem to elasticize the boundaries of truth when it comes to illustrations and humor and many listeners seem to expect embroidering.

Leading your audience to weep is a much more difficult challenge. It's not necessary for actual tears to flow—some moisture on the eyeballs, a quickening of the heartbeat, or a lump in the throat that makes one seem "choked up" is quick sufficient. Novice preachers and evangelists might easily mistake physical symptoms for having hit the conscience bulls-eye or tugged the heart strings.

I well remember in my first evangelistic effort a woman who sat on the second pew seemed to become emotional as I expounded on some heart-rending issue. Her eyes watered and she seemed to have trouble catching her breath. I could not help but notice and silently feel gratified. As the eye-watering and sniffling continued, she rose from her pew, right in the middle of my discourse, and exited the center aisle to the main entrance and out to the front lawn. "I have truly touched this woman," I silently yet proudly proclaimed to myself while continuing my sermon. After the service, the woman approached me and I greeted her with a countenance of tender sympathy as I awaited her apology for slipping out during the sermon and her explanation. Her explanation was both forthcoming and deflating: "I'm sorry that I had to get up and leave right in the middle of your sermon, Brother Cotham, but I was really miserable—that was the worse asthma attack I've had in years!"

How do you make your audience cry? The old story about little Johnny and little Suzy and their mother being unable to buy decent clothes and eat a hearty breakfast because dad is spending all his time and money at the local saloon chasing drink and floozies probably won't impact this generation as it has former generations. Stories about old-fashioned virtues of self-sacrifice (especially for children being raised), fidelity in the face of infidelity, unrequited love, courage in the heat of battle, incredible forgiveness, valiant fights against addiction, and even patriotism should play well.

The best way for the preacher to get the audience to weep is to weep himself. Nothing silences an audience quicker or grabs listener attention instantaneously more than for a speaker to lose control of his emotions and then to pause for regaining composure. Excess display of emotion can seem like a cheap, maudlin trick to some listeners. When a preacher's weeping is considered not to be sincere, such perception will evoke an inner impatience and even disgust.

To my thinking, televangelist Jimmy Swaggert tearfully confessing his big infidelity event on national television, with rivulets of tears streaming down his face and lips and jaws quivering as he looked toward heaven and intoned, "I have sinned against you, my Lord," was a bit overly dramatic. An unforgettable memory was created, for sure, but not a model of adult maturity.

4. Develop skills for making your audience feel pious. Making the audience feel pious or spiritual is the easiest of the major emotions to evoke. And why? Simply because regular worshipers and revival-attendees have attended the service wanting to feel right about their doctrine and morally upright about their lifestyle. Two ways are recommended for helping your listeners to feel righteous and both should be employed generously.

First, attack absentee sinners. It's always effective to condemn scathingly with biting sarcasm such characters as: "those deluded Baptists who strip baptism from the plan of salvation;" "those crazy holy-rollers;" "those mis-guided Methodists who sprinkle babies;" "those liberals who suck every vital doctrine out of the inerrant Holy Bible;" "those perverted Catholic priests who consort with nuns or abuse young boys;" "those liberal preachers in our own fellowship who use modern Bible translations and turn away from sound doctrine;" and so on. Be careful here as better educated and better informed listeners could take offense, especially if they have a family member in another church or faith tradition. Or you could attack to your heart's content the godless, worldly, atheistic movie producers in Hollywood, but be careful not to criticize the local theater lest it be managed by someone in the audience and frequented by three-fourths of the audience. An attack on liberal politicians in Washington or the legacy of the liberal Warren Supreme Court is always effective.

Tom Cook, former Lipscomb English instructor and later an elder at Fourth Avenue, attended a revival back in the early 50s in an Ohio congregation. The guest revivalist lathered up into loud shouting in naming and condemning one denomination after another and then graphically describing the eternal flames that awaited so many in doctrinal error. (Tom did not remember the title for the sermon, so I suggested it could have been entitled "101 Damnations.") Tom then was standing near the front door after the service as attendees filed by the guest speaker, most commending his courageous and condemning candor, but one good sister became especially ecstatic in excitement and praise: "Oh, good brother, what a wonderful sermon! I just loved it. It was great. You just made it seem like everyone is going to hell!"

Second, liberally sprinkle your discourse with words and phrases which are rich in "religious" connotation, the hearing of which will recharge nostalgia batteries in every occupied pew. An abridged listing is thus provided with a rating system (1, 2, and 3, with a "1" being the highest score) on impact on the contemporary audience:

THE ABRIDGED LEXICON

"Restoration Movement" (1)—A powerful expression because everybody believes in restoring something good, whether it's the detailed pattern of the church or the Spirit of Christ; use it copiously.

"Make a joyful noise unto the Lord" (3)—A phrase that should be deployed cautiously or perhaps avoided in most churches because it is drawn from the Old Testament and it sounds like a statement the Pentecostals would use.

"Let's just speak where the Bible speaks and be silent where the Bible is silent" (2)—A time-honored, noble Restoration motto that everyone loves but few follow consistently.

"In matters of faith, unity; in matters of opinion, liberty; in all matters, love" (2)—Ditto.

"The Spirit led me …"(0)—Avoid this Pentecostal phrase like you would any of the ten plagues visited upon Pharaoh's Egypt; it suggests that the Spirit operates apart from the written Word.

"The Lord's Church" (2)—Still has a nice ring to it, but better educated listeners will suspect it is being used in a sectarian way.

"The Lord's People" (2)—Ditto

"Sound doctrine" (2)—Everyone believes doctrine should be sound, and the term is vague enough to be interpreted however anyone desires.

"Thus saith the Lord" (1)—Used properly, the expression renders a point scriptural; the phrase uses the style of the ancient prophets. The chief drawback is that a "thus saith the Lord" is reliance on a proof text that is extricated from its full context, but most listeners are not likely to pick up on this Scripture abuse.

"The Bible says …" (2)—Effective, though some know that the phrase was made popular, not by apostolic preachers, but by the late evangelist Billy Graham.

"Give me that old-time religion" (3)—Sounds a bit too old-fashioned as is the old folk hymn by the same name.

"Unless providentially hindered/Lord willing" (3)—Catchall phrases which can cover a multitude of reasons and excuses for not really wanting to do something you know should be done.

"And all the congregation [or the whole church] said 'amen'" (2)—A phrase gaining in popularity among younger preachers; an effective device for soliciting a lot of "amens" in unison, though many will refuse to say anything orally during a church service.

"Can I hear an 'Amen'?" (2)—Some older church members may not like this question, but it can be an effective way to engage the audience. Be aware that some hear the question and are glad to shout "amen" in unison who do not have the slightest recollection of what you just declared.

"Let's read this text and unpack its meaning" (2)—This phrase is catching hold in modern times, younger worshipers will love it though older ones might deem it ineffective.

"The Bible means what it says and says what it means" (3)—Especially effective when you want the audience to take a biblical statement literally; not so effective when a metaphorical or discounted interpretation is sought, such as in the command "Lay not up for yourselves treasures on earth." The phrase seems based on a premise that every Scripture's meaning and application are immediately transparent to all.

"Come, let us reason together" (2)—A prophetic expression from Isaiah; unfortunately, it sometimes means "Come, let us all see it my way."

"Turn in your Bibles to ..."(1)—Highly effective directive indicating the primacy of the Word even when precious few may have brought their Bibles. Using the phrase in every Sunday's message may entice some to bring their Bibles to the service.

"I'm quoting from the King James Version" (2)—Highly effective with older audiences who could not recognize a single letter in either the Greek or Hebrew alphabet, but who have been warned that the evils of modernism and/or denominationalism may be traced to the Revised Standard or New International Versions.

"This was a 'God-thing'" (2) This phrase is rising in popularity among the younger generation and is used to explain a surprising decision, for example, the decision of a minister to make a surprise resignation to accept a new position with a bigger congregation and large salary increase. A "God-thing," therefore, is irresistible. The older generation will be uncomfortable with the phrase as sounding like a slang or sacrilegious statement.

"Heaven" (1)—Everybody enjoys sermons on heaven and allusions to heaven so long as they are convinced they are going to arrive there and a lot of other folks are not.

5. Preach without a manuscript. If possible, preach without notes of any kind. Use only an open Bible. Use a big Bible that is seen easily when you elevate it high to make a point with one of the above phrases.

A college classmate of mine, a big hulk of a man in his late 20s or early 30s who looked like he could have played nose tackle for the Green Bay Packers, had not learned that lesson by the time he was invited to deliver the homily in the Lipscomb College chapel. Poor Gomer spoke with one of those old-fashioned Southern drawls—when he began a sentence you could have called Domino Pizza, ordered a pizza, and had it delivered by the time he finished the sentence. That elephantine hulk of an imposing man was well into his chapel presentation when he reached into his vest pocket and pulled out a pocket-sized New Testament to read the clinching scripture. Alas, Gomer's point was lost by what seemed to be a wimpish gesture.

6. Quote lots of scripture. Always give the scriptural citation after quoting the scripture. Do not give a second thought as to whether you might be lifting these scriptures out of context.

As a college student I was most favorably impressed by the evangelistic method of George Bailey, at that time the preacher for the College church in Abilene, Texas. In all of his sermons, George quoted some seventy to a hundred scriptures, much like an attorney piling briefly-cited evidence to buttress his case. In fact, George prepared a few sermons composed entirely of scriptures with only book, chapter, and verse citation (zero exposition). Additionally, for most sermons he invented numerous puns, witticisms, and word-plays to reinforce his points. Listeners easily bestowed attention and respect.

The first time I heard George preach was in Dallas Memorial Auditorium in 1958 before 17,000 to 18,000 people, although, candidly, many may have come to hear Pat Boone lead singing. George's deployment of scripture and stories were entwined among the five points of an acrostic on "TODAY" (His five points were Training, Outlook, Dedication, Aspiration, and Yielding.) Once I became a student preacher, I began to imitate his engaging style. Years later I came to know him personally as one of the finest, most genuine people I have ever known. George seemed gratified when I informed him that he had been a preacher role model for me as a young minister.

7. Promote yourself for a follow-up meeting at the host church or at a nearby congregation. The biggest insult is not to be invited for a return engagement. It's acceptable to say point-blank, "I'd like to return in two or three years and

harvest some more souls" or "I just feel like we planted a lot of seed this week that we need to harvest together in another year or so."

Some who are weak in the exhortation department have taken the route deployed by old-time politicians of hand-grasping, back-slapping and baby-kissing. When such politicking is perceived to be phony, such "friendliness" is abominable, indefensible, extravagant, and humiliating. And in contemporary times, baby-kissing without parental permission is a major offense.

A pleasing manner and sincere style, on the other hand, will often be effective in the absence of a powerful, thunderous delivery. Develop some specialty such as an effective "children's Bible hour" before services or slide-illustrated lectures on the Holy Land. It's best if these are pictures you made yourself and that include you and some preacher buddies at the holy sites, but you likely can slip in a few spectacular professional/commercial slides that you have purchased at the gift shop that might make the audience gasp. This presentation might be augmented by wearing an authentic Middle Eastern robe or turban, tooting a few notes on a Palestinian wooden flute that can be bought as a cheap souvenir in some Holy Land tourist gift shop, or narrating how seemingly impossible to drown yourself in the Dead Sea.

Many preachers enhance their take-home pay by bringing a variety of personal tracts and self-published books of sermons which they offer to this new market at a "special discount price." Tables are usually set up in the foyer for the display of these materials and the first five to ten minutes of each night's lesson may be devoted to marketing. You might emphasize that these books make excellent Christmas or birthday gifts and/or that all royalties will be donated to a mission charity or children's home where the Bible is taught every day. Be not concerned that many members who purchase the books will never read them or years later remember where they have placed them. If you autograph them and inscribe the purchaser(s)' name(s), they might be placed on a prominent shelf in their residence.

E. Claude Gardner, then president of Freed-Hardeman College, once made an indelible impression on me and the entire Westwood congregation when he spoke one evening in a special series that featured Christian college presidents.

He and I were standing at the front door greeting the saints he had never met previously as they came marching in for the service. Gardner would carefully ask each adult his or her name and then repeat it a time or two. The sermon he delivered that evening was rather conventional, but what he achieved as the saints filed out one by one was simply amazing—he called everyone by his or her name as he bid each one Godspeed. Sometimes he needed a little pause, occasionally a little hint, but I recall he retrieved all the names correctly. He returned to West Tennessee having made a favorable impression on all who attended that evening.

8. As visiting evangelist, bring some extra sermonettes in case you are asked to speak on the radio or at the local Rotary meeting or some other civic club meeting. You never know when such opportunities might surface. Appropriate themes: "How the Christian Faith Makes You a Better Citizen" or "How the Christian Life Brings Health and Wealth." Check your stock of good, clean jokes. There are plenty of clean jokes available in books or on-line; you can access them and adapt them to each new audience.

9. By all means, avoid controversy. Nothing is more likely to make your tenure at a congregation a brief one than jumping fearlessly into tumultuous controversy. First, avoid religious controversy. While the issues that divide the brothers and sisters may change with the generations, nothing subtracts from the marketability of a local preacher or an evangelist so much as having the labels "modernist" and "liberal" pinned on him.

Much as you might deplore the slanderous techniques of any supermarket tabloid-style periodical that was established for the sole purpose of exposing "false teachers," such a publication does wield much power and influence in the hinterland. Those publications, such as *The Militant Contender* (Thanks, Gary Freeman, for this pseudonym), will not hesitate to call your name and print excerpts of your lectures or articles that may substantiate you have strayed from "the Old Paths." To be exposed as a "liberal" with "an uncertain sound" can lead to the certain dismissal from your pulpit or cancellation of your meetings.

Second, avoid all political controversy, no matter how diligently you seek to be nonpartisan. I made this grievous mistake as a young preacher in my late 20s—so idealistic about our nation and so caught up in both the Civil Rights

Movement and the anti-war movement of the 60s. Probably in every other sermon at Westside Central in Detroit, when as a graduate student at Wayne State University in rhetoric and American history, I would make remarks about the need for social justice in race and economic issues and peace in Vietnam and around the globe. I even had a sermon or two on civil disobedience from a biblical perspective and uttered complimentary statements about Martin Luther King. There was a vocal minority that made clear to the elders the "error" and inappropriateness of my remarks, a few strongly urging my involuntary departure from my position.

In one gospel meeting for a church of around three hundred members in Northeast Ohio in 1969, I devoted one night's sermon to race relations from a Christian perspective and another night's lesson to issues of war and peace. Some of the church leaders refused even to speak to me afterward, and one or two that did speak told me that several members were "infuriated" by those lessons. Needless to say, no follow-up gospel meeting was scheduled for that congregation.

Be aware of this reality: In the True Church the majority of your members will be Republicans, that is, if they have any political party affiliation at all. Thus, if you are a Democrat, best remain silent. Do not state any negative opinion about Donald J. Trump or enter any impeachment debate—his having been the elected standard-bearer for the Republican Party is all that really matters. If a church member(s) ask you what you think about a certain president, the diplomatic strategy would be a retreat to vagueness: "I really am no expert in politics. All I know is that I will be praying for this president as the Scripture commands all of us Christians to do."

Even the most progressive True Church, despite an activist minority of Democrats, will be largely Republican. Most will likely support any military engagement the U. S. is waging at the time, no matter where the conflict or how costly the engagement. They will see it as true patriotism and civic duty. There are a lot of ironies herein as several of the most influential leaders in the Stone-Campbell movement were pacifist; David Lipscomb himself was radically non-involved in political affairs, even contending Christians should not vote because they are citizens of the kingdom of heaven.

Analyze your church audience. Be diplomatic. At times, be vague or equiv-ocal when speaking on political-social-cultural issues. Sure, others may not be diplomatic or tactful when they make political or cultural comments to you or around you. They may not be worried about *your* sensitivities, but you must prudently be concerned about *their* sensitivities.

To cite one example in the early 2000s: Glenda and I were sitting in a Sunday evening home meeting of some twenty to twenty-five Nashville-Woodmont Hills small group members when one good brother asked, in seeming total sincerity, "Do any of you in our group actually believe it is possible for someone to be a loyal Democrat and a faithful Christian at the same time?" My pulse rate elevated immediately and I could only guess how much my blood pressure rose. Nonetheless, after a few seconds I was able to provide what was hopefully a tactful but honest and appropriate reply to such an explosive question.

10. To use the old cliché, last but by no means least, make sure your sermons are not too long. I've always remembered the advice of the late centenarian George Burns: "The secret of a good sermon is to have a good beginning and a good ending and to have the two as close together as possible."

Every preacher will learn sooner or later who among his congregation prefers brief sermons so intensely that "going over-time" is a major offense. And every congregation possesses a separate "corporate culture" that has been conditioned to believe just how long a sermon, as well as the overall tone of the service, should be. To illustrate: When I returned to preach at Franklin's Fourth Avenue Church in 1992 after a long tenure of other positions, my first month of Sunday morning sermons consumed thirty to thirty-five minutes. I did perceive some audience restlessness as I approached the thirty-minute mark.

One senior brother named Fred sat just a few rows from the front and kept his left arm propped up on the end of the pew. From that position he would frequently twist his arm and move his head to the left to check his watch; that happened every Sunday while I was preaching. A few times, when exceeding the half hour, Fred would look at his watch, then look at another brother of like mind at the end of the row, and put a sour and disappointed look on his face and nod his head as though to say, "This fellow in the pulpit is hopeless." A time or two he would rise and walk out of the assembly before I had completed the message with those welcomed and cherished seven words: "And now, let us stand and sing."

A few weeks later, the chairman of the elders, Ron Joyner, asked to meet with me one night after services. He offered some compliments and constructive comments, then he told me, "Honestly, for this church, your content is good and challenging, but your messages are too long, perhaps they need to be broken in half." I was stunned this issue would even be mentioned. Then he explained, "Your predecessor Myron always ended the sermon at twenty-three minutes, and the reason for his brevity was the local Sunday broadcast of our morning services and that was all the time available for the sermon." Thus the congregation had been conditioned to twenty-three minute sermons for some twenty-eight years. Honoring Ron's counsel, I made appropriate and appreciated time adjustments. Indeed, every congregation has its own "corporate culture." It is pure folly to ignore it.

The Warren, Michigan, Church of Christ was the first church I served on a full-time basis. I learned so many lessons in that first full-time job and some were painful. Glenda and I had been married only a few weeks when we moved to this working-class Detroit suburb and several families reached out to us in love and kindness—no family any more than K. C. and Mertie Kinnaird. I learned that just about all the families in that church of 175 or so members were "transplants" from a Southern state, mainly Tennessee or Kentucky, and many of them planned to return to the South upon retirement.

Among the blessings provided by the Kinnaird family, K.C. maintained season tickets to the Detroit Lions home football games, at that time played in old Tiger Stadium along Grand River and Trumbull Avenues. As an inveterate sports fan I was so thrilled to enjoy my first Major League baseball games and first NFL football games that first year in the ministry. Among many games we saw together, K. C. took me to every Thanksgiving game, an annual tradition featuring the Lions at home battling the Green Bay Packers. In those years, the Packers featured Bart Starr, Jim Taylor, Paul Hornung, Boyd Dowling, and others, and the Packers eventually won the first two Super Bowls. After that traditional game we would return to the Kinnaird home where Grannie and Mertie had prepared the most sumptuous Thanksgiving feast Glenda and I have ever enjoyed.

The Lions home games started at 1:00 EST. The Warren worship started at 11:00 A.M. (after the 10:00 Sunday School, of course) and typically went to 12:00 noon or a little after. A full hour was needed to greet the brethren at the end of the service, to drive downtown to the stadium, to park the car, and walk to the stadium seats. The Kinnaird family sat near the front and to my right while I was preaching. As the clock moved closer to 12:00, then K.C. would slowly take out his game tickets and nonchalantly spread them apart and prop them in front of his chin, holding them for me to see easily. The nonverbal message was clear: It was time to be concluding the sermon and neither of us wanted to be late for kickoff. When K.C. displayed the tickets I immediately "put a wrap" on the morning message, sometimes with an irrepressible smile. No one in the assembly complained about a sermon ending too soon.

One more point of pulpit impressiveness: A study of the truly successful evangelists in American history will lead one to a significant conclusion—they all used spiritual music to heighten the emotional impact of their evangelical and revival messages. Even when the preacher is more expositor than evangelist, a positive use of hymns and their lyrics can enhance his exposition. (In the previous chapter we discussed this point in some detail and named the two greatest invitation songs of all time.)

THE NEED FOR COMPLIMENTS

From the first sermon we ever preach until the last one we utter, all preachers need encouragement. The most typical encouragement comes from those listeners who are filing out the doorway in which the preacher is fulfilling his ritual of standing and shaking hands. "Nice job, Preacher," or "Good lesson, Brother" are always welcome comments. In time, the local preacher learns which listeners are more likely to offer compliments and which ones would never utter a complimentary syllable. He will also soon learn of a few who will invariably say "good lesson" or "nice sermon" whom he knows slept through most if not all of the sermon.

We all need sincere encouragement whether we call it compliments or "warm fuzzies." Perhaps the best encouragement comes in an extended personal, written message that highlights the message points that were especially helpful or thought-provoking.

Occasionally there can be an unforgettable compliment. I know no better example to cite than a compliment received by Steven Lemley, who was at that time serving as an associate minister with J. P. Sanders for the congregation in Garden Grove, California. Both Steve and J. P. were also then serving as administrators at Pepperdine University. Within this congregation there was a member who was a captain of a merchant marine vessel. This marine captain was not always able to be present in the assembly, but he attended worship when his ship was in port.

One Sunday when Steve delivered the morning sermon, the merchant marine captain was present. After the assembly worship, Steve was standing in the foyer greeting attendees and shaking hands. When the captain approached Steve and extended his hand, he had tears in his eyes. And then with this sincere but loud voice the captain blurted out his compliment, "Brother Lemley, that was a damn good sermon."

Not your typical compliment, for sure. Perhaps all compliments for a preacher's homiletic efforts should be as sincere and unique!

CORE GOSPEL UNCHANGABLE/PREACHING STYLES CHANGING

Preaching as a medium of communicating divine truth to human beings is, of course, much older than Christianity. Historically, preaching has been, for the most part, a profession held in high esteem. Thoughtful observers often ask two important questions: First, is the quality of preaching getting better or is preaching quality degenerating? Second, do sermons really make much difference in the lives of listeners?

Of course styles have changed, almost dramatically, thanks largely to electronic technology. As a youngster being socialized in the True Church, frequently I would watch and listen as preachers expounded the "five-finger" exercise. They could hold up one hand with the palm facing the audience and then with the other hand point to a finger which represented a point to remember. In our tradition the "plan of salvation" could be explained with this strategy: Point to individual fingers one by one as you explain (and cite scriptures, sometimes out of context): (1) hearing the Word; (2) believing the Word; (3) repenting of sins [preachers usually add that the sins could be "sins of omission or sins of commission];" (4) confessing the name of Jesus as the Son of God; (5) being baptized for remission of aforementioned, renounced sins. If a preacher were missing a finger or two, this might be considered a "speech handicap."

The five-finger exercise also works great for a sermon on Scriptural, authorized worship. Why? Because there are only five acts of Scriptural worship: (1) singing; (2) praying; (3) preaching; (4) communion; and (5) contributing cash, sometimes referred to as "laying by in store." As an aside, Calvinist Presbyterians have received far more attention in church history with their acronym TULIP previously referenced (Total Depravity; Unconditional Election; Limited Atonement; Irresistible Grace; Perseverance of the Saints).

Nowadays, the computer and projection and sound system can provide PowerPoint presentations or showing video clips. Occasionally, I have visited a rural congregation and been amazed to witness the local preacher using PowerPoint and the hymn lyrics have also projected to the screen. The contemporary preacher may be less likely to stand behind a large podium; instead he may walk around in the pulpit while speaking and the Scriptural text and main points get projected to the screen.

One of the biggest changes has been the casual attire of preachers, which, of course, simply mirrors the casual nature of dress and grooming by those in the pew. In past generations a preacher would not mount the pulpit with any less attire than a business suit, dress shirt, tie, and dress shoes. I take minor umbrage when I see a preaching minister walk onto the pulpit wearing running shoes, a pair of low-waisted and faded blue jeans, a pullover short-sleeved sport shirt that barely covers an expanded waist line. Let us comfort one another's wardrobe concerns by the Old Testament Scripture that "the Lord looketh not on man's appearances but upon the heart."

THE PREACHER AS STORY-TELLER

In listing above the ten strategies for being impressive in religious speaking, some facetiously presented, an important one is yet to be seriously cited—the accomplished preacher and teacher must be an accomplished story-teller.

A post-modern approach to Holy Scripture will view the Bible as one long narrative developing the theme of God's love and grace for all his created humankind and his ultimate plan for redeeming, or drawing back to himself, this sinful humanity. The story begins, of course, with Creation and the Garden of Eden and ends in Revelation and the new Zion or heavenly city. The approach is valid, in my opinion, even if I harbor reservations finding an integral role for some Old Testament "components" or details for the grand story. For example, I'm not sure how Proverbs or Song of Solomon or some of the stories of rampage and genocide in the conquest of Canaan fit the over-arching grand biblical theme. Nonetheless, amazing power resides in narrative. A story can fascinate, thrill, and inspire because we as humans can relate to a powerful story that seems to be our own story.

Jesus was constantly telling stories. Some of his stories are embedded not only in our hearts and minds, but in western culture generally. The impressive pulpit speaker is a story-teller. Whether the story is his or someone else's, it may not matter; in case of the latter, then it should be identified as another's story. The entire Bible is filled with briefer stories, briefer in contrast to the metanarrative or grand story. The best stories point listeners in the direction of "the greatest story ever told."

Effective story-telling can hold attention far longer than expert exegesis and can open a window to the soul. Indeed, story-telling can be elevated to an art form. I would not claim to be powerful preacher, but the sermons in which I have elicited the most emotional impact from church audiences have occurred when I told personal stories of my own experiences, especially my own failures, and the lessons learned from them. I'll cite two story-tellers here:

John W. Smith has been a powerful story-teller, spinning stories about his family and life experiences. His first book of stories, *My Mother Played the Piano*, gained numerous positive reviews and steady sales. His second book of stories, *My Mother's Favorite Song*, also, like the first book, placed in print the stories he told orally in churches and lecture programs. John has narrated some of the funniest stories one could ever imagine at Pepperdine Bible Lectures and Nashville's Jubilee. His sessions drew large, joyful audiences. There were moments we listeners could hardly contain our laughter.

Spending some time visiting John and his wife, Judi, and discovering how many interests we shared was indeed grand privilege. (As an aside, when John left San Diego's Canyon View congregation, I auditioned and interviewed for the pulpit position and was impressed by the leadership and ministry outreach in that church.) John has a sense of humor as well as dedication and persistence almost unmatched. I recall a personal notice John wrote for the *Christian Chronicle* seeking a new pulpit position within the fellowship. This septuagenarian was secure enough to be honest in making his case: "Some may consider me, in my upper seventies, to be old, but I am still active and capable as ever and do not want to retire. If you think I am too old for the position, don't blame me—blame my parents. They are responsible for when I came into the world."

How would one describe the best storyteller in our fellowship? That would need to be a speaker who has enjoyed a wide range of experiences; someone highly intelligent and well-trained; someone with positive energy when speaking and able to connect with all kinds of audiences; someone who can make the stories of the past connect with issues and concerns of the current time; someone with knowledge in different fields; and someone with a confident and lively sense of communication while he or she is telling the story.

This could describe several speakers, but I am describing here a Christian educator and gospel preacher: Jerry Rushford. Jerry's range of academic interests is wide indeed! I first heard him telling stories about the composers of the great British hymns, and he naturally and easily expanded his interests to composers and lyricists for great hymns emerging after the Reformation from the entire United Kingdom. Some of his stories required much research and perseverance. Naturally, he establishes criteria for a great hymn and perhaps his favorite lecture—delivered at many churches, lecture programs, and adult retreats—is a discussion of what he considers to be the "greatest hymn" ever composed: "When I Survey the Wondrous Cross."

Originally from Detroit, Michigan, Jerry has long been associated with Pepperdine University and for years served as director for the highly successful annual Pepperdine Bible Lectures, drawing several thousand to the Malibu campus at the end of the spring trimester. Along with other venues, he tells stories each year at the Lipscomb lecture series billed as Summer Celebration. Topics are so diverse. Jerry has told stories about the great hymnists and their classic compositions, of course, but also stories about congregations and Christian colleges established along the Oregon Trail in the nineteenth and early twentieth centuries, William Shakespeare, Abraham Lincoln, James A. Garfield (an effective Disciples lay minister who was elected U. S. president), and numerous others. No one leaves his sessions bored. And we all learn a lot of facts we had never imagined.

A POSITIVE WORD ABOUT OUR CURRENT GENERATION

I have been blessed to hear a number of preachers in my life-time that met a standard of excellence, and, consequently, were a blessing to me and surely to many other worshipers and listeners. There's no way I could name all those preachers, whether they were primarily expounders or evangelists, which have impacted my life.

I would first cite the Bible teachers and preachers who influenced me on the Lipscomb campus, men such as Batsell Baxter and Willard Collins, discussed previously in chapter two. Tony Ash was relevant and inspiring as preacher and long-time ACU Bible professor. I have been challenged as well and, at times, comforted and reassured when listening to lessons presented by Karl Ketcherside and Leroy Garrett. Of course, they used print journalism to reach thousands who might not have heard them behind a podium. I would also place my wonderfully kind and gracious friend, Edward Fudge, in the same category of highly intellectual, provocative, and courageous preachers and teachers. Edward, like Karl and Leroy, used the written medium to reach thousands and his brief GracEmail articles demonstrated openness to technology as well as keen insight on any subject or issue he addressed. The legacy of these three courageous and independent thinkers will live for generations.

Pulpit speakers with a "cerebral" dimension are atypical, in my humble opinion. Those with this "cerebral" dimension displayed depth and profundity of thought. From my younger years, I felt blessed every time I listened to Alonzo Welch deliver a sermon. Ed Neeley Cullum was a profound thinker and conversational speaker; on one Sunday, as he substituted for me at Otter Creek with my series on the Decalogue, he was assigned "Thou Shalt Not Bear False Witness" and I felt it to be one of the best sermons I had ever heard. Every time I have heard a lesson from Leonard Allen, or read one of his books, I have found my mind expanded with new insights. That was also true with Jack Lewis. And my friend Randy Harris always challenges and, at times, entertains, even if I have heard most of his jokes previously, and John Mark Hicks can preach or teach with terrific skills and insights.

Other preachers and teachers come to mind. Lynn Anderson has been one of the most skilled at producing quality messages, but there are times in which he has truly touched the hearts of listeners. After a long ministry career Lynn has devoted his gifts and energies to training and equipping younger ministers. Harold Hazelip has brought such a scholarly approach to biblical exegesis and application and his delivery skills, either in the pulpit or in electronic media, display a direct and near flawless communication style that conveys sincerity and earnestness. My privilege to attend Nashville's Woodmont Hills congregation for more than three years resulted, on most Sundays, being challenged by sermons from Rubel Shelly. Rubel is always prepared, always thoughtful, and apparently an indefatigable professional having written twenty-five to thirty books. While he has reached retirement age, he still preaches almost every Sunday. I once heard him say that he would much rather end his life by wearing out than by rusting out. John York, who later shared pulpit responsibilities at Woodmont with Rubel, also stirs and challenges.

Have you ever stopped to ask yourself, "What is the best sermon I have ever heard in my life?" That "best sermon" is likely one that touched your heart as well as challenged your mind. While I don't think I could name just one, several come to mind. All sermons and lessons I have heard from Mike Cope have combined intellectual and emotional appeals in a highly effective way, usually with a touch of humor.

On one Sunday at Otter Creek, my friend David Fleer was substituting that day for Josh Graves, but David was expected to take the next topic in Josh's current series on the Beatitudes. Now, as an aside, I never relished being assigned a topic in some other speaker's series, and David was assigned "Blessed are the meek. For they shall inherit the earth." As I listened to the sermon, I felt David was a master at displaying all the delivery and rhetorical skills a speaker should possess. He began with a story that left us hanging in suspension; he went next to his brief text and expounded on it using other Scripture and narratives in the life of Jesus; he drew from life experiences and real world events; then at the conclusion he returned to the story with which he had begun and provided enlightening details that rounded out the story and made his application. David's expositional and rhetorical strategy was flawless and impactful. I shall never forget that lesson!

One sermon I might nominate as best I have ever heard came from Jeff Walling and was delivered on a Saturday session of Nashville's Jubilee in the mid-90s. Jeff is truly one of the most gifted and confident public speakers in the nation's entire religious community, at least in my opinion. He is blessed with the ideal speaker's voice that one is only born with. His training and experience in drama and stage performance carry over to his public speaking. (As an aside, I have often told my speech students that training in drama and acting can help them become better public speakers; a great actor can become a great speaker but not all good speakers can become great actors.)

On this occasion, Jeff was discussing the story of Jesus at the Last Supper and the Lord's desire to wash his disciples' feet (John 13). As his lesson neared conclusion Jeff spoke so warmly and affectionately about the gentleman who became a father figure to him after his own dad died at an early age. He spoke of how much this father figure had made a difference for good and how indebted he was to him. Then, as we thought the lesson was concluding, he asked this saintly senior Christian gentleman, Emmett McCreary, to come out of the audience and onto the stage, to sit in a chair. Then Jeff kneeled down and took off Emmett's shoes, rolled up his pant legs, took a basin and a towel, and washed his feet.

Had I known prior to the presentation the way this lesson would climax, I might have dismissed the rhetorical strategy as melodramatic theater. Instead, the event-message, this re-enactment, of what Jesus commanded disciples to do, was incredibly powerful and moving. We all sat in hushed silence. Many of us dabbed away the tears welling up in our eyes.

The principle that preachers, teachers, evangelists, revivalists, and all other church leaders should first and foremost serve others humbly remains a lesson that always applies. In their own ways and styles the preachers and revivalists satirized in the early part of this chapter were surely honest and sincere servants who were being effective within their own culture. And with the change in generations we may appreciate those younger speakers who have walked in their shadows and who now deploy their own giftedness, strategies, and eloquence to be blessing and joy.

6

Priorities, Originality, and Creativity— Pointing the Preacher in the Right Direction on Major Concerns

When being raised in the True Church, what becomes the most important verse of Scripture in the entire Bible?

No quantitative research has been conducted on this issue. Several possibilities emerge: Mark 16: 16 could be nominated for that honor, commanding disciples to go into all the world and preach the gospel to every creature and "he that believeth and is baptized shall be saved." That scripture is likely eclipsed in importance by Acts 2:38 where the apostle Peter on Pentecost instructed the guilt-stricken listeners to "repent and be baptized, every one of you, in the name of Jesus Christ, for the remission of sins, and ye shall receive the gift of the Holy Ghost."

What about those who have already been baptized? Clearly the most important verse of scripture, one that is quoted so easily in sermons and printed in church bulletins, is Hebrews 10: 25 (and always quoted in the KJV)—"not forsaking the assembling of ourselves together, as the manner of some is, but exhorting one another and so much the more as ye see the day approaching." And what is the day that is approaching? Two interpretations have been offered: Sunday, "the first day of the week," or the grand Judgment Day at the end of time.

Suppose "the day" referenced in Hebrews 10:25 is actually Sunday. Can you just see and hear the early disciples talking to each other in the market place: "Hey, Thaddeus, I know it's Thursday now, but in three more days it's going to be Sunday, so be sure to be on time at church and I'll be reminding you again more forcefully on Friday and Saturday."

This command in Hebrew 10:25 clearly means that church services constitute the highest priority and "skipping church" is committing a sin. The next verse instructs us that "if we sin willfully … there remaineth no more sacrifice for sins." Most congregations have been conformist in setting up three times to assemble: Sunday morning, Sunday evening, then a Wednesday evening service that is typically called either "prayer meeting" or "mid-week Bible study." The Sunday evening service is similar in format to the Sunday morning service except that "make-up communion" is served only to those who could not attend the morning service. The Wednesday evening service may have a shared devotional time before or after class study. Usually the "invitation" is offered all three occasions—one never knows when a lost soul needs to repent and/or be baptized or "restored" to the fellowship!

A SCRIPTURAL ESCAPE CLAUSE

Does one need to attend all three services each week to be a faithful Christian? Well, there is the Scriptural "escape clause" that is typically referenced as "providential hinderance" which, incidentally, is a phrase not employed in Scripture. The concept does, of course, square with common sense.

A "providential hindrance," like certain clauses in the U. S. Constitution, could be given a conservative or a liberal interpretation. A conservative interpretation could mean a very serious personal illness or unavoidable Sunday work schedule could justifiably preclude a faithful member from attending a service. A liberal interpretation: Your son plays on a baseball team that has a game on Wednesday night and you go to the game instead of the prayer meeting. Another example: There is a little ice and snow on the road and, even though you traveled on the same icy roads on Saturday to go shopping or attend a movie, you feel best not to risk travel on the same roads on Sunday morning. Or maybe you have a work conflict, but you passively allowed your boss to schedule your work during a service time when you could have emphatically and respectfully informed your boss you were not available during worship service time.

Must one attend on Wednesday nights? The jury might be out on that question. Many preachers and elders insist that "faithful members" will attend "every time the doors are open." An oft-told Church of Christ joke pictures the Judgment Day and a long line of panicking people stretching miles waiting to be judged as saved or lost eternally. Around the "judgment bar" there is a huge cheer and people jump up and down with delirious excitement after Saint Peter makes an announcement. One person runs back from the judgment bar to share the good news with all the other anxious souls waiting in line: "Hey, we just got the ruling—Wednesday nights don't count! Wednesday nights don't count!" Everyone who hears the ruling leaps and shouts for joy.

Preachers and elders use Hebrews 10:25 as a true heavy-duty, workload scripture because no other verse in the Bible can be adduced to lay guilt on those who "forsake the assembly." Those of us who were "PKs"—preacher kids—especially would bear the burden of attending every "regular service," including services of a gospel meeting. After all, we were setting the proper example for the other church families. If any in my family were traveling on the highway on a long trip and "the first day of the week" was the only possible travel date, we had to locate a congregation of the True Church to drop in for the morning worship service.

As a college student and as a young man when I could only best travel on Sunday from Nashville to Dallas, I would typically attend a service in Memphis or in a northeast Arkansas town, then pick up a church bulletin or program to give my dad as evidence of church service faithfulness. If making the long drive between Nashville and Dallas on a Wednesday, typically I would delay travel time, perhaps by stopping to get a hamburger, in order to waive the evening prayer meeting experience.

One summer as a high school sophomore in the Dallas area, I played in a city summer baseball league and some games were scheduled for Wednesday night. Before I could go to the ballpark I was expected to attend my Wednesday night Bible study class, then rush to the family Oldsmobile 88 and change school clothes into my baseball uniform and cleats while being driven to the ballpark. I recall blushing with embarrassment when arriving in the fourth or fifth inning, putting on my ball cap and demurely slipping to the dugout bench. The coach seemed understanding and usually put me into the game at some point before the final inning.

A number of my friends have shared stories of guilt-avoidance on this "forsake not …" command. One way is just take early, pre-sermon communion and get up and walk out of the church house. However, you must not cause others to stumble. Dave and Seanne Brazelton, both raised in the True Church, were married on an April Saturday in 1981. After the first night of their honeymoon spent in a Chattanooga hotel and "sleeping in," they dressed in their Sunday-best clothes in going to a Sunday dinner at a nice restaurant lest, in dressing casually, other diners might realize they had skipped church assembly.

Even as a teenager a lot of critical thinking was not required to know the true meaning of assertions such as "Brother Jones is not a faithful member" or "Sister Smith is out of duty." These sad statements simply meant that Brother Jones or Sister Smith was no longer regularly attending the church services, thus willfully and inexcusably snubbing the clear command to "Forsake not the assembling of yourselves together."

"LORD WILLING AND THE CREEK DON'T RISE"

Our little discussion of Hebrews 10:25 is the backdrop for discussing (in this and the following chapter) "acceptable worship" in the True Church. Adverse circumstances do not alter one iota the need to follow the proper form of public worship at all times. The experience of a young Herman Taylor in the late 1930s, as recalled by daughter Carolyn Wilson, demonstrates the summons to continue steadfastly in "forsaking not the assembly, Lord willing and the creek don't rise."

Taylor, an educator, preacher, and former superintendent at Potter Home in Bowling Green, Kentucky, learned that even during a "providential hindrance" services must be conducted as scheduled. His responsibility to visit the church building at Hermitage Springs, Tennessee, early each Sunday to start the fire which would provide heat for all was discharged amidst a driving rainstorm on this particular Sunday. A creek divided the small community, with residences on one side and the Church of Christ meeting house and a school building on the other. The preacher, an "old Brother Knight," then an octogenarian, arrived early. The creek rose rapidly and no one else was able to cross it.

Taylor expected Brother Knight to say something to the effect, "There's no one but us two here. Let's get home the best way that we can and trust for better weather conditions next Sunday." Instead, the veteran preacher ventured to do more than preach. "I'll lead the singing, lead the prayer, preach the sermon, and you, Herman, can handle the rest." The service began and continued for an hour and a half with only one person in the audience. When the sermon was over, Brother Knight offered the invitation.

PREACHING THE WORD

No one knows what it's like to preach sermons except for the poor souls who have attempted this art. With some "wannabe" speakers in front of large church audiences, drinking battery acid or wearing a garden snake around one's neck would be an easier feat than delivering an effective, challenging sermonic discourse in front of a live audience.

The unalloyed truth: In the Church of Christ, some of the best educated, best qualified, most gifted, and most sensitive men have either voluntarily or involuntarily abandoned a full-time preaching career. The reasons for their leaving are all personal and varied just as were their reasons for entering the preaching ministry. Running through many of those personal dramas, however, are the themes of hurtful church politics, personal theological beliefs changing, feelings of personal inadequacy or unworthiness, pressure, anxiety, alienation, hurt, and even betrayal. Bottom line: The loss of desire to preach.

In other chapters we have discussed some of the special roles and challenges faced by the preacher and the evangelist. At this point we acknowledge additional issues and concerns and offer some practical advice to current or aspiring preachers.

"PULPIT FRIGHT"

Is there a preacher who has never faced his own stage fright? Perhaps there are a few, but one must wonder about their personality and ego if they claim never to have felt speaking anxiety. Often the apostle Paul is depicted as a preacher with confident eloquence, and yet this best-known disciple told the Corinthians he had stood before them with "fear and trembling."

I am hereby coining the term "pulpit fright" and stating that I am an expert in stage fright—mainly through experiencing an abnormal amount of such feelings of apprehension throughout my adult life and through my own study and self-therapy in coping. There have been times I have been besieged so dramatically with stage fright (sometimes called speech apprehension or speech anxiety) that I felt I could not lead a Bible class in a silent prayer.

Some comfort is provided upon hearing that gifted preachers who face big audiences admit to pulpit fright. One Sunday at Woodmont Hills (and remember that many Nashville area congregations have "Hills" in their name), my friend Rubel Shelly was confessing that he struggled with stress and anxiety prior to, and then delivering, a sermon. Of course, I did not believe him at that moment. Then he surprised us when, in the middle of his sermon, Rubel asked any doubters to walk forward and hold his hand for a few seconds and then verify that his hands did not have a normal body temperature. The "doubting Thomas" in me led me to walk forward, take his hand, and, sure enough, I recall his hand felt either very cold or quite hot and sweaty. Immediately, I felt sympathy for him and a measure of reassuring comfort for myself.

Once feeling comfortable in front of the same audience of worshipers, then pulpit fright should not be a problem. But it can rear its ugly head at unexpected times. Maybe the preacher reads strong negative feedback on the face of some important member when he says something controversial and he begins "stressing" over it while still speaking. I have experienced sermon delivery anxiety when, in the middle of my presentation, someone or some group arrives late who months earlier had declared they wanted to hear me preach and would surprise me some Sunday. While the guest(s) are quietly ushered to a vacant seat on the pew and many in the audience turn to see who is arriving late, my heart would start beating, my sweat glands would activate, my pulse and breathing rate would accelerate, and my thinking on sermon points would hit the pause button while new, unspeakable thoughts would emerge.

AUDITION SUNDAY (OR "TRYING OUT")

The audition Sunday is a special concern. Oh how stressful it can be to impress a visiting pulpit committee from a congregation you hope might offer you a new position! You might anticipate the new position will bring a substantial salary increase, yet you can always inform your current congregation that "the Lord has called me to another pulpit position." Apparently, the Lord's callings coincidentally happen to be the positions with the higher salaries and/or better benefits.

Then often the preacher under consideration is invited to visit the church with the pulpit opening. That is equally stressful. Most pulpit ministers have experienced that "try out," as it is called, several times.

My most memorable audition experience came in 2002 when my wife and I flew out to San Diego to visit the Canyon View Church of Christ. Upon landing and picking up luggage, we were greeted by an elder, Mike Osborn, who was gracious, hospitable, and helpful in providing practical information (including how to dress for the Southern California pulpit and to my surprise learning that a Hawaiian shirt was considered quite appropriate preaching attire). Mike delivered me to my first meeting with the church staff. On Saturday there was an all-morning interview with the elders. Later a meeting with the pulpit committee. The next day, Sunday, I preached at an early service, after a brief break then taught the auditorium adult class, then preached at a second morning service, then returned for a different sermon in the evening service, then an informal supper meeting with some elders. Preparation for this weekend involved many hours of planning and consideration, everything from sermon content to selection of Bible versions and apparel choices, and mainly deciding how many of my personal values, theological perspectives, and spiritual insights to share.

Nothing disastrous or embarrassing happened that weekend, at least not like the experience of a new preaching acquaintance I made at a ministers' retreat hosted by L. H. Hardwick, long-time Nashville's Christ Church (Pentecostal) pastor. Incidentally, my getting to know Brother Hardwick and participating/speaking in a service one Sunday morning at Nashville's Christ Church were true blessings in my life.

This new preaching friend, whom I will call Brother Baird, was auditioning for a new pulpit position that would represent quite an advancement up the career ladder. The congregation was considerable distance from his current home, thus he and his lovely wife were offered hotel accommodations for the weekend.

Brother Baird informed his wife they might as well check out on Sunday morning because the Sunday service and a Sunday dinner might put them away from the hotel past checkout time. In the lobby while checking out his wife exclaimed, "Oh, honey, I washed out some lingerie last night and I just know I left it on the curtain rod above the bath. Can you run back to the room and get those panties?" Brother Baird asked the clerk to hand back the room card or key and made a quick run to the room, opened the bathroom door, found the panties, stuffed them in his suit coat pocket, rushed back down to load the rental car and head to the HOW.

Brother Baird was feeling a little more anxiety than he had anticipated while a third of the way into delivering his audition sermon. And it surprised him that his forehead and upper lip broke out into some beads of perspiration while speaking in front of three or four hundred people he was hoping to impress. So he reached into his pocket for his handkerchief and took two or three seconds to wipe his brow and upper cheek. "That handkerchief did not feel like cotton fabric, it felt 'silky,'" he reported, and then there was a sudden panic. "I realized I had just wiped my forehead and my face with my wife's pink, laced panties. Immediately, more sweat popped out. I dug deeper in the coat pocket or went to the other pocket and found the handkerchief. There were some smiles and a few snickers, then much hearty laughter during Sunday dinner when discussing the incident with the church board."

STRATEGIES FOR COPING WITH PULPIT FRIGHT

From a life-time of public speaking in a variety of speech occasions as well as teaching fundamentals of communication at several universities, I offer my own list of a "biblical seven" coping strategies for aspiring preachers:

1. Be honest and admit your stress and nervousness. You are then less likely to attempt repressing your symptoms. The more you try to hide nervousness the worst your symptoms appear. Do not fight the symptoms. Just remind yourself that you are in good company—the Apostle Paul seemed to have speaker fright as did many of the most admired historical characters you might know, including Abraham Lincoln and Mark Twain.

2. Develop proper attitudes toward your assignment. If you are auditioning for a new position, then tell yourself you don't really want that job anyway—that you are just practicing for the next opportunity. That just might relieve the self-imposed pressure and enable you to turn loose and preach your heart out.

3. There is no substitute for full and diligent preparation of your message content. I heard Jimmy Allen once advise young preachers that "you're in trouble if you go hunting with a gun loaded for a squirrel or rabbit and you encounter a big bear; therefore, come loaded for bear and you'll be ready for any animal that appears."

4. Positive visualization means to imagine and even dream of yourself "wowing" an audience with your knowledge, wisdom, and skills—all in front of an audience composed of the people you respect most and would like most to impress.

5. Positive nervousness means transforming that surplus adrenaline into an exciting and dynamic delivery by moving around the pulpit and putting more energy into voice and body which, in turn, burns off some of excess adrenaline.

6. Adding a little humor that goes over well can loosen and relax both you and the audience. *Caveat*: a prepared joke that "bombs" will accelerate your stress and distract you from your main message content.

7. In case the above strategies fail to be totally effective, keep essential supplies needed for controlling symptoms. If your mouth tends to get too dry, keep a bottle of cool water inside the podium or nearby. You can reach for it and take a swig after you say, "Right now I'd like for all of you to turn in your Bibles to our main passage for today." If you break out in sweat then be sure to have one or two handkerchiefs. You might ask the audience to glance at a verse or to look at a screen while you take a quick swipe of your face. Now if you are truly a profuse perspirer in which body moisture can penetrate all layers of fabric, I recommend not lifting your arms high in praise or performing a high sweeping gesture to make a powerful point.

Only a couple of years or so ago during a church service, my mouth became a little dry. I typically have one or two mini-Altoid mints in my shirt pocket, so I reached for one and inconspicuously slipped it in my mouth. After four or five minutes I realized the Altoid did not taste much like a mint and it did not seem to dissolve. Then I nonchalantly took it out of my mouth, held it for a moment between my thumb and a finger, slowly looked down and discovered it was not an Altoid mint all along—it was a very small, circular metal battery for a hearing aid! Alas, my mouth became even drier at that point!

If none of the above recommended strategies is helpful in conquering the bugaboo of pulpit fright, consider the Lord has not actually called you to preach. Seek other employment.

BEING ETHICAL REQUIRES ORIGINALITY AND ATTRIBUTION

The practical matter of finding original material for sermon content is another challenge. Undoubtedly, there is as much hard-core plagiarism in the True Church as in any other institution. Perhaps more. Have you ever considered how many preachers have taken another preacher's sermon verbatim and delivered it as their own without one moment spent attributing the original source? Sad to say, but over the course of a lifetime some preachers have stretched the truth in the pulpit more than they've stretched their waistline at fellowship dinners outside the pulpit.

At Fourth Avenue in the 90s, we invited a young minister as guest speaker for the morning assembly. He possessed a great reputation as an "up and coming" speaker. He was so self-confident, dynamic in a sense, as he walked all around the pulpit without using notes. He delivered a powerful sermon based on Romans 6, used an analogy of slaves being freed after the Civil War yet many of whom preferred to remain with their masters, and how that was akin to Christians being forgiven by God's grace but preferring to remain in bondage to sin. The speaker was well received. Everyone seemed to think he was a dynamic young preacher with a great career ahead of him.

A few days later, one of our church secretaries, Denise Ellis, a spiritual person and well-read in Christian literature, asked me to sit down and listen to a cassette tape of a sermon by Charles Swindoll. We listened to the entire sermon, and honestly, both sermons (Swindoll's and the one from the young minister) were word-for-word identical. A slightly edited version of that sermon is also a chapter in Swindoll's book, *Grace Awakening*.

In the previous generation the preacher's sources might have been Harry Emerson Fosdick, Billy Graham, Gerald Kennedy, Clarence Edward MaCartney, Clovis Chappell, Charles Allen, and Wilbur Smith. The irony: These "denominational" preachers would never have been invited to deliver a newspaper or a pizza, much less an entire sermon, in any pulpit of the True Church any more than today a Charles Stanley, James Dobson, Joel Osteen, Charles Swindoll, Scott McKnight, Brian McLaren, Philip Yancey, or Leonard Sweet would be invited to speak. Truth is, however, those "sectarians" or "denominationalists" have had their messages delivered verbatim and unedited in True Church pulpits throughout the height and breadth of the land through the voices of our own preachers.

All of which reminds me of the old line made by one preacher in his own defense at an elders' meeting. The elders were criticizing the preacher's sermonic content as becoming woefully anemic and inadequate. The preacher defensively replied, "When better sermons are written, I will preach them!"

Plagiarism of sermonic and other religious and spiritual content might be considered linguistic promiscuity. Manifestly, not everyone takes theft of sermon content so seriously. When at Otter Creek, a young Christian sister made an appointment to see me and offer her constructive criticism. One of her complaints was that my sermons seemed too scholarly and overly academic in tone. She pointed me to her model preacher whom I knew to take sermon series on cassette from Lynn Anderson and present them verbatim, even using Lynn's sermon titles. "For me, there's an ethical issue here in terms of this other preacher's pilfering content," I explained to her. "I just don't see this other preaching brother as the proper pulpit model."

"That's doesn't matter at all, even if you preach someone else's sermon word for word as long as it's a good sermon," she countered. "After all, all truth comes from the Holy Spirit anyway." This gave me pause and I offered no follow-up comment.

At McMinnville's Westwood, I spent one year preaching through Acts and in each sermon I would quote William Barclay, Stuart Briscoe, and F. F. Bruce as my major sources, citing each by name in every sermon. Some of my closer friends began teasing me about my constant use of the three B's—Barclay, Briscoe, and Bruce.

How many times have we heard the same clever joke or personal illustration told as actually true by more than one preacher? Let's admit it: It is not very funny or clever to say, "Let me tell you of a funny thing that happened to another preacher when he went to Paris, France, and I read about this story in his sermon book." Sure, it might be a little humorous, but not as humorous as when you tell the story as though it actually happened to you. On the other hand, are you not selling your soul for a few more laughs or other positive responses by claiming the experience is your own?

A pulpit minister walks a fine line here. You don't want your sermons to sound like esoteric academic presentations at a scholarly conference. There's no faster way to put worshipers to sleep even on unpadded pews. On the other hand, global plagiarism is deemed unethical if not criminal. A gifted, popular young minister, who was a personal friend, lost his position with a growing, progressive congregation in the Nashville area because he adduced another preacher's words, even personal illustrations and personal experiences, as his very own—the sermon series, sermon topics, sermon content, and even all sermon PowerPoint visuals! In this case, the elders did their research, engaged dialogue over accountability issues with the young minister, and could not resolve the issue satisfactorily. His tenure in that pulpit terminated immediately even without a farewell sermon. The whole congregation was shocked and spent months in recovery.

One complicating reality: There are several web-based sermon-producing services that provide, for a substantial annual fee, subscribing preachers all the resources they need for a complete sermon series. The consultant-preacher(s) that produce this material must surely be aware that subscribing pulpit ministers will most likely download the entire sermon text, the PowerPoint slides which contain Scriptures, illustrations, clip art (along with template that has decorative art design), the video clips, and other material and present all of this content verbatim without attribution.

My advice: Be original. Make attribution of sources, at least on the screen or the worship guide. Imagine that six hundred people sit in your audience and 598 of them believe all your content is yours alone, but two very bright, well-read, and spiritual-minded listeners know the content is solely the composition of another Christian speaker or writer. Are you willing to kiss your personal reputation and influence with those two people good-bye simply to save preparation time and/or make yourself appear more knowledgeable and eloquent?

All preachers may feel hours of despondency about their occasional or even frequent lack of pulpit effectiveness. Yes, there are quick fixes (although not all "quick fixes" are prudent choices). George Bailey told me about a preaching brother who anticipated an opportunity to boost his morale by accepting an invitation to address an African-American congregation. He visualized an admiring audience of happy faces shouting "amens" and "right on, brother" to even his most shallow exegesis. Several minutes into his address, however, there had not been a single audible validation. A perplexing audience silence greeted his deepest profundities. "I had the sinking feeling that I was in trouble with this audience," he explained, "and my anxiety brought one long pause—a pause in which some woman shouted, 'Oh, Lord Jesus, please help him!' Then I knew I was in trouble."

"NO BEERS IN HEAVEN"

One practical reality that well-educated novice preachers soon learn is that much of their scholarly learning from a graduate department of religion, divinity school, or seminary availeth little in the pulpit. The majority of people who come to church assemblies are less interested in learning some challenging truth or new insight for their personal faith as they are in being confirmed and reassured with their current doctrinal understandings and lifestyle.

Too many of the True Church members seem to long for the dotting of all the doctrinal "i's" and crossing all the doctrinal "t's," for neatly tying up the entire package, for answering every tough question with a simple answer, and having all those with whom they fellowship to read the fine print on the "sound Christian doctrine list" and then sign the bottom line. A list of key doctrines is fine, but I always felt that too much was placed on the list and that the list was handled like a pre-flight procedure list that a jet pilot checks off before confirming the aircraft is ready for take-off.

That church members are not interested in hearing both sides of a controversial issue—instead, only the doctrinally "correct" side—is a lesson I often learned the hard way. A personal example: While serving as minister at Westwood in the 70s, the elders requested that I present a sermon pertaining to an upcoming county liquor referendum.

Warren County was one of Tennessee's few "dry" counties, although it was likely that as much or more liquor was consumed per capita in that county than in any other county in the state. Bootlegging was largely winked at and greatly joked about in a county that boasted fifty to sixty percent of its population as members of the Church of Christ. Several elders were members of a private country club which maintained a bar and one of the deacons, later appointed an elder, made an annual trek to impoverished Grundy County to buy bootleg wine from an old bachelor mountaineer named John Henry.

The issue was an ethically and politically ambiguous one, or so it seemed, but I attempted to throw myself wholeheartedly into my assignment. Not only did I write a sermon which I titled "Is the Steeple Staggering?" but I wrote a special hymn for CALL, the official name of the prohibition camp (Citizens Against Legalized Liquor). The first stanza lyrics (to be sung to the melody of "No Tears in Heaven"):

No beers in heaven

No set-ups given

All will be dairy products there

There'll be no six-pack

There'll be no "on-tap"

When all is prohibition there.

I shared my little song with several church friends who seemed to enjoy it but wisely counseled that it not be incorporated into our regular song service.

My sermon on Warren County prohibition developed two basic parts. Part one was a standard case for legalizing liquor sale. My argument was based on political realities, mainly that citizens who wanted liquor could easily purchase it in adjoining counties. Part two was an argument for voting "no" to county liquor sales and for embracing a lifestyle of abstinence from alcoholic beverages. "You've heard a review of both sides of the issue," I concluded the sermon. "Now, if you choose to vote, please vote your conscience."

Such an approach might have worked in a public forum. But no, not even my jeremiad on the evils of alcohol abuse and the plague of alcoholism could rescue me from the grievous error of encouraging this audience to think and decide for itself. When I observed the redness of face and throbbing of temple of one of the elders sitting in one of the front pews during my presentation, I realized my approach had been all wrong. This elder never forgot; apparently, he never forgave.

Dramatic declarations from the pulpit are usually remembered when everything else about a lesson is forgotten. Harold "Buster" Duncan recalls: "I was attending the East Brainerd church in Chattanooga on Easter Sunday, 1981. The speaker was Danny Cline. He walks to the podium and lifts his arms and shouts 'I need a raise, O Lord, I need a raise.'" Then he paused a while. A few chuckled." Buster continued: "Then Danny said it again, 'O Lord, please, I need a raise. I need a raise.' Then he went on to read the passage about being raised in the likeness of his resurrection. I'll never forget it."

Two generations ago, an influential Methodist preacher named Gerald Kennedy prepared an advice book for ministers entitled *For Preachers and Other Sinners*. We will say more about the practical aspects of a preacher's calling in the next chapter, but conclude here with a most serious point: All preachers, regardless of church or religious affiliation, must realize that we, too, are sinners in need of God's grace. And our own sins may be as grievous, hurtful, and inexcusable—or even more so—as the sins of any people sitting in pews listening to our messages!

7

The Fine Arts of Preaching, Praying, Passing Plates, and Other Public Assembly Skills

Despite the crucial importance of worship services and mandatory attendance, innumerable unplanned and unexpected occurrences have invaded the decorum of sacred assemblies. Because Churches of Christ place much emphasis on the participation of typically untrained men in the implementation of the "order of worship," then any immersed, literate male who is willing to make announcements, usher, orally read the Scriptures, serve communion, collect the offering, and/or make devotional talks can usually be summoned for service when his name turns up on the listing.

PUBLIC PRAYER LEADING AND KNEELING

Effective prayer leading requires only that the person praying is able to express the collective thoughts, emotions, and petitions of the entire church assembled. Many prayer leaders lapse into a verbatim recital of such expressions of gratitude and petitions of request that they seem to come straight from a prayer book.

Actually, a formal prayer book might not be such a bad idea. While it would stifle individual creativity it might prevent some of our more popular redundancies such as "guide, guard, and direct us," "Father, forgive us of our sins, blot them out of thy book of remembrance, and hold them against us no more," and

"If we have been found faithful give us a home with thee in heaven." (See more phrases in the proposed prayer-leading contest at the end of chapter 10.)

The Stone-Campbell Restoration Movement tradition regarding public prayer has changed. In the nineteenth through the early twentieth centuries, many preachers and elders insisted that the men of the congregation kneel during a congregational prayer. The kneeling tradition is a biblical one and reminds the Christian of who is in charge in a dialogue with God. Much of the strength of that tradition in the South can be traced to John T. Lewis of Birmingham. Carroll Ellis knew and remembered Lewis fondly:

> Brother Lewis was a kindly gentleman, loved and respected by all. I knew him as an older man. He was a graduate of the Nashville Bible School in 1889. He was highly influential.
>
> It was Brother Lewis' strong conviction that at the occasion of public prayer every person ought to kneel and that all women should have a covering on their heads. Lewis wrote a pamphlet expounding his views on this topic. It was simply a custom in those days for preachers to set the example by kneeling during prayer.
>
> Years ago Dr. W. T. Brents came to Nashville to hold a meeting. Now Brents weighed some three hundred pounds. Someone in charge of the service said, "We'll stand for prayer" out of courtesy and convenience for Brents. James A. Harding spoke up and said, "No, we'll kneel. The fact that Brents can't kneel won't stop the rest of us from kneeling."
>
> Years ago I visited Alabama Christian College and was called on to lead the prayer. When I got through praying and opened my eyes, I observed that everyone was kneeling. I knew the influence of Brother Lewis was still being felt. Fessor Boyce's father was an elder at Granny White. He saw to it that when their new building was constructed that kneeling benches were installed in the first several rows of pews.

My father told me that one of his most embarrassing moments as a guest speaker was on the pulpit stand at the congregation in Kirksey, a small community in West Kentucky. He had knelt for prayer with the other men nearby. Someone from the audience was leading the prayer in an almost inaudible tone and my dad kept straining to hear the words. After several seconds of silence, and prostrate on his knees, my dad slowly opened his eyes and saw the entire church staring at him. The prayer had ended a few seconds earlier. He meekly rose and resumed his seat.

Most prayer leaders have, during one prayer or another, forgotten something they had planned to say. Some will write out their prayer in small lettering and slip it into a Bible or song book. A few have encountered problems reading their own prayers. In some cases, quite likely, the wife of the prayer leader had written out the prayer for her husband to read or recite.

A story passed along by Carroll Ellis tells how one brother with a failing memory handled the problem in a most unorthodox way. Seems that Howard White, professor of history at David Lipscomb College and later to become president of Pepperdine University, was the guest preacher in a meeting for the St. Elmo congregation in Chattanooga. In one of the services the local preacher called on one of the elders to lead a prayer. The prayer continued to a point where the elder said, "And God, we thank you for our meeting and for sending Brother … uh … Brother …" and then he interrupted his prayer and addressed the local preacher: "Who is this fellow that's doing our preaching this week?" After proper cueing on White's name, the elder resumed his prayer.

Styles of prayer leading vary. A few leaders will raise arms and head and project praise and petitions with a loud voice. Most leaders will bow their heads and pray in a monotone. At one church I served a new convert, also a stage actor, began his first public prayers by shouting, "Good morning, God!" or "Hello, Father!" At the same church another devout man prayed almost in the style of an obscene phone caller—clasping hands around the microphone, whispering his words slowly but dramatically in a low tone and breathing heavily into the much amplified sound system.

Prayer may seem to elicit more than immediate blessings. Years ago a man in a Nashville congregation was leading a prayer during the evening service when, according to Fletcher Srygley, there was a quiet power failure. All electrical current ceased flowing, but the man continued his prayer. When he completed his prayer and opened his eyes to total darkness and silence, the man panicked and shouted, "Please, somebody help me. God has struck me blind!"

The prayer leader certainly must not be guilty of overlooking someone who needs a prayer petition in the assembly—such oversight might be near unforgivable! Thus, the following all-purpose prayer line covers all the spiritual bases and has been frequently uttered: "And, God, we ask Thee to bless all those for whom it is our blessed duty to pray the whole world over, especially those of the household of faith." As an aside, it is best to use "Thee" and "Thou" in referencing God during a prayer, as addressing God with "You" and "Yours" is an unmistakable indicator of insidious modernism and liberalism.

Ambiguity in a prayer enables those praying along to add their own meaning. In the midst of several rounds of intense church conflict at a Grand Blanc, Michigan, congregation, as reported by Minister Hoy Ledbetter, one leader prayed: "Lord, bless those who are sick of this congregation."

Finding just the right language to describe and confess human failure in a prayer is always a challenge. "Forgive us of our sins" is simple enough, but the need for linguistic variety leads to the use of synonyms: failures, frailties, weaknesses, shortcomings, short fallings, iniquities, transgressions, mistakes, misconduct, "things left undone we should have done and things we did that we should not have done" (the last phrase should cover all the sinful bases), and so on *ad infinitum.* This could be stated more briefly by praying, "God, forgive us of all our sins, whether sins of omission or sins of commission." For sheer levity it's difficult to improve on the petition by a brother in a public prayer heard by preacher Danny Cline: "And Father, forgive us of our falling shorts."

PROPER PULPIT DEMEANOR

More advice for preachers: Proper pulpit demeanor cannot be overemphasized. Always conduct a pre-sermon zipper check. I shall always be indebted to Kyle Bills one Sunday at Fourth Avenue. Like many ministers, I find less pressure on my bodily system by quietly exiting to the men's restroom before delivering my sermon. On this particular Sunday, Kyle was sitting next to me on the first pew on the final song prior to my mounting the pulpit and standing behind a glass (acrylic) podium. He whispered, "Your fly is down."

I whispered back, "Don't distract me. I'm nervous enough."

Kyle whispered again right before time to walk to the pulpit: "You'd better believe me."

I looked downward. Wow, he was so correct! Even part of my dress shirt was showing outside the unzipped opening. My pulse rate quickened as I hid my hymnal over the front of my pants and nonchalantly performed a quick zip up. Kyle loved telling the story for months to anyone willing to listen. A mutual friend, Jimmy Gentry, long-time football coach and World War II veteran (also an excellent caricaturist), painted and framed a picture of Kyle and me on that pew that depicted me in a panicked state with my fly open and dress shirt sticking out.

If the preacher is wired for sound but has not commenced the sermon, he best exercise caution in how he sings, what he does, or in whispering to someone. A preacher friend learned the wisdom of this advice one Sunday morning when he switched on the sound for his cordless, FM microphone a few minutes prior to walking up to the pulpit. He then made a last second decision to run to the men's room before delivering the sermon, but failed to hit the "off switch" on his "mic." What several in his audience reported to him after the service was their hearing a water-trickling and then a definite urinal flushing sound just prior to the preacher returning to the assembly and mounting the pulpit.

Sneezing and nasal and sinus clearance should be projected away from the microphone. Yawn if you must, but a system I saw demonstrated by young minister James Carter of the East Detroit church years ago was impressive: During the congregational singing of the hymn prior to the sermon with James sitting in a big chair facing the assembly, he lowered his head and then spread one hand across the upper lip while holding a hymnal open with the other hand, then enjoyed his big yawn. At least at that moment, I thought to myself, he was relaxed if not totally bored with his upcoming assignment.

Avoid showing any leg between the top of the sock and hem of the dress slacks while sitting on the pulpit. Shun the Willard Collins-look of light-colored socks with a dark suit. If the preacher is "hair-disadvantaged" with major forehead recession and he is sensitive about it, then during the prayer he should keep his head at normal level and keep eyes closed intensely, even grimacingly—a posture preferred over the 90-degree head dip with eyes only half-closed and forehead recession on silent but full display.

A preacher needs to watch his moves as he negotiates the pulpit steps. A friend, Wayne Gurley, remembers an embarrassing incident involving a well-known preacher named Flavil Yeakley when he and Nan were members of a church in Irving, Texas. "Yeakley was a big man at that time. He must've weighed something like three hundred pounds," Wayne recalls. "As he was going up the pulpit steps, he lost his footing and fell, landing on his back. He was scrambling on 'all fours' trying to get up in a hurry and for a few moments he looked like a giant beetle on his back moving all limbs trying to get upright. Right away, some deacons jumped up and ran to him and helped him up. He was alright though."

MAKING CERTAIN OF PROPER WORDING

More important than proper pulpit etiquette is the principle "A little learning is a dangerous thing," but when exposed in a sermon as only a *little* learning it becomes a ludicrous thing. To cite but a few examples: A Sunday evening guest speaker at Otter Creek began "lathering up" on how easily Christians fall prey to temptations of the flesh. "Why, it's automatic how some fall into sin. Actually, it's just like Pazloz's dogs," he continued, in a likely intended reference to Pavlov's famous experiment on psychological conditioning that the speaker somehow blended with an Alpo ad—"when the bell rang, the dogs came running."

A preacher for the large McMinnville Central congregation back in the 80s, Jim Gammon, was known for the lengths he would go to avoid publicizing or validating any religious groups other than the True Church. Jim would not use the term "John the Baptist," but instead consistently used "John the Baptizer" to name Jesus' prophetic predecessor. Nor did Jim utter "saint" when the word was part of a non-biblical proper name, presumably to avoid patronizing Roman Catholics. In making announcements, this preacher would say "Sister Jones is a patient in Thomas Hospital" rather than "Sister Jones is a patient in Saint Thomas Hospital." Consequently, among those not enamored, and some being quite amused, by this linguistic strategy, this gave rise to such quips as "Brother Gammon passed through the Minneapolis-Paul area while visiting Canada's Lawrence seaway on vacation, but this year he plans to travel through Louis on his way to Mount Helens so that he can see his friend's litter of Bernard puppies."

A preacher never knows how some listeners will interpret his most innocent comments. George Spain, Christian therapist and counselor, remembers hearing Myron Keith, long-time preacher at Fourth Avenue church in Franklin, Tennessee, expound on the love that Christ has for his bride, the church.

Myron's theme was Christ and his bride, as George recalls. "This morning sermon was delivered in the late '60s, back in the old Fourth church building. Myron was developing the theme in great detail, discussing how much a groom loves his bride and how he wants to provide the very best gift for her to demonstrate his love," George explains. Myron used a fairly recent event the audience could relate to—the wedding of Aristotle Onassis and Jacquelyn Kennedy. Both were quite wealthy, Myron pointed out, and Onassis, who was a full generation older than his new bride, wanted to find something unique that he could give as a wedding gift for Jackie. "Onassis searched and searched the world over looking for the perfect wedding gift. Finally, he settled on giving her an antique organ," Myron reported in his message. "I had to phone Myron in the afternoon and inform him of what he had said and how his story was interpreted by some," George explained.

ISN'T THIS SKILLMAN PRESBYTERIAN CHURCH?

On those rare occasions when the "invitation is offered" and someone responds visibly, a special grace of propriety and empathic receptivity is essential. Never mind that people are sitting out there not wanting a long delay in getting home for a dinner or an NFL ballgame.

Warning: The preacher best not get excited over lateral movement in the pews during the invitation song. One Sunday Hoy Ledbetter was doing guest preaching at Averill Avenue in Flint, Michigan, and everyone had all stood for the invitation. A woman started forward down one of the side aisles. Hoy made a dash to greet her and extended his hand. She ignored Hoy's hand and went right on past him toward a door next to the pulpit. Later Hoy learned that passageway led to the restrooms, where she was obviously going. Others move to the front door during an invitation song to get a jump on everyone else going to the ball game, restaurant, or the lake.

One weekday while cleaning a church auditorium, a custodian found a blank card and simply laid it on the front pew, in a congregation served by George Bailey. The card was not a response card, but was an application card for membership at the local YMCA. The following Sunday a woman walked forward for baptism. George handed her the "Y" card, thinking it was a church response card, and it was routinely filled out until the woman got to the question, "Can you swim?" At that point there was a puzzled and deeply concerned look on her face.

One Sunday a woman came forward to place membership at Dallas' Skillman Avenue congregation. The veteran and respected preacher, John Bannister, began to question her. The woman, sensing she had come to the wrong church, asked: "Isn't this the Skillman Avenue Presbyterian Church?"

"No ma'am," John replied, "this is the Skillman Avenue Church of Christ."

"Oh, no," the woman cried, "I'm in the wrong church. And I just put $25 in the collection plate. Can I please get my check back?"

DEALING WITH SENSITIVE TOPICS

Kids say the craziest things in Sunday School, but then, too, adults can make some incredible statements in class. We can only provide a few samples of the zany and confused statements and misstatements of teachers and students.

One of the more unlikely visual aids for a Sunday School class was provided by Mark Ide, formerly a president of both Tennessee Children's Home and Lakeshore Home in the Nashville area. As youth director for the Central Church in St. Louis in the 70s, Mark was teaching a Sunday School class for junior high boys and girls. The assigned Scripture passage referenced circumcision. Some youngster in the class asked, "What is circumcision?" and others seemed uncertain, too.

"I told them to go home and ask their parents," Mark recalls. "The next Sunday, the class convenes and several tell me that they asked their parents about circumcision but were not given any direct answers. I then go to the board and draw a big visual aid of the procedure. Later, it seems, one girl's father was quite offended."

We might hope that Mark's visual was at least somewhat abstract. On the other hand, circumcision is such a major part of Old Testament Hebrew history, and then the apostle Paul referenced the ritual in several of his major epistles. Lipscomb's 2018 Summer Celebration Lectures provided a "first" for me—an entire lengthy lecture, as delivered by Don McLaughlin, on the topic of circumcision. Don even used PowerPoint slides throughout the lecture though wisely did not present any pictures or artistic sketches of the procedure; nor did he speculate as to whether women in Israel may have felt slighted from being excluded from some parallel, fleshly "badge of membership" in the covenant community.

As an aside, Don did reference the story of Joshua sharpening his knife and circumcising his entire army before all those warriors could be ready for battle (narrated in Joshua 5). I've always wondered about certain unreported details in this biblical story: Did some men cry out, "Hey, you're not going to do that to me!"? Did Joshua need to engage some convincing arguments for men to acquiesce to his insistence on the ritual? How did he convince them? Was there any kind of anesthesia prior to the procedure? There were certainly no bullets to bite, but there might have been super-fermented fruit of the vine to swallow prior to the procedure. Did Joshua have any medical assistants or interns or did he perform all procedures himself? Did he make any mistakes? Who volunteered to go first? Was not the first night after the procedures a night when all warriors tried to sleep on their backs and all that one might hear throughout the entire night was moaning and groaning? One can only imagine!

In the early '80s at the Westwood church, deacon James Dillon was teaching a class for men on contemporary issues. One Wednesday evening his topic was "Pornography and Censorship," and he brought to the class some materials from our church library. One of our elders in the class had a special discomfort with this topic. This elder seemed to bristle like a hedgehog in heat when James passed around a children's illustrated book entitled *Where Did I Come From?* that had been placed in our church library.

Then James started reading a few select lines from a modern translation of the "Song of Solomon" without identifying the source of the reading. This elder's posture and countenance stiffened and his face became livid and flushed with anger that such material would be read in a Bible class even though only males were in the classroom. "Where'd you get that trash?" this elder angrily interrupted.

"It's right out of the Bible, right here in the Song of Solomon," James replied. The silence could then have been sliced.

A chapel class at Franklin's Fourth Avenue was taught by Wert Sanders, a retired school teacher and gracious gentleman. One Sunday, Wert ventured where homiletic angels fear to tread—he started telling the story of King David as an old man.

"Now one of David's problems as an old man was that he got cold," Wert explained. "So his friends go out and get a young woman named Abishag the Shunamite and her assignment was to get in bed with David and keep him warm. Now what do you think that would do for David?"

"It'd about kill him!" one man in the class shouted. We all laughed.

Sometimes a preacher gets some very intelligent, unexpected comments from some point made in a sermon or class. In a Mother's Day sermon at this same Fourth Avenue, I made the point that while God was usually biblically described in terms of masculine traits and in masculine pronouns, there were meaningful exceptions. I cited several scriptures in Isaiah to buttress my claim that God had also been described with feminine traits, imagery, and metaphors.

Immediately after the service Jim McKinney, retired attorney and diligent student of the Scriptures and Bible class instructor, approached me with a thoughtful question: "You made the point that God has certain traits of a woman. Would you say that Jesus has the traits of a hen or chicken?" He paused with this facetious look on his face. Immediately, Jesus' lament to Jerusalem came to mind ("How often I would have gathered you unto me as a hen gathers its chicks under her wings!"). I could only smile at such valid irony.

Not always are comments as thoughtful. Harold Duncan tells an experience in teaching a singles class at Dallas' Skillman Avenue church: "I was teaching a series of lessons on the Sermon on the Mount. This Sunday I was discussing the attitudes that Christians should maintain toward others," Harold stated. He then remembered that as he talked there was "this very attractive young woman" who was sitting close to him and who seemed to listen intently. "I took her to be a highly intelligent, very interested student. She really impressed me."

Harold completed his presentation, then paused and asked for any comments from the class. No one spoke up for a few seconds. "Then, this woman raised her hand. I called on her," Harold continued. "And in a soft, gooey tone she just said: 'Kindness is wonderful. I really love it. Don't you?'"

That comment was similar to one a woman gave me after I commended her for appearing to be such a good listener in my class sessions and for spending free time in reading. "Knowledge is so nice," she said; "I really love knowledge." One would have thought the clouds above Mt. Sinai had parted for the descending of such a profound oracular proclamation.

Naiveté can be blissful in certain worship situations. Janey Gleaves shared a sweet story about the time her mother visited Nashville from her home in Cullman, Alabama:

> Ed and I had been attending Belmont church in the late 70s. We had heard that there had been speaking in tongues since Don Finto became minister there, but we had never heard it there except once. We wanted to take mother to Belmont with us, but we wanted the usual "feel good" service without something bizarre happening that might upset her and then disturb her about us.

We took the chance and brought Mother with us to Belmont on this Sunday that she visited us. The sermon was fine. At the end of the sermon, a woman stood up and started speaking in tongues. She was a real attractive woman named Jimmie Lou Gilbert. She had a turban wrapped around her head. This foreign speech was just rolling off her tongue. I was very nervous and stressed about this whole experience, but Mother seemed calm and unperturbed.

What happened was that for some reason, perhaps the turban around her head, Mother thought that the charismatic woman was a missionary from some foreign soil.

"Wasn't it sweet that this sweet woman could come today and give a mission report in her own native tongue?" Mom said. I had a sigh of relief. We never told her otherwise.

COURTING POTENTIAL DISASTER—HOMILIES HINDERED WITH HOMONYMS

Some of our best preachers and teachers can unwittingly confuse some words with similar sounding words. One preacher reportedly confused "phylacteries," those special arm-bands worn by the Pharisees to signify religious distinction, with "prophylactics," and he kept expounding in a sermon on the Pharisees proudly sporting their prophylactics. One elder that I heard presenting a brief devotional talk before the Lord's Supper spoke about Jesus going through "excretionary pain." On more than one occasion I have heard a lay speaker or a prayer leader speak of becoming "prostate" (instead of "prostrate") before the Lord.

Another preacher, as heard by friend Barbara Enkema when he delivered a radio sermon, might have had "organism" or "organization" in mind. This preacher got excited about the many facets of the church and exclaimed, "Why, the church is a wonderful institution, the ark of the saved from the mighty flood, the bride of Christ, the very kingdom of God, one great orgasm that can shake up the whole world!"

I vividly remember sitting in a pew next to Buddy Arnold, our guest song director for a gospel meeting conducted by Manhattan preacher Burton Coffman. This was the Sunday evening service at Westwood, but we had a full house owing to the Central church combining its own evening service with us in support of the meeting. In the middle of the sermon Burton began to lampoon worship styles within the emerging charismatic movement. "They raise their arms, sway their bodies, and shout 'Praise the Lord' and 'Right on, Jesus,' just getting themselves all worked up into one big spiritual orgasm!" Burton exclaimed. Buddy and I looked at each other at that moment and he displayed a wry grin and raised his eyebrows. I could not repress my smile.

At the Abilene Christian lectureship in 1979, Jack Lewis was addressing a large audience on the topic of divorce and remarriage. He was speaking of the Old Testament character David and his relationship with one of his wives. After several references to the consummation of marriage, I heard him say, "At this time David had not constipated the marriage relationship." In retrospect, I was hoping that I did not hear him correctly, knowing Jack as a scholar of great intelligence.

One of my Lipscomb students from Memphis, Jay Shappley, recalled Jack Lewis delivering a sermon at the White Station congregation and telling a story of washing his car and enjoying a sweet pre-school neighborhood girl trying to assist him. The young girl wanted to be the one using the hose to rinse the car and she had fun pretending to accidentally spray Jack. Jack would fake surprise and pretend he was upset at her; the girl would giggle, then spray him even more. "After she had gotten me fairly wet," Jack told the listening congregation, "I just grabbed that hose out of her hands and I sprayed her **but** good." Little wonder the whole church paused a moment and then laughed, imagining the emphasized word was a body part instead of the conjunction he surely intended. And who knows the point of the little story? Humorous stories only need to evoke laughter, not connect to any sermon point.

PASSING THE COMMUNION

The communion of the Lord's Supper is shared each Sunday in a Church of Christ. Weekly observance on Sunday only is not simply a tradition—it is considered a matter of doctrinal purity that distinguishes the True Church in practice from most others. The unleavened bread and the fruit of the vine are passed separately with a prayer preceding each. In ninety-nine percent of the congregations the collection plate is passed after the communion. The passing of those collection plates is preceded by these seven words: "Separate and apart from the Lord's Supper ..." and these are code words for adults to reach for their purses and billfolds.

Only males, baptized adult men and baptized young boys, are permitted to line up in front of the congregation and pass the trays. After a boy's baptism it is never too early to draft the youngster into a non-speaking, entry-level worship service role such as communion tray passing or attendance car collection. Women are permitted to pass the trays laterally across a pew but are not allowed to enter an aisle or stand to make a passage. They may sit and scoot across unoccupied pew space to hand a tray to a fellow worshiper.

Given the frequency of communion observance, little wonder that many unexpected and disruptive events have occurred during the communion and the collecting of the offering. The accidental dropping of trays and the struggle for proper wording of prayers of thanksgiving are common experiences. Those who plan the worship program soon learn which males are willing to serve and among those willing to serve, which ones will lead a prayer at the communion table and which ones would pass plates but never lead a prayer.

Not every dropped tray has been accidental. A group of high school boys in the 14th and Main congregation in Big Spring, Texas, where my dad was minister for six years, was scheduled to serve communion one Sunday. In the Sunday School class which preceded the main assembly, the young men (including my brother, who tells this story) were discussing their assignment. One of the boys boasted that he would take the dare of deliberately dropping the "fruit of the vine" tray for a five dollar fee. (This may not seem a big cash reward for HOW dare-devilry, but for teenagers such cash went further in the mid-60s.) The other teen boys thought this was a "neat idea." They pooled their personal cash and presented the five dollars to the daring class member before the service began, still doubtful he would actually follow through and make the big drop.

Sure enough, as the teen boys had worked their way toward the rear of the auditorium serving communion, their partner in chicanery simply stood in the middle aisle at the back of the auditorium, looked around to make certain no one was looking, and then released his hands from the tray. A loud echo of clashing metal and broken glass bouncing from a bare linoleum tile floor pierced the silence and filled the building. People reflexively turned to discover who had experienced this "accident" and hence was surely embarrassed by the accidental mishandling. After the service, a number of adults approached the young teen, some giving hugs, and offered him sympathy and encouragement to recover from his "misfortune" and "embarrassment."

I have no doubt of my younger brother's role in this prank and a few other pranks appropriately not named here. My sister and I had already left home with apron strings cut, thus my dad had only my brother Harry as a subject of intense lobbying to enroll in Freed Hardeman College in Henderson, Tennessee, for studies to become a preacher. Harry resisted as long as possible, but when our dad offered him a new car to drive to Tennessee, he relented and enrolled at "Freed." There he made some good relationships yet also discovered a good number of what seemed overly-strict rules, thus laying the groundwork for labeling the institution as "Freedom-Hardly College." Alas, the "Freed" experience did not convince him of any divine calling.

PRAYER BEFORE COMMUNION

A prayer of thanksgiving for either the bread or the cup is usually the first prayer a male learns to lead in public assembly. The most typical prayer sounds as though it comes out of a Church of Christ prayer book: "Our Father, we thank thee for this bread/fruit of the vine which represents the broken body/shed blood of thy Son and our Lord and Savior Jesus Christ. May all those who partake of it do so in a manner well-pleasing in thy sight. In Jesus' name. Amen."

There are several variations on this prayer, of course. One Sunday morning at Detroit's Westside Central church, on a day that Lipscomb's Professor John T. Willis was our guest speaker, a man took the bread plate and gave thanks: "Thank you for the bread which represents the broken body of our Lord Jesus Christ and bless it to the nourishment of our bodies." John looked at me after the prayer, leaned over, and whispered, "That poor fellow must be pretty hungry."

At a Church of Christ in Hawaii served by preacher Danny Cline, a man offering thanks for the cup may have unconsciously been influenced by underwear commercials: "Father, thank you for this fruit of the loom …"

Even a simple prayer at communion can be anxiety-producing. Nan Gurley, a Christian performing artist and entertainer, shared a story about a reluctant participant in public worship in an unnamed congregation. This inexperienced fellow was nervous about any kind of public role in a worship service. He had turned down many opportunities to lead prayer. He finally agreed to co-preside at the communion table one Sunday, but only if he were informed ahead of time which prayer he would be called on to lead. He was then assigned to lead the prayer for the fruit of the vine.

The man wrote out his prayer which included this wording: "…We thank thee for this cup which symbolizes the shed blood of our Lord and Savior Jesus Christ …" Each day he practiced saying his prayer. He had it easily memorized, backward and forward. His budding confidence began to emerge. He could perform this assignment.

When Sunday rolled around the man who had agreed to open the communion service with brief remarks was not present. Another person, one who did not know who was assigned which specific prayer, filled in. He surely assumed, as anyone might, it did not really matter what man would lead which prayer. After his opening devotional remarks, he first called on the poor, anxiety-stricken man to lead the prayer for the bread.

The man panicked. This was not the prayer he was assigned to lead and not the one he had memorized to recite. He struggled to get some words out: "Father, we thank thee for this bread which represents the shed …" The man paused.

He did not know which word to use next. "…Which represents the shed …" He paused again. His stress level skyrocketed.

The third time he completed the sentence: "Father, we thank thee for this bread, which represents the shed skin of our Lord and Savior Jesus Christ. May all who partake of it do so in a manner well-pleasing in thy sight. In Jesus' name, Amen."

MAKING ANNOUNCEMENTS

Official doctrine of the True Church holds "five acts of worship." The making of announcements is not on that official list of five, but it is very much a part of public assembly and may impact the mood of the assembled body. In reality, however, most of the time no one listens much to announcements—visitors find them irrelevant and the locals may find them repetitive or boring. The worst *faux pas* of any kind of public speech in churches is generally not funny because, realistically, people are too bored to listen.

The announcement-making of Willard Collins at Lipscomb daily chapel from the 1940s through the 1980s sets the standard for excellence. Given his booming voice, his knack for pausing where no pause is called for or running words together where there should be pauses, and his penchant for double entendre words and pretentious naiveté, all combined to make announcement time in chapel something more than mere information.

We faculty and students remember the way announcement time at Lipscomb would typically sound on the first day of a new school year in the Willard Collins era: "We welcome all of you to Lipscomb. We should have another record enrollment. We have students here from Columbia, Tennessee, Chattanooga, Gadsden, Alabama, Atlanta, Mobile, Alabama—I was down there for a meeting just last month--Louisville, even Detroit, Michigan—a lotta fine people up there in Detroit," Brother Collins would embellish.

Then the Vice President would make an appeal for Wednesday night church attendance: "Now on this coming Wednesday night, the fine ladies at the Granny White congregation have a tradition. They want all of you to come to the mid-week service and then stay for a special treat. Those good Granny White women have been baking all week--cakes and pies and other good desserts." And seeing student facial expressions expressing interest in home-cooked desserts, Brother Collins might add one more admonition: "So you go over there and eat 'em out, I mean, eat 'em out for me. Eat, eat, eat all you can, and then eat'em out some more. And when you think you can't eat 'em out any more, you're not through. Take some of those pies and those cakes back to your dormitory room and share them with your roommate and keep eating those good ladies out." Non-sensible at times, sincere always, nonetheless.

The more that students and faculty laughed at a Collins announcement the more he kept embellishing. After the laughter continued for several seconds, Collins would turn around to some other administrator or professor on the stage and nod his head as if to say, "I don't know what they find so funny about this announcement."

Ill-timed pausing could evoke laughter. Quite often, Collins would say something such as "Welcome to Lipscomb chapel. We're here to worship God and Buddy Arnold … [then a long pause] … will lead the singing." Students respected Buddy Arnold, but it is doubtful anyone previously had thought of worshiping him along with the Father.

The most quoted Collins syntax involved his announcement about what the students and faculty alike called PDA—Public Display of Affection. Apparently there had been much administration concern about student couples sitting and openly sharing affection on campus benches or becoming romantically passion-ate in parked cars on campus. In one announcement Collins made mention of conferring with spinster Ruth Gleaves, the Fanning Hall head resident. "There is a big problem on this campus, as some of you know," Collins began, "and Miss Gleaves and I got together and discussed it and we decided that the two of us are going to stop all this necking on campus."

Another Collins quote is in reference to him and wife Ruth opening up their front yard on Lealand Lane to all students for an ice cream social: "The faculty will supply the ice cream and Ruth and I will furnish the grass."

Another preaching giant, W. A. Bradfield (already referenced in chapter 4), did not always find it easy to make announcements in front of a large college audience. The following story comes from Harold Duncan, a student at the time, but has been verified by several faculty attending chapel on that day:

> Brother Bradfield was making announcements in the Freed Hardeman chapel. A member of the faculty, Fred Kittrell, had been hospitalized for removal of a tumor. Everyone was concerned about the results of a biopsy.
>
> Brother Bradfield asked if anyone knew the results of his tests. Coach Hoyt Kirk was sitting in the back of the auditorium and shouted out, "The tumor is benign." Brother Bradfield paused for a few seconds, lowered his head, and then nodded in deep sadness as if he didn't know what to say next.
>
> Coach Kirk realized that Brother Bradfield was in trouble and he yelled again, "That means he's o. k." Brother Bradfield then gave a smile of relief. And perhaps he even learned the meaning of a new word.

SHOULD ANNOUNCEMENTS ATTEMPT IRONY AND HUMOR?

Jim Thomas, a good friend and former colleague in Lipscomb University's Communication Department, reminded me of an incident in announcement-making years ago at the Otter Creek Church. One Sunday morning in the assembly, Ed Neeley Cullum, a former Otter Creek minister himself, was reporting to the congregation on the progress of the pulpit committee's search for a new preaching minister. Ed Neeley was a professor in psychology and education. He loved inducing humor by sophisticated irony and satire, but often such facetiousness was not readily identified as such by the majority in his audience.

"Now that our committee has advanced a public notice that our congregation is seeking a new pulpit minister, we have received a plethora of inquiries and applications for this position," Ed began his announcement. Obviously this was a matter of great importance to nearly everyone in the congregation.

"Preachers who have inquired about our position range in age and background, but there is one candidate of interest whose status and qualifications seem totally unlike those of all other inquiring candidates," Ed Neeley continued. "This particular candidate, raised in a small community in a normal-sized family, has not completed special graduate training in religion or biblical studies. In fact, he has not even attended college," Ed Neeley explained. "There has been some public criticism of his preaching and teaching, but on the plus side, he seems to relate well to various audiences. One way in which this candidate stands out from the other candidates is that he is single, never married, and, to our knowledge is neither engaged nor dating anyone."

Ed Neeley closed his announcement by stating the committee "was giving special consideration to this most atypical preaching candidate. He is different from all the other candidates. We will keep you as Otter Creek members updated."

Fast forward to the Sunday evening assembly. Ed Neeley returned to the same pulpit to offer an apology and clarification. "I need to apologize to all of you for what turned out to be a pathetic failure in bringing a little humor to this process of locating a suitable candidate for the preaching position here at Otter Creek," he began. He then informed the congregation that during the past few hours he, the other committee members, and the elders had received a number of calls from concerned members urging them to discontinue further consideration of this one particular, atypical preaching candidate.

"There are two things that have really surprised me," Ed Neeley conceded. "One is that no one recognized that I was trying to describe Jesus as a possible preaching and teaching candidate." He confessed he was simply attempting to add a little humor to close out the Sunday morning worship assembly. Then there was a pause. "And the second thing is even more troubling—If Jesus were to apply for the pulpit position here, I suspect he would not even be considered as a worthy candidate, much less hired."

ELDERS MAKING ANNOUNCEMENTS

In the congregations I have served and others that I have observed, announcements are rendered with precious little enthusiasm or other emotion. Typically, the announcements are typed up by the church secretary as the last assigned task on a Friday afternoon and placed on the pulpit podium for the one assigned to communicate them at the Sunday assembly. Then, on Sunday morning, the good brother making the announcements can just read them off in a monotone voice and his assignment has been completed. Quite often one of the elders regularly makes the announcements.

When I served at the Otter Creek congregation, elder John Crothers often made announcements at the end of the service. Not only was John a sweet and loving person, but he was intelligent and well-educated, having an earned doctorate in higher education and experience in academic administration. His vocabulary was expansive and, without exception, every announcement he made was filled with his trademark verbose and erudite linguistics.

John's typical announcement would sound like this: "And now for our Otter Creek Bible class teachers, be cognizant of the impending convening of our instructional staff to be conducted next Sunday afternoon at 2:00. Pending topics for dialogue and open interaction remain ensconced in our passion for efficacious pedagogical methodology at all instructional levels, even for adults. Please plan to attend, other priorities notwithstanding." After all John's announcement sessions, one could see people in pews with puzzled looks toward each other with a blank expression and almost hear them ask, "What'd he just say?"

John possessed an outgoing personality, so quite unlike another elder for a small Midwestern congregation as served by then Minister Steve Lemley, later becoming the long-tenured President of Lubbock Christian University. This one elder assumed the task of making announcements at the end of many Sunday services, but always in a low-pitched, emotionless monotone that seemed to reflect total boredom.

One Sunday a delegation of visitors arrived by the start of the service. Understandably, these visitors stood out in a small congregation where everyone knew all other members. Their arrival attracted everyone's attention. One rather large and forceful woman seemed to lead the delegation. Nonetheless, the service proceeded as planned and Steve preached the sermon he had prepared. They sat politely through the duration of the service. As the weekly custom, the elder stood before the people after the "formal worship" was over and made his announcements in his dour, low-key, monotone. And, as always, he closed announcement time with the standard line, "Do we have any other announcements that need to be made?"

Immediately, at that point, the large, provocative woman spoke up with a loud and ecstatic voice of excitement: "Oh, yes, brother, I have an announcement for the whole church. I am a member of a special revival team that God has sent to this town," she began. "We have a huge tent set up and each night there is powerful preaching, soul-stirring testimony, great music, the sick are being healed, the dead are being raised, and other wonderful miracles are happening, and praise Jesus, hearts are set on fire. I have come to invite all of you to attend."

When the vivacious visitor had completed her stirring announcement, the entire church sat for four or five seconds of total and expressionless silence, and then the dour elder still standing quietly at the front simply said in his restrained monotone: "Are there any other announcements? If not, Brother Jones will lead our dismissal prayer."

WORD CHOICE, SYNTAX, AND LEGIBILITY

The proper pronunciation of names of people and places is probably the most difficult challenge in making announcements. Sometimes an announcement and a name provide an interesting juxtaposition. "There's a little community near Murray, Kentucky, called Sawdust," relates Porter King. "A person known to our West Seventh congregation in Columbia had died and his body was taken to that community. The man making announcements stated, '… and his body lies in Sawdust.'"

Tom Carr, a good friend whose life-time career has been Christian benevolent services, heard an elder discussing the plight of a workaholic church member who had been stricken with a near fatal stroke and lay hospitalized in a comatose state. Standing before the entire church assembly, the elder spoke in a somber tone about how indefatigably the stricken brother worked: "Our poor brother worked so hard on his job and then he worked constantly at home. His hobby was his vegetable garden. I'd pass by his place on weekday afternoons and he'd be gardening. I pass his place on weekends and he'd be sweating in his garden. Garden, garden, garden—that's all he knew at home. Now he's become a vegetable."

At another church service, Carr heard another brother making another serious announcement about a member who had suffered a fatal heart attack. The announcer inadvertently reversed two of the letters on "fatal heart attack" and declared: "We regret to announce Brother Smith has suffered a hatal feart attack."

Shoddy syntax and improper word choice deployed by men making announcements have produced some interesting statements. The following announcements have been actually rendered in church assemblies:

--"We are sorry that we don't have many sick to announce. However, we are happy to announce that sister Smith has the flu."

--"We are thankful that Reggie Jones had the audacity to respond to the invitation and be baptized."

--"As you know, we like to have the truth properly confounded here, so we invite you to come back tomorrow night to hear Brother Green dispense with the gospel once again."

--You'll see a number of songs listed in the program. We're going to be singing these songs simultaneously without any interruption."

There would have been many more smiles and laughter after these announcements except for the fact that, quite manifestly, few people were listening to the announcement ritual and many in attendance might not have known the true meaning of some key words.

To her immense embarrassment, one elder's wife participating in a Sunday evening small fellowship group failed to use the proper abbreviation of a five-syllable word. During open social discussion after the group's Bible lesson, this woman was praising the generosity of another elder's family in the same congregation. She told the group that she and her husband would be traveling to Destin, Florida, for a "weekend getaway" for just the two of them. She then commended this elder, Brother McCree [not his actual name], "for loaning us his condom to use on this little trip to the beach." Just as some group members were attempting to stifle their smiles and emerging chuckles, she added: "This condom is fairly new and modern and has only been used once or twice this year." Group laughter then was unrestrained. When this elder's wife displayed a puzzled look on her face, another female group member leaned into her face and whispered revealingly into her ear the nature of her linguistic *faux pas*. This woman's stunning countenance of shock and embarrassment could not have been greater.

Illegibility created problems for some. As a guest at the Homewood congregation in Birmingham, Alabama, speaker Joe Beam was sitting through announcements. A man walked to the pulpit and handed the announcer a late notice scribbled on a piece of paper. "The brother making announcements read the note: 'Sister Smith is one hundred and eleven and needs our prayers,'" Joe remembers. "After a pause to reflect on this unlikely age for a good sister, the brother read the note again: 'Sister Smith is ill and needs our prayers.'"

Let's conclude: The church assembly is vitally important to the community of faith. It should not be frivolously forsaken. The "acts of worship" should be conducted as effectively as possible. Given the lack of formal training of most men for worship leadership, as well as the general anxiety most people feel while standing in front of an audience, it's probably by the grace of God that services turn out as well as they do!

8

Homileticus Interruptus and Other Distracting Acts of God, Acts of Men, Acts of Women and Children in Church Assembly

Only one solitary event in this poor man's life is all that he has ever been known for.

He wrote no book, invented no system, experienced no epiphany, authored no epistle, wielded no political power, nor headed a famous family, at least so far as we know. He preached no great sermon. In fact, he didn't even hear a great sermon. Not for long, at least.

No one would have thought anything about poor Eutychus falling asleep—God knows how many others might have been asleep that fateful night in Troas when Paul droned on until the bewitching midnight hour—if he had not selected such a precarious perch for a private pew. When the poor chap fell, the whole congregation likely gasped in horror.

Imagine how the apostle Paul must have felt the moment Eutychus dropped from his deep, slumberous state of dreamland at a third story window facing to the cold floor of reality. He was "picked up dead," according to Luke in Acts 20. Did Paul blame himself ("God, is this an act of you or an act of me? I know I should have wrapped this sermon up thirty minutes ago")? Or did he begin intense prayer ("God, if I never get to perform another miracle in my life, please enable me to bring ole Eutychus back to life. If you don't raise him up, God, you know I may never get invited back to Troas for another meeting.")?

You probably know this little story has a happy ending. Paul threw himself on the young man, embraced him, reassured the congregation that all would be well, and brought the poor fellow back to life. You can imagine how embarrassed both Paul and Eutychus might have been. At that point, Paul takes a break, probably wipes sweat off his brow, goes upstairs and has a meal, then he resumes his speaking until the break of dawn.

Most of us can understand Eutychus. We'll hold no personal grudges against him if we happen to spend some time together with him on one of the clouds of glory. (I wonder, will there be sleep in heaven?) Let's face it: The vast majority of us have slumbered at one time or another during a sermon. A wonderful friend and true Christian gentleman, Fletcher Srygley, often physically in my audience, is typical of so many ecclesiastical slumberers. The times he does *not* drift off to sleep during a sermon I begin to wonder what is wrong with him. Fletcher has slept through sermons delivered by some of the most renowned preachers in our fellowship and retains a sense of humor about this proclivity.

I am reminded of a Sunday School teacher of preschoolers, who, right before dismissing her class a few minutes prior to their meeting their parents to sit in the main worship assembly, asked: "Why is it important to be quiet when we sit in church?" Immediately, one little boy replied, "Because people are sleeping!" If all the people who slept in church were laid end to end, the old saying goes, they'd all be a lot more comfortable.

Thus Eutychus' notoriety was not his failure to maintain attention for the elongated duration of the famous apostle's stem-winding sermon. His claim to a place in even the abridged Bible dictionaries (the kind you find in the back of bigger Bibles) was his startling, unusual, and non-intentional interruption of a church service.

How heartening to consider that of all the developments the historian of Acts could have reported of that Saturday night service, including something of the content of the sermon or how many people were present, this interruption draws special mention in the divine record. And surely more important biblical characters are referenced in New Testament Scripture (such as the Samaritan woman at the well or the adulteress Jesus forgave), but who, for some puzzling reason, are left unnamed. This poor soul got named.

Do you know anyone today named Eutychus? This hapless worshiper probably had worked hard all week. He may well have been a slave or over-worked servant. What further endorsement do we need for chronicling our more colorful interruptions in the post-Eutychusian age?

Most interruptions are not welcomed by preachers. After all, what is more important and worthy of attention than the absolute gospel truth they are freely dispensing? The real reason, of course, is that most preachers have a massive egos and crave that "undivided attention" they so often commend audiences for giving them.

Let's acknowledge up front that not all interruptions are created equal. Sadly, in fact, there can be tragic interruptions. On Sunday morning, September 24, 2017, Emanuel Samson arrived at the Nashville-area Burnette Chapel Church of Christ with guns, a knife, and a stockpile of ammunition. Claiming to be motivated by vengeance for Dylann Roof, the white supremacist who killed nine black churchgoers in Charleston, South Carolina, in 2015, he pumped four shots into the first worshiper he saw in the parking lot; then he entered into the church house and sprayed the crowded vestibule with bullets. In May 2019 Samson was convicted of one murder and attempted murder and injury of seven other church members.

Apart from these very rare tragic and inexplicable occurrences, there are three other kinds of interruptions: the good, the serious, and the funny. We'll cite some examples of each.

GOOD INTERRUPTIONS

Good interruptions are few and far between. When the Holy Spirit interrupted that Pentecostal prayer meeting in the upper room and sent down tongues of fire and a mighty wind, then strange and wonderful phenomena started popping around Jerusalem. A little later a big audience started experiencing an old fashioned, heart-pricking sermon and interrupted Peter's message even before he got around to offering the invitation: "Men and brethren [admittedly somewhat redundant], what must we do to be saved?"

Several preachers brag about their successes and prowess as soul-stirring evangelists. Some have persuaded the weak and erring to stream profusely and tearfully down the aisles to the front pew. But I have never heard a single preacher claim that his sermon was so convicting, so piercing, that some group of people or even just one person charged the pulpit and loudly demanded the sermon be halted so that an important question be answered and obedience to a crucial command could proceed without further delay.

Our best church interruptions, which usually happen in classes or in less formal assemblies, typically occur to announce a new birth to the wife of the song director or youth minister, a contribution or attendance record just having been set, some congregational goal having been met or exceeded, or a victory by the regional Christian college baseball or basketball team in the national tournament (just to cite a few examples).

SERIOUS INTERRUPTIONS

The serious interruptions are those that make us pause, if only for a few moments, and reflect on who we are, what life is all about, or where we stand on some issue. A few dramatic interruptions of church services which impacted mightily on me and a number of my friends merit recounting briefly.

One interruption that was widely discussed on the Lipscomb campus and in some local church circles involved a sharp disagreement between one of Tennessee's best known preachers and one of the state's most respected political leaders. The context for this story was the closely contested 1960 U. S. presidential campaign.

As soon as John F. Kennedy was nominated by the Democratic Party as its candidate for president of the United States in the summer of 1960 at the Democratic National Convention in Los Angeles, a wakeup call was sounded for many conservative and evangelical church leaders. Kennedy, a young, popular, and ambitious senator from Massachusetts, was Roman Catholic. No Catholic had ever been elected U. S. president. Since Democrat Alfred Smith, the first Roman Catholic to be nominated for president by a major party, was defeated in 1928, the issue of Roman Catholicism and American freedoms had remained dormant.

There was a great deal of opposition in the Church of Christ as well as in other conservative Protestant groups, especially Southern Baptists, to Kennedy's nomination and bid for the White House because of the religious issue. From mid-summer 1960 through Election Day, I heard a number of sermons in various congregations about the dangers of Roman Catholicism as a political power.

Some preachers and elders opposed Kennedy and his Catholic faith undoubtedly out of sheer prejudice and bigotry. Most opposition among our thinking brothers and sisters, however, emerged out of genuine conviction that a Roman Catholic in the White House would be the first step in moving the nation away from religious liberty and the historic doctrine of separation of church and state. Though not so explicitly stated in all sermons, many conservative Southern church leaders and members feared both that a Catholic president would concede American freedoms and rights to the wishes of the Pope and that a major growth in Catholic parishes and membership that might eventually surpass the ranks of Protestant adherents.

On October 9, 1960, Batsell Barrett Baxter, my major adviser at David Lipscomb College, delivered his own personal message on this important subject in full sermon form to a typically full house at the Hillsboro Church of Christ, at that time meeting on 21st Avenue South and Ashwood Street. The audience was composed of the congregation's regular membership of several hundred and then possibly one to two hundred additional college students (most from Lipscomb, some from Vanderbilt/Peabody). College students generally sat in the wrap-around balcony on three sides above the main floor.

Most coincidentally, NBC had sent a camera crew (some of the crew and cameras came on loan from the NBC affiliate station WSM-TV, I was informed) to the Hillsboro service that morning to film a report on Bible Belt preaching on the "Roman Catholic-presidential election" issue. The film would be edited and shown with commentary on "Chet Hundley's Views," Huntley being the respected co-anchor of network news with David Brinkley. What no one connected with NBC at the time would have imagined, and yet what they likely welcomed and embraced for the sake of viewer interest, was the drama at the end of the worship service.

Brother Baxter's sermon was entitled "A Dangerous Doctrine." The message did not, as I recall, mention John F. Kennedy by name. The sermon did adduce a number of quotations, some from other centuries and from non-American Catholic authorities, in support of Brother Baxter's thesis. This respected preacher's conclusion: Any Catholic placed in high political position will be pressured to acknowledge that "absolute authority rests in Rome." Such an acknowledgment at the highest executive level of national government would indeed place the entire nation and citizen liberties in peril. If the Catholic Church became large enough and powerful enough to dominate the nation, then all non-Catholics "would lose their religious freedom." And it might even make the nation vulnerable to Soviet Communism or some other form of totalitarianism.

Sitting in the audience as a visitor that Sunday, and quite coincidentally (due to a Lipscomb board meeting the previous day), was U. S. Representative Joe L. Evins, a respected and long-time political leader from the sixth district in Tennessee. Evins was a Democrat. He was also a member of the Church of Christ. The two men—the preacher and the politician—respected and liked each other personally, but they saw this high voltage issue from radically different perspectives.

After the sermon had been delivered, but before the service was concluded and dismissed by prayer, Evins marched to the front of the assembly and declared that there were some impromptu remarks he felt compelled to make. He asked if he might speak for a few minutes before the closing. Many in the audience knew Representative Evins, how could anyone have spoken up and said, "No, you must not speak at this moment"? Stark silence fell upon the congregation. This was already an unusual and most unexpected interruption.

Representative Evins proceeded to explain why he disagreed with Baxter. The congressman's true conviction (paraphrased): In time of conflict between an American president's responsibility to his nation and political principle, on the one hand, and his personal, private religious faith on the other, the president would first and foremost abide by the U. S. Constitution he has sworn to uphold. In fact, Evins was basically reiterating what the candidate himself had clearly explained and promised a month earlier (September 12) in his famous address to the Greater Houston Ministerial Alliance.*

Though this unscheduled confrontation during the hour of worship was professionally courteous and orderly, it left the congregation shell-shocked. Wanda Baxter, wife of the late preacher, remembered that Sunday: "On that day I was sitting with my sweet little boys. When Evins came to the front and strolled to the microphone and then starting talking, there was a feeling we all had of absolute shock. No one spoke from that pulpit without special permission from the elders and without prior arrangement," she told me. "We certainly never entertained any bad feelings about Congressman Evins. He [Evins] just felt like this sermon stoked a fire that he needed to put out in front of the whole audience. Batsell knew that it was a touchy subject. Sure, there was a great deal of opposition to Batsell but at Hillsboro there was a whole lot more support. The general sentiment of the entire church was that Evins' public reaction was inappropriate."

One of the Hillsboro elders at the time, Prentice Meador, Sr., remembered: "We tried to play the incident down and, frankly, I don't remember too much about it. We said nothing more about it publicly. Evins did offer to us a private apology for interrupting the service. This is just indicative of what happens when people get excited about some political issue and what have you."

Though I sat in many classes and had private conversations with Brother Baxter, I never heard him refer to the incident and I'm not sure why. This had to be one of the stirring moments in his preaching career. His sermon that day was

---

* The incident of Congressman Evins interrupting the closing of the Hillsboro Church of Christ worship assembly in October 1960 is also narrated in Richard T. Hughes' definitive study, *Reviving the Ancient Faith: The Story of Churches of Christ in America* (Wm. B. Eerdmans, 1996), chapter 11, pp. 265-66. An excellent study of the entire issue of the making of a Roman Catholic president was researched and written by a respected colleague and friend, also a speaker and teacher in the Church of Christ, Shaun Casey. His study: *The Making of a Catholic President: Kennedy Against Nixon 1960* (New York: Oxford University Press, 2009).

published in an edited "tract" form by the same name, "A Dangerous Doctrine," and widely distributed. Brother Baxter received support and understanding from scores of church and school leaders and faculty. With one exception: Athens Clay Pullias, president of Lipscomb at that time. Pullias and Evins were life-long friends. When Evins died, Pullias traveled to Smithville to preach his funeral.

SOME DRAMATIC INTERRUPTIONS

An even more dramatic interruption of a worship service occurred at a Nashville church on February 4, 1973, illustrating the force of Emily Dickinson's words: "Because I could not stop for death, he kindly stopped for me." This was an incident where one man, in essence, unknowingly preached his own funeral.

On that Sunday at the Otter Creek Church of Christ, Henry Arnold led the congregation in singing "How Great Thou Art." Dr. Thomas W. Rogers, an elder of the church and respected faculty member at Lipscomb in business administration, went to the lectern, offered a few remarks about forgiveness, read Psalm 32, and then led the congregation in prayer. In his prayer he spoke of being in the presence of God and closed with a plea for forgiveness.

As soon as Rogers returned to his special seat on the pulpit he slumped into an unconsciousness. Rogers received first aid from several physicians (William Gray, Larry Arnold, and William Gaw) who were present in the assembly. Otter Creek's preacher, Carroll Ellis, would always remember the power of that service and he told me the story from his own perspective:

> It was obvious to most adults that Dr. Rogers was having a heart attack. While the three doctors were working, one of them giving mouth-to-mouth resuscitation, Henry Arnold led us in prayer. I continued to pray and then Brother Arnold led us in a song during the time. Without any struggle or fight, Dr. Rogers was dying. In spite of the fact that an ambulance had been called, Dr. Gaw suggested that we get a station wagon and take him to the emergency room.

During this time, Sister Rogers, who had rushed up to the platform, knelt beside him and tenderly said, "Thomas, I love you." Two of the ladies arose and stood by Sister Rogers as she quietly wept and prayed. Carolyn, his daughter, was there with her mother … Several of the men quietly slipped from their seats and helped move his body … Approximately thirty-five minutes had already elapsed while the congregation sang and partook of the Lord's Supper.

I arose and informed the whole congregation, "The sermon I had prepared is not appropriate." I walked over and picked up Dr. Rogers' Bible and read from John 11: 25 Jesus' statement: "I am the resurrection and the life; he who believes in me shall live even if he dies."

One of the Otter Creek elders received a call from the hospital stating that Dr. Rogers was dead on arrival. Later, Dr. Gray said that for all practical purposes Dr. Rogers was clinically dead when they were administering mouth-to-mouth resuscitation on the platform.

No one lost composure in that day's assembly, an audience enhanced by a large number of out-of-town visitors who had attended Lipscomb's homecoming that weekend. Some quietly wept, but, understandably, no one left the assembly. The entire service was a poignant demonstration of the Christian view of death and the hope of an eternal life. Periodically, the incident is recalled in a public way at the Otter Creek church. One might ponder if there is, indeed, a more appropriate setting for a godly man or woman to make the ultimate departure from this earthly existence.

While delivering one of my Sunday evening sermons at Westwood only a few years later, a Christian gentleman named Noel Womack passed out in the pew. Three or four people quietly gathered around him; they determined that he was seriously ill. Noel was soon taken by ambulance to a local hospital where he regained consciousness. Obviously, this was a sobering interruption of our evening assembly worship.

Noel was the most stoically serious and reserved deacon in our congregation.

Though my family had often visited with him and his wife Margaret in their home, I had never seen him smile. That night in the hospital room I attempted to add some levity to his situation. "I just hope my sermon was not a major factor in your getting sick and passing out in church," I offered, perhaps subconsciously fishing for a compliment. "Oh, no," he replied expressionlessly, "the sermon wasn't *that* bad."

Noel never recovered. A few weeks later I preached his funeral. Months later, I officiated at the remarriage ceremony of his widow, Margaret.

LESS SERIOUS INTERRUPTIONS

Then there are those less serious interruptions which serve to remind us that we live in an imperfect world where people and machinery experience failure and breakdown and where humanity and nature are not always in perfect harmony.

Many less serious interruptions are totally unpredictable. Steven Lemley, a professor and administrator for Pepperdine University at the time, was delivering a sermon on a Sunday evening at a Southern California congregation. "As I was reading this Scripture text before expounding on it," Steve reports, "there was this loud and almost angry voice from the back of auditorium that shouted out, 'who wrote that material—was he a human being or just what?'"

Steve was startled but calmly replied: "This writing comes from the apostle Paul." The immediate response seemed one of relief. "Well, then, I'm glad you are willing to acknowledge it," the man said. Steve's sermon continued.

God only knows how many times preachers have interrupted sermons in order to reprimand teenagers misbehaving in the audience or to instruct mothers to remove their crying babies from the auditorium. Some have rightly wondered how some preachers could virtually humiliate a young mother for the behavior of her innocent baby, especially in the older church buildings that provided no nursery or what is known in our circles as a "cry room."

What needs to be remembered is that some preachers have massive egos. How impertinent that a mother and child are confined to sitting at one spot on a hard bench for what seems like an eternity—both mother and child as well as everyone else within earshot are expected to sit in rapt attention to the preacher's every word.

NATURE'S CREATURES AND THE CALL OF NATURE

While standing and "delivering the Word," most if not all preachers are certainly accustomed to seeing presumed listeners appear to be drowsy and drifting off to sleep. Sometimes there are unexpected distractions. Trey Morgan was preaching for a small church in Ojo Felix, New Mexico, on a Sunday in which a large mouse trap had been placed in a dry baptistery tank. The trap went off and a big rat started flopping, flailing, and screeching. Morgan reported that "for the next twenty minutes I tried to preach over those sounds of a dying rat just behind me."

Charlie Harrison, preacher for the Brunswick, Maine, Church of Christ, enjoyed watching one mother's approach to corralling her rowdy children on the pew with her. He reported this young mom would stuff jumbo marshmallows into their mouths when they began to wiggle and make distracting noises. Charlie warned against using this strategy with talkative adult members of one's family as "they might take it the wrong way."

Animals have been, on rare occasion, brought to the HOW. I once taught a college class in which a bright, blind student typically brought his big leader dog to class. The student sat on the end of the second row of the classroom with the dog in the aisle at his feet. The dog seemed as well-behaved and respectful as did some of my students and might well have learned and retained as much as a few of those students.

Bobby Ross tells of an East Hampton, New York, preacher who spotted a small cat peeking out of a woman's purse. My friend Bryce Grissom laughed as he remembered a story from the 50s. Seems an elementary school lad enjoyed concealing a live garden snake in his jacket's inside pocket and bringing it to church services at the Graymere congregation in Columbia, Tennessee. The youngster seemed to enjoy slipping the snake from his pocket and shocking his school pals at the least appropriate times. Interestingly, the kid's name is Lowell Mosley, the son of Graymere's preacher at the time, Fred Mosley.

In a class at Nashville's Woodmont Hills about fifteen years ago, a young single woman named Melissa quietly informed me that she brought a miniature Chihuahua to each Bible class session during the winter. When I expressed disbelief, thinking she was only joking, she led me aside to the corner of the classroom, slightly opened her coat, and, sure enough, there was this bright-eyed and alert miniature dog. I softly welcomed the Chihuahua to our class and pledged not to announce his presence to the other class members.

Some interruptions are predictable. In my experience, every church has at least one or two members who are known for walking out, either for home or for the rest room, at some point in the service (especially during the sermon). If you understand the legalism of so many members in the True Church, then you know why, in those Sunday morning services where communion is served prior to the sermon, that a sprinkling of members stand and walk out after taking (many prefer the prefix form: "partaking of") the communion—the minimal requirement has been met and they can move on with their day! Some ingenuously exit the HOW just after the "emblems" are passed but before the collection plates are passed.

At the Westwood church a young father whom I'll call Joe Roy rose from his pew each Sunday during my sermon and slowly led his young daughter up front past the pulpit and then out a side exit to the restroom. Alas, five minutes later he would return across the same conspicuous route, moving slowly, stooped over and holding the little girl's hand. Several wondered why the little girl's mother, also always present, did not make this mission of relief (one inferred that perhaps Joe Roy, too, "had to go").

These two never missed a Sunday answering the call of nature and "the call" could come indiscriminately during some major point or dramatic illustration in my sermon. At any rate, the weekly round trip of dad and young daughter soon became the source of a private joke for some worshipers, so much so that I nearly lost my composure on several Sundays when they made their move. With all the control at my command, I continued to speak while looking out over a profuse sprinkling of smiling faces.

A preacher always dreads the times in which the most important point he wants to make or the most emotional statement he has planned to utter gets totally lost by some unexpected interruption or distraction. How many great statements in a sermon have been barely heard when a book or children's toy drops loudly on the pew or the floor, a glass breaks, a child shrieks, a police car or fire truck with siren screaming as it passes outside the door, or a jet aircraft flies overhead with what seems like a sonic boom?

Indeed, assembly worship amidst the gathered saints can be a mixture of the sublime and the ridiculous! We have all experienced this absurd mix on one Sunday or another.

UNPREDICTABLE INTERRUPTIONS

Most interruptions are not predictable, of course. Some interruptions seemed to be divinely timed. From my boyhood days I recall several occasions wherein a big bolt of lightning knocked out lights in the house of worship for a night service, accompanied by a deafening roar of thunder. Typically the preacher would attempt a little impromptu humor by asking some stupid question such as, "Where was Moses when the lights went out?" Then he would keep on preaching in the dark as though everything was normal. Of course, no one was listening to the sermon during those moments.

Early in his preaching career, a young Batsell Barrett Baxter was delivering an emotionally charged sermon on heaven and hell for a Los Angeles area congregation. As the emotion revved up, more than the sinners started trembling. The whole church building frighteningly shook. Earthquake tremors were rocking the whole area. The lesson was more soul-shaking than Baxter could have dreamed when he prepared it. This might have been a great occasion for a sermon on Paul and Silas and the Philippian jailor's traumatic conversion experience.

A young Steve North once was delivering a Sunday sermon at Spring Hill, Tennessee, in the late 60s. North, who claims he got his theological education by car-pooling from Spring Hill to Nashville each day with the city's clergy (North was riding to Vanderbilt Law School along with the Baptist preacher to Belmont College and the Episcopal preacher to Vanderbilt Divinity School), served the city's one Church of Christ at that time as minister. In the middle of the sermon a man burst through the front entrance and shouted, "The barn at the [Tennessee] Children's Home is on fire!" Sure enough. North ended his sermon immediately and everyone filed out of the church house and went out to fight the fire or watch the others fight it.

Some instances of *homileticus interruptus* challenge both the nerve and creativity of the preacher. Jim Bill McInteer told about an incident in the 70s while speaking in a meeting for the large Skillman Avenue congregation in Dallas:

> As I was delivering this meeting sermon at Skillman, back when Virgil Trout was minister there, a man strolled into the assembly. He was dressed quite casually and was unkempt in appearance. The pulpit covers a wide area there and he began to make his way toward me. All eyes were focused on him. When he got to me I just stopped my sermon. He plopped a letter in an envelope on the podium.
>
> I looked at it and saw that it had the wrong address and I just calmly said, "Young man, I believe you have the wrong address." Quickly, some men from the congregation rose and went to the pulpit and escorted this man, who may have been deranged in some way, away from the assembly.
>
> Later, Gwen Trout [the preacher's wife] who was sitting close to the front, said, "Wow! That was scary. I was sure frightened for your safety. I quickly put all my jewelry in my mouth till he was out of here."

NO INCENSE BUT INSECTS IN OUR WORSHIP

Sometimes the animal kingdom and the spiritual kingdom become dangerously entwined.

For several years I served as preaching minister for the Owen Chapel church in Brentwood. The church, founded in 1859, continued to meet in a building constructed just after the Civil War. Originally a one-room building which held two hundred worshipers, the sanctuary had a high ceiling. To our chagrin, this historic building, at least in the 70s and 80s, was seemingly the perfect environment for a large collection of wasps to reside.

The wasps seemed to live below the floor level in this old building. In the cold winter, once the building became toasty warm which was usually near the start of my sermon, the pesty little stingers began emerging from the many openings where a big base board separated from the wall. The drama seemed all too much like one of those Hollywood natural disaster horror films.

Sunday after Sunday a new brigade (sent by the devil?) emerged from their safe abode and started buzzing around. No matter what the sermon topic, people's attention was understandably focused on the stinging insects in flight. Any speaker's effort at eye contact with listeners was typically futile. At times there would be a loud shriek when some unsuspecting woman, teenager, or child suddenly spotted one within striking proximity. Sometimes people would suddenly jump jack-in-the-box style out of their seats. Often some worshiper would try to swat one with a Bible or hymnal. We killed several each Sunday, but they seemed especially prolific in multiplying and inflicting their pestilence.

During one my Sunday lessons, one especially persistent wasp was making several buzz dives and was so distracting and menacing that every worshiper had adopted a self-preservation mode. After the critter made a threatening move in my direction, I simply interrupted my lesson, walked away from the podium, picked up a swatter (we always had one, along with a can of insect spray), swung with gusto and nailed the noxious pest to a century-plus old pew on my first swing—its life cycle had been brought to sudden termination!

The congregation applauded as I walked back to the pulpit and resumed the lesson with this comment: "I always hate to mow down one of God's little creatures, but I think the wasp, along with all the flies and stink bugs, is a remnant of the fall of man."

"NO FLIES ON JESUS"

Most preachers have encountered distracting troubles with flies buzzing around their faces during summer season message delivery, especially in rural churches where windows might be raised, and, in the old days, some church houses did not have screens. Something about pastoral sweat seems to attract flies. Gordon French, preacher at a church in Lapeer, Michigan, and director of the Michigan Christian Youth Camp, once preached for several long seconds with a fly left unmolested while perched on his nose—all to the amusement of happy campers present that day.

My approach to a distracting fly has varied from a nonchalant and hopefully inconspicuous flick of one finger to an all-out effort to swat with my Bible the nasty pest which dared to enter God's house uninvited. After all, there's an old country hymn once sung in lower socio-economic regions titled, tasteless as it may seem, "No Flies on Jesus." When people see that a fly is buzzing around my face and the distraction persists, I share an experience of G. C. Brewer, a very capable Bible scholar and grace-oriented preacher of the early to mid-twentieth century.

During a summer revival at a rural church a collection of flying insects encircled a light bulb extended from the ceiling above the pulpit. Seems that one bug of unidentified species somehow took a nosedive into Brewer's mouth when he had opened it widely to articulate first a consonant and then a prolonged vowel in the King's English.

The sermon came to a precipitous halt. The preacher could have quietly and "tastefully" removed the insect using his handkerchief. But no! With a mighty sound of forceful expulsion, Brewer spat the bug to the floor, paused for a moment, and then informed his amused congregation: "He was lukewarm, so I spewed him out of my mouth."

As a young preacher, Hoy Ledbetter was delivering a Sunday sermon to a rural church in Arkansas. If a lesser man than Hoy had told the story, then I would not have believed this one: "A dog apparently had been chasing a rabbit outside around the building. We kept the front door open for ventilation," Hoy reported. "The rabbit must have circled the building. The hound dog came running into the building, down the center aisle, then made a skidding halt in front of the communion table. It quickly turned and ran out the building just as fast."

BEWARE OF RHETORICAL QUESTIONS

Preachers need to be especially careful when inviting the congregation to be involved in a lesson. Every preacher seeks positive responses but not always immediate answers. This is true, apparently, even when asking a rhetorical question. The preacher hopes to gain better audience attention, but does not expect an oral reply, possible exception being in African-American congregations.

One Sunday morning before a full house at Otter Creek Church in the 70s, Carroll Ellis was expounding on the wiles of the devil. Never mind that few listeners know what "wiles" might be. Dr. Ellis walked down from the pulpit to the main floor, as the manner of some preachers is, in order to conclude his sermon with an emotional impact and one final spurt of focused audience attention. With a curled fist moving in a knocking motion, Ellis he shouted these words: "And so, what are you going to do when the devil comes knock, knock, knocking at your door?"

Immediately from the audience came a loud answer from preschooler Christopher Jennings: "I'd let him in!" The entire congregation roared in laughter. No one in the family of Jerry and Nancy Jennings has ever been shy! Dr. Ellis laughed and then regained his composure: "Well, Christopher, many people would indeed let him in, but that's the wrong thing to do. That's the time to send for Jesus!"

Poor ole Eutychus might have been one embarrassed soul. His fall-out from drifting off to sleep during an apostle's lengthy discourse has earned his only place in sacred history. At least he lived (or got resuscitated) to tell his embarrassing story to all his friends. Eutychus certainly could not have harbored any long-standing grudge against the long-winded apostle. He might have lived long enough to read, perhaps with a smile, some of that apostle's epistles to various churches.

And slumbering Eutychus certainly has a lot of kinfolks in the True Church— even if they don't sit on a third floor window sill!

9

"See, Here is Water! What Doth Hinder Me ...?"

The story is told of a minister who always managed to work into every sermon a five to ten minute discussion of baptism. On numerous occasions his entire sermon was devoted to the topic of baptism.

Knowing the vital importance of baptism, and yet ever hopeful of some fresh thinking on other topics in the sermon content, the elders in this congregation mustered all their collective diplomacy and requested the preacher to preach a series of expository sermons from some book in the Bible. "You might just start in chapter one of some book and work your way through from there," one of the elders suggested helpfully and hopefully.

What better place to implement this excellent suggestion than with the first book in the Bible, the preacher reasoned. On the following Sunday the newly commissioned preacher mounted the pulpit and began reading: "'In the beginning, God created the heavens and the earth.' Now scientists and geographers tell us that two-thirds of the earth is composed of water. You know, of course, water is necessary for there to be Scriptural baptism. And while I'm on that important subject ... [and the preacher droned on another ten to fifteen minutes on the topic of baptism]."

If that is not a true story involving a Church of Christ preacher, then it should have been!

The scriptural doctrine of baptism has intrigued and challenged the vast majority of preachers and Bible students within the Restoration movement since the days of Alexander Campbell and Barton Stone. No subject has been more important, perhaps because this understanding and the practice of baptism have separated Churches of Christ and the Christian Church from most other Protestant groups. So important was the subject of baptism that Campbell traveled to Washington, Kentucky, in October 1823 to debate W. L. McCalla, a Presbyterian, on the subject and, in 1836, he debated another prominent Presbyterian, N. L. Rice, on this and other subjects in Lexington (interestingly, the Campbell-Rice debate was moderated by Henry Clay, a highly regarded national political leader).

How many debates and arguments over baptism have been waged between preachers in the True Church and the "denominationalists?" God only knows. And God only knows how much mud-slinging and sarcasm have been leveled against those who dared to differ with our preachers on this important subject.

THREE CARDINAL POINTS ABOUT BAPTISM

Three cardinal points compose the true New Testament doctrine of baptism. First and most important, baptism is intended for believing adults and is absolutely essential for their salvation from sin. Mark's version of Jesus' great commission is the much to be preferred rendition: "Go ye into all the world and preach the gospel. He that believeth and is baptized shall be saved."

One is not a true disciple until he or she is baptized. As a college student I once traveled one summer evening with my lovely date Faye Creel, whose spirituality I vainly thought to be an acceptable match for my own, to Fairview, Tennessee, to hear the most respected African-American evangelist in our fellowship, Marshall Keeble.

Keeble, by then an octogenarian (b. 1878), was conducting another one of his many tent revivals. I had heard him and his young preacher students on numerous occasions as a boy, but this was my last time to hear him. In retrospect, seems a little strange now that I recall that hundreds were present that hot summer evening in 1962, perhaps almost a thousand, but I do not remember that any African-American listeners were in attendance; however, there may have been some black worshipers present and supporting Brother Keeble that I did not notice.

The venerable evangelist kept all us listeners under the big tent chuckling with his front porch interpretations and commentary, all of which were standard fare in Brother Keeble's Traveling Salvation Show. The subject of baptism elicited his greatest "wax of eloquence": "If you're trying to get salvation before you get baptism, you're trying to move too fast!" the noted evangelist exclaimed. "God's not in the dry cleaning operation. If you're trying to get saved before baptism, you're just trying to put God in the dry cleaning business!"

Second, baptism is intended for believing adults only. By adults, I do not necessarily mean adults by legal age such as eighteen years of age in the United States. Actually, many children have been baptized. I have seen some children so young and small in size that it appeared the church was closer to practicing infant baptism than adult believers' baptism. There are times in which some water should have been drained from the baptismal tank, usually referred to as a baptistery, because the young convert was nearly self-immersed when taking the last step into the baptistery.

The story is told of a clever fellow who hoped to embarrass the aforementioned Brother Keeble after his typically simple and understandable exegesis on the text from Mark 16: "Go ye into all the world and preach the gospel to every creature."

"Would you baptize a mule if it walked forward to where you were standing when you were singing the invitation song?" This fellow asked what he deemed a clever question. "After all, a mule is one of God's creatures."

The man's query might not have been so farfetched when one considers that many of Keeble's evangelistic efforts were outdoors in the South from mid-spring to mid-fall, and many listeners undoubtedly rode to services by horse or mule as did Keeble on many occasions himself.

"I certainly would," Keeble retorted immediately, "if that mule walked forward and openly repented of his sins and confessed his faith in Christ, then I would baptize that mule!" The man had no further questions.

Third, baptism must be done in the right way, namely by total immersion in water. Preachers who did not know their alpha from their omega when it came to the Greek language have often taken great pains to explain that the Greek word *baptizo* means to "immerse" or "bury."

Years ago I heard one of our preachers use a clever analogy. "Just suppose," he asked his already concurring audience, "that your pet dog died and your dad commanded you to go in the backyard and bury the dog. You get one shovel full of dirt and sprinkle it over the dead dog and then go tell your dad that you have obeyed his command," the preacher paused. "What do you think your dad would say when he goes to view your 'obedience' and sees a dead dog with a few clods of dirt sprinkled on it?" The preacher had made his point. Several smiled and nodded agreement. There's nothing quite as satisfying as a preacher using a light-hearted, over-simplified analogy to reaffirm what the listeners already believe from the "get-go."

PENTECOST, THE JAILER, AND THE EUNUCH

Baptism should be done immediately upon conviction of sin and faith in Jesus as God's Son and Savior.

No doubt the number one baptism narrative in the New Testament is the story of the Jewish people in Jerusalem on the Pentecost Day after the crucifixion. The story is told in Acts 2 of how listeners to Peter's address were "pricked in the heart" and desperate to know what immediate action should next be initiated. Such is the backdrop for the second most popular scripture in the True Church, second in import to John 3:16. That scripture is Acts 2:38, commanding repentance and baptism "for the remission of sins." On Pentecost there seemed no delay between apostolic command and listeners' eager compliance.

Perhaps the second favorite baptism narrative in the New Testament for gospel meetings is, quite arguably, the conversion experience of the Ethiopian eunuch narrated in some detail in chapter eight of the book of Acts. Some evangelists might opt for the story of the Philippian jailer narrated some eight chapters later. Like the story of the eunuch, the jailer is unnamed, but he winds up with his entire household being baptized. If the gospel meeting were long enough, there should be enough nights for a separate sermon on each character.

The jailer's story is not quite as popular on the meeting circuit for three reasons: It does not have a "confession" step for the convert; Paul's first response to the jailer was simply "Believe on the Lord Jesus" and, quite naturally, the Baptists have adopted that text; and the supernatural earthquake scared the living daylights out of the jailer, heavy-handedly influencing his decision to get on with his salvation experience, no doubt.

Back to the eunuch. The story involves international travel for one character (an anonymous political official on a special mission), hitchhiking for another (an actual apostle), cross-cultural preaching, intense soul winning, and, for the eunuch, an immediate and fortuitous discovery of adequate water that surely was knee deep if not waist deep.

I must confess that I was a freshman in college before I was educated by a fellow classmate as to what a eunuch actually was. Imagine my embarrassment over such woeful ignorance! I had heard the story all my life. Any reference to this emasculated convert in my own sermons for the next few years employed the expression "the Ethiopian nobleman."

Now this poor eunuch is every true evangelist's dream. The sermon's not even over when he spots a body of water deep enough for immersion. The newly enlightened eunuch interrupts the exposition of Scripture with an exclamation and a question: "See, here is water! What doth hinder me from being baptized?"—a question which has been quoted in fervent appeals and special pleas long after the sermon is over in the case of modern hearers. (Of course, modern hearers will not interrupt a sermon in that manner. Their only interruption would be simply walking out the nearest exit from the pew on their way to a scheduled secular activity.)

This was one lucky eunuch—if, in fact, a eunuch can be lucky! Had the eunuch not sighted the water in this dry, arid desert land, how would the story have been written? Imagine the eunuch saying: "Philip, I'll keep giving you a lift, but I've heard enough preaching for a while. I'm going to check my map for the nearest lake or river and see if my horses can stay fresh enough to get us there today."

A former professor of mine at Vanderbilt Divinity School, the late Herman Norton, was not as fortunate in desert baptisms as the first-century Philip and the eunuch. The professor told our class an interesting story. Serving as a chaplain stationed in North Africa during World War II, Norton taught and counseled a young soldier who wanted to be baptized. Norton, a kind gentleman devoted to the Stone-Campbell Restoration and Disciples' tradition (thus we can claim him), could not collect and spare enough drinking water for a full immersion. Of course, sprinkling with water would have been an option. But there was indeed a burial for remission of sins. Norton dug a shallow grave in the desert sand and then covered the soldier with sand before he quickly arose, presumably, "to walk in newness of life."

DIVERSE SETTINGS FOR IMMERSIONS

The settings for baptism in this country have been as diverse as the climate. Some of my most vivid recollections of boyhood religious experiences involve baptisms. I've witnessed baptisms in rivers, lakes, creeks, and ponds. Harold Thomas, long time missionary in New England, baptized a woman in the frigid winter outdoors when a layer of ice on a swimming pool had to be broken, a testimony to her desire for obedience. I have a picture of a woman being baptized in Russia wherein several inches of ice had to be chiseled away to reach the water. What amazing resolve!

Recalling from my boyhood, there were outdoor baptisms in rural Western Kentucky after an evening evangelistic service when cars circled our granddad's farm pond at water's edge and turned on the headlights to illuminate the scene—what a fascinating setting to stage a special Sears Diehard battery commercial! Yet in that setting, with friends and neighbors who were willing to delay their bedtime by another hour or so, and in the few moments when all that is heard is the gentle rippling of water and the croaking of frogs, a new child of God was born. In some cases, I have been informed, baptizees walked a few feet into the darkness to get behind a tree or a bush to change back into dry clothing before heading back to their homes.

Many rural churches built an outdoor baptistery with building blocks and steps on one or both ends. This was a progressive step away from the creeks and ponds. Despite the fact that the water temperature could not be controlled, the congregants were spared the journey to a natural water site. I recall baptisms in such an outdoor baptistery next to the Antioch church building, an old congregation founded *circa* 1820 and located between Murray and Mayfield, Kentucky. As an aside, this was the home church in the boyhood of my paternal grandparents, dad, two uncles, and other relatives. We returned to visit Antioch for a meeting every summer.

This accommodation of an outdoor baptistery was not without its objectors, even apart from the fact that "baptizing season" could only run from late spring through early fall. Some church members claimed that the act was only "scriptural" when performed in running water, as might be inferred as the exclusive practice among the first century Christians. To counter this objection, some ministers have offered to accommodate the demurrers by turning on the faucet and pulling the plug during the indoor baptismal ceremonies; this legalistic strategy was a little more challenging with outdoor baptisteries.

I have seen baptisms in bathtubs, in hospital whirlpool baths, and have performed baptisms in swimming pools with witnesses in swim suits. A considerable number of Pepperdine University students have been baptized in the Pacific Ocean.

A few years ago I witnessed some baptisms in a livestock watering trough, part of a Sunday morning service conducted in the ballroom of a Nashville hotel. The trough was aesthetically skirted with a short curtain. Manifestly, the eunuchian pattern of "they *both* went down into the water" could not be followed as there was insufficient space for two adults in the trough at once, but the sanctity of the act was honored, nonetheless. Afterward, the preacher offered a corny quip that he could borrow the trough "only for that Sunday with Mr. Ed's permission." That was a line he likely used after every trough baptism if there were guests and first-time visitors at the service.

Nowadays, almost every building in the fellowship of the Church of Christ has its own baptistery. Usually it is slightly elevated in the center of the building, directly behind the pulpit, enclosed by a curtain. Newer church buildings may place the baptistery to the side of the pulpit area. Older buildings may have a baptistery at the level of the pulpit platform with a glass wall on the front side, thus giving viewers a chance to see more of the actual immersion. God forbid that the glass should crack. The back wall of many of these older baptismal tanks is often adorned by some amateurish color mural with no artistic appeal, usually depicting a clear, unpolluted river or stream with some trees and flowers on the banks.

A FOUNTAIN AND A BAPTISTERY

One of the newest and most intriguing constructions on the campus of Lipscomb University is Osman Fountain, which includes Jones Baptistery, added to Bison Square at the center of campus. Bison Square is situated between the steps of the Collins-Alumni Auditorium and the wide, bricked walkway that leads to the modern student center. The names Osman and Jones honor families that contributed generous gifts that made these structures a reality. Ty and Nancy Osman offered their gift in memory of their 18-year-old son Ty, who died tragically in March 2012 while helping a woman who had been in an accident along an interstate highway.

This outdoor baptistery is indeed a structural beauty with such eye appeal and fascination to anyone walking in the heart of the campus. Water is easily heated when necessary so that baptisms can be performed anytime. Since its dedication in June 2013, there have been hundreds of baptisms in this structure, a large number of baptisms resulting from biblical teaching and inspiration of IMPACT, a spiritual formation camp that hosts thousands of teenagers each summer.

The purpose of the fountain is intended to serve as a constant reminder of God as the source of life and redemption. Certainly it will always be a place of deep sentiment and nostalgia for those who experience or witness the new birth process there. Such architectural beauty and central location announce to all who walk by this fountain and baptistery that Lipscomb is an "intentionally Christian" university and baptism by immersion is central to New Testament faith and practice.

"IF YOU'RE HERE TODAY …"

Here's the way a baptism usually works today: The preacher always closes his sermon by a ritual called "offering the invitation." (Technically, of course, only Jesus offers the invitation and the preacher simply passes it along; preaching, of course, usually does not deal with such technicalities.) This "invitation extension" is usually a fervent plea super-infused with some heavy emotion. The preacher closes his invitation with these words: "If you are here today and not a Christian, please come forward and give me your hand and God your heart and Christ your life. Won't you come, right now, while altogether we stand and sing?"

As an aside, the phrase "if you're here today …" always struck me as a rather curious expression. Should the preacher add a corollary: "…and if you're *not* here today, please disregard what I am going to say next"? Perhaps the phrase plays best when the entire service is broadcast over the local AM radio station which reaches shut-ins and nursing homes throughout an entire ten mile radius, a not uncommon small town phenomenon in the Bible belt region.

When the congregation is standing and singing, it is much easier for the "alien sinner" (a phrase I heard frequently in sermons but did understand at least until my junior high years) and wayward Christian to walk forward. One night after traveling to a revival service alone with my dad, I asked him what "alien sinner" meant as we drove home. I had heard him use the term so many times in sermons that I felt I needed to ask. Nowadays, some pre-teens hearing about "alien sinners" needing baptism might conjure images of immersing the malevolent "aliens" they see in science fiction or adventure movies.

When a person walks forward the sensitive preacher will walk the distance of two or three rows to greet the respondent with earnest countenance and extend a hand. Keep in mind that in most churches an actual response is pretty rare and the entire congregation may be surprised and fascinated when someone "walks forward;" some members will need to strain their necks a little to see who has actually come forward, especially if they need to silently speculate on why the person responded. Those who come forward are called "responses," although technically everyone present "responds" to the sermon one way or another. Those who walk forward are often labeled "visible responses."

The sinner is then ushered to the front row to take a seat and may be asked to fill out a card which solicits name, address, and reason for coming forward. I've never used the card system believing it impersonal and bureaucratic, but I must confess to occasional mental blocks and having to whisper during the last stanza to a nearby deacon: "What's that person's name who just came forward? I should know, but the name seems to have slipped my mind." Sometimes the nearby deacon does not know. Blessed indeed are the preachers who know in advance of someone's desire to publically "obey the gospel."

The preacher then delivers a little impromptu talk about the one who has responded to the invitation. He then asks the baptismal candidate to stand and confess faith in Christ as God's Son. Given the emotion of the moment, I have found it is better not to ask the respondent for his or her own formulation of faith but to ask for a simple yes or no. The confession is usually inaudible to most of the audience anyway.

The preacher then points the sinner toward the dressing room. Immediately, two or three people jump up from their pews to assist in preparation. The men's dressing room is on the right and the women's on the left (well, almost always). The candidate will then usually strip down and put on a white baptismal robe; a rubber cap is optional gear for the women. The congregation will usually sing some songs while waiting for the baptism ("Have Thine Own Way, Lord" is an excellent choice).

The preacher leads the way into the water, then turns and offers his hand. The hand-offering is a nice gesture; besides, the steps can be treacherously slick. When both are in the water the preacher whispers some last minute instructions to the baptizee, who by then may be traumatized over the prospect of placing his or her life into the hands of another person: "Just layer your hands together; hold this handkerchief; after I announce the reason for your baptism then take a deep breath and put the handkerchief over your mouth and nose; it'll be a piece of cake [or some other reassuring figure of speech]."

The preacher then signals for his assistant to pull open the velvet curtain.

He then shuts his eyes, quite possibly looking heavenward, and, for some in-explicable reason, raises his right hand high with an open palm, and projects a brief declaration that the imminent baptism is by Christ's authority and for the remission of this person's sins. He then braces the backside of the person while lowering him or her into the water until the person is totally immersed and then quickly brought to a standing position. The curtain is pulled immediately and the song leader springs to his feet and leads a song, usually "O Happy Day" or "Tis So Sweet To Trust in Jesus."

To recapitulate, baptism must be performed on the proper candidates ("adult" believers), for the scripturally correct reason (remission of con-fessed sins) and in the right way (total bodily immersion). As the minister for Brentwood's Owen Chapel, on the rarest of occasions we might have someone requesting baptism. Owen Chapel did not have a baptistery and in the earliest decades of the church's history (founded in 1859), baptisms were done in the nearby Little Harpeth River. In modern times we had access to the building and baptistery of the Concord Road congregation, less than two miles away from our little HOW.

In the men's dressing room that accessed the baptistery at the Concord Road building, there were two messages posted for the one doing the baptism. One of the signs gave a formula by which the one doing the baptizing could recite or read aloud: "Upon your confession of faith that Jesus is the Christ, the Son of God, I now baptize you in the name of the Father, Son, and Holy Spirit and for the remission of your sins." The lettering was large enough that the declaration could be read by baptizers with 20/20 vision while standing in the water. The other message stated: "To the one baptizing another person—be sure that you get all of the body submerged below the surface of the water."

I always wondered if some body part or some few inches of epidermis any-where on the body did not make it to heaven, then whether the explanation is that somehow this missing corporeal flesh did not get totally submerged during the act of obedience. I had one private baptismal experience where an observing minister-friend on our staff noticed that the sizable gentleman I was baptizing had a few centimeters of one elbow that did not get submerged; this witnessing friend soberly recommended a re-baptism. (Yes, I know the apostle Paul informed us the redeemed will all have new bodies, so a few centimeters of dry skin after immersion just might be a moot point.)

BAPTISMAL STORIES

"Age of accountability"—an expression heard in the sermons and teachings of most True Church evangelists and preachers. As a preschooler and then in early elementary school, I heard the phrase so often (along with other phrases that were foreign to my child-like understanding) that I had to ask my dad what it meant. I'm not sure I understood it when he first attempted to explain it. Gradually, I began to understand. If some youngster has not crossed that accountability line as yet, he or she is in safe spiritual territory. Presumably, telling little fibs to mom or dad or snitching a cookie from the cookie jar without mom's permission or hiding little sister Nan's favorite doll just to see her cry in frustration might not rise to the accountability threshold.

If a person has not reached "age of accountability," one is not a fit candidate for Scriptural baptism. Eventually the concept was explained to my understanding. Somewhere there is a line to be drawn at a point in life when one hasn't the faintest clue some thought or action is actually morally wrong, and then it suddenly dawns on the person that what he or she is thinking or doing is morally wrong and even hurtful to another. Once that line is crossed, and who can say when that point is reached, remission of sins is in order—that person should and must be baptized.

All baptized believers, most surely, have a baptism story. Each story is as unique as the individual. What people believe about baptism and what they expect to happen at baptism factor into their stories. As is true for other religious rites and ceremonies, both humorous and sad experiences can happen at baptisms. Over the years I have heard more than my share of baptismal stories, and while they contain several common elements, there is uniqueness in each one. I conclude this chapter by sharing a few personal baptismal stories and in the next chapter will pick up the theme with a few wild and crazy baptismal stories.

"In the Church of Christ, getting baptized is paramount," states Stacy Clayton. "It is the occasion that all parents long for their children." Stacy, along with her husband Daniel, has been a dear, loving Christian friend for almost thirty years. She is almost a walking/talking paradox with such a wild, zany wit and sense of humor, on the one hand, and a profound Christian commitment and deep sense of empathy and compassion for troubled and hurting people, on the other hand. Those wonderful traits led her to become a professional therapist and counselor with a special emphasis on women's issues.

"At a young age I began asking my father when I would know that I should be baptized," Stacy writes in an essay about her baptism. "He always said the Lord will speak to your heart and you will just know."

As an eleven-year-old, Stacy and her family lived in Germany where her dad was stationed while serving in the U. S. Air Force. Her parents were devout Christians, and their family attended a German-speaking mission church: the Frankfurt Church of Christ. One Sunday her parents, exhausted from a busy and hectic weekend, dropped Stacy and her sister Ellen off at the building for the morning service. "Well, who would have thought, lo and behold, the sermon was over and the singing began and I felt the call! This would be the day," Stacy narrates. "So I left my sister in our pew and walked down the aisle. It never occurred to me at that moment that my parents would care if they missed it. I felt moved to do the right thing."

Stacy's walking forward must have seemed out of synch with the set pattern of the order of worship. She told the preacher she wanted to be baptized, but his immediate response was to pat her on the head and then announce to the congregation that she did not understand the German language and had walked forward on the closing hymn and not the official "invitation song." The preacher then asked the congregation if anyone objected to her being baptized before the service was dismissed. "No one opposed," Stacy reports, "so I went to a dressing room and changed into the white gown and was immersed before a large congregation of Germans. I then went back behind the curtain and changed into my regular clothing."

When Stacy emerged from the dressing room she was expecting to be met by scores of church members who would be greeting, hugging, and congratulating her on her decision for baptism. Instead, she was greeted by the preacher who had a seriously somber countenance and a disturbing bit of information. "The preacher told me that one of the congregants had noticed that my right knee did not go under the water and therefore I would need to be baptized again," she reports. "At this point I began to panic as I knew my parents were waiting outside and church had already gone over the typical time by at least twenty minutes. I rushed behind the curtain and redressed in the white robe and bathing cap and proceeded to be immersed a second time, focusing on getting my knees down."

A full forty-five minutes had passed since the time the worship service would typically have concluded. Walking to the family car, Stacy's sister Ellen kept whispering, "Why did you do that? Mom and Dad are going to kill you." Immediately upon getting into the car, the new convert explained the delay to her tired, exhausted parents. They grew silent. No one uttered a word the entire way home and little was said the rest of the day.

"That night as I lay in bed, my father walked in and sat beside me. He began to cry and told me that I made him miss the moment he was looking forward to ever since I was born," Stacy recollects. "He told me he was very proud of me, but he and my mom were also broken-hearted."

As I learned of Stacy's story, I thought of similar stories where young teenagers, and even pre-adolescents, at summer church camps are emotionally swayed by a persuasive youth minister and/or peer pressure to get baptized before the encampment concludes. Sometimes parents are called to witness their children's baptism and sometimes they are not called. In the latter case, "hard feelings" have been engendered by hasty youth camp baptisms.

Stacy concludes her baptismal story on a paradoxical note: "So, collectively, I responded to the invitation on the wrong Sunday, I responded at the wrong time during the ending of that service, I failed to make certain my knees were immersed, was subsequently baptized a second time, and then I made my dad cry," she writes. "However, now I look back with some smiles and laughter but most of all with great joy. I have been blessed by great parents whom I have loved and they loved me. I was truly revived then and have been revived in different ways again and again!"

REMEMBERING MY OWN BAPTISM

How well I remember my own baptism. No July 15th passes but what I do not think about it as a special anniversary—the beginning of a new life. I am aware that most people cannot remember the exact date of their baptism—while baptism is so important, birth dates and anniversary dates seem far more important to remember if one values peace and harmony within the family.

I had heard my father preach the gospel many times and as I moved inexorably to adolescence and witnessed my peers' baptism, my guilt and shame welled up inside. Sure, I was guilty of those early adolescent indiscretions which emerge from the desire to experiment with adult privileges, from the need to be scornful of authority at home and at school, and from the onslaught of bodily change and thoughts ushered in by normal pubescence. I had played "hookie" from public school only once, slipping off to an afternoon movie ("Picnic," with Kim Novak and William Holden, a "sexy for its time" romance story), but my guilt precluded enjoying the pleasures even of contemplating Ms. Novak's ample charms and, hence, burdened with my guilt I returned to school with a special fabrication to cover my brief absence.

A double bind had enslaved me. I wanted and needed to walk forward, but I was too shy. When my family visited other churches for gospel meetings, there were times I was called on to take a role in the service, such as read the Scripture or serve Sunday evening communion (the latter an entry level public service position for new converts). How humiliating for me to hang my head and confess that I had never made the Great Confession and been buried with my Lord in baptism! Therefore, I did not technically qualify as one who could perform any role in the service, not even a non-speaking role such as passing plates or collecting attendance cards.

But the most embarrassing experience was replayed each Sunday morning as I sat in my pew with my teenage peers and passed communion to the next person without partaking. I kept my head low during the sermons about hell and the wrathful judgment to come. As the invitation was offered, I nervously pulled my song book from the rack and pretended to have trouble finding the announced number for an invitation song. Those were the moments I felt as though I was already in hell. I had a sigh of relief once the invitation song was completed. I had made it through another Sunday service.

Sometimes just a simple statement of advice and support can turn a life around. One day my mother casually encouraged me to be baptized. "Aren't the other young people your age [I was nearly fourteen] already Christians?" she asked non-threateningly and tender-heartedly. "Wouldn't you also want to go ahead and be baptized?" This brief conversation was an encouraging relief I had needed for months. I never talked to my dad about it ahead of time, but surely he must have been tipped off by my mom. "This coming Sunday will be my D-day," I determined. I needed now only to plan the details.

When that next Sunday, July 15, 1956, in Duncan, Oklahoma, rolled around, I had opted in my mind for a Sunday evening baptism. Here was my logic: If I went forward on Sunday morning I would have a much larger audience to witness my act and then on Sunday night I would be expected to stand up from my pew in front of everyone present and take communion along with the few others who, for one reason or another, had been "providentially hindered" from attending the morning service or, in a worst case scenario, had "forsaken the assembly, as the manner of some is." I would have been embarrassed by the attention given me by my standing to take "make up" communion.

That Sunday night when the congregation stood to sing the invitation hymn, "Only a Step" (number 62 in *Great Songs of the Church*), I was resolved not to move forward on the first stanza lest the church view me as one conscience-stricken and miserable sinner who could hardly wait until the end of the sermon (a la the Jews on Pentecost). Neither did I want to wait until the last stanza, lest my move be interpreted as flippant afterthought; then, too, the song leader could have prematurely ended the song before singing the last stanza (a truncation sometimes done on Sunday and Wednesday nights) and I'd be left holding the empty spiritual bag for another week and having to re-live all my stress and anxiety for another week.

I had thus calculated that the middle stanza was the right time to make my move. My head was spinning. I felt like I had climbed the ladder to the top of a high diving board and was peering at the long distance to the water and dreading the jump but could not turn and climb back down the ladder; all you can do is say to yourself "here goes" and you jump.

My dad was happy. I don't remember a word that he said to the gathering after I had walked forward and sat on the front pew. Upon the expected cue, I stood and made the "good confession." He kissed me on the cheek in the baptistery after the immersion. I was feeling warm, supported, and satisfied, too, as well-wishers of all ages came around to congratulate me. I was born again. I was saved. O happy day—when Jesus washed my sins away! I could now serve communion or perform other small assignments in the assembly.

Two of the most emotional moments of my life involve my baptizing a daughter and a son. Our older daughter Teresa was one of a group of young teenagers who had heard one of fire and brimstone evangelist Jimmy Allen's closing revival sermons at our home congregation. Too shy to walk forward, but too scared to go to bed and attempt to sleep, I baptized the entire group about midnight after returning to McMinnville from delivering Allen to the Nashville airport. These teens and their families had remained up late that Sunday night, sitting in pews at the building while awaiting my return and, of course, there was no cell phone to alert me they were awaiting my return or to how that Sunday would close. What a huge surprise for me!

Our son Prentice's twelfth birthday fell coincidentally on a Sunday. A few days in advance of the birthday, I walked up to his bedroom, sat down with him, and talked quietly and seriously about his baptism. I know he would have preferred to join the trend of private, family baptisms, but I encouraged him to make his obedience public on the possibility that someone else might be encouraged by this example. He respectfully accepted my recommendation.

My personal remarks to the Otter Creek Church on this occasion included this statement:

> Exactly twelve years ago on this morning, at about 2:00 A. M., Glenda and I experienced a special and momentous event—the birth of this boy sitting before you now. He is our own flesh and blood; he bears our name.
>
> Today, there is going to be another birthday. It will be a new birth. He will acknowledge another Father. He will begin to wear a new name. I continue to be his father, but now the two of us will be brothers.
>
> He had no choice about his immediate family. He has power of choice about his spiritual family. So there will be a new birthday and a new celebration, for we believe that those who are born twice need die only once.
>
> This baptism does not mean that a boy is turned into a man; that all traits of personality are changed; that this boy has or ever will have perfect faith; that he has been a bad boy or that some great moral change in behavior is needed (for he has been neither rebellious nor disobedient, but kind and sensitive always); that he knows all about life, its struggles, challenges, and temptations.
>
> What this baptism does mean is that there is adequate faith already for this decision; that a process has been at work in his heart and mind that leads him to this moment; that along with the word being planted in his heart, there has developed a sense of moral accountability and discretion as well as the belief that he is responsible for his own attitudes and actions and must assume the consequences; that this Jesus he has studied and sung about since he first recited "Jesus Loves Me" is not a fictional character, but that he is real, not only as a model to follow, but as our Savior; that this boy is starting

a journey of faith; and that, for whatever faults and shortcomings his mother and father have had, that we have done some things right (a credit we joyously share with his grandparents, teachers, and friends in this very church family).

To be a father means to have trials, struggles, and pains; yet, "a wise son maketh a glad father" (Proverbs 10:1). To see a precious son grow into likeness of a Christian father and even closer to the image of Jesus is life's greatest delight. I commend his example and now solicit his confession of faith in front of you, his extended family, as his witnesses.

O Happy Day!

10

"A Snake? Baptize Me?
The Hell You Say ..."

One of the most practical and interesting courses I ever took in college was intended for aspiring preachers. For two quarters the course was entitled "Preparation and Delivery of Sermons." The spring quarter the course was called "Practical Aspects of Preaching."

The class was taught by Batsell Barrett Baxter, perhaps the best known and most respected preacher of the Church of Christ at that time. Baxter was a kind and humble man, unpretentious in all his ways. You felt as though you were in the presence of a truly godly man whenever you were around him. He possessed the potential for enormous influence in the True Church, but, being very conservative culturally and politically, he steered a mostly moderate and non-committal course on nearly all controversial issues.

Because he was so widely experienced in preaching, his advice was valued by the "preacher boys." Brother Baxter, as most students called him, taught us the differences among textual, expository, and topical sermons and instructed us so wisely on the importance of *ethos* (character persuasion). He also taught us about practical ministerial matters: how to plan a gospel meeting; how to conduct funerals; where to stand at the gravesite; how to plan for a wedding; how to offer the invitation (walking slowly two or three steps up an aisle and deploying that earnest facial expression with slightly tilted head as the invitation song is sung) so that sinners are more likely to walk forward; and how to relate to females in the congregation.

One highly important subject was omitted from the homiletics syllabus, however. There was no specific instruction on how to conduct an immersion in a dignified, fail safe manner. Perhaps Brother Baxter simply assumed each of us had witnessed enough baptisms that we student preachers could just pull off the act intuitively. Or that in our youth we had practiced baptism on our playmates while "playing church." As a preschooler, I inadvertently drowned some neighbor's kittens in our home bathtub while overzealously practicing the coveted technique of biblical immersion.

Given its importance in the scheme of salvation, as well as the symbolic beauty of an old life of sin buried and a new creature being born, one would think novice preachers should be given a special course or be required to pass a special test, much like the required road test for driver's licensing, before licensing a preacher to practice immersion.

While teaching at Lipscomb in the 70s, I proposed a "baptizing contest" to be conducted once each year in the college chapel; occasionally I would discuss my proposal among a few Lipscomb Bible and preaching majors. They all seemed to enjoy hearing my ideas.

My proposal: Contest finalists would baptize ten different body types of varying difficulty (including, of course, one tall male [in 6'6" to 6'10" range], one large, obese person, one pre-adolescent child, one physically-disadvantaged person) in the makeshift baptistery that was built below the stage when Alumni Auditorium was first constructed.* Judges would rank the contestants using a system much like Olympic judges rate gymnastic, skating, and synchronized swimming events. The judges would hold up a card after each contestant's round on a scale of 1.0 to 10.0. In case of a first round tie for first place, then a "baptize-off" would be conducted by lowering the water level eighteen inches and the same subjects would be re-immersed before the judges, presumably veterans of the revival circuit.

Some people found my proposal humorous and others found it to be patently absurd and utterly ridiculous. One or two felt it bordered on being sacrilegious. No one took it seriously. However, at the time of my proposal, Lipscomb College sponsored an annual song leading contest (near co-founder James Harding's birthday) and an annual oratory/preaching contest (near the other co-founder David Lipscomb's birthday) and one of the categories for competition in the intramural forensics contest was Bible-reading.** Lipscomb offered an entire course in Bible reading, more formally known as "Oral Interpretation of the Bible."

Surely, then, a baptizing contest is equally justifiable as would be a preaching contest, song leading contest, and Bible reading contest. Since the baptismal tank (or whatever body of water is used) is like an enemy harbor filled with explosive mines just waiting to be set off, figuratively speaking, any strategy that enables a minister to avoid a literal baptismal *faux pas* and adds dignity and grace to this beautiful symbolic act deserves consideration.

There is no way of knowing for certain who has been the most prolific baptizer in the Church of Christ. Most likely no one has come close to the number of people baptized by African-American evangelist Marshall Keeble. Keeble's total number of baptisms over his career, it is claimed, reached 40,000. Yet, like other preachers, I've enjoyed considerable experience in baptisms and feel qualified to pass along some practical advice to young preachers.

This same advice may be useful to the fathers who may be considering baptizing their own willing children. Preachers "come and go" and some "fall from grace." If the father is willing to assume the role of spiritual leader in his family, then it is highly appropriate for him to baptize children and other relatives and thus strengthen the family through shared memories. Honestly, in more recent years, I have encouraged both the mom and the dad to get into the baptistery and share the responsibility of baptizing each of their children who wants to be baptized—after all, they co-operated in bringing the first birth of each of their children and thus why not share the experience of facilitating their new birth?

GUIDELINES FOR NOVICE BAPTIZERS

Some principles and guidelines for all novice baptizers to consider:

1. Make certain that you have an adequate amount of water and that the water is kept at the right temperature. Three feet of water which is kept at the

68 to 75 degree range will meet my minimal recommendation. The higher the water level then the less strength and skill are prerequisite for the baptizer.

A few years ago, I led an elderly woman into a baptistery during the winter at a Sunday morning service. The water was quite cold, even to my mind. Before the baptism, I sent word to her dressing room that she might choose to delay until another day, but she was not to be dissuaded. She impulsively began quivering and cringing just by placing her leg on the first step in the water. Once standing in the baptistery she began quivering like crazy. When I immersed her and brought her up out of the water, the quiet solemnity of the occasion was pierced by her loud shriek. Then it took several seconds for her to draw her next breath. For a split second or so I seriously felt we might need to summon a physician or nurse. She continued to shiver and loudly holler "Brrrrrrr" as her head shook and her lips quivered. The congregation of some four hundred sat in stone silence. This was a new birth. Assuming she was a mother, her first birth at delivery time could not have been more traumatic than her own "new birth."

How vividly I recall the second Easter Sunday of my full time preaching career! Our church building in Warren, Michigan, was filled with over two hundred worshipers, some twenty or thirty above our average attendance. After a more or less stirring sermon on the resurrection we stood on cue to sing the invitation song. Immediately a woman I had never seen before started marching down the aisle from a back pew to the front. I didn't know her from Adam, or Eve, in this case. Rather attractive in the face, this young woman appeared to be almost six feet tall. She had one of those bee-hive hairstyles with an Easter bonnet topping off a stiffened concoction of coal-black hair wound around the top of her head. The most concerning dimension was my perception that this plus-size respondent might have easily weighed between 225 and 250 pounds, perhaps even more.

As this woman sashayed down the uncarpeted, linoleum center aisle of the church building in high spike heels, sounding rhythmically something like a Tennessee Walking horse whose steps were easily heard over the discordant notes of the congregational singing, I immediately prayed a silent but intense and sincere prayer: "O Lord," I thought in half exclamation and half petition, "please let this woman be a restoration!" (A "restoration" requires only the preacher's impromptu declaration of some encouraging remarks about the sinful nature even of stalwart Christians, a commendation to the erring child of God for walking forward and confessing wrongdoing, and is followed by ministerial prayer for forgiveness.) Appropriately I extended my hand and immediately she proudly declared: "I came to be baptized." So much for an easy restoration! I next motioned for her to take a seat on the front pew and I scrambled to get her name, writing it on a card. I then announced her decision to the assembled saints, just wondering if any of our worshipers knew her identity.

After communion and before the contribution, a nice time for the preacher to make his exit to the dressing room (which at Warren also doubled as my personal office), I donned my baptismal suit and opened the door to the baptistery. Lo and behold, much to my surprise and chagrin, there were only a few inches of water. I surmised that had the woman laid flat on the bottom of the tank there would not have been sufficient water to cover her body. A less anxious preacher would have postponed the baptism until the afternoon, but, no, I sent word to the song leader to start singing several hymns and I immediately got the wrench and used it to turn on the big faucet. Fresh water was gushing into the tank. With curtain already pulled and closed tightly, I strolled across to the women's side and shouted instructions for the baptismal candidate to take her time getting changed: "No hurry here. It'll be a few minutes before we're ready."

After seemingly fifteen to twenty minutes and realizing some of our members might well be considering slipping out to enjoy their Easter dinners, there appeared to be enough water to give it my best shot. Besides, I risked the whole church walking out on me. Most churchgoers don't like to be late for Sunday dinner, "preferring the pot roast over the Holy Ghost," as I heard it expressed once by Carroll Ellis in one of his corny rhymes. I tightened the faucet to stop the flow of water, my attendant sent word to the song director that the singing could cease, and I summoned the woman into the tank while the curtain was still closed.

Knowing there was no way that anyone short of an Olympic weight lifter could gracefully swing this soaking wet sinner-turned-Christian convert to a vertical position, I asked her to sit down on the floor of the tank and allow me to lower her back from a sitting position. Insensitively, perhaps, I suggested our procedure would be very much like her doing a sit-up. She seemed both sweet and understanding.

With the woman sitting on the floor of the baptistery, I then signaled to my attendant that the curtain should be pulled open. I then raised my right hand and stated my memorized declaration about the purpose of baptism, then lowered her gently into the chilly water. Once I got her face under the water, I did a quick body check. Either a portion of her stomach was above the water or an air pocket had formed under the waist of her robe. Taking my left hand from her submerged face, perhaps out of some legalistic fear that some part of her body would not make it to heaven, I rapidly slapped that part of her anatomy under a rising water level. It was the tightest burial I have ever conducted. As I later reflected on my reflex action, I had to admit that I did not know if a part of her stomach was above the water line or some small air pocket had elevated her robe.

What a memorable Easter Sunday! Naturally I had to explain privately to inquirers why there had been a long delay although some had heard the sound of a non-mighty rushing water. I asked several friends what the baptism looked like from the vantage point of their pew. Everyone told me that all he or she witnessed of the baptism was a stack of black hair that was lowered into the water and brought back up in a state of wet collapse. I hoped that the rest of this new convert's Easter Sunday was good. I felt certain she was a very sweet and sincere person, and I knew even then as a beginning, full-time minister there must never be tolerated any unkind comments or hints of body-shaming of any kind. However supportive and accepting that Easter Sunday we all attempted to be, this woman did not become active in our fellowship.

2. Treat each baptismal candidate as a special, unique physical and psychological challenge to your baptismal skill.

As for the physical part, well, quite frankly, you need to know how to pull it off without botching the ceremony so bad that it must be repeated. The main principle: Just as marriage therapists inform us that the physical size of a husband and wife has no bearing on their sexual compatibility, the differences in physical size (weight and height) between baptizer and baptizee have no bearing on the efficiency of the baptismal experience. Water, and enough of it, is the grand neutralizer for weight differentials. Training in technique will take care of the height differences. It's a piece of manna!

A rule of thumb: The taller the baptismal candidate, then the further the baptizer should establish position laterally in the direction he is laying the person into the water. The easiest baptisms, of course, are pre-teenagers who have taken swimming lessons at the Y and are totally unafraid of water.

The rule is a simple one but, according to Jim Bill McInteer, was forgotten by a youthful Charles Brewer. Jim Bill reported that, in his early days of preaching, Brewer won a response for baptism. The congregation went to the creek at night to see Brewer baptize a man into Christ. But the two found it necessary to keep walking up the creek bed to find water deep enough for a burial. The already-redeemed who were present as witnesses understandingly trod their way up the banks parallel with the two men in the water with only a lantern to light the way.

Finally, enough water was found in a little pool. The stage was set. Brewer raised his hand, recited his declaration, and began lowering the man. The man, already frightened by the prospect of a late night drowning in near total darkness, dug his heels deep enough into mud to push his body back in resistance. Brewer seemed stuck in mud, kept trying to hold on, and the man kept back pedaling at a fast pace until he was out of sight.

Exasperatingly, and embarrassingly, Brewer called out softly to the man, beckoning him to return and try again: "Hey, come back. We can get this done tonight." No answer. Brewer then walked toward the saints on the shore and announced his need: "Could I borrow a lantern from you? I've lost the man I'm trying to baptize."

The Brewer baptismal experience, or non-baptismal experience as it turned out, also points to the need for the preacher to realize the psychological as well as the physical dimension of baptism. How many of us feel totally comfortable voluntarily placing an immobilized body in the hands of another person pushing us into an oxygen-free environment? Of all my baptisms (again, I hold no world record on number of baptisms), I can only remember very few candidates that were, pardon the pun, totally laid back and relaxed about the watery grave.

The point is clear: Baptizers, do your best to allay the fear of those you lead to the water and exude confidence that you can pull off the ceremony without a drop of water getting in the lungs. Let's be honest and concede that despite your best efforts, some people will remain fearful, as illustrated by a personal story related by Carroll Ellis:

> Back in the '50s every community had two-week meetings. In a lot of those meetings we had two services, one in the morning to go along with one at night. I was holding a meeting down at Hill's Chapel, near Nolensville [Tennessee]. This building at Hill's Chapel had no baptistery. At one of the services a young man, somewhere in his 20s, came forward to be baptized. That afternoon we went into Grandview Heights in Nashville to hold the baptizing. There were about ten or fifteen present for the occasion.
>
> Now this man was rather tall. Of course, I'm not tall. I'm about 5'6", maybe not quite that tall. I have always had a special way of baptizing folks so that I don't have any trouble. I have the candidate take hold of my right arm with both hands. Then its easy to pull them up out of the water.
>
> I could tell this man was frightened. He must have thought to himself, "That little fellow is going to drown me." As I was putting him down in the water he let go of my arm and grabbed my head. I tried to immerse him but it was easy to see that I didn't get him all the way under.
>
> I said to him, "I'm sorry, but baptism is a burial, and we didn't do it, so we've got to try this again." So I lowered him into the water and once again he let go of my arm and grabbed my head. Then, without any further instruction to this man, I just took a deep breath,

grabbed him, and we both went under as deep as I could go. I got just as wet as he did. We got the job done.

Jerry Tallman, for years the loved and respected minister for the Rochester, Michigan, church, experienced his own new birth traumatically. Every time he freely recounts it to friends and church gatherings, the story evokes great laughter. Once again, the context is one of fear and seemingly physical mismatch in the baptismal tank.

As an older, and quite large adolescent, Tallman was led into the baptistery by a minister much smaller in size. As he was lowered into the water, young Tallman grabbed the preacher in a valiant effort to keep his head above the water. The preacher, already water wrestling in trying to subdue the panic-stricken teenager, then hollered at the attendant on the sideline: "Hurry, pull the curtain!" The preacher was thinking he could gain the upper hand in the fight without having a live audience to cheer him on, calm Tallman, give more instructions, and try again.

When the attendant pulled the curtain, Tallman grabbed it reflexively as if to find something stable to get himself under control. Under Tallman's weight and mighty tug the curtain came tumbling down, covering both men. Panic then turned to noisy desperation as both men fought and thrashed about in the waters of baptism like two demented water buffalo, ingloriously splashing water in all directions. America's funniest home videos could not have topped this scene. Bottom line: Tallman got immersed and became a preacher.

These stories lead us to a third principle related to the other recommendations.

3. Do not rush the baptism. Handle the pre- and post-baptismal periods carefully and thoughtfully.

Most preachers have a memorized declaration to make in the baptistery right before the immersion. The declaration is usually made by raising the right hand, even though no preacher seems to know the reason for raising that hand. After several baptisms, the declaration is generally "set in concrete" and may be recited verbatim for the rest of the preacher's life. Young preachers pick it up from older preachers. How easily one can become so relaxed during this ceremony that he says literally anything liturgical that may have been already memorized.

Jim Bill McInteer told me of an incident involving Howard Horton, long-time preacher and interim Bible department chair at Lipscomb, who, in the water with his baptizee raised his hand and thoughtlessly uttered: "Our Father which art in heaven. Hallowed by thy name …" After some laughter, Horton said: "Well, I can see this place is really jumping today."

As for the amount of time for the baptism itself, an impressive baptism will fall into the five to ten second range from the lowering stage to the raising stage. Please avoid the extremes here. You are not trying to impress the audience with how long you can hold a person under the water.

Lou Pfeiffer once told the story of his first baptism. Seems the candidate for baptism was a cattle rancher who wanted to be baptized in his cattle farm pond. The two had to wade out some distance to get into water deep enough for baptism. Pfeiffer neglected to stand back the recommended step, put the rancher under the water, then found himself stuck in mud and unable to leverage the burly convert out of the water. The rancher was under the water for some twenty seconds and started blowing bubbles. He finally got the man up, leaving him puffing and wheezing.***

On the other hand, don't try to be the human dunking machine for the *Guinness Book of Records* by baptizing with lightning speed no matter how many baptisms you have lined up. Sure, I've often wondered how fast the apostles were baptizing those three thousand people on the day of Pentecost and where they actually did the baptizing. How long did all that immersing take, especially allowing two or three minutes for each one? Did they have to finish the last several hundred baptisms under torch or moonlight?

I'd like to think those Pentecost baptisms weren't quite like those done by a Nashvillian named Jack Rankin. Rankin was in our entourage of summer missionaries to Great Britain in June and July 1963, and he seemed to pride himself on the vast number of conversions, veritable stars in his crown, he could gather. Unlike Paul at Corinth, Jack did his own baptizing rather than delegating to others.

Unfortunately, however, Rankin was to baptizing skill and dignity what mud wrestling is to the fine arts. In rapid fire speed he would sling his subjects under the water and bring them up with the same lightning speed. No one had time to be scared. I recall a few times at Aylesbury, England, that after a Rankin baptism there seemed as much water on the pulpit floor as remained in the baptistery. Thankfully, a bucket and mop were available.

As for speed in baptisms that I have witnessed, no one could baptize more people faster than Jimmy Swaggert. Yes, I know Swaggert is Pentecostal, thus not in the True Church, but my witnessing his personal style bears mentioning. On a trip to the Holy Land in Y2K guided by good friend and wonderful preacher and writer Philip Morrison, we stopped one day at the Jordan River. Apparently, getting baptized, or maybe in most cases getting re-baptized, in the Jordan River is quite a tourist experience. Those in our group who were uncomfortable calling their experience a "re-baptism" opted to use the phrase "re-enacting my baptism." Either way, quite a few Christian tourists wanted to get immersed in the same river in which Jesus was baptized. Guessing that proprietors who ran the gift shop and renting baptismal robes, towels, and dressing rooms did, indeed, reap some profit year round.

Along this stretch of the Jordan River there are several small outdoor arenas with small theater seating and a concreted walkway and railing that go down into the river. The people awaiting baptism at Swaggert's little arena were lined up; I am thinking there could have been up to two hundred people in the line. Swaggert impressed me as an automated baptizing machine—he so rapidly raised his hands, made a quick declaration, then plunged the person under the water, and brought him or her up from the water all in a matter of two or three seconds. Assisting ministers led each candidate to Swaggert and then led each one away from Swaggert so the next candidate could step up and be plunged into the Jordan. Pictures and videos could be made of personal baptisms by a celebrity revivalist. A lot of hands were raised and spontaneous shouts of "praise the Lord" were exclaimed and heard by all.

A few minutes later, Swaggert took a break and he and I met on the river bank and enjoyed a brief conversation. I informed him of my research and writing on the "electronic church" (in which I had featured Swaggert and other televangelists), but otherwise that did not seem to impress him and there was nothing particularly profound exchanged between us.

4. Demonstrate always a high measure of aesthetics and sensitivity.

Perhaps the most sensitive matter on this subject involves a preacher's baptism of mature members of the opposite sex. A female candidate will usually wear a white robe, occasionally without sufficient foundation garments. Just stepping into warm water can produce air pockets which float the garment; a good garment will have lead weights in the bottom seams. After the baptism, the preacher must guide each new babe in Christ up a treacherous stairway to the next awaiting hand, and he must learn to avert his eyes as much as possible away from a female who, in any other situation, would be embarrassed to display the true form of her God-given physical endowments.

Since the preacher takes off only his shoes and steps into what is hopefully a water tight wading suit (I'd look for a warranty which guarantees the suit for fifteen years or 1500 baptisms, whichever comes first), he may enjoy impressing the majority of his audience by reappearing so quickly from the changing room and in time to make some closing exhortation or announcement before the service is concluded. Some in the audience may wonder if the preacher has something akin to an Indy 500 or NASCAR pit crew to help him change clothes; the new Christian convert appears half hour later with wet hair and pleasant smiles. The baptized female typically takes a little longer than the male baptizee to emerge from the dressing room. Sometimes communion has been brought to the newborn babe in Christ before that person even leaves the dressing room or turns off the hair dryer. Such moments would be unforgettable.

Some preachers have developed a practice of standing in the baptistery after the baptism(s) and making some closing remarks. That, of course, is a nice change of pace. Careful here. A number of years ago a Baptist preacher in Louisiana baptized a person, turned to the audience to make some appropriate remarks, grabbed a microphone to amplify his voice and electrocuted himself; this tragic event was reported in the national wire services.

5. Finally, always remember that the presence of a baptistery can present certain hazards and temptations.

The hazards are much greater in older church buildings where the water tank is level with the pulpit. According to McInteer, Granville Taylor witnessed a man fall in a baptistery during public prayer. The man, who had a part in the service and was standing on the pulpit for the prayer, must have lost his balance. Taylor, doing a little peeping during the prayer, saw the man at the baptistery precipice with arms extended and waving them furiously trying in vain to catch his balance.

Horace Busby and S. H. Hall, two early twentieth century gospel preachers, are among the ones with the "distinct honor" of having fallen into baptisteries while hyperactively delivering sermons. Such accidental immersions were likely rare but highly entertaining. There are rumors of others who have experienced the same fate, a phenomenon that I call SISIS—Sudden, Involuntary, Self-Immersion Syndrome.

Who knows what private uses baptisteries have been subjected to over the years? A friend, Dan Smith, knew a member of a small Tennessee church who had acquired some tropical fish and needed a place to keep them for a few days until he could buy his own sizable tank. There had been no baptisms at this church in many months and the man felt free to turn them loose in the baptistery while making preparation to keep them in his home. Lo and behold, the one Sunday that the fish were being kept in the baptistery a person walked forward requesting baptism.

Remember that everybody wants to see a baptism. No one I know ever drifted off to sleep during one. Children and youth are especially fascinated by an old fashioned immersion. People have often moved to another pew to get a better view of a baptism. Night baptisms in church buildings have been enhanced by the turning off of all lights except the one over the baptistery.

When considered within the entire sweep of Christendom history, one must remember, the baptismal tank—first made of concrete blocks or metal and now made of molded fiberglass—is a rather modern invention. For at least nineteen centuries the majority of baptisms occurred outdoors in natural bodies of water, settings in which almost anything could go wrong. (True, several hundred years ago in the European Catholic tradition, some larger parishes built special baptistery buildings with the tank in the center and a large seating capacity surrounding the tank. The most impressive baptistery I have seen, mounted on colorful statues of bulls, with marble and ivory all around, is in the Nashville [in Franklin] Mormon Temple.)

G. C. Brewer, who told the following story about himself in Lipscomb chapel as remembered and shared by Carroll Ellis, once presided over an instance of *baptismus interruptus*. Brewer was baptizing people outdoors in a river when a man rode up on his horse, dismounted, and hitched his horse near the stream. The man announced that he was seeking baptism. He was then instructed to wade out to meet Brewer and thus commenced his move to immersion.

As the man got near the preacher, Brewer spotted a water moccasin gliding across the water surface near the man. "I never thought of a man being afraid of a snake, but I didn't want to immerse him and bring him out of the water with a water moccasin across his face," Brewer told his audience. "If you'll hold right still for a few seconds, there is a snake near you and it will move on out of our space in just a moment or two and then I'll baptize you," Brewer reassuringly announced to the man.

"A snake? Baptize me? The hell you say!" the panic-stricken man instantly shouted. He turned immediately toward the shore, scurried out of the water, ran to his horse, unhitched and mounted it, and rode off in his wet clothes without further word. "And I haven't seen him since," Brewer concluded his story. Not only did Brother Brewer not see this man again, but it is unlikely this chapel audience at Lipscomb ever heard a preacher again use a profanity—even if quoted from another source—in a chapel speech.

NOTHING TO HIDE AT BAPTISM

Perhaps the most widely known story of a disastrous *faux pas* during a Church of Christ baptism involves one person understandably seeking a better view of a baptism. There are slightly varying versions of the story. This version was pieced together after my conversations with Nashville veteran preachers McInteer and Ellis, already cited in this chapter.****

A well-known Texas preacher named Horace Busby traveled to the little Texas town of Ozonia to hold a meeting. The brethren there had rented a public hall for the meeting. They had put out chairs, put up a pulpit, and arranged for a portable baptistery to be installed front and center. Make-shift dressing rooms were also provided by roping off some space around the baptistery and suspending a curtain for privacy.

One night Brother Busby preached a powerful sermon. Several people, men and women, responded for baptism. Baptismal garments had to be shared as they were in short supply.

A relative of one of the women who had walked forward to be baptized had gone to the dressing room to assist in the preparation. This woman, the relative, was rather large. When it came time for her kin to be immersed, the woman decided she should witness the event. Rather than leave the dressing area and join the audience, she sought some elevation from a folding chair or other prop and braced herself by holding onto the wire which suspended the curtain.

As the baptism process began, the woman, standing on her tiptoes and holding the wire, leaned forward a bit too much in seeking a better view. Losing her balance, she started falling forward and, in attempting to stop her fall, gave a heavy tug on the cord. The cord snapped and she fell with the curtain on top of Brother Busby and her relative in the baptismal tank. The hefty Christian relative panicked and thrashed about in the tank for space and oxygen, thinking she was about to drown.

Seems that on the other side of the tank, the makeshift underpinning of the curtains for the dressing rooms also collapsed under the weight of the falling woman. More than just a man's sins were precipitously exposed that night. A man who was in the process of changing all his clothing was standing there naked as the proverbial jay bird before the whole church. Without a room to run toward or a barrior behind which to hide, he quickly grasped for any garment or towel to cover the privacy of his manhood.

The congregation did its best to keep emotions and attention under control for the remainder of the service. None had ever seen anything like this before. The local preacher called on a brother to lead the closing prayer—a brother who was always grave and serious about everything and always under control. He started his prayer: "Our Father in Heaven, ha, ha, ha, ho, ho, ho …." and struggled throughout the prayer with even more irrepressible laughter.

After the services that evening the leaders of the small community church came up to Brother Busby and confessed with regret, "We're going to have to close the meeting as of right now. This whole fiasco was just too embarrassing. We're going to be the talk of the whole town."

"No way we'll close the meeting," Busby replied. "This is the best advertisement this small church will ever get." The next night the crowd at church was even larger. The meeting continued with success.

Each year for several years Brother Busby was invited to Ozonia for a repeat gospel meeting. Nothing like this event ever happened again. The church loved Brother Busby. Each year Busby was given some kind of sheep skin gift as Ozonia was a community in the heart of sheep-raising country.

"IT'S NOT EVERY DAY SOMEONE COMES ALONG AND SAVES YOUR SOUL"

One of my own memorable baptisms was conducted in McMinnville, Tennessee, for a younger friend named Jim Woodard. Jim was a congenial and affable young man in his mid-twenties who had been raised as Methodist. We shared many interests. He was a part of a group of young men with whom I would play basketball and tennis. Together, Jim and I had long conversations about life in general and religion specifically. After thought and study, Jim concluded that scriptural baptism was an immersion and he told me he would like to be immersed soon on a Sunday morning.

Not wanting Jim's baptism to look like the typically rushed job at the end of a service which would delay everyone's Sunday dinner, I planned his baptism for early in the service after several songs. I had listed his name in the printed Sunday worship guide. The baptism went smoothly. Later I preached the morning message and announced I was willing to return to the baptistery for any other person seeking baptism (all the while silently doubting anyone else would come forward).

Jim was so happy. He gave me my first copy of a New Testament in the New International Version. I have used it in the pulpit frequently ever since he gave it to me.

I have saved and cherished the brief message that he included in this New Testament. It closes with words he wrote in all sincerity: "Perry, you have already become a very special friend to me. After all, it's not every day that someone comes along and saves your soul."

We Christians have long taught that baptism is the second birth that inaugurates a new beginning in life. All services and occasions of baptism, no matter where they occur or how artistically they are conducted, should conclude with such heartwarming, ineffable joy.

END NOTES

*The Granny White congregation once assembled and worshiped in the Lipscomb Alumni Auditorium and their baptisms were conducted in this baptistery in the back part of the stage before the construction in the mid-50s of a commodious and modern church building that was actually on Granny White Pike. The congregation always aimed to attract Lipscomb college students to its services, though for many students it was a "back up" place to attend when time was short or transportation not available to another meeting place. The church was often dubbed by students as "Chumley's Chapel," in "honor" of the long-tenured, melodious and soft-voiced gentleman preacher, Charles Chumley. As noted in chapter 4, the congregation has now changed its name to incorporate "Green Hills" into the name. In the last two generations, Green Hills has become an upscale Nashville neighborhood.

**How intriguing to think of contests that measure skill in various acts of assembly worship! Admittedly, a baptismal contest is totally facetious and satirical. So also might be the "communion passing contest" as designed and revised by two witty Srygley brothers, Bill and Fletcher, along with other cohorts of theirs. Because of the difficulty in measuring skill in communion passing, mainly due to so many variables such as density of worshipers on a pew or some pews involving young moms with babes in arms, I decided not to report on the Srygley communion passing contest in this book. How could judging criteria be determined? Might some pew occupant deliberately speed up or stall the passage of a tray in order to influence the outcome of the contest? However, the idea of a prayer-leading contest seemed both clever and appropriate. Read on:

In my files of pleasurable reading that I have maintained over the decades, I have an old, mimeographed copy of the *Bald Bison*, an underground paper of religious satire. The bison has long been mascot of David Lipscomb University. The "bald Bison" might be a not-so-veiled reference to President Athens Clay Pullias. This document was produced in the late '60s. The reference to "ansem" in this piece might be a reference to Anselm Mount, a religion reporter for *Playboy* magazine at the time and who, in the late 60s, was known for debating the *Playboy* philosophy with Bill Banowsky, another Lipscomb graduate whose career path took him to distinguished pulpits and university presidencies at Pepperdine and Oklahoma University.

No one knows for certain the authorship of the *Bald Bison*. Conventional wisdom holds that it was written and circulated largely by Philip Roseberry, a young man of intelligence and deep spiritual commitment but also a person of great wit and satire, while he was a student at Lipscomb. Philip was keenly interested in social justice and improving race relations, and he emphasized the importance of personal relationships.

After college graduation, Philip left the comforts of middle-class life in the South and became a director of one of the full-time inner-cities ministries by Shiloh Inc., a special ministry for inner-city youth in the New York City area. On June 26, 1975, Philip Roseberry, while escorting a group of females in the program to their apartment in an especially dangerous area of East New York, was senselessly and tragically murdered.

The following is taken directly from the underground paper. It explains the prayer leading contest in some detail:

THIS STARTS THE bald bison's RELIGIOUS SECTION. ansem [sic] WAS NOT AVAILABLE, BUT WE DID THE BEST WE COULD.

Already, lusty voices have begun to train themselves for the song leaders' contest. This contest certainly presents an excellent opportunity for various young men to demonstrate their ability in leading us in praise. Whoever does the best in this aspect of worship receives a reward. This is all fine and good. However, a very interesting question presents itself. If we have a contest for song leading, why not for other aspects of worship? For example, why not have a prayer-leaders contest?

If this seems irreverent, may we suggest that there is little difference between communicating with God with your head up, eyes open, and singing and with your head down, eyes closed, and speaking. This idea is so intriguing that we present a plan to implement the idea.

First of all, the contestant would submit a written prayer to a judging panel. The prayer would consist of an arrangement of selections from the following list:

1) We come before thy throne of grace.

2) We thank thee for this day and all its many blessings.

3) Help us to avoid the sin that doth so easily beset us.

4) Thank thee for our many blessings, both spiritual and temporal.

5) Thank thee for this opportunity to worship you in spirit and in truth.

6) Thank you for this land where we can worship without fear of molestation.

7) Help the rulers of our land that they may rule wisely.

8) Be with the sick and afflicted wherever they may be, especially those in the household of faith.

9) Bless the one who is to speak to us, may he have a ready recollection of that which he desires to say, and may we, as eternity-bound creatures, listen intently to that which is said.

10) Guide, guard, and direct our every move.

11) We pray for those whom it is our duty to pray for.

12) Be with us now as we go to our respective places of abode.

13) In the name of your Son and our Savior.

14) If we've been found faithful, give us a home in heaven with thee.

In order to facilitate composition and judging, all the contestants have to do is write the numbers with conjunctions that are appropriate. For example, one might choose: 1 and 2 and 7; or 2 and 8, Moreover 11; etc.

The judges, men who have used and organized those prayers *ad infinitum*, will select the three finest efforts. These authors will then have the opportunity to present their prayers to chapel. They will be judged on content, presentation, usage of "thee", "thou", "hath", etc., instead of common English, and several other vital facts. An applause meter could be used.

An appropriate reward will, of course, be given. However, several other positive goods will be derived from this exhibition. First, it will encourage our young men to pray beautiful, articulate prayers, according to the pattern. Moreover, it will preserve several archaic phrases which otherwise might totally drop out of the language. I mean, how many times have you turned to your friend and said, "I'm going to my respective place of abode"? Ten? Twenty? Well, perhaps you've got the point.

If this contest is a success (and how can it fail?), we can envision a chain of contests. How about a Lord's Supper contest with the social club seeing how fast they pass out the emblems? Or an announcement contest? Or a baptismal contest (with off-campus Presbyterian judges)? And many more!

We have only begun to tap the vast area of worship contests. Why stop with song leaders? Amen.

***Story is told in Gary Holloway's interesting and entertaining book, *Saints, Demons, and Asses: Southern Preacher Anecdotes* (Bloomington: Indiana University Press, 1989), p. 55. The book is a scholarly study and Gary compares written and oral anecdotes about Southern preachers.

****This story is also told by Gary Holloway, *ibid*.

11

"Sing On, Ye Joyful Pilgrims"

It's only seven or eight minutes before the scheduled time to begin the Sunday morning worship service. The congregation's regular song leader, Brother Sangster, is sitting on a front pew to the side of the auditorium, frantically flipping through the pages of the hymnal. Every few seconds he spots a song which catches his eye. "Humm … we haven't done that one in a while," he mutters to himself as he writes that number down on the backside of a used envelope. The preacher joins him on the pew two or three minutes later.

"Got any songs you want me to lead today?" Brother Sangster asks the preacher. "Nope. You jus' pick 'em. Better not throw me any curve balls, though," Brother Preachitt replies. Both song director and preacher know the congregation may not be greatly in the mood to sing and they certainly know by name the ones who will sing out heartily and those who either seem to mumble the lyrics or keep lips pursed and not even pretend to participate. The better singers know they may be tapped to sing voluntarily in a small group for a funeral or a wedding within the church family.

Brother Sangster knows the authorized order for that Sunday and every Sunday—he's followed it for decades, as did his father, also the church's song leader, before him. He picks three songs. He looks around for some man to call on who is willing to lead a prayer, then jots his name in the proper slot on the envelope. (At this church, Brother Sangster has mentally divided every adult male into one of three categories: those who will lead a prayer at any time, those who will lead a prayer if given advance notice, and those who won't lead any public prayer under any circumstance.) He has also picked a communion song ("'Break Thou the Bread of Life' will be just fine," he says to himself, oblivious to the fact this hymn is not about the communion) and an invitation song.

"Number 429. [Pause. He takes out a pitch pipe and softly blows the first note] That's four-two-nine. [Pause again]. Let's all sing," he exhorts the congregation as he begins leading that first song. The congregation sits and sings half-heartedly through the first three songs, and they stand for the first, second, and last stanzas of the song before Brother Preachitt's lesson. Most congregants do not need the hymnal—after all, they have sung most of these hymns all their lives.

Brother Sangster may sing a little off-key but no one seems to notice as they are quite accustomed to hearing his voice each Sunday; he does wave his right arm and beat out the time of the song but no one pays any attention to his arm movements. Any connection between a lyric in one of the hymns and a point in the day's lesson is purely coincidental. "Mark number 622, that's six-two-two, as our song of invitation." (Most will "mark" that hymn by turning to the assigned hymn, pulling the eight inch ribbon down in the middle of the opening, then closing the book, possibly keeping in the lap to prop up elbow and upper arm on which to rest a chin.)

At sermon's end, three stanzas of number 622 are sung. And with one stanza of a closing hymn, thus enabling Brother Preachitt to make his way to the front door to greet the exiting saints, especially those who offer a compliment on the day's sermon, Brother Sangster's responsibility has been fulfilled until that evening.

TAKING CHURCH MUSIC SERIOUSLY

Contrary to what outsiders may think, members of the Church of Christ take their music seriously (at least in some sense of the word). They know full well that the Scriptures command Christians to "sing and make melody in your heart" and that the purpose of singing is to "teach and admonish one another with psalms, hymns, and spiritual songs."

Church music must be performed according to the Scriptural pattern--*a cappella* music only. Perhaps no trait of the True Church is better known to outsiders than its unyielding, steadfast insistence on vocal music only. The doctrine is still maintained rigorously, at least among conservative and mainstream congregations. Some church members will even refuse to visit services of other denominations because of the use of instrumentation; or, they may visit but refuse to sing along with the instrument lest they worship falsely and offend God.

HISTORICAL PARTING OF ECCLEISIASTICAL WATERS

This staunch stand for exclusively non-instrumental music is truly the crown jewel in the Church of Christ doctrinal headpiece. That crown jewel is revered, respected, and polished to perfection on almost any homiletical occasion—regular sermons, lectureships, periodical publications, Bible classes. Perhaps because the experience of church music is such a visceral experience, it has become the most important and most sensitive issue dividing the Church of Christ from the Christian Church and the Disciples of Christ. The issue led to a division within the Stone-Campbell Restoration movement in 1906.

Since that historic parting of the ecclesiastical waters, non-instrumental Christians could maintain different points of view on a wide range of subjects, including whether Christians have the moral right to take up arms in military combat, and still remain in fellowship with one another. Once, however, some Christians brought an organ or piano into the meeting place, that congregations had fallen into "digression" or apostasy.

The Westwood church I served for six years constructed a church building and classroom wing on several acres of land donated by the Boyd family. Several brothers in the Boyd family prospered from their nursery business and the entire family was kind and generous. Correct doctrine was important to them. In the deed to the property there was a stipulation that if instrumental music was ever used in a worship assembly that the property would revert to Boyd family ownership again. This type of provisional deed making *a capella* congregational singing the chief standard of authentic Christian doctrine is not at all unusual.

In November 2019 the *Tennessean* announced that, seventy-five years after the death of Robert Wickliffe Comer, the wealthy Nashville businessman had made *a cappella* singing Churches of Christ the beneficiaries of a $35 million trust. "Not incorporating instrumental music in their worship services would be deemed 'loyal to the Church of Christ,'" the Chancery court ruled. (*Tennessean*, Nov. 2, 2019, p. 1). Indeed, adherence to "sound doctrine" has its reward.

SHUNNING THE INSTRUMENT/EMBRACING THE LEGALISM

The measures to which some members of the Church of Christ have gone to find peace on this issue would seem astounding to many. To cite just one example: One evening a number of years ago, I received a call from a mother whose voice of desperation seemed near the panic point. Her daughter was scheduled to be married in a large church wedding the next evening. She was calling me from the church building where the wedding rehearsal was in progress and both families and the full wedding party were in consternation. Seems that their family minister, a Church of Christ preacher, had not realized until that evening that an organ would be used in the ceremony. His scruples would not allow him to perform the ceremony with an organ playing in the church house and the family would not relent in their choice of music. The local preacher stalked out of the rehearsal and the frantic MOTB (Mother of the Bride) called me and apologetically, and tearfully, asked for my assistance as a substitute officiant. I immediately and gladly obliged and forever won this family's respect and best wishes.

Some wedding parties have gotten around the dilemma of "to play or not to play" by striking compromises which provide instrumentation but keep the accursed instrument out of sight. The most typical "end around reverse," to borrow football jargon, has been to play recorded music. This might be a suitable alternative for weddings if churches had elaborate sound systems. All too frequently in the old days, however, I have witnessed a home stereo unit brought to the building with a microphone stuck in front of it and a scratchy, old record placed on the turntable and operated by a young usher who must aim the needle for the right groove. On other occasions, pianos have been played for weddings "off stage" in some room adjacent to the auditorium or chapel.

One nomination for the Legalism Hall of Fame was submitted by a friend, former preacher, and now retired psychology professor emeritus at Western Kentucky University, Sam McFarland. Sam reports on proceedings for a wedding at a rural Church of Christ near Woodbury, Tennessee, for which he was officiant. The bride and groom were both alumni of Freed-Hardeman College. For the processional and recessional and other musical selections, a piano had been placed on a flatbed truck which had been backed next to a window of the building. The window was opened and the pianist mounted the truck bed and played the traditional music during the ceremony—all the while the instrument was never in the building nor did it technically even touch the building. Indeed, there was innovative adherence to sound doctrine.

EXPLAINING THE UNEXPLAINABLE/SCRUTINIZING THE INSCRUTABLE

A challenge I had as a teenager and young man was explaining to my "denominational friends" the Scriptural logic for our insistence on "singing only" and why we rejected "mechanical instruments of music." (Only in the True Church have I heard the expression "mechanical instruments of music," and the phrase must be an ancient one simply suggesting an instrument humanly made and having moving parts such as strings, bows, valves, and keys.) The basis for such a practice is rooted in the Campbellian formula of speaking where the Bible speaks and being silent where the Bible is silent. Applying such a formula, Christian actor and friend Chip Arnold points out, is intended to "explain the unexplainable."

Here's the hermeneutical principle: There is certainly no command to use an instrument in worship. Thus a strict, clearly stated prohibition against instruments is not necessary. The silence of the Scriptures is honored only when Christians do not take the liberty to implement some practice not mentioned on any page of the Holy Writ. To blend instrumental music with vocal music would be summarily condemned by the same God who struck down Nadab and Abihu for offering "strange fire" on the altar, even though who on earth knows what "strange fire" was?

True Church preachers have needed the assistance of Noah and his ark to advance a clear and irrefutable case against the use of instruments in worship. A cartoon published in *Mission Journal* years ago, as remembered by Richard Hughes, depicted Noah and his ark and the text read: "God told Noah to build the ark out of gopher wood. He did not say to build it out of maple. He did not say to build it out of oak. He did not say to build it out of hickory. And that is why we do not use instrumental music in worship."

For today's younger generation—a generation that attended youth retreats where Christian rock bands performed Christian music and a generation not emotionally committed to old traditions—the old arguments against instrumental music simply no longer "hold water."

Actually, some older Christians in this tradition join the younger generation in contending that the New Testament contains no set pattern or blueprint for public worship assemblies, either in worship forms or styles; that commands for singing were not intended as divine prescriptions for public worship but applied to a Christian's personal life; that the lack of references to instrumental music is based on cultural incidentals, not divine commands; that whatever aids people in bringing genuine praise and adoration to God cannot be reasonably condemned; that we should praise God with all our gifts, talents, and means; that our God is great and grand and not small and petty.

"THE BEST SINGING THIS SIDE OF HEAVEN"

The quality of a song service in the Church of Christ varies widely. There are at least three variables to be considered: (1) the congregation's abilities and attitudes toward church music; (2) the ability and training of the song leader; and (3) the value of the hymns selected.

Some congregations are filled with talented singers who sing out joyfully and enthusiastically, most of whom may be on key. In many congregations, the singing drones on without much purpose or energy and seems only to serve as that mandatory prelude to the sermon, itself often as boring and hapless as the singing.

Most preachers have visited a church they consider to have "the best singing this side of heaven." Which church, lectureship, rally, or encampment has the best singing will always be debated. There are hundreds, perhaps thousands, who will contend that the annual all-night singings conducted twice annually at tiny Diana, Tennessee, literally in south central Tennessee pasture land near the Alabama border (about sixty-five miles south of Nashville), constitute the most heavenly *a capella* efforts "this side of heaven."

DIANA SINGING

The Diana event is the brainchild of respected evangelist Tom Holland, and over the decades since its founding in 1969 has evolved into a veritable Church of Christ Woodstock event. Tom spent his life in preaching (especially holding meetings), teaching, and writing, having a long tenure at Freed Hardeman College (now a University), and his endorsement and leadership of an area-wide singing insured its success. In 1969 the event began in the Diana church building but soon outgrew its small seating capacity. Organizers bought property and built an outdoor pavilion for the event, eventually expanded to accommodate three thousand of God's singers.

Christian women and men travel from many counties in Tennessee, Kentucky, and Alabama, as well as from all over the United States, in cars, vans, trucks, and campers for the privilege of "catching up on news," meeting new people, and cooking out. When I have visited Diana, my nostrils easily sensed the aroma of country ham sizzling on the grill. God's singers were very much at home meeting each other again, swapping stories, and touring a miniature museum which features old song books. The highlight of the weekend, however, is singing for as late into the night as God's singers choose to sing.

Scores of area song leaders sign up and wait their turn for the privilege of leading their favorite hymn under the big shed. Some leaders will select a hymn they know cannot be led easily in their home congregation, but they choose it as a personal favorite. The *Tennessean* called the event a "gospel sing-along," but also noted its reputation had been sullied after a Confederate flag was displayed at the event's fiftieth anniversary celebration and posted in the Diana Singing Facebook group by an attendee (*USA Today* Network—Tennessee, July 21, 2019).

An undeniably sweet fellowship and loving spirit permeate the Diana singings. What a warm feeling—devoted Christians, most middle-aged and older, demonstrating love and respect for each other and lifting their voices in *a cappella* praise! There is also a preference for the hymns of the 30s, 40s, and 50s, especially ones with simple lyrics expressed with long soprano and bass parts. Stamps-Baxter lyrics and arrangements are standard fare, kind of the "fast food" of American hymnody—fast food being known for its speed and tastiness, not necessarily for nutritional value!

Those old hymns sung with such joy and happiness can bring tears of nostalgia and memory to the faces of many. As for expressing sheer joy, it's hard to beat the hand-clapping (though seldom heard at Diana), and foot-patting (often seen but seldom heard on soft soil under the big tent) rendition of "I'll Fly Away." You won't hear too many contemporary and modern hymns sung under the big tent, nor are there many requests for "O Sacred Head," "Breath of Heaven," or Handel's version of "I Know That My Redeemer Lives," but the joy is irrepressible. One will often hear, on the other hand, "Our God, He is Alive!"—the "national anthem" of the True Church.

ALLENSVILLE SINGING

Another continuing tradition is the annual area-wide singing in Allensville, Kentucky, held the first Sunday in June. The tradition was begun by Robert G. Neil in 1969; Bob was preaching for this congregation at that time. As an accomplished singer, he invited folk who shared his love of singing such as Phil Cullum, Bud Morris, Paul Brown, and Jim Jackson—most of whom enjoyed some connection with church music at DLC—to participate in leading the hymns and encouraging congregations to support the event.

Allensville is little more than the proverbial "wide spot in the road" just across the Tennessee state border above Clarksville. On this Sunday each year there are song directors and Christians who love singing all kinds of hymns who travel from several states to the Church of Christ building to sing for ninety minutes. The wood-frame church house is an old-fashioned in design, but acoustics remain ideal for *a cappella* singing. The auditorium, which I estimate holds 250 or more, is always packed tightly and there is typically an overflow into an open annex foyer. Folding chairs are opened for seating on the pulpit platform though only males will sit there. The "amen-corner" to the right has two or three pews that are usually occupied by the men who expect to lead at least one hymn.

This annual Allensville event seemed to grow larger each year with numerous participant song leaders from area churches in both Nashville and Clarksville. And though there could be 150 or more guests, the local brothers and sisters will cater a big barbecue dinner for everyone before the singing begins. While the smoked barbecue is catered, side dishes and abundant homemade cakes and pies provide more culinary temptation than many of the good brothers and sisters could bear. Dessert lovers often rush to grab and zealously guard their favorite pieces of cake and pie even before sitting down to begin the outdoor feast.

If the hymn is published in the "old blue" hymnal, *Great Songs of the Church* (with the appendix of approximately fifty or so additional hymns), that hymn was subject to being selected. With two or three outstanding soprano voices emanating from the very front pew every year (young single women who had driven down each year from Indiana), without exception "O Lord, Our Lord" (number 562) and the Hallelujah Chorus (number 548) were selected at one point or another. Literally any male of any age could lead a song at the Allensville singing. All one needed to do was stand behind the pulpit, announce a number, pause a few seconds, lift a hand, and then drop the hand, and the congregation sang in forceful unison.

Among the singing traditions that developed at the Allensville singing, Mack Craig would lead his dramatic rendition of "Just As I Am," a hymn that he would always introduce by declaring Paul Brown had pledged to lead in the same dramatic style at the Dean's funeral. For the concluding number Robert Neil would stand on a pew in the middle of the assembly and lead "How Great Thou Art." Paul Brown and son, Larry, both accomplished song directors, were always present to lead a hymn or two, as were accomplished choral directors such as Lester McNatt and James Jackson.

EXCELLENT SINGING AT LOCAL CHURCHES

In the 70s and 80s, the Crossroads church in Gainesville, Florida, had a reputation for great singing. This church had experienced phenomenal growth under the teaching leadership of Chuck Lucas. During this time Lucas became a highly controversial preacher for advocacy of "discipling" strategies and teachings regarding "total commitment" of new converts. So much of the explosive growth at Crossroads came from University of Florida students. Their participation in enthusiastic and expressive singing was the force driving their worship in song. Thus one year on a Florida vacation I took our family to a service there to hear both the congregational singing and the preaching of Chuck Lucas. The Crossroads singing was spirited and moving, to be sure.

The Otter Creek Church in Nashville was, and remains, the best singing congregation I've ever had the privilege of serving as pulpit minister. The church is composed of many fine singers, a few of which have sung professionally in musical drama, musical comedy, and even European opera houses. At least a dozen or so highly competent song directors have been members at Otter Creek. Literally anyone, any male that is, could lead a song there if given the opportunity. Just as with the Allensville singing, all one had to do was stand before the gathered saints, announce a selection, extend an arm with open hand and then drop it to signal a beginning.

For many years Otter Creek's song director was Henry O. Arnold, known affectionately as "Bud" or "Buddy" by his friends (he had no enemies). During two different tenures Buddy had been both a professor in music and the drama director at David Lipscomb College; he also led singing in daily chapel; he was also music critic for the *Nashville Banner* and always found something positive to commend in every performance he reviewed.

Buddy enjoyed leading selections with a classical music score, always integrated selections with the theme of the service or the sermon. He assiduously avoided the Stamps-Baxter genre of hymns which he considered to fall within the campfire genre of non-sophisticated "fun-songs." What an honor and a joyous privilege to work with Buddy! He was more than simply a gifted "song director"—he was truly a worship minister in every sense of the title. Most of all, he was truly one of the kindest, most loving and humble Christian gentlemen I have ever known.

In time we Otter Creekers all knew Buddy's favorite hymns. He maintained a fondness for Moravian hymns, his favorite being "Hallelujah, Praise the Lord." We knew also that when a special guest speaker was scheduled to present the lesson and a large audience with many visitors was present that Buddy was a surefire bet to lead the "Hallelujah Chorus." Otter Creek could sing through Handel's majestic hymn quite impressively with neither instrument nor hymnal. Buddy liked to nonchalantly announce "Number 548" as though he were announcing some simple hymn such as "Trust and Obey," and he would never make any preliminary comment such as "This is an audacious challenge" or "I think we can do this classic selection if we all join in." Buddy did not need to prompt the congregation to stand as we all rose spontaneously and immediately.

The "Hallelujah Chorus" would typically be the last hymn before the guest speaker began his lesson. One Sunday evening the guest speaker was William Teague, president of Abilene Christian University. I remember the opening statement of President Teague's address: "Well, this is impressive. I've known several churches to begin singing the 'Hallelujah Chorus,' but this is the first one I've known to complete it."

Actually, there are a number of churches with outstanding singing and there seems to be no correlation between the size of the congregation and the quality of the singing. Some large congregations have sounded as anemic and melodic as wounded buffalo on the prairie during a draught season. Conversely and encouragingly, some small gatherings have been able to sing with such quality, spirit, and enthusiasm that no one could fail to "catch the spirit."

Acoustics play a far greater role in quality of singing than most church members are aware. Even the most harmonious of vocal offerings can be greatly absorbed in padded pews, fully carpeted floors, and acoustic tile ceilings. An official diagnosis of all singing factors was often offered to individual churches by Ralph Casey.

THE "MUSIC DOCTOR"

In 1970 Ralph Casey initiated a career of traveling from his Atlanta home to congregations around the country to conduct weekend "Singing Emphasis" workshops. Throughout this career, Ralph conducted nearly over one thousand of these workshops in the United States and a few others before English-speaking audiences in the Orient. In the workshops these churches were given lessons on reading music; the males, including the very young and the very old, were drafted for special training and private tutoring; a final diagnosis, prescription, and initial treatment were then given by the "M. D.—Music Doctor." This "M. D." would tell the "patient" congregation that every church is as different as every individual patient's fingerprint and individual prescriptions are necessary.

In Ralph's training sessions, the males were taught how to beat musical time patterns such as "plink, plink, plink," "plink and scoop," and "slap and scoop." I found that keeping all the plinks and scoops in the right order to be a formidable but entertaining challenge, and the levity I brought to Ralph's academy did not prevent me from "graduating" on the last evening of the workshop. Ralph remembered the time that one student song director, a grown man, started weeping while attempting to lead a song; the next evening at graduation the man blamed the trainer publicly for his failure by declaring "Brother Casey embarrassed me!"

On another occasion, Ralph was conducting a workshop in Louisiana and "tutoring a big lumberjack of a fellow trying to follow directions." This fellow had a young son sitting on the front pew. The young son jumped up from the pew and charged at Ralph, put his hands in a defiant posture, shouted "I don't think that's funny," and threatened kick him in the knee caps. Who would have thought instruction in song directing to be a hazardous profession?

There is as much variety in song leading skills as there is in preaching skill. Some Church of Christ worship ministers, but not many, have been skilled in both pulpit arts. L. O. Sanderson could preach with power and simplicity, but the legacy of this fine man will be etched for generations in the hymns he composed under both his own name and the pen name Vana Raye. Paul Epps could perform well in either music or spoken word as did Ralph Casey.

Paul Brown, an excellent teacher, maintained a reputation as one of the most loved song directors in this fellowship. Paul led singing for nearly four hundred meetings and many more special occasions such as funerals, weddings, and lectureship programs. For my weekly contribution (sounds nicer than "for my money"), Mack Wayne Craig was the most gifted at both singing and preaching. Many are the occasions in rural congregations when ministers have been summoned both to lead singing and preach in the same service. There are a few occasions in which I have done both, perhaps at LBC (Ladies Bible class) or when no male in attendance was willing.

GETTING THE RIGHT PITCH

Getting the right pitch on a song is the first major hoop a song director must jump through. This is particularly challenging in a tradition where no piano or other instrument is allowed—the one exception being a pitch pipe or tuning fork which may be blown or struck scripturally on the first note only. As an aside, one of my close Bible-major friends in college, Ron Powell, I deemed to be "soft" on the issue of instrumental music at the time. In visiting with Ron one evening in Lipscomb's Elam Hall, Ron asked, "We use a pitch pipe to make a musical sound to get assistance on the *first* note of the song. What's wrong with using an instrument to gain assistance with the pitch on *every* note of the song?" "Whoa," I thought at the time. "Ron is doctrinally weak on this issue. I fear he will backslide from the faith." Then as I reflected further, I realized Ron offered a thoughtful question.

The first requirement is that the leader knows where his pitch pipe is located. Buddy Arnold remembered a day of Lipscomb chapel programming that was being taped for broadcast to radio stations on a national network. While Willard Collins read Scripture, Buddy gave the pitch to the students except on the day he put his instrument in his hip pocket and spent the remainder of the chapel session gently patting every other pocket in an effort to locate it.

A pitch pipe that remains stored in a suit pocket may need to be tested prior to the service. A song leader directing for a congregation near Columbia, Tennessee, brought inadvertent laughter to his audience when it was apparent that some lint had lodged in the instrument. He nearly brought down the house when he kept trying to blow the note and then apologized with a firm voice: "Sorry, folks, I'm having trouble getting started because I have something jammed into my A-hole."

Actually, the congregants can always spot an inexperienced or diffident song director by the length of delay in starting a song. The monologue of the diffident song leader typically proceeds thusly:

"Take a song book and turn to number five-thirty-one" (Pause)

"The Lord's my Shepherd.' That's based on the Twenty-third Psalm." (More pausing)

"That's five-three-one." (Pause again as he intones the pitch)

"We'll sing the first, second, and last verses." (Still more pausing)

In time, of course, the song begins. Note a musical rule of thumb: If the hymn has four stanzas, there's a 90% odds that the third stanza will be omitted even if the omission truncates the thematic scheme of the hymn—such an established True Church tradition!

Obviously, launching a song on the wrong pitch is a fairly common phenomenon that embarrasses some leaders but is seldom noticed by others. Pepperdine Bible Professor "Big Don" Williams was guest speaker on an occasion when the Church of Christ song leader encountered a typical problem. The leader announced and then pitched much too high the beginning of the majestic hymn "Holy, Holy, Holy." This song leader, like many others mired in the same musical *faux paus*, was willing to abort the song at the end of the first line, but unfortunately he ran together words of the hymnist and his own exclamation with great volume. His rising inflection made it seem he was taking the Lord's name in vain: "Holy, holy, holy, Lord God Almighty I've got this song pitched too high!"

Dress and grooming issues for the song leader may not be as important as musical concerns. In rural areas, leaders rarely wear a coat during the hot summer months.

Hoy Ledbetter was once teamed with a song leader in an Arkansas church who was not aware of how a failure to zip up his trousers impacted on the congregation's ability to sing. Seems that a good portion of the leader's shirt tail was protruding through the unzipped opening as he stood to begin the song service. The leader always stood to the side of the podium or on the main floor where his entire body could be seen.

After announcing and beginning the first selection, half the congregation tried to sing while the other half tried unsuccessfully to suppress their chuckling. Thinking the song was pitched improperly, the leader stopped the song and announced: "I think I must have this pitched too high." Twice he pitched the song again and after the second re-start his efforts were greeted with even more laughter. He then slammed his hymnal shut and exclaimed to the church: "What's the matter? Can't you grab hold of it today?" The laughter nearly ended the entire service.

HARROWING EXPERIENCES FOR A MUSICAL MURPHY'S LAW

In addition to getting the right pitch, the song director knows that any one or several of the proverbial one hundred and one things that could go wrong just might go wrong. Song leading is, as Dennis Crawford put it once, "an emotional minefield" and "humiliation looking for some place to happen." Little wonder that the role of song leader is one that most fellows shun and few seek.

In addition to improper pitching of a hymn, numerous additional harrowing experiences may be faced by the song leader. We will state ten common errors only briefly:

1. Selecting a song which no one knows. (The leader may then abort the effort or proceed to sing a solo which, alas, is something that would have been considered unscriptural and unacceptable had it been an intentional solo.)

2. Soliciting requests from the audience and receiving one that you do not know how to lead. (Mack Craig, who often led from memory, once admitted to me he would simply say, "I don't believe this group knows that number well enough to sing it now. We'll sing it another time.")

3. Soliciting requests and receiving one you are not willing to lead. (Paul Brown once asked for requests and a young boy who likely had just seen "Song of the South" shouted out "Zippety Do Dah;" when Paul paused to think of a response, the boy shouted, "You do know it, don't you?" I was doing both singing and teaching in a Franklin, Tennessee, nursing home and I always began by asking for song requests. Once a woman blurted out, "Would you lead 'the Chattanooga Choo Choo?' I really like that song." My reply: "I really like that song, too, but think we'll just save that one for another time.")

4. Losing your place in a song. That's when humming comes in handy and with proper facial expressions you can make it appear the humming is intentional.

5. Unintentionally singing one stanza twice.

6. Trying to lead a song that you thought you remembered.

7. Singing the wrong melody on a lyrical text that has two melodies.

8. Having a congregation that won't follow a lead. Most worshipers will simply sing a song exactly as they have learned it and sung it for decades. In most churches the beating of time and waving of the arm are perfectly useless motions except for the aerobic exercise it provides for the leader. It can be fun to imagine what some arm motions seen without sound might remind us of, such as patting an animal pet, hammering roofing tiles, or milking a cow.

9. Giving special instructions for singing a certain hymn (such as, "Let's sing all three stanzas of 'Low in the Grave He Lay' before we sing the refrain") that most don't hear or follow. Or perhaps failing to give instructions such as

allowing the church to stay seated while leading "Stand Up, Stand Up for Jesus" or "Standing on the Promises."

10. A loud interruption of a song, such as a baby falling out of a pew or a fire truck passing with its siren screaming.

Song leaders deserve our highest respect for daring to make their way through those mine fields. Most song leaders, at least for smaller congregations, are not paid for their services.

Song selection always hinges on a number of factors, not the least of which is the size of the leader's repertoire and the randomness of his flipping through the pages of his hymnal on any given Sunday. A little known fact is that many song services have been totally planned by the leader's wife. The weather and biochemistry of a song leader on a given Sunday may influence selections. I once heard Otis Henry begin a song service at Fourth Avenue church in Franklin, Tennessee, by saying: "We've had a lot of clouds and frost here lately, so let's sing 'Heavenly Sunlight.'"

Harold N. Roney, my respected friend and the song leader at the Westwood church, practiced his own unique system of song selection. His typical approach was to sing through the song book one hymn at a time, thus our printed worship program would read number 688, number 689, number 690, prayer, number 691, sermon, number 692, and closing hymn number 693. Any conceivable connection between the lyrics of a song and the theme of my sermon was purely and remarkably coincidental. Harold's real force was derived in large part from his wife Judith who coached him instrumentally before the service and lovingly critiqued him afterward.

"RISE UP, O MEN OF GOD" AND "O, WHY NOT TONIGHT?"

Sometimes the selection and timing of certain hymns has been particularly unseemly. Two incidents involving Harold come to mind. One Sunday evening while preaching a series through the Sermon on the Mount, I presented a lesson entitled "Sex and the Christian." I also deployed 1 Corinthians 7 as a text to contend that in Christian marriages the body of the husband belonged to his wife and the wife's body belonged to the husband. "So, then, sex may be considered a responsibility, perhaps even an obligation, in Christian marriage," I concluded and then closed the lesson, asking everyone to stand and sing. Lo and behold, Harold then led "O Why Not Tonight?"

In the same series, upon reaching Matthew 6 and Jesus' comments on personal piety, I presented a lesson on "Fasting and the Christian." As we stood to sing, Harold then led "All things are ready, come to the feast." To be honest, I really doubted that many worshipers recognized the coincidence. Yet I knew for certain that Harold had chosen those invitation hymns for his own devious sense of irony and humor.

Hoy Ledbetter informed me that on several occasions his song leader would lead the congregation in the hymn "Ready to Suffer" right before he entered the pulpit to deliver the Sunday morning service. The same leader would occasionally and thoughtlessly lead "O Why Not Tonight?" on Sunday morning. Obviously, nobody was being rushed to respond.

The combination of preaching on sex and selecting hymns is a tricky challenge at best. One Sunday evening at Otter Creek, Tommy Daniel spoke on Christian sexuality. In his closing point he touched on the topic of sexual dysfunction and made reference to male impotence. When the congregation stood to sing the announced number Buddy Arnold led one of his favorite hymns, "Rise Up, O Men of God."

No one should argue that Divine Providence influenced hymn selection and sermon content or events and sounds outside the HOW, but then again who knows? One Sunday when Buddy was leading the hymn "Revive Us Again," as remembered by daughter Nan, the congregation came around to the lyric "May each soul be rekindled with fire from above." At the very moment that lyric was being sung a fire truck came barreling down Granny White Pike with the loud blare of siren that almost drowned out the singing. "Dad smiled about it as it happened," Nan recalls, "and he was confident to enjoy the moment and not let it distress him."

HYMNODY AND IMAGERY

Sometimes lyrics of a song conjure interesting images in the minds of worshipers. A friend, Ed Gleaves, called my attention to the rich possibilities for gleefulness as the second stanza of "It Is Well With My Soul" begins—"My sin, O the bliss of the glorious thought. My sin, not in part but the whole …" Ed's wife, Janey, once asked if I had ever said "'You-hoo' to Jesus," a misreading of the first stanza of George Keith's hymn "How Firm a Foundation" ("…You who unto Jesus for refuge have fled?"); the same hymn contains "I, I am thy God," suggesting a naval salute. "Spirit pants" and "bosom fly" can be found in classic hymns. Judith Roney, a marriage counselor, discovered a secret to sexual bliss among marriage partners as the second stanza of "Blessed Assurance" begins—"Perfect submission, perfect delight!"

A cynic might contend, with much evidence, that most Churches of Christ are wary of new hymns and prefer that the majority of their hymns meet three standards—time, triteness, and triviality. I will contend, however, such cynicism is no longer justified, at least in more progressive congregations.

There's nothing wrong with old hymns, of course, and some of the greatest hymns of all time were composed centuries ago. The hymns of the bygone age of Martin Luther and Charles Wesley are not necessarily True Church favorites, but some rather interesting hymns of the early twentieth century have become standards.

The hymn writer would be in the throes of frustration without the liberty to draw creatively upon figurative language and lyrics. For decades churchgoers have sung "In vain in high and holy lays, my soul her grateful voice would raise" and "Here I raise my Ebenezer, hither by thy help I've come" without having the foggiest notion as to the meaning of either phrase. Certain petitions to God the Father seemed puzzling to me as a youngster: "Do not our suit disdain" and "Bid my anxious fears subside" were among the puzzling lyrics.

For many childhood years I wondered where is "Beulah land"? I was confused by the Christmas carol "Away in a Manger" when lyrics claimed "the cattle are lowing." Also I often pondered the meaning of such phrases as "night with ebon pinion" (wondering if Ebon might be some fellow we all should know, and what kind of experience did ole Ebon have when he was "brooded o'er the vale"?); "peale out the watchword, silence it never;" "cherubim and seraphim, falling down before him;" "when upon life's billows you are tempest-tossed" (I knew about pillows being tossed but had no idea what "billows" were). Nor could I define the "asunder part" that gives us all "inner pain." And then I wondered about "the bomb in Gilead" and "a bomb for the weary." Perhaps in junior high I learned that "balm" and "bomb" did not have the same meaning, but I still had no idea what "balm" meant. As a young boy learning the standard hymns I was perplexed by "the whelming flood," and even "toiling on," a phrase which conjured imagery only of childhood constipation and toilets.

When Cheryl McFarland was a young child, her congregation sang the old standard "Bringing in the Sheaves." She and a close childhood friend questioned the meaning of "sheeve." Her young friend thought the congregation was singing "bringing in the sheets." She had observed her grandmother bringing in dry clothes and sheets from the outdoor clothing wires and noticed the grandmother seemed relieved when the laundry was all done. After all, the long sheets were the last fabric items to be removed from the clothesline, thus little wonder "we shall come rejoicing, bringing in the sheets."

After getting into elementary school and learning to read, my fascination with hymnals expanded by conjuring images based on the unique names of some of the hymn writers. (Yes, some of my childhood friends and I could sit quietly on a pew when the sermon seemed boringly long and just turn pages in a hymnal.)

A few hymnists whose names seemed to jump off the pages of song books still come to mind: Fanny J. Crosby (an outstanding hymnist who gave us, among so many great hymns, "Blessed Assurance," "Praise Him! Praise Him!" "Jesus, Keep Me Near the Cross," "Tell Me the Story of Jesus," "A Wonderful Savior," "Redeemed," "Rescue the Perishing," "Jesus is Tenderly Calling," and "To God be the Glory"); P. P. Bliss, who gave us both hymns and melodies ("Hallelujah! What a Savior," Almost Persuaded," "Wonderful Words of Life," "I Gave My Life for Thee," "I Will Sing of My Redeemer," "Let the Lower Lights Be Burning," and "More Holiness Give Me;" as a boy I sometimes wondered if

Brother Bliss was called by his initials or by a nickname); Jessie Brown Pounds ("Anywhere With Jesus," "I Must Needs Go Home," "Will You Not Tell It Today?"); Augustus M. Toplady (the classic "Rock of Ages"). W. T. Sleeper and the angelic sounding Charles H. Gabriel were two more interesting hymnist names.

The prolific hymnist Tillit S. Teddlie was a member of the Church of Christ with a number of popular hymns to his credit, none better than "Worthy Art Thou" though "Heaven Holds All to Me" might be a close second. When Teddlie turned one hundred years of age, I asked Wayne Gurley, our song director for that Sunday, to lead a "Teddlie Medley" in this hymnist-centenarian's honor.

PRAISE AND ADMONITION OR AN EXERCISE IN NOSTALGIA?

The following are some particularly rich and nostalgic phrases and lyrics that joyful pilgrims have sung many times in popular hymns in recent years:

--"*I've got a home in gloryland that outshines the sun.*" This meaningful description of heavenly real estate is drawn from the classic "Do Lord." The imperative petition "Do Lord" is meaningfully repeated some eighteen times in this hymn.

--"*There's a church in the valley by the wildwood, no lovelier spot in the dale, no place is so dear to my childhood.*" Everyone remembers visiting a country church. The very thought of such a wood frame house of worship recharges the nostalgic batteries and reminds us of that "ole time religion."

--"*What a song of delight in that city so bright, we'll be wafted 'neath heaven's fair dome. Having overcome sin, hallelujah amen will be heard in that land o'er the foam.*" These poignant lyrics are drawn from the first stanza of that favorite "When All of God's Singers Get Home," composed by Luther Presley in 1937. Many of God's singers may not clearly fathom the anticipated rapturous experience of being "wafted neath heaven's fair dome in the land o'er the foam." I work diligently to repress thoughts of domed football stadiums, filled beer mugs, and shaving mugs.

--"*Come, then, o come glad fruition*" is a wistful longing expressed in that funeral favorite "Whispering Hope" even if mourners have no idea of the meaning of "glad fruition."

--*"Precious memories, how they linger,"* another funeral favorite, seldom fails to bring a tear to the eye.

--*"It's the glory hallelujah jubilee"* from "There's a Land Beyond the River" suggests that heaven may be more like a Pentecostal revival than most True Church singers have ever imagined.

--*"Troublesome times are here, filling men's hearts with fear. Freedom we all hold dear, now is at stake"* sounds adaptable to anything from "America First" to "American Civil Liberties Union" rallies. "Jesus is Coming Soon" is fun to sing, but interestingly was written in 1942.

REAL ESTATE ESCHATOLOGY

Both preachers and song writers have labored to conceptualize the eternal abode of bliss awaiting those wayfarers who journey unswervingly the straight and narrow path. While some may conceptualize eternity as an ineffable quality of life in the presence of the Lord, most members of the True Church might surely think of heaven in terms of real estate—land, property (usually with water), streets, housing (all in the neighborhood of angels, many of whom are singing and playing) and ideal climate and weather conditions—a concept I call "Real Estate Eschatology." Consider a few lyrics lifted from some of our most popular hymns:

--*"The summerland of bliss ... Land beyond, so fair and bright, where is no night."*

--*"To Canaan's land I'm on my way ... a love light beams across the foam, it shines to light the shores of home."*

--*"We're marching to Zion, the beautiful city of God."*

--*"There's a land that is fairer than day ... we shall meet on that beautiful shore."*

--*"I've got a home prepared where the saints abide, just over in glory land ... I'll join the happy angel band."*

--*"I've a home prepared where the saints abide, just over in glory land."*

--*"Just beyond the rolling river lies a bright and sunny land ... soon we'll join the happy band."*

--*"O they tell me of a home where no storms clouds rise, o they tell me of an unclouded day."*

--*"There's a land beyond the river, just beyond the shining river, when they ring those golden bells for you and me."*

--*"Beautiful robes so white, beautiful mansions bright."*

--*"Then we'll all go strolling down God's avenue."*

--*"We will rest in the fair and happy land."*

--*"Shall we gather at the river where bright angel feet have trod?"*

--*"In the land of fadeless day lies a city foursquare."*

--*"There is a habitation."*

--*"No tears in that bright city."*

--*"In the mansions bright and blessed, He'll prepare for us a place, when we all get to heaven."*

--*"Then we shall meet Him in that bright mansion."*

--*"I've reached the land of corn and wine and all its riches freely mine ... O Beulah land, sweet Beulah land ... where mansions are prepared for me."*

These songs are mere samples of some heavenly hymns sung about the "land fairer than day" located on the "beautiful isle of somewhere" to be reached in the "sweet by and by."

SOME GOOD, OLD-FASHIONED HYMNS

There are, of course, great hymns in most of our hymnals—hymns that express the majesty of God and the beauty of Christian sacrifice and commitment. Hymns that come to mind are: "A Mighty Fortress;" "God of Grace and God of Glory;" "All Hail the Power of Jesus' Name;" "Lord of Our Highest Love;" "Sing Hallelujah to the Lord;" "O for a Thousand Tongues to Sing;" "Come, Thou Fount of Every Blessing;" "How Great Thou Art;" "Lord of All Being Throned Afar;" "Joyful, Joyful We Adore Thee;" and "Christ We Do All Adore Thee;" just to name a few.

Unfortunately, some of these great hymns are not favorites among most in my religious heritage. Many True Church worshipers had rather sing the highly sentimental and personal song "I Come to the Garden Alone," which suggests a secret trysting during early morning hours, yea even "while the dew is still on the roses." While this A. Austin Miles classic does not once mention the name of God or Jesus, it uses the personal pronouns of "I," "me," and "my" numerous times. This hymn makes sense for me only when I imagine I'm Mary Magdalene, something I do not imagine very easily.

Another favorite is "The Old Rugged Cross," which, of course, is linked to the sweet themes of redemption and sacrifice, but suggests tenaciously cherishing and clinging to a relic of our faith rather than to the author of our salvation and the object of our faith.

Two hymns deserve honorable mention for their state of the art hypocrisy when sung by prosperous, well-trained, and sophisticated Christians who have made their peace with affluent American culture. "There's a Mansion" is one of these hymns bemoaning the arduous struggles of a poor working class Christian struggling to secure adequate housing: "Here I labor and toil as I look for a home, just a humble abode among men. While in heaven a mansion is waiting for me." Imagine the wealthy but rather shy and inhospitable Christian gentleman singing: "I'll exchange this old home for a mansion up there and invite the archangel as guest."

The other hymn, "Mansion Over the Hilltop," elevates the ludicrousness level several notches. "In your mind's eye" (a popular sermonic phrase), picture the worldly successful, hard-nosed corporate executive and his family leaving their brick mansion in the wealthiest neighborhood in the city and driving to the church grounds in their new Lexus, Mercedes Benz, or BMW, then sitting in a padded pew wearing his designer clothes and heartily singing with sincere countenance this Ira Stamphill classic composition of 1949:

> *I'm satisfied with just a cottage below,*
> *A little silver and a little gold;*
> *But in that city where the ransomed will shine.*
> *I want a gold one that's silver lined …*

And though I find here no permanent dwelling
I want a mansion, a robe, and a crown.
I've got a mansion just over the hilltop.

Can you imagine the handsome bachelor in the congregation whose social life with an impressive list of pulchritudinous women and a collection of slightly off-color stories, widely known to his business friends and associates, heartily singing "More holiness give me … more freedom from earth stains" or "Purer in Heart, O God, help me to be … keep me from secret sin, reign thou my soul within"? Imagine also the hard-nosed corporate executive who makes no effort to control his selfishness and explosive temper in the business world prayerfully singing: "Prince of Peace! Control my will, bid this struggling heart be still."

THE HYMN THAT TOPS THE CHARTS

There is one hymn which tops the charts for its unique and incomparable rendering of those noble character traits of grief, consternation, and self-pity. W. B. Stevens' lyrics and music "Farther Along," composed in 1911, has long been a classic hymn and favorite of thousands and ten thousands of God's singers who apparently have known both economic deprivation and social molestations. (The hymn begs the question: Would we really want people who are "wrong" to be "molested"? If so, what kind of molestation might one prefer for those living in error?):

Tempted and tried, we're oft made to wonder
Why it should be thus all the day long
While there are others, living about us
Never molested, though in the wrong.
… Then we do wonder why others prosper
Living so wicked year after year …
Farther along we'll know all about it,
Farther along we'll understand why
Cheer up my brother, live in the sunshine
We'll understand it all by and by.

How amazing the holy horsepower that gets generated from lyrics that never seem to be carefully pondered or lyrics that do not even seem comprehensible! Consider, in the case of the latter, one lesser known stanza of that grand old favorite "Sweet Hour of Prayer," words by W. W. Walford, composed in 1845.

> *Till from Mt. Pisgah's lofty height,*
> *I view my home, and take my flight:*
> *This robe of flesh I'll drop, and rise*
> *To seize the everlasting prize*
> *And shout while passing through the air*
> *Farewell, farewell, sweet hour of prayer.*

If you did not know this stanza was part of a hymn which has strengthened and comforted innumerable Christian souls, then you might mistake this for an anthem from "Top Gun" sung by military pilots in flight. (Admittedly, this stanza is omitted from many hymnals, though most hymnals include these lyrics: "And oft escaped the tempter's snare … To him whose truth and faithfulness, engage the waiting soul to bless.")

Many of my friends are men and women with a healthy self-esteem who appreciate and truly enjoy their family life, their children and their grandchildren, their careers, their material comforts, and their recreation and vacation time. They have a sense of humor about all dimensions of life, and they welcome the dawning of a new day and do not face life with a sense of dread. In the church's song service, however, they are often asked to sing some old standards that seem to say life is one dreaded, miserable experience after another, a "vale of tears" in which one continually faces "losing and weeping"—"thus for the showers of blessing we plead"—as though the current level of blessing is woefully insufficient for emotional well-being. This earthly life is a place one's "raptured soul would here no longer stay." Such incongruity with reality!

The glimpse of heaven provided in Revelation informs us that all the redeemed will be gathered around the throne and singing praises. I've wondered about this heavenly song service: What about those who do not like to sing? How about those saints who have refused to sing on earth? Will they bring out the instruments and, if so, which ones? Will anything be amplified? Who will be leading the singing or might there be a praise team? Will they need song books or might lyrics be posted in the clouds? And will they have hymn request time? And how long will the song service last? Would they lead "invitation songs" just for the sake of nostalgia?

I wonder also if they might change some lyrics of some of the all-time song-fest favorites to reflect the rapturous state. Might they change "When We All Get to Heaven" to "Now That We've All Got to Heaven" and "When the Roll Is Called Up Yonder" to "When the Roll Was Called Here Yonder, I Was There"?

I don't know the answers, but I'm convinced that "Do Lord" and "I'll Fly Away" will not need to be sung there and that there will be perfect pitch and perfect harmony. For the redeemed it will mean "joyously singing with heart bells all ringing, oh, won't it be wonderful there!"

THE POWER OF MUSIC: A SERIOUS CONCLUSION

Music provides the emotional substance of worship. It can take us places that our intellect alone cannot go. Music has the ability to express every conceivable emotion and it can impact the human being in ways that simple spoken expression might never reach. Music that is offered and performed with excellence has the capacity to richly express joy and praise, sorrow and sadness, relief and concern, majesty and despondency.

Ideally, music complements and enhances every other act of worship during the gathering of God's people. Music is a medium through which every attitude and act of honor and adoration can be expressed to God and one another. True enough, there are many congregations who still sing some of these old hymns that have miniscule spiritual content; apparently those hymns tap their memory banks and recharge their nostalgia batteries (for that reason many of us still enjoy the songs of our childhood). On the other hand, some of the greatest hymns with the deepest theology are old hymns too, for example, as in the many hymns of Charles Wesley.

In the Church of Christ, worship music is changing in the more progressive congregations. We have some new and creative composers. Ken Young, for example, has composed many new, meaningful hymns and led the Hallal ministry since 1989 with the mission of helping people experience the power and presence of God through music and worship experiences. Ken's ministry has taken him into congregations in various states and several foreign countries and how naturally he taps and blends the gifts and talents of his own immediate family and some close friends. There are excellent new songs being sung by a wide variety of composers, though admittedly some new songs have little spiritual content and seem totally focused on personal feelings. Great hymns are addressed to and/or focused on God, not so much on human beings.

Many congregations now use amplified voices of a praise team to lead the singing, and then lyrics are projected by PowerPoint onto overhead screen(s). The old-fashioned hand-held hymnal seems moving toward becoming a relic of the past. Some progressive Church of Christ congregations have now incorporated the use of instruments in their worship assemblies or may provide an alternative instrumental service to complement an *a capella* service.

Many people in commenting on the music in their home congregation have found some trait they can highly praise and appreciate and then, often, find some other trait they find disappointing and displeasing. The best spin on this reality is to conclude that Christians know that church music is important and it should be conducted and offered as meaningfully and effectively as possible.

Music is a marvelous gift from the Creator and one does not need to be able to read music to sing or hum along with the music of others in assembly. An anecdote is told of a minister urging his congregation to sing out with volume and enthusiasm. He offered this admonition: "For those of you whom God has blessed with a great singing voice, it's your way of saying, 'Thank you, Lord.' For those of you God did not bless with a great singing voice, it's your way of getting even."

12

Distinguishing Between Adultery and Fornication and Other Services Rendered by a Competent Church Staff

The right church staff chemistry is absolutely crucial today to the resident preacher's success in each congregation he serves.

And how times have changed! In my first full-time local ministry, called to a working class congregation of almost two hundred members in the Detroit area, I was not given the services of a secretary, much less of any other staff member. Whatever church office work had to be done, I was expected to perform it. Which was satisfactory, of course. For example, one of my weekly assignments was to write all the content for the weekly church bulletin, type it up on a stencil, run it off on a manual (hand-cranked) A. B. Dick mimeograph machine, address and then mail copies to members and Sunday guests. Additionally, the Warren church offered a modest residence only two or three blocks from the church house.

I commenced this job in August 1964 as a recent college graduate ready for my first big career challenge. As the bleak winter months passed it became increasingly difficult to rise each morning, open a cold, empty church house, and sit in an empty office waiting for a visitor or even a phone call. I gave attention to any members in the hospital and went to visit them even though a few hospitals were at some distance away in this big metropolitan area.

Those were the idealistic days I labored under the delusion that the main task expected of the minister was to study the Word diligently and deliver eloquent, insightful messages. I was so pleased to learn that Harding Graduate School would offer courses by extension into our Detroit Metropolitan area, thus my first graduate training entailed enrolling in two graduate classes, "Revelation" and "New Testament Theology," under Dean and Professor W. B. West, who flew up from Memphis and taught classes all day on each Monday of the semester. "Revelation" was Dean West's special academic love. He seemed to have a world of stories to buttress his points.

In more recent years I served a suburban congregation which provided a two full-time secretaries, a full-time administrator, a part-time accountant, a full-time youth director, a fully supported missionary, a minister of music (sometimes called a worship minister), a full-time custodian, and a pre-school/ kindergarten program with a director, ten to twelve "Little School" teachers; the "Little School" program engaged its own full-time secretary. Back in the 70s, some congregations even employed a "bus minister" to invite and provide transportation, mainly for school-age children from lower income families, to attend Sunday School classes or other activities.

IMAGINING THE MINISTRY OF JESUS AND THE APOSTLES IN MODERN TIMES

The concept of a church staff is a fairly recent development in the whole sweep of church history. Can we imagine the apostle Paul who, for example, spent eighteen months as a preacher and teacher in ancient Ephesus, partnering with an assistant minister, a youth minister, and an administrative assistant? He did, of course, have other disciples who assisted him in various phases of ministry, though safe to assume these were not salaried church employees. Paul was always mindful and considerate to commend many of those brothers and sisters for their personal encouragement and assistance.

What if Jesus, Paul, and the other early apostles were living in contemporary times? If Paul called the first century Graeco-Roman world "the fullness of time" when God sent his Son into the world, how might he describe our world today? How many of the advanced means of transportation, communication, and public relations would Jesus and the early disciples have employed to advance their cause?

Would Jesus have a website with all kinds of links to information and perhaps a new video lesson each week? Would the Master have delivered his "Sermon on the Mount" in a domed football stadium that holds at least 100,000 and has massively huge screens for those who cannot sit close to the speaker's podium? What kind of food and drink would be sold at the stadium concessions? Surely loaves and fish with a few olives thrown in, but what else? Carbonated fruit of the vine? Fermented fruit of the vine for adults?

Would Jesus use FaceBook and announce that he wants everyone to be his friend? Knowing many followers would want brief messages, Jesus would surely carry a smart phone and tweet instructions and commentary each day. He would surely command his disciples carrying smart phones to "tweet others as they would like to be tweeted."

Would Paul and the other apostles be interested in building a mega-church with full staff? If so, then Paul could certainly have profited from an assistant minister, a youth minister, a minister for seniors, a children's minister, a capable administrative assistant, travel agent, and a limousine. A body guard and a good attorney might also be beneficial considering all the persecution and life-threatening scrapes Paul experienced. This apostle would certainly employ a media specialist as well as a technician. He could set up satellite congregations all over North America, Europe, Asia and other areas, and while his sermons might be preached in only one worship assembly they could be beamed to countless other locations and close-captioned with translations in the dominant language of each nation. Of course there would also be closed-captioning on telecasts for the deaf and hard of hearing.

Modern churches use a marquee along the street or highway in front of the church building facilities to make some witty statement that might catch attention or to make announcements such as for an upcoming gospel meeting or guest speaker. Sometimes new members are announced on the outdoors marquee and sometimes congratulations to the newly immersed are posted at street level. Would the early churches put up a giant "Baptizotron" on the street corner where passers-by could see continuous playing of videos of the most recent baptisms?

Items that all the apostles, especially Paul, could use today would include a lap-top computer, an I-phone, a fax machine, a photocopier, a life insurance policy, a double-knit comfort robe, and a pair of prescription sunglasses. Paul would surely have a concordance of all Old Testament Scripture downloaded on his laptop, thus not only sparing him the need to memorize so many ancient prophecies but also the embarrassment of a mistake in quotation or citation. His epistle-writing time could be greatly reduced when using a cut and paste function in dropping the Old Testament Scriptures into his text. With his laptop in full use while serving prison time, one might only guess how many electronic epistles Paul could send to all the congregations, brothers, and sisters that he knew; he could call them "e-pistles." Perhaps he could use Skype or FaceTime to stay in touch with most of them. Satellite technology could be useful in so many ways!

Would Jesus and the apostles have been willing to be interviewed on the major networks and on cable news? If so, on which networks? Surely on Fox News in order to reach so many of his evangelical followers. What about CNN? And MSNBC? Would Jesus call any of these networks purveyors of "fake news"?

In the mid-twentieth century, several preachers wrote gospel tracts (pocket-size booklets of fifteen to twenty pages typically) on a wide variety of topics. My dad was known for wide distribution of tracts he authored on at least a dozen titles. Most True Church lobbies had a tract rack where copies were freely available. During the 50s and 60s, many preachers and others interested in "soul-winning" would set up "cottage meetings" for showing "Jule Miller filmstrips" that were intended to perform the heavy load of personal evangelism. It would seem wise in the twenty-first century to dispense with tracts and film strips and just produce podcasts. Can one feature Jesus and his apostles each making a series of podcasts? Might we feature them speaking in a series of TED Talks? Perhaps even making a movie that utilized all the technology and special effects of modern movie production?

Of course, worshipers and listeners in the church assembly would enjoy a different experience. Sermon points and colorful images could be projected to one or more elevated screens while speaking in tongues would be fully amplified by a dynamic sound system. Imagine all the early disciples sitting in assembly with their smart phones. How would the youth be attentive to some apostle in the pulpit? Already in contemporary times we can glance at a row of teens in a worship service and see that sending text messages to some pal on the same or a nearby pew has replaced the writing of hand notes and sending them down the pew to the intended recipient.

THE INDISPENSABLE INGREDIENT FOR LOCAL PREACHER SUCCESS

Regardless the availability of technology, the value of maintaining good relations with all the church staff cannot be overstated as an ingredient to the local preacher's success. Chauvinist as this may seem, I've witnessed more envy and fighting between females on a church staff than between males. The preacher's mediating skills become especially important because he will need full cooperation from his support staff to achieve what his congregation and his elders expect of him. The elders often run the whole show or at least they have the "final say" and retain "veto power" in all areas of ministry. For a minister or other church employee there is little or no job security—one is only as safe and secure as the last elders' meeting!

A loyal, competent secretary is indispensable to the preacher's ministry. She (a pronoun used thoughtfully, since 99.44/100 percent of all church secretaries share gender kinship with Eve) is especially helpful to the preacher when the preacher first assumes a new position in a new community.

The secretary can provide a background overview on the entire church and especially on certain families and their trials and woes to which sensitivity is best exercised, fill the new preacher in on all the quirks and idiosyncrasies of key church members, brief him on what to expect at the office, warn him about certain chronic "drop-bys" and complainers who will drain his schedule of any office study and work time, provide him with directions for finding certain streets and addresses if he hasn't mastered satellite/GPS directions, and offer clues on what to expect in certain home visits (*egs.*, an unruly toddler with a perpetually soiled diaper, a vicious dog, a long-haired and shedding cat, a dirty and cluttered house, just to name a few undesirable possibilities).

All this information has no bearing on sermon preparation, but it has immense practical value in "pastoring." As long as his relations with her are discrete and diplomatic, the loyal secretary can also inform the preacher of everything he ever wanted to know about the previous preachers or some current members but was afraid to ask. And quite often the resident preacher will be providing valuable advice and counsel to his administrative assistant or secretary as well as to other members of the church staff. Ideally there is much mutual respect between preacher and staff.

In due time this loyal secretary will know what to tell inquirers when the preacher is away and can cover for him when he is attending private matters which are no one else's business. She will know how to "keep her ear to the ground" and be the first to inform her preacher-supervisor of rumbling against him within the local household of faith. All these services are infinitely more important to the minister than how efficiently she types the church newsletter or files the visitors' cards.

What a blessing, of course, if the church secretary is efficient in more skills than cheerfully greeting office visitors, pleasantly answering the telephone, and watering office plants! In our electronic era the church secretary absolutely must possess computer skills for word processing and record-keeping. Skills at computer research, desktop publishing, and preparing PowerPoint presentations would be added "pluses." And if she brings in a home-baked delicacy occasionally, or, as did a lovely secretary named Kathy Lawrence Green at Westwood, brings in a vase of fresh wild flowers almost every day and places them on the minister's desk, then count your many blessings, name them one by one.

Several excellent secretaries have blessed my daily church office experience. One of the best church secretaries who ever worked for me, Emma Phillips at Otter Creek, seemed as quiet and shy as the proverbial cat in a room full of rocking chairs. However, she completed her work efficiently and speedily—so much so that there was considerable free time for her in the afternoons. Emma then removed her portable television from the closed cabinet and watched the daily soap operas, all the while keeping eyes open to visitors dropping by or taking incoming phone calls. Precious little work for the kingdom was done by her during those mid to late afternoon hours, but, on the other hand, given her efficiency then precious little actually remained to be done at that point in the day.

While I did not have the time or interest to join her in viewing such daytime drama I was deeply grateful that Emma was willing to keep in touch with the world and keep me updated on changing story lines and plot twists. As she shared them with me, then I facetiously claimed that with such updates my sermons could assume a greater measure of contemporary relevance.

The real test for a secretary comes when the minister is pulled into severe conflict with any governing gerontocracy and his pulpit position is on the line. The secretary knows she is supervised by the minister in day-to-day work detail and may regard him highly, yet her salary and position are secured by the same people who hire, retain, and could possibly fire that minister. Occasionally she cannot avoid choosing sides. Church fights over a preacher's effectiveness and tenure are all too common and frequently messy.

A church fight is not required to divide a church staff. Personality and ideological differences are quite enough. A few years ago a large church in Nashville employed two pulpit and teaching ministers. To say the pair worked "hand in glove," or "palm in Bible," or whatever metaphor suggests respect and camaraderie, would assault the truth. In fact, each reported he neither saw nor spoke to the other except when passing in the office hallway once or twice a week. Ironically, each stated that he got along beautifully with the other. Apparently, each appealed to a separate constituency within the congregation. Church life and church business moved forward!

THE CHOICE OF "E. F. HUTTON"

The most colorful and most unforgettable character I ever worked with on a church staff was a young man from Russellville, Kentucky, named Dave Dockins. Dave was employed by the McMinnville's Westwood elders during my tenure as pulpit minister for the dual role of music minister and youth director.

This position was the first career opportunity for this young man, fresh out of college with a history major and degree in hand.

Dave received an opportunity to candidate for this music and youth position because of a strong recommendation by Dr. Robert Hooper, the chairman of the Lipscomb's History and Political Science Department from which the young man emerged, and whose daughter, coincidentally, Dave was dating at that time and nigh unto matrimony. Bob's letter of strong recommendation acknowledged that Dave had no prior experience in any aspect of church ministry, but that he was a young man of sterling character and unrivaled dedication to the Lord.

I remembered Dave as a student. He was a member of Sigma Chi Delta, a social club for which I was faculty sponsor on the Lipscomb campus. His reputation as a student was that he was a great young man yet anything but serious. He liked to stage pranks and practical jokes. I liked and respected that in a young man. I figured I'd like that that trait in a youth director and assistant minister, too. I knew we'd get along beautifully.

Westwood contacted one other candidate for this open position. He was a handsome young man I judged to possess outstanding credentials in music and untested abilities in youth work. He performed one Wednesday evening and interviewed quite well. The elders announced emphatically they would hire someone with great musical knowledge and leadership skills so I felt certain this other prospect would get the presbyters' nod.

The Sunday that Dave auditioned for the job remains unforgettable. Dave was asked to lead songs pre-selected by Harold Roney, our interim song leader. Harold picked some well-known standards so that they could be printed in advance in our "worship guide" and would be easily known by Dave and the entire congregation. The first hymn began with the words "Of one Lord has made the race, through one has come the fall," the beginning of "The Gospel is for All." Dave stammered and struggled through one stanza and honestly, to this day I cannot tell you what musical melody he sang solo—I just know it wasn't the melody in the hymnal.

The song ended abruptly after one stanza and Dave announced the next number. "My Lord," I prayed in a silent, private panic, "this is embarrassing.

What's more, if all songs move as rapidly as the first one, then I'll have to stand and start preaching my sermon within the next minute or two." Dave managed to induce a few others to sing along with him on the other hymns. Manifestly, he did not have a singer's voice and did not know how to keep musical time. Imperturbable about these and any other reality was Dave, however; leading four hundred people in singing praise was a lark.

Later that Sunday the elders huddled with Dave in a private conference and learned that he had been raised on a farm in Western Kentucky. Country expressions dotted his linguistics and syntax. He had worked many hours in a tobacco patch and tended livestock. Words cannot describe the funny sounding laugh with which he concluded nearly every statement or the way he tilted his head and maintained a unique, whimsical expression. He was a genuine country comedian, a rural Peter Pan who resisted growing up.

After his tryout Sunday visit, I just knew Dave would be reimbursed for his travel expenses and sent on his way back to his family's Kentucky farm rejoicing. How very wrong I was! The elders were mesmerized by this young man. The "power elder," Chester N. Womack—the elder I called E. F. Hutton because when he spoke everyone listened—announced that Dave had been hired. "While he needs some polish in certain areas," E. F. conceded, "we elders believe that Dave is a diamond in the rough."

IN AND OUT OF THE PULPIT

An entire book could be written on the uniqueness of Dave Dockins as youth director and music minister. We suspected Dave did not know a note of music and his youth work was confined mostly to playing touch football with other kids in the big churchyard after school with junior high school kids and basketball with high school boys in the evening.

During office time before local schools dismissed, Dave typically pulled his chair up to our secretary's desk and visited with her. Dave visited a number of his favorite families around suppertime, a time-tested ministerial maneuver designed to maximize impromptu invitations for a free supper. It's so much easier for a single minister to garner supper invitations than for a minister who is married with children.

Making his "pastoral" visits, Dave drove a time-worn, road-tested '68 blue and white Ford F-150. Accompanying him on many of these visits and riding compliantly and respectfully in the cab was his English setter, a handsome dog which probably spotted more quail than Dave spotted stray souls. Dave also kept a mongrel named Ugly, a dog which, unfortunately yet candidly, was aptly named. Every home visit for Dave was an occasion for storytelling and jocularity. Seldom was any serious topic discussed. Every family seemed to love a visit from Dave. And each family likely needed the "laugh therapy" that Dave brought.

Occasionally, young people visited Dave's Morrison Road duplex apartment where he lived alone, just across the highway from the Westwood church building. On my impromptu visits there I observed a few stark rooms with little or no furniture and floors bare except for the manifestly dirty garments distributed evenly throughout the living area. It did not matter. I, along with anyone else, was always welcome there. Dave's bed consisted of seven to eight twin size mattresses evenly stacked on the bare floor and, of course, easily dissembled to accommodate overnight guests.

One might think that working with Dave was a spiritual ordeal. Nothing could be farther from the truth. Elementary children and junior high school students loved him dearly as a big brother. High school students found him always at their level. Adults loved and appreciated Dave, too, but for reasons different from the ones for which the elders hired him. Dave loved life. He seemed to take few concerns seriously. He told farm stories. He seemed like an innocent farm boy who wanted to keep himself unspotted from the world. His laughter was infectious. He and I got along marvelously. He was simply a fun person.

Any given Sunday with Dave sitting on the pulpit and leading singing could easily became a *tour de force*. Dave always arrived in the nick of time before the start of our 9:30 morning assembly. When he stood to lead his first song his tie might be a little crooked and his face always had a sleepy look, conveying the "I just got out of bed" countenance.

Dave's blond hair was typically still wet in the early minutes of his pulpit experience, thus adding a "just showered" dimension to his appearance. (Rumor had it that Dave's mother called him long distance from Kentucky every Sunday to make certain he was awakened in time to get to the HOW on time; on weekdays we did not see him at the office until 11:15, the exact time that our church staff and preschool teachers shared lunch each school day in the church kitchen and to which Dave was always invited.)

When it came time in the Sunday service for the sermon Dave put on his best Ed McMahon's *Tonight Show* impression and loudly announced, "And now … [long pause, of course without a drum roll] … hereeeee's Doctor Cotham." Prior to this position, Dave had known me only as a college professor and his nomenclature was both genuine and natural. The elders soon asked him to cease all public introductions and references to me as a "doctor." From that point on after their instructions, I was introduced by him as "Brother Cotham."

Dave was a blond-headed, six-foot plus a few inches, highly active young man who seemed more like an energizer bunny on steroids. In our worship services, when it came time to exit the pulpit platform right before the sermon, he would jump down to the floor and sit on the front pew. At the end of my sermon, rather than walk around to the three or four steps at either side of the pulpit, he would jump to his feet and then leap directly to the pulpit floor, turn around, and start singing his announced number.

Dave and I became the best of friends. He was courteous, well-mannered, and willing to perform any errand for me or anyone else on our staff that might be required. Every day at the office Dave was always asking what he could do to help. The two of us shared a lot of interests. One major mutual interest was our appreciation for a beautifully staged practical joke.

WILD GAME, WILD BASKETBALL, SHARP PHOTOGRAPHY

One year the Westwood deacons planned and announced a "wild game and fish dinner" for the entire church. The dinner was held in the fall near the end of hunting season for certain wild game. People were encouraged to bring exotic dishes based on innovative recipes including animal meat caught on land, in the air, or seafood from any lake, river, or sea. A lot of venison and fish platters were brought and laid on the table. Fresh vegetables from the home gardens were plentiful. This seemed such a unique idea, such a novel way to foster "the ties that bind our hearts in Christian love," the likes I had never experienced in any other congregation.

Just prior to the dinner, Dave summoned me outside the fellowship hall where he had spotted an opossum amidst the shrubs. He then taught me how to "sull" and then subdue the slow moving, defenseless, and harmless creature. We then announced to the church that he and I had a contribution to the dinner which was both wild but very fresh meat. Dave saved it for a special table around which our clerical and preschool staff were eating. He and I placed it in a big cooker, asked no one to open it until after the blessing and everyone was ready to eat. Once the prayer was offered Dave lifted the top and the live opossum slowly and bewilderingly moved out onto the set table. The response was something more than total surprise, yet something less than total panic and horror. Once the humorous surprise effect had worn off, Dave carried the poor creature back outdoors and set it free.

Dave was outstanding in sports. He competed aggressively in basketball. Playing with him and the teen boys outdoors after classes on a cold late October Wednesday night after Bible classes, I received a broken nose from some hard foul from him that sent me tumbling hard and face down to the asphalt basketball court. Unable to get my arms under me to break the fall, this was excruciatingly painful and my nose bled profusely. Needless to say, I was stunned and did not even attempt to return to the game; after getting home our family summoned a nurse rather than deliver me to the ER.

On the following Sunday I had two unsightly black eyes and a skinned face noticed by everyone present when I stood to deliver the message. Deacon Carl Stanley could not resist calling this sad appearance to the entire church's attention as he opened the service with announcements. "Just look at Perry's face," he invited, "and then you'll see what happens when a Tennessee Volunteer tangles with a Kentucky Wildcat on the basketball court." Most people laughed. I mustered a smile of some kind.

Dave's main hobby was photography. He was quite proficient, so much so that I commissioned him to travel about the county and take photographs of forty or more church buildings which later ran in a county church history I authored. The most innovative photo of Dave each year was something of a "selfie" (an unheard of term at that time) that made its way to his annual Christmas greeting.

The early greeting cards depicted Dave's horse or his dog. Another showed Dave in swim trunks swinging by rope over a river. Each card included the words "Merry Christmas from Dave." One year's card depicted Dave pointing a big pistol into the eye of the camera and, surely influenced by Clint Eastwood, his caption read: "Go ahead. Make my Christmas." Another of his later renditions showed a couple of shapely, casually-clad young ladies sitting on Dave's lap; Dave sported a Santa pose and props and the caption read "Dave Dreams of Christmas."

Surely pranksterism was Dave's main hobby. During his college days, Dave was "mooning" through the raised glass of an automobile when one of the unappreciative "moonees" hurled a big rock at Dave's bare *derriere*. The glass shattered and left his buttocks cut and bleeding. A visit to the emergency room was required for some stitch work on his *gluteus maximus*. When some Westwood teen boys in a locker room inadvertently noticed the scars, then Dave explained that once in college he had accidentally sat on some glass and injured himself.

"WELL, BACK TO NASHVILLE!"

In time, the church elders seemed defensive about Dave's undeveloped song leading and teaching skills and felt the need to provide growth opportunities. Dave was granted several weeks leave of absence and instructed to stay in Nashville and receive private church music and song leading lessons from an accomplished hymn director and music critic, Henry "Buddy" Arnold, at that time worship leader at Nashville's Otter Creek. After several weeks of private training, Buddy informed our elders that Dave had been adequately tutored and that, quite possibly, he could lead any hymn in the church's song book.

On the first Sunday after Dave's return from Nashville, we congregants noticed and appreciated that our young friend was deploying hand and arm beating of rhythm for the first time. Indeed, the church funds expended for Dave had borne musical/metrical fruit. Then, an emboldened Dave announced the congregation would next sing "Consider the Lilies," an opportunity for a more daring display of an enhanced song directing and hymnodic expertise.

Dave led the church through all the lyrics once, unmindful that the bass lead off a refrain that begins with the words "And yet I say unto you …" Dave ended this lovely hymn prematurely, backed up a few steps to his pulpit chair and began to sit down. At that moment, both Harold Roney and I from our seats led off the bass part, "And yet I say unto you," and the sopranos joined in at their echoing part.

Dave catapulted from his seat like a spiritual jack-in-the-box and began to sing along and wave his arm rhythmically, yet again displayed that familiar pained and perplexed expression on his face. Clearly this was a case of the church leading the leader, a not unheard of phenomenon in the True Church. When the song was concluded, Dave stood there, compelled to say something before resuming his seat. He then noisily slammed the song book shut, threw up his arms, shrugged his shoulders and loudly proclaimed, "Well, back to Nashville!" The congregation roared in laughter.

FAITH, HOPE, AND HILARITY: DAVE DELIVERS THE WORD

The elders' well-intentioned attempt to compel Dave to gain experience in preaching and teaching adults turned into another public occasion for raucous hilarity. Seems that Dave had served as a staff minister for over a year without having delivered a public speech, preached a sermon, or taught an adult class. To correct this glaring imbalance, the elders asked Dave to make the brief, five-minute devotional talk before the entire Wednesday evening assembly. This seemed a rather safe and easily managed assignment. He was given a couple weeks' advance notice which, to anyone else, would surely seem more than adequate time to prepare appropriate remarks.

The challenge stirred the first anxiety in Dave I'd ever witnessed. Day by day, hour by hour, for two weeks, he sat in a chair pulled up to either my desk or our secretary's desk and ponderously grunted and moaned about this new assignment. He turned through pages of Scripture, examining them carefully with the expression of a paleontologist scrutinizing a new fossil. Still, Dave could not think of a topic. He kept asking Karleen Rogers, our secretary, and me for our opinions on Scriptures and topics he might deploy.

Late on the afternoon of the Wednesday evening the assigned talk was due, Dave seemed discouraged and desperate. Despite two weeks' advance notice, he still did not have a topic. He sought my advice once more. This was a conversation in which, for a change, he was not cracking jokes or chuckling.

"Dave, get your pencil and paper," I suggested, "and I'll give you a little sermonette that you can use verbatim. Now, since you're a youth director, I'd read Ecclesiastes 12: 1 and make a few random comments. The young people will think you are speaking to them. Their parents will appreciate it. The elders will love it. You can't fail."

Dave sat quietly, read the passage while moving his lips. He paused a few moments. Despite a lifetime of Sunday School and four years in a Christian college which required him to attend daily chapel and daily Bible classes, nothing came to his mind when he read this most familiar passage in Ecclesiastes.

"Here. You take notes and I'll tell you what you should say. First, read the verse through. Then, go back and read a word or two at a time and explain the meaning of each word in the text," I counseled, without any thought that he'd remember what I would tell him. Given our sense of humor, I never thought he would take my facetiousness as serious exposition.

Thus began my exegesis: "'Remember.' That means 'not to forget,' 'keep it in mind,' 'tie a string around your finger.' 'Remember NOW.' That means 'don't remember yesterday and don't remember tomorrow, but remember today.' 'Thy Creator' means 'God made it.' The verse does not say to 'remember thy evolutor.' Here you can talk about the heresy and shame of biological evolution."

My farcical exegesis continued. Though I was being totally facetious, Dave wrote every word down. In my heart I knew he might actually use some of this nonsense. The possibility intrigued me. What I did not imagine was that he'd use all of it and then spontaneously compose a lot more, too.

Standing to speak that evening in our church auditorium, Dave looked awkward but determined. After telling how glad he was to have the opportunity to speak he related his difficulties in finding a topic and acknowledged gratefully my assistance. He then read the verse I had suggested. He had gained everyone's attention. Then he began his explanation and application: "'Remember' means 'don't you forget,' 'keep it in mind,' and 'tie a string around your finger if you have to.'"

Line by line, the entire church, save the elders, roared in laughter at such simplistic nonsense. Dave was so inspired by the laughter that he began to add even more inane commentary in addition to what I had given him. At one point he left my script and somehow started talking about belief.

"You know," he said, "sometimes you believe but someone else doesn't believe." Profound enough, I thought. Then he threw in an illustration I had never heard before or since as related to the theological concept of belief. This was a case of turning scatology into theology or vice versa.

"I remember back in my elementary school days. I was a little boy and my mom had fixed something for supper the night before that didn't agree with me," he started.

We all wondered where this was going but would never have guessed.

"Well, the next morning at school, I got real sick at my stomach. I had the trots real bad. You know what it's like to have the trots real bad when you're sitting in class or at work?" Dave laughed. We all laughed an incredulous laugh. People looked about the auditorium with expressions which asked "Can you believe this?"

"I was gittin' up out of my chair every few minutes asking my teacher if I could go to the john," he continued. (I just knew next Dave would throw out the old line about the Christian school bathroom which had three commodes and the students referred to them irreverently as first john, second john and third john. That one hadn't occurred to Dave at the moment.)

"After a while the teacher said to me, 'Dave, I'll excuse you just once more, but I can't believe that you really need to go to the bathroom that much. What are you up to?' So the teacher did not believe I had the trots, but I did believe and I could provide them proof for my beliefs," Dave explained.

I sat on the front pew and thoughts of the absurdity of the whole occasion crossed my mind. In a pulpit where men have broken the bread of life now stands this young minister with open Bible discussing a malfunction of his lower gastro-intestinal track and drawing a spiritual analogy. Yet we all laughed uncontrollably. Honestly, I never recall laughter any longer or louder in any venue (even in a comedy club), much less in the HOW, than we experienced in that Wednesday night church service. Some of us could have rolled out of our pews. Indeed, revival of some sort had come to Westwood Church of Christ that night!

ON THE AIR: A RELIGIOUS BOB AND RAY SHOW

The elders never asked Dave to deliver another speech. I was favorably impressed, however, with his ability to win an audience with spontaneous comments.

In the last few days of my tenure at Westwood, the time of my "lame duck" ministry, I faced the dreaded task I had committed to fulfilling several weeks earlier—filling in as guest speaker for a local religious radio show. My lack of enthusiasm was not an opposition to the show, an AM broadcast that seemed innocuous enough. I did not want expend the time to prepare scripts and did not know of anyone at Westwood who had confessed to actually having listened to this daily radio broadcast. Yet, perhaps, there were a lot of elderly and other shut-ins who listened each day.

Out of the blue an idea came to me. I would invite Dave to be on the program with me and we'd conduct on-air time like a Christian talk show. As always. Dave was agreeable. I envisioned little preparation on my part and absolutely no preparation on Dave's part. I thought it would be an easy way to fulfill the assignment and might even be fun.

The show was broadcast daily around noontime for fifteen minutes. Each day the two of us sat behind the microphone and I took the lead. I introduced Dave as an "expert" in various subjects, such as church life and hymnology, and I began asking him questions such as "What's your favorite Bible story?" "What do you enjoy about church work?" or "What's your advice for young preachers today?"

"Dave is Warren County's expert in church music," I announced to my radio audience one day, "so for today's show I'd like to ask him a few questions about music in worship."

"Just anything, Doctor Cotham," Dave replied with either cockiness or facetiousness, not sure which. For this radio show he stuck with my academic title rather than calling me "Brother Cotham."

"Dave, you've studied the lyrical qualities of hymns as well as the underlying theological premises of the songs you lead. Tell me, what are some of your favorite hymns?"

"Well, Doctor Cotham, I've always liked 'I Come to the Garden Alone.' There's just something about a garden. I can't put it into words. There's something really special about a garden with roses. This song reminds me of my grandmother's garden. She had a lot of flowers in her garden" Dave reminisced. "You'd have to get there real early after the crack of dawn if you wanted to see any dew on her roses."

"Any other hymns come to mind, Brother Dockins?"

"Oh yeh. I like 'The Old Rugged Cross.' There's just something about an old rugged cross. I don't know who wrote that song, but whoever it was surely had a real knack for writing hymns about crosses."

And so the non-sensible, trivial dialogue continued. Early in the week we both informed a few friends about our program. Word spread rapidly. New listeners started tuning in on their AM dial. By the time we got to our last show on Friday, Dave and I were loving it. Not only did the show require no preparation on our part, but it became fun improvisation.

One of our friends, Carl Stanley, perhaps the only church officer (an elder at this point) who knew how to place such levity in perspective, appreciated our efforts and urged others in our church family to tune in to what he called a "religious Bob and Ray Show." I just sensed that show may have had more listeners and stirred more discussion than any previous week of programming.

The last show on Friday was unforgettable in my mind. We had exhausted our supply of topics and decided to present a question and answer session between the two of us. Dave threw out a few questions and I played straight man, trying to give serious answers. I shall never forget one bit of dialogue on that last show. (As an aside, I have saved cassette recordings of these broadcasts which can verify my descriptions of such hilarious outlandishness.)

"I've had this question a long time and have not been able to find an answer to it," Dave began with seeming seriousness. "What's the difference between fornication and adultery?" We never rehearsed any script and this question surprised me. I always tried to give a straight answer to any question he proposed.

"Well, Dave, the traditional answer is to say that fornication means 'uncleanness' and it often refers to immoral sexual acts by single people. Adultery is unfaithfulness by married people. However, the dichotomy is really not that clear. The New Testament seems to use these words interchangeably," I explained. "That's a challenging question you posed."

"Well, Doctor Cotham, I see you're having the same trouble defining these two words as the old Kentucky preacher I heard about," Dave declared.

"Really?" I asked.

"Years ago, when someone asked him about the difference between fornication and adultery," Dave answered, "then this old Kentucky preacher said 'Well, I reckon there ain't much difference in the two. I've tried 'em both and they seem about the same to me.'"

I was at a loss for words trying to maintain some seriousness. Sure, I'd heard that old joke before, but I had not expected to hear it again at that moment while conducting a Middle Tennessee religious radio show.

A SAD OCCASION BRINGS SWEET REUNION

My ministry at Westwood ended in a few days after these broadcasts in the summer 1982. Dave's tenure there continued for a few more months. Then one day he precipitously resigned and left town. Nothing shameful happened, as best anyone could tell. Dave's feelings were hurt about something and he refused to talk about it. He's been on the farm ever since. Everyone that knew him well possessed nothing but love and appreciation for him.

The first year out of his church job Dave drove his big motorcycle at a fast speed on a farm road into a barbed wire fence. The barbed wire wrapped around his face and body. He nearly died from injuries suffered in the accident. Once the slashes and cuts were sewn together with hundreds of stitches, my erstwhile ministry associate looked akin to Frankenstein. Dave wrote a letter of thanks to his Westwood friends who offered help and concern during his hospitalization. The letter was published in the church bulletin and contained a brief message: "Thanks for your prayers and your support throughout my recent entanglements."

A sad occasion brought Dave and me to the same platform again. The event occurred a few days before Christmas of 1988. A young man with whom Dave had established a close friendship when he was a teen in the youth program had been killed when his truck slid off a road rendered treacherous by an ice storm, leaving behind a young widow and child.

The family asked me to officiate at the funeral service at High's Funeral Home in McMinnville. I drove down from Nashville for the service. Much to the pleasant surprise and appreciation of the young man's family and many friends, Dave drove down from Kentucky for the service. The family appreciatively asked him to make a few remarks after my eulogy.

Dave spoke to a full chapel of mourners as a friend of his lost buddy. He spoke seriously and wisely. For the literally hundreds of times that he had made us laugh, for once he had made us cry. I felt he had offered as much or more support and comfort in a few short minutes as I did with my longer eulogy.

Dave continued farming with his dad in Russellville, Kentucky. He later married a woman named Paige. It was a joy to see him recently at the 2019 Lipscomb homecoming reunion. I informed him that he would be highlighted in this chapter, and he offered his approval for my telling this story of our ministry together. We look forward to his zany Christmas card each year-end holiday season.

13

Bounteous Blessings and Perilous Pitfalls—The Many Roles of the Resident Preacher Outside the Pulpit

A complete education for a preaching minister, thoroughly furnishing him unto every good work and insulating him unto every ruinous temptation, consumes a lifetime. Quite literally. By the time a preacher is properly educated and emotionally equipped to maintain a lengthy tenure with some sizable congregation he is then, ironically, too old to be considered as a serious applicant for the position.

As an aside, the ideal age for a minister to get a prime pulpit position is in the thirty-five to forty-five-year-old range. Churches would not seek a pulpit minister in the sixty to seventy-year-old range, though some ministers that age might land an associate position such as "associate minister" or "minister for seniors."

In the True Church, the ideal candidate is "husband of one wife" (a nice term that ordinarily would mean he is not practicing polygamy, but in this case means he is not in a second marriage or, God forbid, a third marriage). Furthermore, the ideal candidate has between two and four children "in subjection" (meaning they behave during worship services and do not wear outlandish or immodest clothing, nor do they attend high school dance parties, or go to youth parties where there is laxity about drinking beer or other alcoholic beverages) and is "sound doctrinally" (meaning the candidate accepts ultra-conservative, party-line interpretation of Scriptures). If an unemployed preacher is over seventy and has no interest in selling life insurance, he might best consider a job giving food samples at Costco or Sam's or he might practice the following brief greeting: "Welcome to Walmart."

One basic premise: What a terrific blessing to work with people in some of the most important and life-changing situations in their lives and, subsequently, to come to know them with some depth and intimacy! To make these relationships even more important, then the minister is partner in helping his church family develop the values and priorities that make huge differences in their lives. The flip side of this reality coin: The resident minister can face all manner of perilous traps and pitfalls that potentially bring sadness, stress, and even unhappy termination of his tenure with the congregation that hired him.

WHY IS A PREACHING CAREER SO CHALLENGING?

There are two reasons for ministerial peril especially in resident, full-time positions. (The typical term for a resident preacher is "located preacher," presumably in contrast to one who cannot be located or is not willing to be residentially located.) First, the public and private lives of the preacher are totally merged. Unfair as this may seem, such is reality. In no other profession, not even in political life, is this merging of private and public lives so fulsome.

Every word the preacher utters away from the pulpit, the automobile he drives (perhaps even the dealer from which he bought the car), the way he spends his leisure time, the style that both he and his wife groom and dress, the stage productions and movies the two attend, the demeanor of his children, his guests in a public restaurant, the places he or his entire family take vacations, his closest friends, the topics and jokes that elicit his interest or his laughter, anything he does with a member of the opposite sex outside his immediate family, the establishments at which he and family members shop for clothing, and so on, *ad infinitum*—all are vital concerns to certain members of his congregation.

If church members could read their ministers' minds and heart, would they also invade this last bastion of privacy? You can jolly well bet your eternal life that many would and feel they were justified in doing so!

Sooner or later, and usually sooner, even the most morally strong and

?

carefully discrete minister will do or say something that will cross some influential member or fanatical faction in his home church in a doctrinally or morally wrong way. Let's face it: The minister may have given years to Bible study, even learning biblical languages, and achieved graduate degrees in religion and have subsequent years of Bible study completed, and there can be some sitting in the pews who have never spent one minute in academic study of the Bible who are confident they know more about biblical exegesis and interpretation than anyone else knows!

Second, the modern preacher is expected to play many roles well. He is expected to be, in addition to an eloquent pulpit orator, a Bible scholar, a skilled teacher, church administrator, business manager, marriage counselor, hospital chaplain, psychologist, fund raiser, public relations expert, community leader, civic club member, and omni-purpose speaker and "prayer" (*i.e.,* one who prays publicly at civic organization meetings, public functions, banquets, etc.), and master of ceremonies (just to name a few roles). Whether the congregation he serves actually grows numerically or diminishes numerically or simply stagnates—all these numerical outcomes rest squarely on his shoulders.

At times the preacher may wear the hats of chauffeur, youth chaperon, softball umpire, church custodian, song leader, cheerleader (literally and figuratively), and van or bus driver. He needs at least a good library, hard hat, tough skin, steel nerves, chauffeur's license, a convincing Santa Claus suit and a scary Halloween costume. No mortal, of course, can excel in all these roles.

Many freshly minted Bible and preaching majors leave the college, university, and/or graduate school of Bible/Religion with the delusion that the churches which call them to a pulpit position expect them to devote the quantum bulk of their time to diligent study, meditation, and excellence in sermon delivery. Such wishful thinking is ecclesiastical poppycock!

Any resident preacher, though possessing an eloquence that would make the apostle Paul jealous and the forthright courage of the prophet Amos, may as well draft his resignation letter if he makes an unforgivable mistake—paying no attention to human relations and the scores of minor roles he is expected to fulfill while in the midst of the brothers and sisters. That does not require excellence in *all* roles—only excellence with great flair in a few roles and at least a feigned interest and passable competence in the others. All these talents should be combined with a humble acceptance of whatever salary the elders have determined is merited.

BURTON COFFMAN AND J. EDGAR HOOVER

Among my blessings of associating with some terrific evangelists has been the opportunity to work in two meetings with Burton Coffman. Short in stature (guessing around 5' 5" or 5' 6"), Burton was the proverbial "live wire" and a bundle of energy. This indefatigable preacher/evangelist and fundraiser's efforts and perseverance in New York City and throughout the Bible Belt firmly established the Manhattan Church of Christ. I always remember counsel he gave as a guest lecturer to our class of young preaching students at Lipscomb. Burton declared there are three words which form the key to the success of the local preacher— visit, visit, visit! A visit from the local man of God sends a message to the visitee: "The church is important to you and you are important to the church."

Burton most surely recognized some of the hazards of pastoral visitation. The first time I met this courageous, colorful bantam of a man was on a Saturday morning before his scheduled meeting began the next morning with our congregation at Westwood church in McMinnville. My enjoyable assignment was spending the day with this illustrious pulpiteer, and thus I took him visiting with me, stopping first at the home of Bob and Mary Winton.

The Wintons owned two English setters and another dog of unknown pedigree named Gidget and, though all of them were quite friendly, they would commence fierce barking when a stranger arrived. One of the English setters, named J. Edgar Hoover but called Eddie for short, had an especially menacing bark while alternately nuzzling his sniffing nose into the body of a male visitor, usually at his crotch.

As we walked up the back sidewalk from my car, Burton got the standard loud barking and assertive sniffing welcome from Eddie. The guest evangelist suddenly stood rigid like a wooden Indian on the porch of an old country store while the dog both barked loudly between sniffs and wagged its tail. No doubt about it. Burton was alarmed. I felt a little embarrassment for him.

"Don't worry about that dog, Burton," I advised him. "His name is J. Edgar Hoover and he's very friendly. I've been around him a lot. He won't bite you."

Burton walked slowly up the walk. The Wintons walked out on their back porch and immediately apologized for their obstreperous canine.

"Well, I could see that the dog was giving a friendly message at one end and at the other end I was getting a hostile message," Burton explained. "I just didn't know which end of that blamed dog to believe." Burton always possessed a great sense of humor and laughed frequently. He seemed to have a ready joke or quip for every unusual occasion.

NHC NEEDING A THERMOSTAT ADJUSTMENT?

On my last tenure as pulpit minister at Brentwood's Owen Chapel, my family and I came to know and love the family of Keith Crow. Keith had a lengthy and quite successful career in sales with the 3M Corporation, and yet I am convinced his first love was pastoring a church family. He loved pastoral visiting and consequently was frequently called for officiating at weddings and funerals. When I "stepped down" from the pulpit at Owen Chapel, then Keith took my place and preached each Sunday for another two or three years, delivering substantive and carefully crafted sermons. Besides a love for all kinds of sports, Keith and I bonded through talking politics, playing tennis, attending concerts, biking, walking, hiking, and partnering in pastoral visitation.

On one Sunday afternoon following our typical Sunday lunch at Cool Springs Schlotsky or Red Lobster, we decided to drop by the nearby NHC where one of our older church sisters (guessing around seventy to seventy-five years of age) was a resident. Our wives, Glenda and Sandy, opted to relax in the lobby living room as Keith and I made our way to this good sister's private room. She seemed glad to see us and sat on the end of her bed and invited us to pull up chairs. As an aside, I recommend that if the pastoral visitor only wants a brief visit with a patient, for whatever reason, then best to say, "No, thank you, I'll just stand. I can only stay a few minutes."

After ten minutes or so, this fine church sister asked us, "Aren't you fellows hot in here? I'm burning up." And instantaneously with her last statement, she crossed her arms in front of her, used her hands to take the front tail of her sweat shirt, and jerked that shirt completely off so rapidly that we were at a loss for words. As she rolled up the shirt and put it beside her on the bed, Keith and I stood speechless for a few seconds. Ordinarily, Keith and I closed our pastoral visits with one of us offering a prayer. Catching his breath, Keith said, "Well [calling her name], our wives are waiting for us down in the lobby, I think we need to be going now." Nothing was said about one of us leading a prayer to close out the pastoral visit.

Keith and I left the room with the topless sister in Christ still sitting on the bed and seeming a bit perplexed at our precipitous departure. I exited with a smile of incredulity. Keith had a much more serious demeanor and went to the nurses' station and asked a nurse to go to that room and check on the resident. When we both arrived at the lobby to meet our wives, one or both of us first exclaimed something to the effect, "You won't believe what we just experienced!"

A year or two later, Keith and I were co-officiants at this good sister's funeral service. Quite prudently, in sharing our memories of her, the story of this visit at NHC was not conveyed in our eulogies.

OUT ON "VISITATION"

Most churches will tolerate a minister who maintains a recreational hobby if it is kept in moderation. A preacher I succeeded at the Westwood church, Harold Jones, was reported to have headed to the golf links every late spring and summer afternoon and into early fall, but he wisely muted criticism of this passionate devotion to his game by always including church buddies and prospective converts in his foursome. The fairways and putting greens were indeed, it was argued, the environs of true ministry and were allegedly alive with the sound of gospel music and spiritual talk as well as sliced balls. As an aside, Harold achieved something I had never heard before—he enjoyed three separate tenures, with other ministers between these tenures, as pulpit minister at the Westwood congregation.

At that time in my life, tennis was my game and, fortuitously, the back corner of the church grounds included a tennis court. I recall on several summer Wednesday or Sunday afternoon matches that a final set would last longer than expected and the early arrivals at the church building could be seen from the court driving into the parking lot. Immediately, I ended the game, dashed around the end of the church grounds and into the church home while hoping not to be seen, took a quick shower, dressed in befitting ministerial apparel, and rushed over to the church house to discharge my priestly responsibilities.

Demands of resident church work can come closing in on the minister. Time for study or time for hobbies may be cunningly arranged in a variety of ways. Generally speaking, for example, gospel meetings are virtual vacations for the visiting evangelist. The local minister might consider the gospel meeting a "break" from his routine and thus sit back and leave the spiritual "driving" to the guest evangelist.

One of my students at Belmont University (known as Belmont College when I taught there as adjunct professor in the late 80s) told me about a preacher friend, a Baptist minister. This pastor enjoyed fishing and other water sports, yet experienced difficulty getting away from demands and expectations of his calling. The preacher devised an ingenious solution. He purchased a new, fully equipped motor boat and privately christened the craft "Visitation." When anyone in his congregation sought him by calling his wife or secretary, the inquirer would be "honestly" informed, "Sorry he's not available right now. He's out on 'Visitation.'"

SPECIAL SPEAKING INVITATIONS

The preacher is considered first and foremost a public speaker. If he is not effective in public speaking, at least with minimal skills, he needs to pursue another calling.

The congregation, in fact the entire community, believes that since the preacher is a public speaker then he is an appropriate candidate to speak in nearly any venue or occasion and on any subject. From my experience I could propose two speaking opportunities that may be welcomed and then two speaking opportunities to be avoided.

My advice: Accept opportunities to speak for local civic clubs or other local organizations either as featured guest speaker or introducing another speaker. What a great opportunity to make contact with community leaders outside your own congregation, to share interests and concerns in light-hearted conversation, and to make new friends!

Also accept opportunities to present after-dinner speeches. Everyone needs to laugh. Humor is essential to emotional wellness. Laughter in a social setting builds relationships. Laughter recharges our hearts and souls, making us feel more fully human and alive. I find myself agreeing with Texan Liz Carpenter, who quipped, "I find laughter more necessary as I enter the springtime of my senility." Develop an inventory of appropriate, clean jokes you can adapt for almost any joyful occasion. The speaker will elicit more hearty laughter if he is able to inject the names of people sitting in the audience into his standard repertoire of stories. Among fellow preachers I always felt Jim Bill McInteer to have been a master at after-dinner speaking.

Two speaking opportunities might be avoided like the proverbial plague. One is speaking in a high school or college chapel service at a Christian institution. Both as Lipscomb student and faculty member I was expected to attend daily chapel services. I have also spoken in several chapel services at two or three Christian institutions. These students have already heard just about everything in the way of biblical exposition, correction, counsel, and warnings. Thus, many students despise the requirement to attend. In more recent chapel visits I have observed that the number of cell phones outnumbers the open Bibles and hymnals sitting on student laps by about ten to one. The guest speaker who skillfully captures and engages a chapel audience and leads attendees to listen attentively, laugh, or cry is rare indeed.

The other non-desirable speaking invitation is a commencement address. Yes, here is an opportunity to tap into your storehouse of wisdom and knowledge and eloquently present great counsel to high school or college graduates moving out into the "real world" or the next step in their education. Who are you kidding when you think these newly-minted graduates are going to remember your immortal words to cope with an uncertain future? The only concerns on their minds at that moment are getting the commencement service concluded, getting out of their uncomfortable caps and gowns, greeting and hugging family members and friends, and exiting promptly to the festive party!

In general, excluding speeches delivered at assisted living facilities (what my generation always called "nursing homes"), high school and university students compose the toughest audience a speaker can face. These kids have been raised in the bosom of all kinds of electronic nurturing, from television and movies to video games and computers, and awakening them to your personal wisdom delivered in a speech may be life's greatest oratorical challenge. Be ready for your deepest profundities and wisest observations to be met with blank stares and icy silence. (Yes, admittedly, the preacher can receive the same congregational responses while passionately delivering some of his cherished Sunday sermons.)

ASSEMBLY, CEREMONIAL, AND DEEPLY EMPATHETIC—THE VARIETIES OF PASTORAL PRAYER

There is such variety in the occasions for a preacher to lead a public prayer and a preacher needs skills of effective public praying. If the preacher excels in public praying, then he will be remembered for that fact alone. If the congregation is sizable, there are likely enough men willing to lead a prayer so that the minister need only lead special prayers in the assembly.

In assembly prayer, best to guard against overuse of pet petitions and phrases no matter how well-worded they may be. Judge Robert Brady, who was often called on to lead assembly prayer at Westwood, would invariably include this petition: "And, God, bless us in all our laudable undertakings." At that same congregation, the prayers of Dr. Glenn Davis never failed to move me for their connection to deep human concerns, current events, originality, and creativity in eloquence. As in preaching, when the minister prays in assembly it should seem as though every prayer thought is earnest and the minister has kept one hand on his Bible and the other hand on the current newspaper.

Some prayers can be blunt and brief. My last Sunday at Westwood, when the church seemed deeply divided and many felt at odds with the elders, deacon James Dillon was slated to lead the "main prayer." James walked to the microphone and bowed his head. I shall never forget that emphatic, passionate prayer: "Oh, Lord God, I just pray that our elders here will come to their senses and do the right thing for this church before it is too late. In Jesus' name. Amen." Then James seemed to hold his head high as he walked down the steps of the pulpit to his pew, pleased with his blunt courage for the moment.

Some preachers begin their sermons with a prayer. This hits me as a fairly recent and unusual trend—I always believed the time for a preacher to pray about his upcoming sermon would be at the conclusion of his last private moments of lesson preparation. Of course, if prayer is sincere and earnest, it can come at any time. The hymn "Lord, Speak to Me" is always appropriate before sermon presentation.

CEREMONIAL PRAYER

Let's face it: The preacher is going to be the one called on in a public setting to lead a prayer whenever event organizers deem public prayer appropriate. In past years, especially in the Bible belt, there could be a wide variety of occasions where the preacher is asked to pray publicly.

For at least one of the games each season of the Warren County High School Pioneer football team, for example, I was scheduled to lead the prayer. The whole occasion seemed a bit artificial to me. The press box announcer would ask everyone to rise and bow their heads and then declare: "The Reverend Perry Cotham of the Westwood Church of Christ [the announcer should be forgiven for not knowing the True Church minister is never referred to either as "Reverend" or "Pastor"] will lead our invocation." (I am always comfortable with the word "invocation," all the while aware that a majority do not know its technical meaning.) I would then take the microphone in hand, pull out an index card on which I had written what I deemed to be an appropriate prayer for the occasion, and read the prayer with enough volume that I could hear some echo from the amplifiers around the stadium. My assignment was completed and I had received free admission to the game—now on to the bleachers and the game!

While serving as one of the ministers at Franklin's Fourth Avenue congregation, I had two invitations for leading a public prayer that were challenges. One was the invocation prior to start of the annual Franklin Rotary Club Rodeo. I knew surely I needed to pray for the safety of the cowboys and cowgirls competing, but should I also pray for the horses, ponies, bulls, calves, and steers? Should I refer to these animals as "equine and bovine athletes" and pray for their safety, too? Again, I wrote out and read that prayer over the public address system, but the challenge was a unique one.

The other invitation came from my dear friend William Walker, Sr., upon the grand opening of his new and modern showroom and garage for his Chevy-Olds dealership at a brand new location in Franklin at Highway 96 and Carothers just off I-65. Billy planned a special occasion and reception that included the mayor, city commissioners, prominent businesspeople, and personal friends. My invocation was the first part of the program. Again, I pondered a long time on what should be prayed.

As a stress reliever to entertain our church staff, I first wrote out a facetious prayer: "O Lord, we pray that customers will be convinced of the value, either in first sale or trade-in value, of these Oldsmobiles and Chevrolet cars and trucks. We pray that all these engines and other automotive parts will perform to expectations, even well beyond warranty. We pray that young people who have dates in these cars will behave morally and the music they play in these autos will be appropriate music, and ideally Christian music. May these automobiles protect occupants in any kind of accident." Of course, I ditched the facetious prayer and wrote one I trusted to be much more appropriate for the occasion. Billy, an elder and very ethical person, had honored me by this invitation.

Sometimes a minister may not want to lead a prayer in a setting where he is called on only because it seems "the right thing to do." A minister often gets the feeling there would not be a prayer if he were not present. For example, at wedding rehearsal dinners where the wedding party and wedding families did not strike me as spiritually-minded, and everyone is already drinking and talking loudly and young children noisily running around, and then the father of the bride or the MOTB feels that a prayer should be offered before the food is served. I have prayed publicly in those situations only because I am called on, though it seemed awkward and difficult to get everyone quiet and in the mood for prayer. The human side of me was always tempted to say, "Let's just skip the prayer and sit down and eat."

DEEPLY PRIVATE, PERSONAL, AND EMPATHETIC

There are prayer occasions for the preacher that are simply unforgettable and often tragic. And sometimes the immediacy of the tragedy means that no prayer can be effectively uttered.

Every minister needs to be able to pray almost anywhere when prayer is needed and appropriate. When Philip Morrison served a congregation as pulpit minister in the Washington D. C. area, he frequently addressed Congressional Representatives in his listening audience; occasionally, one or more were regular members. During the 1974 Watergate hearings, a member of the House Judiciary Committee called Philip in his office and reported his distress: "As a member of this committee, I have just been permitted privately to hear the secret Nixon tapes, and this political situation is far worse than anyone might imagine. I need you to pray for me." Philip replied: "I'll be glad to do that." There was a long, awkward pause. The congressman asked if Philip had heard his request. The Representative wanted prayer right then on the phone. This was a new experience for the young minister and seemed a bit awkward. Later, praying on the phone or even writing out a prayer in an email or text can flow naturally. I have prayed on the phone with some distressed person on several occasions, the only drawback being inability to see facial expressions of the other person—never attempted praying by FaceTime.

In 99% of my hospital visits I would invariably offer to pray with the patient, typically clasping the patient's hand. If the patient is in a coma or asleep, I could still pray with the attending family members. As a Lipscomb Bible and preaching major and still in college, I recall making hospital visits with Myron Keith, a respected minister who was exactly (to the day) ten years older than me. I would follow Myron on his pastoral rounds and learn from him. Once he surprised me in a hospital room by asking me to pray for the patient. I recall how awkward I felt at the time, but early on I began to feel much at ease in offering a prayer to any patient that wanted it. Sometimes it seemed a little awkward when there were other family members or friends in the hospital room that I had never met and especially when some of these other visitors seemed not at all spiritual-minded.

Two tragedies are unforgettable. In one situation, my basketball playing at the "Rec" Center in Franklin was interrupted by an emergency call. I ended my "pick up" basketball game immediately. Two teenage brothers had been killed instantly when the pick-up truck they were driving home from school hit the concrete siding of a new bridge and flipped over onto the dry, rocky bed of a creek; the older brother was driving. Their parents were wonderful people and faithful members at the Fourth Avenue church.

Slowly, various members of our church gathered at Williamson Medical Center. We offered the parents hugs. All of us spoke in hushed tones. Neither I nor anyone else offered a prayer that early evening. We all just stood by, taking deep breaths but unable to find any appropriate words. Any conversation was sparing and always in hushed tones. What an immense and unspeakable tragedy! The next morning, Richard Ellis, our youth director, and I went to the boys' home and conversed in subdued tones with the mom and dad, both understandably still in deep shock and near denial. A few days later there was a double funeral conducted in our church auditorium.

Williamson Medical Center was also a place where I was asked specifically to lead a prayer by a mother who was totally stressed out from horrifying information—one of her twin sons was being delivered by ambulance to the hospital after a terrible ATV accident on high school grounds after a school day. As minister in their church family, I was requested to come to the hospital and inform the mom that her son had not survived this freakish accident. This mom was a teacher at a local elementary school and many of her teaching colleagues and other friends also gathered with her, some surely knew or suspected the news was tragic. More and more people gathered, hugged the mom while saying nothing, adding to the mom's stress level. The group got large enough that a hospital supervisor requested we move from the hallway where ambulances unload patients into a large adjoining room.

Once we got into the room, everyone remaining silent with a sober countenance, the mom nervously spoke up and said, "I'm asking Perry to lead us in a prayer that my son will not have been seriously injured." This was the most difficult prayer situation I have ever experienced. I knew the boy had been fatally injured. The mom did not as yet know the terrible news and I kept dreading and delaying for the proper time to inform her.

Those are times in which one "hopes against hope" that somehow there was misinformation and that the loved child was still an accident survivor. While I knew the ambulance could arrive at any moment, I knew also I could not ask God that the boy would not have been seriously injured when I already knew, as did likely many others in the room, that the youth did not survive. About all one can pray aloud in those pastoral situations is that, no matter what news we are soon to receive, those who know and love someone who is suddenly in peril can learn a sense of acceptance and peace with reality, however harsh and devastating that reality may be.

I stayed at the hospital another hour or so that afternoon, always knowing that physical and emotional presence is worth far more than any words that could be uttered. I recall being with the family in a waiting room—not speaking, just sitting with them. Another minister came to the door, quietly entered, and softly announced he had come to pray with the family. One of the family members told him, "Thank you for coming, but, please, we don't need or want any prayers right now." He quietly and respectfully exited the room.

On two other occasions that I recall when offering to pray, I was told by the person (each was a male) that he did not want a prayer from me. One was beside a hospital bed and the man, an Otter Creek member, answered, "No, I don't want your prayer, but I will pray for myself, if you don't mind." "Please do," I said. And thus he prayed: "Dear Lord, I am getting sick of being in this hospital. I am sick of doctors not knowing what is really wrong with me. Thank you for sending Brother Cotham my way, but who I really want you to send my way is a doctor who can give proper diagnosis and treatment and send me home to my family.

The other time a man refused a prayer was in a counseling situation wherein his wife had accused him of infidelity. This man said he did not want my prayers or anyone else's prayers. That session did not last much longer.

A lighter story is needed to conclude this topic. An older preacher friend in the Pentecostal tradition, L. H. Hardwick, founding and long-time pastor at Nashville's Christ Church, experienced a unique sensation. After visiting a middle-aged fellow in a hospital, Brother Hardwick offered to pray and, as Pentecostals are more likely to do, raised one hand, placed the other hand on top the patient's head, closed his eyes, and began his prayer. "My hand kept sliding all over the man's head and I could tell the patient was moving his head, so I pressed harder and gripped tighter," L. H. said. "The strange head movement continued with my hand sliding everywhere, so I decided to end the prayer more quickly. When I opened my eyes," L. H. chuckled, "I discovered the man had been wearing a toupee. This hair piece had been sliding all over his slick head during the prayer and was pretty much covering his face and eyes when I said 'Amen' and opened my eyes."

THE "GIFT" OF CHURCH ADMINISTRATION

Church administration may be considered a "gift" or a "calling" that is given to at least a few devoted individuals. Is not such a premise drawn from no less than the Apostle Paul himself? The KJV translates Paul as saying "there are differences in administrations, but the same Lord" (1 Cor. 12: 5; the NIV renders this as "different kinds of service.") Of course, there is no divine command that a congregation should purchase real estate and build an expansive church edifice equipped with an education wing, an office suite, a multi-purpose building, an elevator to lift people or cargo between floors, a paved parking lot with a covered "drive through" near an entrance, and other conveniences. Realistically, the larger the congregation and the more property it owns, the greater the need for a church administrator.

For ten years I was assigned to be "Minister of Administration," among other titles, for the Fourth Avenue Church of Christ in Franklin. I could not begin to list all the responsibilities and interactions this role required: securing the building; making certain the building was opened and locked at the proper times; maintaining comfortable facilities' temperature in heating and cooling; hiring clerical staff; hiring and monitoring custodial employees and their performance; maintaining church vans and other vehicles; maintaining proper lawn care; meeting drop-by visitors and answering their questions; supporting church communications; dealing with salespeople and vendors dropping by the offices unannounced; dealing with "drop-by" poor or indigent people asking for financial aid for food or paying their utility bills or transportation expenses; and on and on.

Of course, some of those duties could be shared or delegated. In time, an administrator learns vigilance as visitors would drop in and wander through the building with "itchy fingers," a nice euphemism for stealing anything they can hide under their clothing and then exit another door (our building had at least eight entrances/exits).

As administrator, with the assistance of our secretarial staff, I always needed a scheduling book for the rental of our facilities. For a number of years our congregation possessed the largest auditorium in Williamson County; counting the balcony, the auditorium seated around a thousand people. Thus, outside parties who expected a sizable turn-out for a wedding or funeral would seek to reserve our auditorium, and often the fellowship hall below it, for their special event.

Working with the elders and ministry staff in formulating rules and guidelines for church building rental was essential. We established one rate for outsiders and another, more economical, rate for our members. Membership had its privileges. In the case of reserving the building for weddings, the elders determined the spacious fellowship hall on the lower level could be used for a wedding reception: a set rate for auditorium rental and a higher rate for additional use of the fellowship hall for reception; a rental deposit was required; a key could be checked out by a family for use in rehearsals; a pre-determined fee for custodial services (clean-up) would be paid in advance by the family doing the rental; the serving of alcoholic beverages and dancing were strictly forbidden during the reception. Rules for use of our building for a public funeral service were not nearly as detailed, understandably.

As for church weddings, reservations were often made many months in advance of the joyful event. Sometimes prominent citizens, such as entertainers within the country music field, rented the building for weddings. One movie producer, making a film set in historic downtown Franklin, rented our building for use by director, producer, and actors to take breaks, change clothing, store props, and enjoy catered meals and drinks. Our church building was only a half block away from Main Street. Sometimes there were weddings within families of local political officials. I always looked at this role in church administration as opportunity to meet and serve new acquaintances. Of course, I personally did not need to be present for weddings or funerals within families I did not know personally, though sometimes I chose to attend.

CAN A SWEET FAMILY TRADITION BE HONORED?

One wedding occasion remains unforgettable. The father of the bride-to-be, whose family were not Fourth Avenue members, came to my office in a sense of urgent panic. When this father had mentioned to our secretary that there would be a quintet from the Nashville Symphony that would play for the dancing at the reception, she reminded this gentleman that the contract he signed had stipulated no dancing or alcoholic beverages in our fellowship hall.

"I was told you are the one I need to see about this," the father (guessing around 50 years old) soberly said to me. "Your secretary just told me that we cannot do dancing in your fellowship hall."

"Well, that is a rule in the regulations you signed when you reserved the building and paid your deposit," I reminded him calmly.

"I see that in writing now," he said, with paper in hand. "But, honestly, there are several other stipulations and I just did not read them carefully and I don't remember reading that prohibition about dancing," he explained. "I just never thought polite, social dancing would be a problem in your church fellowship hall or in any church for that matter."

"I sympathize with you," I stated with empathetic tone, "but on the other hand, even though I did not write all the rules, I am expected to support them and request compliance."

"Well, it is too late for us to change the venue for either the wedding or the reception. Invitations were sent out three or four weeks ago," he pleaded politely. "Had I known about this prohibition on dancing, I would never have rented your facility. I can live with the prohibition on alcoholic beverages. We already have sparkling grape juice for the toasts that looks like champagne, but we also have paid big bucks for the quintet from the Nashville Symphony."

"Well, that quintet can still play," I countered.

"But it's not the same. Could you please make this one exception?" he pleaded. I told him I would see what I could do, that I would need to talk to our elders. He was a polite man and seemed a loving father and I truly felt his pain. "I will go home and discuss this with my wife, but I assure you she will not be a happy camper. She didn't see that rule in print either." The father of the bride left my office.

The next morning I received a call from this father. He was very polite and said he understood my predicament, but he wanted permission for one "small family tradition" to be honored at the reception. "That's fine," I replied, "and what is that?"

"Our family has had several weddings, each of which my father-in-law has enjoyed a first dance with the new bride in the family. At first, my wife's dad had that one special dance both with her and then with my sister-in-law and then at the weddings of two granddaughters. It's a real sweet, innocent tradition and we want to maintain it," he explained. "So, may my immediate family have your permission to gather over in the corner of the fellowship hall just in front of the symphony quintet, and my daughter and her granddad experience this one dance for sake of family tradition? The others present will surely hear the music but likely not even notice the one little dance."

"That seems so sensible to me, just honoring your family tradition in a sweet way, so I, personally, would approve it," I replied, "however, perhaps I need to run this past our elders. I will urge them to approve this proposal. I don't think there's a problem."

"Thank you so very much," the dad said with relief in his voice.

I asked our secretary to contact the elders about a very brief meeting after the upcoming Wednesday night classes. We then gathered in the minister's office. We shut the door and sat down together and I told them our meeting need not last more than five minutes. I then explained the entire situation, said that I had given permission to this family for the one dance tradition with a granddad at their daughter's wedding, but that I wanted to inform them (the elders) that this family had originally wanted everyone to feel free to dance but was attempting to honor our rental regulations.

Once I explained the situation, I expected an immediate rubber stamp approval, perhaps even commendation that I had secured a sensible, even sweet, compromise. Immediately, one elder, Jim McKinney, declared, "Perry, I have four daughters, that tradition seems like a sweet one, I have no problem with it." Two or three other elders made very hesitant and slight affirmative head motions but no spoken words.

A pall of silence then fell on the other elders. I looked at Harry, who was sitting in the minister's chair, his head was down and nodding in a slow, negative fashion and his lips were pursed. Then he spoke: "Well, this might not be sinful, but I'm just thinking it will set a bad precedent and any other family could claim a right to dance here at their wedding reception." "I agree," Walter said, "It would be a bad precedent. And word will probably get out around the church and even around town. We must remember the 'weaker brother.' Sure can't cause that 'weaker brother' to stumble."

Another long uncomfortable period of silence followed. I started to inform them there is a difference between causing "a weaker brother to *stumble*" and "a weaker brother to *grumble*" and that some of *them* were seemingly acting like "weaker brothers" looking for justifiable reason to grumble. Of course, such a statement would have been the height of imprudence on my part.

"So should I inform this father of the bride that as a group our elders are denying the request for one musical number to be enjoyed with his daughter, the new bride, dancing with her grandfather?" I asked.

The response was all non-verbal communication. All but one slowly motioned his head in affirmation, that is, they agreed I should inform the father that his daughter and his father-in-law could not dance to a single musical selection. The elders could surely see I was crestfallen. I dreaded calling the father of the bride. I waited till the next day to make that call, lest our elders talk again by phone that evening and hopefully later report to me a change of collective mind.

The next day I called the father as I had promised. I told him how sorry I was for the situation, that our elders had opposed the grandfather and new bride dance for one musical selection and that I had attempted to convince them otherwise. "However, let me tell you one thing," I said to the father. "I personally think the grandfather-bridal dance is a sweet tradition. Now I am not going to be at your family wedding and I doubt any of our elders will be present," I continued. "Therefore, whatever happens at your wedding and your reception is beyond both my personal concern and my personal business. And, personally speaking, it's pretty hard for me to be shocked or offended."

The father thanked me graciously and our conversation ended after I declared, "I wish all of you the best." The wedding was upcoming on that Saturday night.

Postscript to the story: On Sunday morning when I am entering our church building from the back entrance, Opal Anderson, the sweet wife of elder Ed Anderson, who was in charge of locking up the building even late at night, came running to me in a state of near panic. "Oh, Brother Perry," she said in a frenzied and trembling voice that momentarily reminded of Edith Bunker of *All in the Family* fame. "Ed and I came over here last night between 10:00 and 11:00 to see if the custodian had cleaned up the building and then locked all the doors and you won't believe what we saw happening!"

"No, please tell what was happening," I implored, knowing she would tell me anyway.

"We heard music and went down the steps to the fellowship and, lo and behold, I have never seen a sight like this before, especially in a church house!" she exclaimed.

I tried to be calm. "What was going on?"

"There must have been two or three hundred people, all of them dancing away like crazy," Opal said. "I just couldn't believe it. I've never been so shocked in my life! And we had to wait a long time for them to stop dancing so we could lock up the building."

"Pray tell, surely that's not so! How could that possibly happen?" I then declared, giving very little thought at the time that I had totally faked my surprise, pretending to be horrified at what had occurred the night before in our house of worship.

Though I had truly expected there to be only the one grandfather-granddaughter dance, I had no reason to doubt Opal's report. Ed, having been in the previous elders' meeting, said nothing at the time. When I delivered the eulogy at Opal's service a few years afterward there were several sweet and funny stories that I shared about Opal. She had been active in various areas of service, including supervision of our clothing ministry. I did not tell the fellowship hall dancing story, however. Even telling it here is meant as appreciation for her values and concerns as a sweet Christian lady.

My immediate, first response to Opal was indeed hypocritical, but on that Sunday morning the full story was much too long to explain to her with the worship service beginning momentarily. I have hoped to be forgiven the hypocrisy in feigning moral indignation.

THE ART OF PASTORAL COUNSELING

Every resident preacher is expected to devote a certain amount of his time to pastoral counseling. This art has become a special academic discipline nowadays complete with its specialized journals, jargon, and curriculum. Some larger churches have wisely sought the employ of a full-time therapist or family counselor.

This premise cannot be successfully refuted: The most important work a resident minister achieves is performed *outside* the pulpit. An hour of effective counseling to a person or family, it may be contended, is worth more than ten hours of pulpit preaching to the same party. On the other hand, pastoral counseling is a field of land mines waiting to be detonated. Any immature or inexperienced preacher must "guard his heart" and not harbor secret ego-satisfaction from receiving the deepest confessions of evil thoughts or moral transgressions from his parishioners.

My advice to the novice pastoral counselor: Do as little counseling as possible. Sometimes a "one shot" effort will be sufficient either to close out counseling or refer the person or the couple to a certified therapist. Here are four special problems:

First, the preacher may present himself as an expert in either therapy or biblical theology and, in reality, he may be expert in neither. A young preacher, or even an older one who seems to have lived his life mostly insulated from the real world, may seem all too naive or ever so shockable for some parishioners to share all the failures and sinful nitty-gritty of their personal lives.

Some preachers know just enough about relationship dynamics, personality theory, and family systems to be innocuous at best (by uttering some vague, vapid spiritual advice such as "You two need to go home and start loving each other more because Jesus loves both of you) or outright dangerous at worse (as in the case of the preacher who told a battered wife, "You don't have a scriptural right to leave your husband just because he slaps and pinches you when he's angry. Just get ready to bop him on the head next time with a big skillet!").

Second, pastoral counseling can consume a huge amount of time. An old fashioned spiritual and emotional bean spilling does take time when it's done right. Generally speaking, spilling the same beans to a psychologist or psychiatrist might not be as time consuming since forking over a hundred dollars or more per session performs wonders for clients in producing succinctness.

Third, the pastoral counselor runs the risk of being misquoted or misrepresented by someone in the counseling session. The minister must maintain confidentiality, but the counselee is under no such ethical mooring. In the True

Church, issues related to divorce and remarriage are particularly nettlesome, a lesson I learned in a painful way at the Westwood church.

In this case I was counseling two young women in joint sessions, both sisters, and both experiencing the pain of divorce. I attempted to share concepts of God's grace, concepts joyously received by the two and which they shared with their mother and friends. The mother, for some reason, preferred a hard line solution to their complex marital situation and shared her own filtered version of my counsel with one of my elders—a professional in his field whom I knew had been lobbying many months for my involuntary departure from the church's pulpit.

This gave my non-supportive elder all the ammunition he needed to file a formal grievance with the other members of the "board." When I met with the elders and some mediators to add light to this confusion by explaining my doctrinal position undergirding my counseling advice, this elder was unrelenting in his vocal criticism of me.

I addressed him personally and respectfully, politely calling his name: "The way you talk about me is troubling," I confessed. "Why, you make it sound like I'm a heretic and a blasphemer."

"I never said you were a blasphemer!" the elder snapped back immediately. I thus found some measure of comfort that I was only considered to be a heretic. (Before this conference had ended, by mutual agreement a date was set for me to terminate my ministry at this congregation. I had learned a painful lesson.)

Fourth, it should be mentioned that the counseling session is often filled with interesting revelations and tough challenges to the preacher's empathetic skills. Any preacher who comes across in the pulpit as compassionate and understanding will likely, over the long haul, have confessed many times over to him a breach of every command in the Decalogue with the possible except of the sixth one. There are plenty of Christians who will silently utter some equivalent of the prayer of Augustine: "O Lord, help me to be pure, but not yet." Sooner or later the counselor will encounter a Mae West-type churchgoer who confesses that "whenever I'm caught between two evils, I take the one I've never tried."

Within a few years of counseling ministry, the preacher will concur with "the preacher" of Ecclesiastes that, at least when it comes to church members' misbehavior, there is indeed nothing new under the sun. In fact, after a while the minister can, upon hearing the prologue and opening incidents of a marital conflict, fill in the rest of the story with amazing accuracy.

Also, with years of experience and maturity, the preacher in his early years of ministry who is almost shocked over some deeply true and heart-rending confessions in time learns the same sins, mistakes, shortcomings, and dysfunctional behavior may be confessed again and again. There are two sins the pastoral counselor is much less likely to hear confessed—the hunger and thirst for personal wealth and the inordinate desire for enhanced social and professional status among one's peers. The counselor will seldom, if ever, hear a fellow church member confess, "I've been far too materialistic and too desirous of acquisition."

Like any counselor, a minister in a pastoral role must learn to be non-shockable (or at least to appear non-shocked) at any true confession! The minister who is an authentic counselor must possess genuine love and unconditional positive regard for those who seek his advice and support.

A PASTORAL COUNSELOR FALLS OFF HIS ROCKER

Sometimes the story is not so unusual as much as it is the people who bring the story to the counselor. A friend and Christian professional counselor, George Spain, tells of a couple who had been married for over sixty years who came to him for counseling. The man was in his upper eighties and the woman was in her seventies. "The long steps leading to the front door of the office building in which I practiced were like climbing the steps of a Mayan temple," George remembers. "By the time the old man finally reached the top, he was wheezing and breathing heavily. His wife started berating and ridiculing him for being so slow in climbing the steps. The man had to sit for a while and catch his breath before he could answer her" George explained. "It was obvious to me that some of their relationship problems were aggravated by aging and degenerative processes."

Becoming too relaxed and too informal in a counseling situation is easily possible. George relates another experience which illustrates this problem:

> In one counseling session, just as emotions were heating up, I struck an informal pose. I leaned back in my swiveling, pedestal rocking chair. Then I relaxed my arms above my shoulders and clasped my hands behind my neck and maintained that posture for several minutes while listening to my client. Suddenly, one of the caster roller wheels on my rocker chair snapped and I went flying backward to the floor on my rear end. In those few moments as I slowly picked myself up, I tried to "get outside my body" and imagine what it would be like to see a counselor flip over on his back. It seemed so absurd. Suddenly, it came to me what I should say. "You have just seen a demonstration of someone falling off his rocker," I told my client.

On another counseling occasion, George lit a pipe and puffed away during a client's recital of a laundry list of personal woes. (Of course, no preacher should light a pipe or any tobacco product while counseling or doing anything else in public! He might could indulge if so inclined when hundreds of miles away from all his parishioners on a vacation.) As the session continued, George routinely knocked ashes out of his pipe by hitting the rim of the metal waste can. Before the session was over, and quite suddenly, George saw flames jetting out of the waste can. The counseling session came to an immediate halt.

CLOSE TO GOD IN THE NUDE—IS THIS POSSIBLE?

Occasionally, however, someone comes along with a tale of hanky panky or genuine distress so unique, so titillatingly interesting, that the pastoral counselor discovers a personal challenge to his skills. One example for me arose years ago in the context of premarital counseling for a middle-aged couple engaged for a second marriage for each party.

The two, whom I will call Luke and Rhonda, seemingly shared an intense relationship based on a mutual spiritual commitment. Verbally and nonverbally, they frequently expressed their love for one another. They had asked me to officiate at their wedding and, given their maturity and age, I felt confident about the success of the union, especially when they both concurred that a few sessions of premarital counseling would be beneficial.

After a long opening session in which I explored with the pair all the usual kinds of issues—economic, in-laws, religious commitment, sexual compatibility—I felt even more confident about their chances of fulfillment and happiness. In subsequent sessions Rhonda seemed reluctant about commitment though she longed for intimacy and partnership. She was a devout Christian woman who had experienced much pain and ostracism from leaders in her home congregation because of her divorce years earlier and did not want to risk such pain again. I did not understand the real reason for Rhonda's hesitancy until Luke invited me to join him alone for supper one evening. I allowed him to name the time and place.

The two of us met at the Green Hills Shoney's family restaurant in Nashville. Luke informed me that the meal was on him and I rightfully concluded that my supper would be his only free-will offering for my hours of counseling (I have never charged for counseling services). Somewhere between the visit to the salad bar and the main course my counselee broached the main point for discussion.

"The main reason Rhonda is hesitant about this marriage is that for years I have enjoyed visiting nudist camps," Luke stated matter-of-factly.

"Hmm," I intoned, continuing to chew slowly on my "half pound ground round" and pretend an unshockable nonchalance.

"Furthermore, I want to continue spending my weekend and my vacations at various nudist colonies. There's one in Murfreesboro for weekends and one family camp in Florida that I enjoy for longer vacations. Rhonda doesn't seem to like this idea at all, in fact she's vehemently opposed, but I want her to go with me. I want her to try it just once," Luke continued. "I know she'd like it."

"Why do you personally like it? And why do you think she would like it?" I asked earnestly, harboring some ideas of my own about his possible interest.

"Well, it's all so natural. That's how God created us. I feel close to God and nature when I'm there. There's no greater feeling in the world than to go swimming in the altogether. And nothing is better than a total tan."

"Well, it doesn't seem all that natural to me," I replied. "Have you ever injured yourself jumping off the high board or standing too close to the campfire? And what about sitting on an old splintery picnic bench at the nudist camp?" I thought I had asked some pertinent questions, though I confess to an internal smile as I raised them. "Why don't you just invest in a private pool or get a Jacuzzi for your back porch or deck and get your nude water thrills at home and away from total strangers?" I reasoned with him.

"No, you don't seem to understand that I am serious about this. Rhonda thinks that I am sinning because I like to enjoy nature this way," Luke explained. "I told her to show me one solitary scripture that calls social nudism a sin. She can't do it. You're not the first preacher I have talked to. I've talked to several other ministers. They can't find a scripture either. One or two of them didn't even want to talk to me about it. At least you are willing to sit and talk to me about this topic. The other ministers think I'm either crazy or sick."

I remained silent. He seemed surprised that I did not blast him with words of shock and condemnation.

"Rhonda and I have agreed to let you settle this dispute. Rhonda's known you for a long time and respects you as a preacher and she'll abide by your judgment. I just ask for a scripture," Luke pleaded.

"I don't have a single scripture for you, but what about those New Testament principles of modest apparel and decency and Jesus' condemnation of lust?" I offered, knowing he had already formulated an answer for each.

"Modest apparel is always relative," Luke countered. "What's modest in the South Sea Islands would be indecent in a Nashville shopping mall. There's a time to be fully clothed and a time to be naked. We were born naked. Isaiah pulled a public protest by walking and preaching nude in the streets, didn't he?"

"Interesting point, but …"

"As for lust, I'll tell you the truth. I don't lust at all in a nudist camp. If I lust it's when I visit the poolside at an adult singles' apartment complex or walk on a beach where there are lots of shapely women wearing bikinis. Just looking at naked bodies won't make you lust."

"I can see that," I stumbled, "or I don't see that, as the case may be." I wanted to be fair and I was at a loss for words and I sensed he was in no mood for any impromptu humorous quips from me.

"Besides, there are some wonderful, family people who are practicing nudists," Luke argued his case. "There's absolutely no crime there. Nothing ever gets stolen. There's no hypocrisy. When you meet a person in the nude you can't tell if he's a pauper or a millionaire. We're all equal."

"But can you tell if that new person you meet is a 'straight' or a 'weirdo'?" I queried.

Luke ignored my last question. "A lot of them go to church."

"Maybe you could establish a special ministry there, maybe build an outdoor chapel for weekend services. Think of some catchy name for your ministry, such as 'good news for good nudes' or something like that," I countered, unfairly subjecting his statement to *reductio ad absurdum.* I thought he was Luke!

The curious side of me led me to ask James some questions about nudist camp life in general—the personalities and ages of folks one would find there, the cost, operation, attitudes of first-timers, and so on. I was certainly hard-pressed to find a single scripture which specifically addressed Luke's interest. My counselee interpreted my lack of wholesale condemnation of his recreation and my questioning mode as acceptance of his recreational preferences and reported to Rhonda that I was the first minister to give his penchant for nudism a personal stamp of approval.

Nothing was further from the truth, however. When the three of us met for the next counseling session, I continued to raise questions about normal behavior and the "need" for this kind of recreation on a continual basis and the attitudes toward personal uniqueness and the sanctity of the body that nudism conveyed. Ultimately for me, the bottom line (pardon the pun) was summed up in my question to Luke: "Since Rhonda opposes your frequenting nudist colonies and will be highly uncomfortable accompanying you there, are you willing to forego this component of your lifestyle for the sake of a meaningful marriage relationship?"

Luke's reply was an exercise in circumlocution. Through the verbiage he never convinced Rhonda or me that his answer was lovingly affirmative. A few days later Rhonda called and informed me that she had cancelled the engagement and therefore I would not be needed to officiate at their wedding.

DANGEROUS MEN AND DANGEROUS WOMEN

The pastoral counselor profits from an advantage in counseling church members that other counselors seldom employ, namely intercessory prayer. If the counselee believes that God may be summoned for aid for any human problem, the use of prayer provides mighty spiritual and psychological assistance.

On the other hand, pastoral counselors have been known to put prayer to dubious and devious use by subtly giving further direction to the counselee. I've heard prayers in which a Christian counselor asked God for his counselee to receive the spiritual strength to know and do certain specific actions and strategies which the counselee might challenge during the regular part of the session but will not find it proper to interrupt a prayer.

Many a Christian counselor has attempted to referee a verbal shouting match. Sometimes one does not get at the truth of a situation until hostility gets expressed before a counselor. I recall one or two marital counseling situations where the wife and husband sat at opposite ends of a sofa in my office, with arms folded and body language that bespoke hostility, and commenced accusing and blaming each other in loud, angry voices. Some couples seem to have come to near physical blows in a session. Nothing is more frightening, however, than actual physical threats of one party upon another.

One Church of Christ preacher witnessed a tragic event in a counseling session. In April 1991, Ft. Worth College Hill Church minister Robert Waller was counseling a couple which had been married nearly forty-three years. The differences between this couple may have been far greater than anyone suspected. In the midst of an afternoon counseling session, the 67-year old husband pulled a .38 caliber pistol from his pocket and fired four shots into his wife's body. He then dropped the gun to the floor and made no effort to flee. The sixty-year-old wife underwent two emergency surgeries but died the following morning. Three days later Waller spoke at the woman's memorial service.

The neophyte preacher will soon learn that the majority of the church members who come to him for counseling will be female. This will be true in any congregation he serves. One reason for female openness to counseling is cultural—women in our culture are more open to sharing feelings and basing friendships on the sharing of feelings than are men. Cross-gender factors may play a role, *e.g.,* a woman may feel that a male counselor will be more sympathetic.

Another reason is that women easily transfer to a male counselor, especially a minister of the church, feelings which more appropriately should be attached to another male such as a husband or a father. Some devout women finally reach the conclusion that the only time a woman succeeds in changing a male, it is facetiously claimed, is when he is a baby. The minister then becomes the most likely candidate for sainthood and the female client may subconsciously begin to idealize him. (How true the old saying that Mahatma Gandhi was what some wives wish their husbands were: thin, tan, and moral!)

Every preacher must resolve for himself how he relates, both physically and emotionally, to the women in his congregation. This is the precise issue that many preachers refuse to discuss in any public forum, but it is both real and crucially important.

My Lipscomb college class in homiletics did not deal with this sensitive issue. In retrospect, I have always felt this omission was a major neglect and deficiency in our ministerial training. There was one statement, however, offered by Brother Baxter which I'll never forget: "There'll be women in your church who'll want your attention. Some of these women can get you in deep trouble," the Bible department chairman counseled. "My advice and personal policy is that a preacher never touch a woman physically except in the area from the tip of her fingers up to her elbows." One older minister I knew quite well maintained a policy of never riding alone in an automobile or having a lunch alone with any woman other than his wife or sister.

Brother Baxter's advice seemed rather conservative even for the mid-1960s. Hyper-cautiousness would make any minister about as warm as a halibut on ice, seemingly. However, following that advice is indeed, to use the old expression, "playing it safe." Furthermore, if an adult female were in that class, she would have been justified in arguing that it's not simply a woman that gets a minister in trouble—the minister also makes choices and bears at least equal responsibility if not greater responsibility for improper conduct and its consequential pain.

In the intervening years since having heard our godly Bible chairman's advice, on the other hand, I've learned that not a few ministers wish they had adopted and implemented such safe, wise counsel.

WATCH OUT FOR "THE PIE WOMAN"

"Watch out for the pie woman in your congregation," a co-worker within Tennessee's Department of Human Services named Thelma Berry once told me. For three years between university professorship and church ministry I worked in the staff training division of DHS and met many interesting, hard-working, and underpaid professionals. Thelma was raised in the African-American church, her parents were educators and her grandfather served African-American churches as minister and was the founding president of Tennessee's Lane College. Thelma is a most intelligent and very sweet person, thus I figured she had learned something from her heritage worth passing along to me.

"Who is the pie woman?" I asked, thinking I already knew the answer.

"The pie woman is the lady in the congregation who is always bringing a freshly baked pie to the minister," Thelma explained. "Of course it doesn't have to be a pie. It could be a favorite cake, a vase of roses, a neck tie, a new book or anything else she's selected, purchased, or baked that she thinks he'll like— whatever it takes to make the minister feel special. Whether the pie woman is aware of it or not, her purpose is seductive."

"Really?" I asked. "Seductive" seemed too strong of a word at the time.

"Well, not always sexually. At least not at first," Thelma continued. "The seduction is emotional. The pie woman has a neurotic need to feel special and important to the preacher. If he is seduced emotionally, she can then control him, even if she may be unaware of what she is doing—her own needs have so blinded her."

"How's that?"

"By telling him how to conduct his ministry. What sermons to preach. What he needs to do to placate his harshest critics, or maybe even how to survive in the ministry. The preacher then thinks of the pie woman as a special life support system. He starts confiding in her, depending on her."

"Are some of these pie women would-be female preachers?"

"Of course, they could be. They're usually pretty intelligent, too. They're also frustrated. Neurotic, to some extent," Thelma explained. "Your church doesn't give women any real, official power. So this is how they exercise their need to control what happens at church or to preach through somebody else's presence and language."

The "pie woman" is not the figure of speech I might have employed, but it was as descriptive as any other. I felt Thelma might have been a bit harsh and over-stating her point, and her dialogue was offered in the late 80s and might be discussed today with different sensitivities.

I knew even then that the male minister was equally if not more responsible when any moral indiscretion occurs. There is no doubt that an alarming number of ministers/preachers have taken liberties and advantages of Christian women who trusted them for empathetic counsel and support. And sometimes the devastating consequences have spilled over to impact painfully the entire congregation.

"There's no way that you can win with the pie woman," Thelma concluded with great expressiveness. "If you graciously receive the pie and warm up to the other favors as they are increasingly laid at your feet, you will find yourself so emotionally involved with her that disaster is a sure thing. On the other hand," she continued, "if you spurn her favors and try to keep your distance, this pie woman becomes an enemy for life. And if you think hell hath no fury like a woman scorned, wait till an entire church feels the fury of a scorned pie woman."

Of course not every woman who brings a pie, cake, or other delectable dish to the minister harbors a devious hidden agenda. Each church will usually nurture its share of kind, generous people—men and women—who gladly share their talents and blessings with the man who brings them good news and refreshing insights from the Holy Scriptures on a regular basis. Most ministers can never fully match for others the favors they have received from them unless one weighs the expressions of gratitude and support proffered orally.

Thus, to preachers young and old, remember there is no substitute for the simple yet sincere expression of gratitude when some good deed or some nice gift is given to you. Never feel you deserve it, that it should have been given you earlier, or that it is not enough.

As rare as thunder clouds over the desert are those gifts of nourishment which the preacher or his household cannot honestly appreciate. I can't think of a time that a home-made cake or pie or other delicacy has been delivered to the church parsonage that was anything but delicious and deeply appreciated even if the excessive calories were not needed.

There was one preacher, on the other hand, who received a homemade cake which had been delivered to his family's door while he was away. The baker was a wonderfully kind and devout woman, but, unfortunately, a terrible cook. After one or two bites of the cake that evening, everyone in the family turned up noses in culinary revulsion. No one in the family wanted to eat any more of it.

The preacher immediately carried the cake behind the fence and laid it amidst the garbage cans for the stray dogs and cats. "Who knows? At least some stray creatures might find some delight in this cake," the preacher silently rationalized.

The preacher then faced a dilemma. He had not been at the house personally when the cake was delivered when he could have sincerely said "thank you, we will enjoy this." He was loathe to say anything which might hurt his parishioner's feelings, but neither could he live with himself if he fabricated a total lie. At the next church assembly, he spotted this kind woman who had baked and delivered the cake and scurried over to her.

"Thank you so very, very much for that freshly baked cake you delivered to our house, and I'm just so sorry I was not at home when you dropped by" he gushed profusely. "That was so kind of you. And I just want you to know one thing—that's the kind of cake that doesn't stay around long at our house!"

14

"Is It Kisstomary to Cuss the Bride?"—Some Reflections on the Art of Conducting Weddings

Church weddings, and sometimes even private weddings, are fiascos waiting to happen.

Most God-believing families, even those who proverbially "never darken the doors" of a church building, believe that a preacher and a religious service are essential for either a funeral service or a wedding ceremony. The local preacher, consequently, will get requests for his special services from people who know and respect him as a minister of God as well as from families who know him remotely or who might have been selected because some acquaintance recommended him. Or, possibly, his name may have been picked at random from the Yellow Pages—the difference is between those family members who must engage a *special* minister and those who must have just *any* preacher.

Some preachers are able to earn a little extra cash from officiating at weddings and funerals although for most the amount is pitiably low. Guessing here these extra earnings for a few preachers are as likely not to be reported to Uncle Sam as they are likely to be reported. Who can say?

I shall never forget my first wedding. Glenda and I were living in Warren, Michigan, just above Eight Mile Road which divided Warren from the Detroit city limits. I was serving in my first few weeks of full-time ministry. A young couple had been given my name as a possible officiant for their private wedding.

The couple even agreed to come to our house. They dressed in their "Sunday best," as did I, and I performed that ceremony.

I well recall that when the happy couple was in the process of leaving, and a hard rain was coming down outside, the fellow pulled out a five-dollar bill from his trousers that was curled up in his hand. He kept the hand with the bill close to his pocket as though he were ready and hoping to stick it back in the pocket.

"Would you like this cash for your services?" he asked. I had never met this couple prior to the impromptu wedding and I was not about to go to the trouble of making quick preparation, dressing in my Sunday clothes, and signing the appropriate papers, and so forth, all for nothing. "You're jolly right, I would like to have that five dollars," I declared unhesitatingly. If the amount seems a pittance, indeed it was, yet that cash could buy two adequate suppers back in 1964.

As an aside, a few weeks later I officiated at my first funeral service on behalf of a U. S. serviceman killed in an automotive accident. In this case, too, I knew neither the serviceman nor his family. In both cases, at least at that time, I felt it almost providential that in performing my first wedding and first funeral service that I did not personally know any of the families. My reasoning was that expectations of my performance would not have been established, and if I "messed up" big-time in some way by appearing nervous, life would go on satisfactorily as I would never likely be seeing any of them again. I looked as these early invitations as sort of "practice sessions" for future rites of passage among people of "like precious faith."

The original draft of this book entailed a single chapter combining discussion of both weddings and funerals. There were too many stories on each topic, however. Because both weddings and funerals can be conducted amidst immensely stressful circumstances, sometimes family ties are strained and actions or words spoken, even with all good intention, that produce pain and regret that is not easily forgiven, much less dismissed. From this point we deal with weddings in this chapter and more specifically with the experience of funerals in the following chapter.

ARRANGEMENTS AND COUNSELING

A formal wedding, like geography in the state of Tennessee, is divided into three grand parts: the initial arrangements, including a counseling session with the presumably happy couple, the wedding rehearsal, and the wedding itself.

A pre-ceremony counseling session is quite helpful whenever it can be arranged, if for no other reason than to finalize procedures and schedules for the "big day."

Sometimes an advance planning session is not possible. I have conducted weddings for couples that I met for the first time only five minutes prior to the beginning of the ceremony. Such couples, along with a few of their friends and/ or family members, will usually come to the church office and ask for a preacher. My *modus operandi* is to ask the starry-eyed couple a few questions—the main one being, "Do you already have a marriage license from the county court clerk?"—to satisfy my concerns about being party to this act of matrimony.

At one impromptu wedding request, an early-middle-aged woman unknown to me just walked in the Franklin Fourth Avenue church office door and introduced herself and asked if I would do her wedding ceremony on that day. I asked this bride-to-be why she wanted to get married so quickly. "Because my fiancé has just been released from prison," she replied. Reason enough, I thought. Why should they wait? After a brief interview with her, I agreed to honor her request. I then apologetically informed her that I did not have a coat to wear during this impromptu service. "That'll be no problem whatsoever," she told me.

Soon the groom arrived wearing blue jeans and a plaid sport shirt. A bootenaire was then pinned above the shirt pocket. I grabbed my Bible and led them to the chapel, turned on the lights, and gave this grinning couple their ten dollars' worth of vows and wedding homily. Actually, it seemed a sweet occasion and I was happy to add my personal smiles to their own. The bride's sister, who also served as the witness who could sign off on the marriage certificate, made a few pictures. The pair went on their way rejoicing.

The trend nowadays among younger, better-educated clergy requires couples to participate in several lengthy counseling sessions, perhaps even employing a battery of written tests to determine compatibility and readiness for life-time commitment. This process will satisfy the conscientious minister that he is offering the highest level of service to the prospective groom and bride.

In most cases, however, I find that merely determining the time and place of the wedding, asking about special scriptures and themes, and reviewing ceremony procedures quite enough to cover in this session. I've rarely known a premarital counseling session by an officiating minister to change any couple's mind about what they are planning to do, and the average wedding fee hardly justifies an excessive investment of time in light of other pressing pastoral responsibilities.

In the True Church there are many preachers who agonize over a decision to officiate at the wedding of a person or persons who have been married previously. Some preachers resolve this quandary by invoking a blanket refusal to conduct a wedding for a second marriage for any reason except for someone widowed. They explain their judgmental enactment as "playing it safe rather than sorry."

Once I was called by a preacher friend and Lipscomb colleague, namely Rodney Cloud, who made an unusual request: "Would you conduct a ceremony for two of my best friends? I'm convinced they have a scriptural right to marry, but I fear that my elders will not agree and there will be negative consequences, so I wonder if you can conduct the ceremony for me? I really care about this couple so naturally I'll be present for the wedding." I was happy to oblige. Rodney attended the ceremony and sat silently among other attendees. I did wonder how he explained his non-involvement/cop-out strategy to the couple he cared about, but had "handed off" to me.

I always believed an officiating minister is providing a service to a couple of people who love each other, not passing eternal judgment on their spiritual status and their odds of eternal salvation!

The matter of sex almost never comes up in a pre-wedding counseling session. I certainly never raise the topic. However, I shall never forget a time the issue was raised. A woman in her mid-sixties named Margaret, who had just been recently widowed, had asked me to officiate in her marriage to Bill, another widowed person who had been a long-time friend. After I asked her a number of questions, she bluntly raised the issue. "You may wonder if we've talked about sex in our marriage," she offered. Truth is, I had not really wondered nor even thought about it. "We've talked it over and we know that we can still enjoy it—it will take us a little longer and it won't happen as often, but we can still do it." I could only smile and say nothing more on that topic other than "thank you for sharing."

In the pre-ceremony session it is always helpful to read the vows to which the prospective bride and groom will affirm. On many occasions a bride will ask, "You're not going to insert that part about 'obey' in the ceremony, are you?" I assure her that I have never used that four letter word ("obey") in a wedding message or in vows. Furthermore, I've never had a bride request that wifely "subjection" or "obedience" remain in the traditional vows. In fact, I always invite, and even urge, each party to write and recite his or her own personal vows and then read or recite them to each other. Not all couples want to do this, but I think it renders the ceremony much more personal and impressive.

DAVE AND HIS BRIDE-TO-BE, THE PLAYMATE OF THE MONTH

One never knows how friendship with a single person may evolve into an important role in a wedding ceremony. Case in point: my experience with Dave Turner and Dorothy Mills.

Dave was a computer consultant contracted by the Center for Labor-Management Relations at Tennessee State University for which I worked as education specialist for three years in the late 80s. Dave and I worked together closely for many hours while I was researching and writing a book on U. S. labor history.

Dave was a handsome, winsome young man. He was bright, a graduate of Vanderbilt University. We developed a good friendship. He proudly told me he was engaged to a beautiful woman and expected to be married in the indeterminate future.

On several occasions Dave would transfer our computer work on our office Mac SE to a floppy disk, and the two of us would go to his apartment on West End Avenue to continue our project on his personal computer with a huge screen and Pagemaker program. There we laid out the work, selected pictures, and designed the cover for the book. I was fully aware my fledgling computer skills were minuscule compared to his expertise.

While in his apartment, though highly impressed with his desk-top publishing techniques and modern computer equipment, I was equally impressed by the framed photos of a beautiful woman that adorned his tables and walls.

"That's Dorothy, my fiancé," he proudly informed me.

Dorothy Mills was pretty indeed. She worked in a business office downtown and was a part-time student at Belmont College, Dave informed me.

As time passed, Dave told me more about Dorothy. Seems that she had spent considerable time in California and that she had been a model and had appeared in a number national ads. Some of those ads featuring Dorothy were also framed and displayed around the apartment. "Lucky young man," I thought about Dave. One day, while working at his apartment, Dave was willing to share more about Dorothy.

"Perry, would you like to know what Dorothy's greatest claim to fame is?" I assumed he would inform me of her being on national television or winning a national beauty contest.

"Sure. If you want to tell it," I replied.

"Dorothy was once a Playmate-of-the-Month."

"You're kidding. Do you mean that she was featured in some way in *Playboy* magazine or that she was actually the featured centerfold?"

"She was Playmate-of-the-Month. The centerfold. Back in July, 1979. Do you want to see her in that issue?"

"Well, I'm not so sure," I said haltingly. The offer seemed a little strange to me. "Wasn't this before you met her? Are you sure you have that issue?" I tried to think of several questions while pondering my willingness to see the issue that featured his fiancé.

"Of course I have a copy. You're a good friend. I don't share that fact with just anybody." Without getting explicit approval from me, Dave went to his top closet shelf and then plopped a copy of the July '79 issue of *Playboy* on the table in front of me. Incidentally, at that time Dave did not know me as a minister, only as friend, professor, and labor-management education specialist at Tennessee State University.

Legions of preachers in my position at that point would never have picked up that magazine. Lifting my nose and turning away would have assertively informed Dave that viewing such a magazine was not a wholesome thing to do or that any appearance in such a publication was inappropriate moral behavior. I, on the other hand, did or said none of that—I was too human and too curious. Besides, Dave would have been offended if I had not glanced at his fiancé's greatest claim to fame, I thus rationalized.

I turned slowly to the middle pages of the magazine. There emerged a curvaceous Dorothy, appearing more candidly exposed than in any photos I had seen previously displayed around Dave's apartment. One or two photos, I felt, struck especially immodest poses.

I turned the pages much more rapidly than I would have if Dave not been standing right beside me and awaiting my response. I uttered several nasal sounds intended to convey objectivity and overall disinterest. "Hmm. I see. Ah. Hmm. Interesting."

Then, of course, I had to turn the magazine sideways to allow the third page of the fold-out to unfurl. I quickly folded the page back into place and moved to the next opening. Honestly, I've never had such a bizarre feeling—a feeling that comes only when a young man willingly shows you nude photos of his bride-to-be. I was almost speechless.

"Well, thanks for sharing that little bit of personal history. By the way, how do you feel about this whole adventure, your fiancé having shared her entire body with the entire nation?" I inquired. "Doesn't this embarrass you?"

"I'm rather proud of Dorothy," Dave replied. "These photos are tastefully done. I consider them to be works of art. I don't see them as pornographic in any sense," he explained. "I don't look at them any differently than I might look at some of the great sculptures of ancient Greece or paintings of Renaissance Europe."

We returned to task on my publishing project. A little time passed. Dave soon had another request for the day.

"I'm scheduled to pick up Dorothy at 5:00 downtown at Fourth and Deaderick Streets, but I need to complete some work on our project here. Would you be willing to drive downtown, pick her up, and drive back to my place?"

"Well, of course, I'll do you that favor," I replied all too matter-of-factly. By now I was all too anxious to meet this lovely woman in real life. "Tell her I'll be there on curbside at 5:00 sharp and to look out for a man driving a red Toyota Celica."

When I arrived at Fourth and Deaderick I did see a blond-haired woman in professional attire standing on the sidewalk corner, but who did not strike me as someone with extraordinary sex appeal. "Are you, Perry?" she asked me as she opened my passenger-side door. "And you are Dorothy?" I replied.

Dorothy got in my Celica and I shall always remember what she stated next: "And I'm guessing you were expecting someone much more glamorous?"

I paused without knowing a good answer, but I knew then that she was most likely aware Dave had shown me those intimate pictures. "You've seen my pictures and now you see the real 'me,' and all I can say is that it's amazing what bright lights, a lot of make-up, and a little air-brushing can accomplish for a picture in a national magazine." At that moment I could only look at her and smile.

That was the day I met Dorothy, who turned out to be a bright, well-read, and charming individual. She had met Dave while he was providing computer consultancy for firms and individuals; she claimed that her meeting Dave was "love at first byte."

Dorothy was particularly interested and well-read in Native American culture and history. She offered me the insight that whenever political and religious conservatives talk about returning to the principles of the Founding Fathers they ought to return to the ideas and values of the Indian cultures who had settled here before the Europeans arrived and made contact. She contended the natives were more "founders" than Europeans.

I later wondered if I should have been surprised that she was highly intelligent, her language was always appropriate, her vocabulary was expansive, her clothing was always stylish yet modest. She seemed anything but a "Playmate of the Month." Now the three of us—Dave, Dorothy, and I—enjoyed the opportunity to become friends, sharing meals and visits together when I was at TSU Downtown campus (now Avon Williams Campus). The following semester, quite by surprise, I found Dorothy had registered for a class in communication I taught in the evening at Belmont College.

Dorothy was the brightest person academically and the best student speaker in the Belmont class. Not surprisingly, Dorothy never once informed the class of her modeling history or the intimate photography that was published nationally. The two of us visited several minutes after every class that met one night a week for the entire semester. On many of those nights I gave her a "lift" back to her apartment. Along with Dave, the three of us talked much about life, values, and relationships.

Dave and Dorothy planned a wedding at a retreat center on a mountain-top in the Blue Ridge Mountains. Their knowing that I was "clergy," I was not surprised when they asked if I would officiate at their wedding ceremony. Neither had been married previously. I had never spent as many hours informally counseling a couple before marriage than I had with Dave and Dorothy. I was confident at that time such a marriage would succeed.

THE REHEARSAL

There's hardly one positive thing to say about wedding rehearsals. I know of no interesting stories to tell about rehearsals.

Most rehearsals can be fairly boring events. A few will be a trial of the preacher's ingenuity and patience. My recommendation is that preachers ask for a waiver from mandatory presence at the rehearsal; after all, the preacher does not have any meaningful role to rehearse in the wedding.

If the bridal party feels the need for a minister in rehearsal, one strategy would be borrowing and dressing a "male" mannequin in formal attire and standing it right in the middle of the line-up so everyone can "visualize" the ministerial presence. Actually, a preacher may be useful in a rehearsal if the couple has not contracted the services of a wedding director. His experience in officiating can be tapped in terms of making suggestions or reporting how the format is typically arranged.

Remember that wedding rehearsals typically do not begin on time—well, almost never on time. Members of the wedding party are busy meeting and greeting one another and there are usually participants who are late arriving from out of town.

Nor do wedding rehearsals end on time. Most rehearsals last two or three times longer than necessary. What must be allowed is time for the prospective bride and all other members of the wedding parties and the two major families to argue about any number pointless procedures—the proper musical cues, the pace of the processional, the up-front spacing of the groomsmen and brides-maids, the order of the ceremony, how the bride and groom should be addressed, how to hold the ring until it is requested, how to train and control any preschool children who are selected to participate in the ceremony, and so on, *ad infinitum*.

As if this were not enough, time is usually allotted for some good arguments about protocol at the reception. I have found it a prudent use of time to bring to the rehearsal a good book or magazine and retreat to some pew or chair in the church house or chapel for silent reading during the more lengthy family negotiations and harangues.

There is one participant to watch out for during the entire wedding ordeal—the Mother of the Bride or MOTB. The MOTB believes that just because she once gave birth to the bride, nursed and gave first solid food to the bride, often gave advice to the bride, and is footing a major part of the bridal bill, that she has earned the right to order, boss, cajole, even humiliate if necessary, all other members of the wedding party and families. Stay out of the way of the MOTB. A wedding does not need to be performed according to any certain order or ritual, so as for my part I usually simply tell the MOTB and her daughter, borrowing language from an old MacDonald's commercial, "have it your way" and "what you want is what you get."

With freedom for the blissful couple to plan their own ceremony, might the ritual include kneeling and praying at an altar? Sam McFarland recalls of-ficiating at a wedding in Junction, Texas, in the early 60s wherein both parties and their families were Church of Christ members. The MOTB was insistent the bride and groom kneel at an altar for a prayer during the ceremony. She felt this added class and dignity to the ceremony. The groom, a student at Abilene Christian College, was equally determined. "I won't do it!" he insisted. "This is what the Catholics do!"

Both parties dug in and it appeared as though the wedding might be called off right there at the rehearsal. "I finally persuaded the groom that it was neither Catholic nor against the Scripture for him to kneel at an altar while a prayer was being offered for the success of this union, thus the wedding proceeded and the altar prayer was offered," Sam recalls. "I have no idea how that marriage went, but it definitely was not getting off to a good start."

Ideally, rehearsals should be relaxed and enjoyable occasions. In reality, however, they can be a foretaste of the tension to come during the ceremony itself. I heard of one prospective and often tongue-tied groom who found his nerves own edge by a tedious work schedule and the barking of orders by his future mother-in-law, the MOTB, during the rehearsal. When the preacher finally had an opportunity to allow the beleaguered young man a question, the poor soul was anxiously concerned about his role at the end of the ceremony. "Is it kisstomary to cuss the bride?" he nervously stuttered.

At rehearsals I always tell the wedding party what I have seen confirmed as useful advice: "There will be at least one procedure that will not go as you have planned. Don't let anything distract you and just enjoy participating in this important production. No one should expect perfection and just adapt or roll with the realities—you two will get officially and legally married one way or another even if someone else in the wedding party drops dead during the ceremony."

THE ACTUAL WEDDING CEREMONY

While most religious wedding ceremonies are conducted in a church building or chapel, consider that wedding ceremonies can be held literally anywhere—in lawns, gardens, boats, private homes, lake shores, beaches, balconies, athletic fields, campuses, even airplanes or parachutes (you name it!).

As for wedding sites, I've had two rather interesting requests. One from a couple who wanted to be married the first or second day in January in an outdoor chapel on a mountaintop in Beersheba Springs (Grundy County), Tennessee. I consented to this nonsense. On the day of the wedding, several carloads of friends twisted and spun their way upward through treacherous ice and snow-slickened roads to finally reach the Methodist Youth Campgrounds, a converted antebellum grand hotel, at the top of Beersheba Mountain. Being the New Year Day holiday, nobody else was on the mountaintop that day.

All participants and witnesses except me wore heavy overcoats or parkas and head coverings. I generally get warm while conducting weddings and funerals and was content to wear my regular Sunday suit, dress shirt, and tie—no overcoat or hat at all. Our troupe walked slowly across treacherous ice to the outdoor chapel with a scenic view of the snow-covered mountains of the Cumberland Plateau. The wind-chill factor was near zero if not actually below zero as the wind whistled through the pines moving up the mountain.

The wedding began promptly. I could not resist making some apropos comments about marriage and the prevailing wind and temperature, how that marriage is an honorable institution to which "many are cold, but few are frozen."

All participants and friends stood during the ceremony, spurning the frozen, ice-glazed log pews that had no backing—no one dared to sit down. Two or three minutes into my remarks I noticed that the bride and groom were bouncing around on their toes to ward off frigidity. Their noses began to whiten with frost bite and their teeth began clicking. Others in the wedding attendance began bouncing rhythmically on their feet. We could see everyone's breath as it vaporized in the frigid air on each exhalation.

More of my traditional remarks, stock literary quotations, and witty sayings remained to be uttered, but I perceived that everyone's thoughts were now turning to mere survival against the elements. "I'll end my remarks now and turn to the vows," I announced, "allowing you to chatter your vows to one another as we close this service." Thus, the service was closed with my prayer and pronouncing the couple "husband and wife." And not a minute too soon.

We quickly made our way back up the edge of the mountainside to our cars and then motored cautiously down the mountain, intermittently sliding from ice patches to clear pavement. We arrived back in McMinnville safely and enjoyed a nice reception and, praise the Lord, the new husband and wife had the remainder of the day to thaw and warm each other from that frigid nuptial experience.

In general, plans for an outdoor wedding should always include a "back up" plan if needed. I was asked to officiate for the early spring wedding of a former Lipscomb student secretary, Nancy Gist, which would be conducted at the edge of the Camp Marymount Lake (near Fairview, Tennessee) in early morning. This was intended as a heart-warming sunrise wedding. The "dawning of a new day in their lives" could be the wedding theme. Seems twenty to thirty close friends were invited to attend. I set my alarm and allowed enough drive time from our home in Franklin. The only problem: A thick fog had descended on the area that early morning and, even standing near the water's edge, no one could really see the lake. We waited a couple of hours or so with no comfortable place to sit except in our vehicles, hoping a rising, brighter sun would burn off the fog and we could begin the wedding.

On another wedding occasion, I had agreed to officiate at the wedding of a wonderful, bright faculty colleague at Nashville State, Michelle Adkerson, an English professor. As I recall, the bride-to-be had no church affiliation. Michelle wanted to marry her chosen fellow on April 1 in Nashville's Centennial Park. At the appointed hour, a huge thunderstorm hit that area. In the torrential downpour and wind, even umbrellas seemed much inadequate. Each attending party had only about an hour to spare before returning to campus obligations. We were able to move the ceremony to the top step of the Parthenon and stand under the high roof of that majestic structure, but the stiff breeze blew cold rain on the entire wedding party. I felt it appropriate to make some little impromptu quips about Greek Stoicism and the ironies of wedding, weather, and April Fool's Day.

ROSE'S TATOO PARLOR

The second highly unusual request for a wedding site was made by Bonnie McNally, an adventurous and vivacious young woman who worked with me in Staff Development Unit at the Tennessee Department of Human Services. Bonnie was refreshingly and, at times, embarrassingly honest about all matters, including details about her rather checkered past. As an attractive young woman, she had modeled, sung in rock groups, posed as a model, and even worked for an escort service, the latter being a business in which she claims to have made good money. Appropriately, perhaps, she never discussed services rendered with the escort agency.

With self-determination and encouragement from others, Bonnie began the process of spiritual restoration. She already possessed an infectious and joyful laughter and a terrific sense of humor to infuse it. Along the way she fell in love with Ron, a man to whom she was certain she could be faithful.

"Perry, Ron and I would like for you to conduct our wedding ceremony for us," Bonnie told me one day. "We've talked about different locations for the wedding. Venues such as Shelby Park or the Rachel Jackson Chapel on the grounds of the Hermitage."

"Either of those places sounds fine," I said. "Or you might consider having the wedding in Centennial Park, Warner Park, or around Radnor Lake."

"Well, here's where we really want to do it. And don't laugh, because we're serious and we've thought a lot about it." Bonnie quickly stirred my curiosity. "We want you to marry us in Rose's Tattoo Parlor down on Church Street. Won't that be unique?"

"Wow. It would be unique. I've never thought about a wedding in such a place!" I responded. Actually, I was stalling for more time to process this absolutely zany idea.

"And instead of exchanging rings, we're going to exchange tattoos and place them on some part of our anatomy. My tattoo will have his name and his tattoo will have mine."

"Bonnie, I'd really like to help you out with your ceremony. I was convinced that you wanted to settle down with one man for the rest of your life. But if you and Ron have your wedding in a tattoo parlor," I reasoned, "it's going to look like to me and your friends that you aren't taking your marriage that seriously, that the whole thing's a joke."

"Well, it's not a joke," Bonnie immediately countered. "If we were taking this wedding lightly we wouldn't be getting permanent tattoos punctured into our skin. Anyone can take off a wedding ring, but exchanging tattoos symbolizes a fairly major commitment."

I had never thought of it that way. Still I wrestled with whether I wanted to be involved in this affair. Sure, it would be a novel experience to officiate for a wedding in Rosie's Tattoo Parlor and to think of something clever to say during the tattoo exchange.

Bonnie told me of another part of her wedding plans that helped me resolve my indecisiveness. She told me that she was so enthralled with the whole concept of a tattoo parlor wedding that she would call some contacts at the local newspapers for a feature story and photographs of the wedding. She also informed me that she knew Catharine Darnell, a newspaper gossip columnist for the *Tennessean,* and that a special column could be written about the ceremony and published on the first page of the "Living" section of the paper.

That was enough for me! I could see photocopies of any *Tennessean* stories and pictures appearing in the brotherhood muckraking publications ("PREACHER MAKES TRAVESTY OF HOLY MATRIMONY" the headline in *Contending for the Faith* might read). I was already preaching every Sunday as interim pulpit minister once again at Fourth Avenue Church in Franklin, and I just knew some of those brothers and sisters might likely be offended by my officiating for a wedding in such a venue.

I still liked Bonnie and wished her the best. I was honored that, after she considered various possibilities, she came back with another idea: getting married in the ballroom of a Nashville hotel. She was persistent and still wanted me to officiate. Thus I agreed to officiate in the more sedate venue. When I came around to the segment of my remarks that asks, "And what do you give one another as symbols of these vows of love and fidelity you have taken today?" then both Ron and Bonnie modestly lifted part of their garments, one at a time, to expose the personal tattoo that each had given the other.

Years later, Bonnie asked if I would be willing to officiate for a female friend of hers whose wedding was planned for the front steps and porch at Nashville's Two Rivers Mansion. I agreed to honor her request. Bonnie's sense of humor had not changed, I could tell that from the message on the bumper sticker of her car (a message best not shared here). Her giggling and laughter remained undiminished. When I had a free moment, I asked her about Ron. She informed me that he had died a few months earlier.

"PLEASE GET ME TO THE CHURCH ON TIME AND THEN HELP ME KEEP STANDING"

Be prepared for anything to happen during a wedding ceremony.

First, a preacher must make certain he arrives at the wedding site on time. One hot summer Saturday afternoon in the mid-1980s, my '79 Mercury Cougar sport coupe developed vapor lock and sputtered to a complete stop, leaving me stranded on Nashville's Lebanon Road on the way to Andrew Jackson's Hermitage grounds to perform a wedding. Rachel's Chapel had no phone. Already late, I grabbed my coat and Bible with wedding notes, approached an unknown woman entering her car in a parking lot, and asked if she would kindly transport me to the wedding site. Despite much reluctance at first, she obliged; I assumed I looked both desperate and safely non-threatening in my Sunday suit and tie and carrying a Bible.

When I arrived at the Rachel's Chapel, there were no groomsmen—they were trolling the highway looking for me. (Of course nowadays the anxious moments could have been easily assuaged by cell phone communiques.) The ushers eventually returned just in time for us to settle into place and conduct the wedding as the chapel could only be reserved for an hour before the next wedding party takes custody. After the reception at another venue, I engaged an auto mechanic to retrieve my abandoned car and get it started and running again.

One Saturday the beloved Madison minister Ira North was working in a field on his farm. A car came speeding up the road way. A young man, dressed in tuxedo, jumped out of his car and hollered: "Brother North, we're waiting for you at the church. You're supposed to perform our wedding ceremony." Ira apologized profusely. He had forgotten his commitment to perform the ceremony. Possibly he had obtained a waiver from the wedding rehearsal, so that the wedding was not foremost on his mind. The wedding party was standing around and ready to march, and Ira was far from ready to change roles from farmer to preacher. Another minister was called and fortuitously available to perform the ceremony on a moment's notice.

Preachers who have been veteran officiators have witnessed many a groom and many a bride become highly nervous. During nuptials on summer afternoons in churches and chapels which have become virtual sweatboxes, beads of perspiration will form on the upper lips and foreheads of the bride, groom, and/or father of the bride. I've seen eyeballs roll around in their sockets and a dizzy sway by a bride or groom.

In a wedding I was conducting at Nashville's Hillsboro church for two young Lipscomb graduates and former students of mine, Croley Graham and Joy Sanders, a groomsman fainted and dropped to the floor. I immediately stopped the ceremony, if for no other reason than attention to the proceedings was totally lost at that unexpected point. The other groomsmen carried him out of the chapel feet first and inadvertently allowed a swinging door they kicked open to swing back and give the poor groomsman another hard lick on the head. There was an audible groan from all of us in attendance as we imagined pain the groomsman must have felt.

A few moments passed. I then resumed speaking to the bride and groom, all the while wondering if the poor groomsman had survived the hard blow. Indeed, he had survived but he did not return to the chapel. Praise the Lord, he felt well enough to attend the reception, though he had to endure a fair amount "ribbing" for his novel way of being transported out of a very warm chapel where the air conditioning seemed to have failed.

Charles Chumley, long-time preacher at Nashville's Granny White church (long enough for the church to be dubbed "Chumley's Chapel"), once officiated his most unusual wedding ceremony. A couple that he had known fairly well had asked him to officiate, yet days before the wedding the two were injured in a bad car accident. Invitations had been sent out and the bride did not want to delay. She felt recovered and strong enough to appear at the church and be rolled down the aisle in a wheel chair, and the groom, though scuffed up and bruised, was fully ambulatory. During the ceremony, the groom was quite nervous and his eyes were rolling around some. Then he fainted, dropping hard to the floor. The ushers carried him. Charles and the bride stood silently in front of the church gathering. Minutes passed. The bride kept muttering, "They'll never let us live this down. They will always remind us." The groom was eventually revived, returned to ceremony, took his place beside the bride, and Charles reported that "I hurried up with the rest of the ceremony."

Brides have been known to either weep audibly or even laugh out during the ceremony as a release to pent up anxiety. This is not at all unusual. After all, the bride likely perceives the entire audience is looking directly at her and making judgment calls on her wedding dress and her overall appearance.

I was performing a wedding ceremony for two middle-aged adults at Owen Chapel one Saturday evening in front of a number of distinguished guests. For vows I have often used an original contemporary pledge of love and fidelity that is poetic; I will read a line of the poem and ask each person repeat that one line after me. I felt it more meaningful than just asking a long question that begins with "Wilt thou ..." and the bride and groom need only utter two syllables afterward ("I do" or "I will").

As I read one of the lines to the groom, he started to quote it, stumbled, forgot the next words and said aloud, "Come again?" After hearing it again, he recited it verbatim. However, this may have rendered the bride, Jane Greer, even more nervous. When I read that same line to her, she stated the first two or three words, paused, and then broke into uncontrollable laughter. Her laughter stopped and then started again. She stooped a little in her laughter and for a moment I thought she might fall to the floor. The congregation began laughing, too. It was almost sheer pandemonium. Then I announced to everyone: "I trust Jane is taking these vows more seriously in real life than she appears to be during this ceremony." Overall, everyone seemed to have a good time that evening.

Myron Keith once revealed a strategy he typically used for defusing the anxiety of the bride. "As soon as she has marched down the aisle and takes her place next to the groom, I ask the bride softly, 'Did you remember to brush your teeth?'" Myron reported. "The bride usually smiles at such a ridiculous question and forgets her anxiety. One time when I asked a bride that question she got her back up and stated rather audibly, 'What's the matter? Do I have bad breath?'"

Unexpected developments may be the result of planned surprises. When

Rubel Shelly called for the ring to symbolize the marriage of his son Tim to Sherry Lassiter, Tim handed his dad an old plastic toy ring which had come from a Cracker Jack box years earlier. This evoked some surprised facial expressions, but the wedding continued without hiatus. I have occasionally witnessed a best man silently handing over a contraceptive device along with the wedding band when the moment had come for ring exchange.

Some weddings do not require much formality or even dignity. Hoy Ledbetter officiated for a wedding in a rural home in Arkansas: "This was what I would call a crude wedding. While I was officiating with the wedding party standing in front of me, there was a television blasting out sound in another room. There were kids running around the house. And the bride and groom and some of the adults would make comments to each other during the service."

Even preachers can be nervous. George Goldtrap worked as a Nashville television weather forecaster before entering the ministry full-time. He would end his weather forecast with the same little comedic routine. He'd announce "And that's the weather," at which moment he would toss a piece of chalk or colored marker high into the air and hold open his vest pocket to catch it, and then end with the words "by George!" I've often wondered if he concluded his sermons in the same fashion, flipping a pen or pointer and then declaring: "And that's the gospel, by George!"

George often shared his experience of performing his first wedding ceremony. "I was as nervous as I could be," he recalled. "I had rehearsed over and over what I was going to say. I was every bit as nervous as the couple getting married. Well, everything went fine until after I'd pronounced them man and wife. That's when I announced: "'You may now cuss the bride.'"

"THIS LITTLE LIGHT OF MINE"

I've sat through a number of wedding and funeral services over the years. My conclusion is that nobody in the True Church was more eloquent in special ceremonial speaking than Jim Bill McInteer, a long-time pulpit minister at Nashville's West End congregation.

Jim Bill surely conducted hundreds of both weddings and funerals—a testimony not only to his oratorical skills as a communicator but also to his sterling character and congenial personality. He was always personal in his remarks, conversational in tone, and a quick thinker on his feet. In his sermons and after-dinner speeches, this godly gentleman could draw from a repertoire of great jokes and could tell them with perfect timing. Jim Bill, nonetheless, had proven himself to be human a few times.

When his daughter was getting married Jim Bill experienced a mental block. In her wedding, on February 5, 1973, the avuncular preacher could not think of his future son-in-law's name.

"Boy, what's your name?" Jim Bill asked. The audience chuckled.

"I'm so nervous I don't remember myself," the groom replied. The big crowd at the West End church roared in laughter.

After the recessional, with the large audience in attendance still seated, the music stopped, and Jim Bill then made an announcement: "Thanks to all of you for coming. You are all invited to the reception in the fellowship hall. However, I am going to be slipping out early because I've got tickets to the Vandy-Ole Miss basketball game."

Jim Bill told me, on one of our walks around the Lipscomb track on Lealand Lane, about the only time he "lost it" while conducting a wedding:

> I was conducting a wedding at the beautiful Wightman Chapel on the Scarritt College campus. During the middle of my message, the bride winked. I thought, "Woman, don't wink at me. Wink at your husband-to-be."
>
> Then the bride began to wink convulsively. Seems that she had displaced a contact lens. It got out of place and was moving out from under the eye lids. While I was talking she slipped her hand up under her veil and retrieved the contact.
>
> During the remainder of the service she kept the contact balanced on the tip of her index finger and held it up right in front of me. It was an amusing sight. Then I thought, "I believe I'll sing 'This Little

Light of Mine'" and when I thought of that I lost it. I got tickled. My voice cracked. I tried to restrain myself. Then I just pretended to be crying to save the embarrassment of laughing during a wedding.

WEDDING MUSIC IN THE TRUE CHURCH

A final word may be offered about wedding music. Harsh as this may seem, I doubt that any denominational body can ever claim as much uninspiring wedding music and ineptitude as experienced in some True Church weddings. Churches which would not allow a "mechanical instrument of music" in their building have permitted cassette and scratchy records of instrumental renditions to create the desired mood. *A cappella* quartets and solos have been permitted. At one wedding Paul Brown stood with three others behind a curtain in a dry baptistery tank to serenade the audience. At a Church of Christ wedding in Michigan in the 70s, the bride and groom had selected a few Perry Como LP recordings as wedding music.

At Fourth Avenue Church in 2001, my good friend and former Lipscomb classmate in Religious Education courses, Don Smithson, asked me to officiate at the wedding ceremony for him and fiancé Connie in the church's chapel that seated approximately two hundred people. Don had once been married, then was single for many years. I felt he was a truly good man with a soft-spoken sense of humor. My only question regarding his critical thinking skills was a firm belief he held since 1978—that Elvis Presley was alive and in hiding in a witness protection program and would one day resurface publicly. Don could not be dissuaded in this belief. I almost felt he believed in the second coming of Elvis more than in the second coming of Jesus.

Needless to say, Don loved all of Elvis' songs. He selected two or three of them for the wedding ceremony. In rehearsal a cassette player which was wired to speakers was placed on a shelf in the walk-in closet to the left and front of the chapel. My wife Glenda was sitting in rehearsal and Don drafted her to graciously sit secluded in that closet with a pin light and program in hand and play the recorded Elvis songs at the assigned time in the program. The recorded music was interspersed with my comments as officiant.

The processional went well, my comments were delivered as planned, and then, we gave cue for the next Elvis song to be played (remembering that it was "I Can't Help Falling in Love with You"). There was a long pause. No Elvis music. I knew that Glenda was encountering trouble operating Don's cassette recorder. I ad libbed for two or three minutes, cracked a joke or two about the technical difficulties, just trying to camouflage our emerging embarrassment.

Don, standing there with his lovely bride Connie, turned to the audience and declared: "I think I need to fix this." So he stepped down from the low pulpit stand and walked over to the closet, opened the door, took the light, and proceeded to get the music back on track while Connie and I stood alone (except for best man and matron of honor). As the desired Elvis tune was being played, Don made his way back up front and center to continue proceedings. I could not resist ad libbing more comments about what a good handy-man husband Don would be for Connie.

As an aside, within two or three years, Don and Connie divorced. But then, working on their differences, these two remarried each other again, this time getting married at Owen Chapel with another officiant. I doubt the second marriage ceremony was as memorable as the first one, but perhaps another officiant could bring the couple better fortune and more marital longevity.

UNUSUAL WEDDING PARTICIPANTS

A bride may not necessarily be escorted down the aisle by her father. In some sad cases, the father may have died. Or the marrying couple might be middle-aged and the parents quite aged, maybe even unable to attend. On a rare occasion, a mother might walk the aisle with her daughter. Sometimes it is a brother.

On two occasions I have officiated where a dog was part of the wedding ceremony. One was a semi-private wedding in the Fourth Avenue church building where a white poodle was one of the "bridesmaids." I have forgotten the dog's name, but was hoping that no canine misconduct would occur during the service.

The other occasion was an outdoor wedding for Everett Lowe and Fay Gannon, conducted on Fay's beautiful patio with bright, colorful flowers and a well-manicured yard. At this wedding the bride's pet dog was also the ring-bearer and entered on a leash with the bride. When I asked if there were a symbol to represent the vows to life-long commitment, love, and fidelity, then Everett bent down and disconnected the small package from around the dog collar and handed the rings to me for inclusion in the ceremony.

Finally, from Tennessee DHS colleague Shirley Gaudain, someone I deem credible, I reference briefly the most unusual "participant" at a wedding I could ever imagine—a deceased best man. This best man's friend was scheduled to marry his fiancée and the date was set and invitations mailed out, yet, sadly, the best man was fatally wounded in an automobile accident a day or two before the wedding. The bride and groom, and especially the groom, were devastated. The groom very much had desired his friend in the wedding. A decision was then made to re-locate the wedding venue to a funeral parlor. The groom's best man lay in an open casket and the wedding party lined up around the casket (not sure if the best man "held" the bride's wedding band until it was called for). Vows were exchanged. The wedding ceremony was thus conducted on the announced date, and the best man was "present" in the line-up of the wedding party.

WEDDING RECEPTIONS IN THE TRUE CHURCH

This topic deserves brevity. And why? Not much goes on at wedding receptions in the True Church. Well, perhaps what is most important does actually occur—good friends in the fellowship greet and visit with one another, people are dressed at their best, a line forms wherein the guests may kiss the bride's cheek and shake the groom's hand, offering both best wishes, a few late wedding gifts are dropped off, and young kids run around and play. What a joyous occasion!

What doesn't happen at a wedding reception in the True Church? The answer is obvious immediately, assuming the reception is in the church's fellowship hall. There are no alcoholic beverages, and there is no champagne toast to the newlyweds. Wedding guests line up around a buffet table, pick up their paper or plastic plates, paper napkins, and plastic utensils, and help themselves to cookies, mixed nuts (with a small dip for scooping the nuts), a few little round colored sugary mints, and a slice of sugary wedding cake. Then guests are given a cup of sugary fruit punch from a punch bowl with Canada Dry ginger ale, fruit flavoring and with a big glob of sherbet floating on top. For more elaborate wedding receptions, there might be other delicacies such as small sandwiches and some chips and dip, maybe some bits of chocolate candy.

There may be some recorded music, in rare receptions there may be live music, but there is definitely no dancing, thus no chance (or at least little chance) of lust arising. Nonetheless, laughter and smiles seem abundant, and indeed, "blest be the tie that binds."

While serving congregations in Michigan, we learned that a full course meal was often served at a church wedding reception. These congregations were typically composed of working class people, many being transplants from Southern states who migrated for jobs in automotive factories (especially during World War II), and a traditional wedding reception could be expensive for the bride's family. Thus, in some church families a real sweet tradition emerged. Rather than the family of the bride hosting a full course meal, the church members considered the wedding reception to be a "pot luck" or "covered dish" event wherein wedding guests brought one or more dishes to the table and everyone enjoyed that meal together.

My first church wedding in Warren, Michigan, was for the K. C. Kinnaird family, whose beautiful daughter Linda was marrying a fine young man in the same church family, Sonny Carmack. Incidentally, this marriage is still happily intact after all these years. However, I understand when some preachers report their estimate that half the weddings they have performed have been for couples who moved from "I do" to "I'm done" within a few short years. Indeed, there is a lot of "asunder-putting" in today's modern society.

Sonny and Linda's wedding seemed awkward for me at the time as I was only a year or two older than the bride and groom. I recall the ceremony being in the Warren Church of Christ building and there was recorded instrumental music, thus no precious soul could be offended by live instrumentation. However, the reception dinner, at a classy restaurant in East Detroit along Eight Mile Road, was another story.

A full-course dinner with restaurant servers was planned. The menu and drinks were pre-selected. Adults were seated and served a plate of delicious food and a drink, children were given a smaller serving and what Northerners called "soda" or "soda pop" to drink. The chilled drink was poured into wine glasses and, sure enough, tasted something like what I imagined wine might taste like. At the time I was a total alcoholic-drink virgin myself, though I never believed total abstinence was ever commanded or even implied in Holy Scripture.

One by one several of our congregation quietly came to my table and whispered in my ear, giving me (with slight variations) this basic question: "Hey, Brother Cotham, I think this drink tastes like wine. I am shocked it is being served. I don't believe the Kinnaird family would have approved this. I think the restaurant is to blame." These concerned church members talked to me in tones that seemed to say some huge, abominable sin had been committed.

I would quietly say to each person coming to me on this concern, "Hey, don't worry about it. Drink if you want to. Don't drink if you don't want to. Either way, don't make a big deal about it."

A few others approached me with the same concerns and questions. Finally, I just stood, clinked on my glass with a utensil to get attention, then made an announcement: "Several of you have come up here with concerns about your drink. You know at the first wedding feast that Jesus attended he turned water into wine. Now this is the first church wedding I have ever officiated and seems you are coming here wanting me to turn wine into water!" I announced. "If you like how it tastes," I concluded with emphasis, "then drink it and be joyful. If you don't like it, just request some soda or water, but still be joyful."

That message seemed to come as a relief to quite a few True Church diners that evening. No one expressed any more concern. Maybe all those concerned just needed "official permission" from "the clergy" to go ahead and enjoy their drink.

Little wonder that so many True Church couples have gone to one of the "denominational" church buildings or chapels or some other special venue for their wedding ceremony and reception!

15

Honoring the Dearly Departed— Reflections on Funerals and Recommendations for Meaningful Memories

Death and taxes are allegedly the two absolutely unavoidable realities for human beings. A sizable number of devious folks with scheming strategies in accountancy and/or politics have been "successful" in avoiding taxes, perhaps even making the tax system work to their financial advantage. I am rather doubtful that any man or woman of any previous generation has successfully avoided death though many will contend that Enoch of Genesis fame was an exception.

Given the universality of death and the human need to mark that final rite of passage, then the effective pulpit minister must be equipped, both by study and emotional stability, to perform whatever last rites may be requested.

An entire volume could be written on the varied and unpredictable experiences that preachers have encountered in the conduct of funerals. Any veteran preacher has likely conducted scores, perhaps hundreds, of funeral services. Each is different from all others. In the years and perhaps even the decades that pass, the preacher may have forgotten the names of people involved. There's an exceptional few services, however, that he will never forget throughout time and eternity.

When engaged in preaching the pulpit minister practices an art of homiletics, the presentation of homilies. In conducting weddings and funerals, the preacher is doing ceremonial speaking, what Aristotle called *epideictic* speaking. Surely, therefore, in those moments of deepest joy or deepest sadness we learn some of life's greatest blessings—as well as experience some of life's little serendipities.

References to funeral incidents will be brief. Not that funny and unusual events do not occur. They are plentiful, to be sure. During times of greatest solemnity, mistakes and miscues are bound to happen. Indeed, funeral services and other last rites constitute a landscape filled with land mines ready to explode; however, the slip-ups during a funeral service are more likely to be distracting and embarrassing rather than instantly humorous.

What is the difference between conducting funerals and weddings? The preacher of Ecclesiastes informs us there is a time for mourning and a time for rejoicing, and on rare occasions there are intimations of both in the same assembly and the same ritual. Though without close connection to the True Church, other than being in the western part of the Bible Belt, the story of Texas state troopers H. D. Murphy and Edward Wheeler illustrates how joy and sadness might be unequally yoked. Both officers stopped their motorcycles near Bonnie and Clyde Barrows' car on April 1, 1934, thinking two motorists needed assistance. When they approached the car they were both shot and killed in the line of duty by these notorious gangsters. Officer Murphy was twenty-two and had been on the job just six months and was soon to be married. Instead, Murphy left behind a grieving fiancée. In cruel irony, the fiancée wore her wedding dress to the funeral of the man she had planned to wed that day.

Years ago Palmer Wheeler, well-known song director in the Dallas-Ft. Worth area in the 1950s and 60s, was making some announcements in a church service for the Turnpike church in Grand Prairie where my dad served as full-time minister. Brother Wheeler mistakenly announced that there would be a funeral service for some brother whom he apparently did not know well. A male voice from the pew spoke up immediately and corrected Wheeler: "It's a wedding service and not a funeral. Brother Jones is getting married!" Undaunted and unembarrassed, Wheeler then exclaimed: "Funerals, weddings. Funerals, weddings. What's the difference? They both put a man out of circulation!" The entire congregation roared in laughter at the spontaneous though irreverent humor.

THE GREATEST HONOR

The greatest honor a family can give a minister, in most cases, is being asked to officiate at such final rites. I shall never forget this point as taught Lipscomb Bible and preaching majors over a half century ago in our homiletics class.

"And what kind of preacher would a family that is suffering such a huge loss call when they need a comforting funeral message delivered?" Brother Baxter asked. "Do they turn to the preacher who is the most dynamic in his speech delivery? Or one who is the youngest or most handsome preacher they know? Or one who is best known in the fellowship or maybe even the most popular preacher around?"

The questions provoked our thinking. "No, the typical family will turn to the minister they love and respect the most for his personal character and devotion to the Lord," our professor informed us. Brother Baxter then made his application: "Then serve unselfishly and live sincerely the kind of life that inspires such high measure of love and respect wherein fellow brothers and sisters will come first to you in time of their deepest need."

If the minister serves a congregation of any size, he will be called on, either occasionally or quite frequently, to conduct funeral services or serve as a participant along with other speakers. I was always glad to share the eulogy time with other speakers, whether another preacher or perhaps even a family member(s). My reason: If I "screwed up" and did not speak at my best, then perhaps the other speaker(s) could compensate for any inadequacy. And if family members were speaking, I truly believe the funeral service is much more personal and sweetly appropriate. So I always encouraged family members to participate and, if they felt they could not emotionally handle the situation, to write out a statement of memories and I would share that by reading or paraphrasing it for those in attendance.

There can be a difference of twenty to thirty years between the age of the ideal ministerial candidate when the church seeks to hire a new minister, and the average age of the minister who is sought and requested to officiate at a funeral service. And why? Likely the deceased Christian man or woman was closer in age to the older minister, the latter being able to draw from his memory bank of stories and experiences that paint the character of the one eulogized. Also, the older minister may be retired, thus having time for pastoral visitation of older members, especially if they are residing in assisted living or nursing facilities.

Over the years I have had a number older Christian brothers and sisters who have told me, "When I die I want you to do my funeral." I have a standard reply: "I'm honored and willing to do that for you, but I am hoping I won't be called on anytime soon for such duty. Furthermore, I warn you that I won't be having any but good things to say about you." That usually brings a smile. On some occasions, when that person dies, the immediate family may not call on you to do the eulogy if they do not share the same church background or share the same closeness with you as did their loved one. In those cases I have been quite content to attend the funeral service and remain silent, putting my thoughts in writing if feeling compelled to express them.

THE STEWARDSHIP OF THE EULOGY EXPERIENCE

When a person—minister, friend, or family member—is called on to present a eulogy, the invitation should be considered high honor. If you feel close to that person, then it bestows a unique opportunity to appreciate again your personal memories of that person and to share your own special experiences with others who also loved this person. In fact, you can have a deeply emotional experience when contemplating and then preparing your eulogy.

So often on occasions when I have retreated to privacy for formulating my thoughts and then later sitting down behind a keyboard to write the eulogy, my eyes have filled with tears and began running down my face. Eulogies for family members tug at your heart, because you know them so intimately and they have been so much a part of who you have become. I have written and presented eulogies for both my mom and dad, for one aunt, and then participated in services for two uncles. I have felt that presenting a eulogy for a loved relative or close friend is the last public honor one can bestow on that person—which is not technically true, of course, but that is how I view it at the time of preparation and presentation.

There is place for appropriate humor that emerges from the life story of the person being eulogized. No eulogy should be considered entertainment, but humor can render an effective salve to soothe wounds of the grieving family and friends. Occasional and appropriate laughter that is integral to the person's life experience can provide emotional release during the service.

Eulogies should give a flavor of the person being honored. Draw from personal experiences. I find it helpful to reserve some time for visiting with family members prior to writing the eulogy and asking them to share their favorite memories and/or share what character and personality traits they will miss most in their loved one.

My advice for eulogy presentation: Don't give a resume. Don't take precious time to read aloud the obituary—in most cases listeners have already read it or know its content! Use eloquence of language to share the essence of the person, to provide some facts or insights that many may not know, to share a message of hope and grace, and to impart in a highly personal way how much the listeners meant to the departed loved one. The memories that are shared eloquently should speak a message of love to every family member and friend.

The preacher likely will mention cause of death for the person eulogized. Exact time of death and those near the death bed, or other place of passing, might be appropriately mentioned and with commendation for those lovingly present at the time, especially in the beginning of the eulogy. Then again, perhaps not always. One Sunday afternoon I received a phone call with a tearful wife on the other end of the line. She informed me that earlier in the day, her husband, for whom I had conducted their wedding ceremony, had died. The husband, whom I will call Charlie, around sixty-five years of age, had battled severe cardiac issues for years. "I'm so sorry," I told the distraught wife whom I will call Ethel. "Was his passing sudden and totally unexpected?"

A long pause followed. "Brother Perry," she said with this prolonged Southern drawl, "we wuz in the bed having sex at the moment he died."

Then I was the one with a long pause, just contemplating what to say next. Thoughtlessly I dared to say what first came to my mind. "Well, Ethel, I hope you don't feel offended when I say you were the one who enabled Charlie to die with a smile on his face."

"I'm not offended at all, Brother Perry," Ethel told me. "In fact, there are two or three others who have already told me the same thing." I felt silent relief that my comment seemed to reinforce a sense of comfort.

CHILDHOOD MEMORIES/COUNTRY FUNERALS

Strange and unexpected occurrences at funerals are seldom humorous at the time. Some are sad and remain sad.

A case in point: Some twenty to thirty years ago, a Church of Christ preacher from the Clarksville Highway congregation in the Nashville area was preaching the funeral of a young man who had died of an AIDS-related illness. In his eulogy the preacher began to condemn the deceased's sexual preferences and "life-style contrary to God's will."

Within minutes into the eulogy, a number of the young man's friends stood up and walked out of the funeral service in protest. Later the preacher told of this "prodigal son's" repentance, but those who had protested and departed did not hear the conclusion of the eulogy. Regrettably and inexcusably, this preacher felt compelled to inject his own personal judgment into his message. The incident was reported in the two Nashville daily newspapers.

My earliest childhood memories of funeral proceedings were that these services were not "hurried up" affairs. Funerals seemed more likely to be conducted in a church building, especially if the family attended a rural congregation, than in a funeral home. The coffin containing the body of a dearly departed brother or sister was brought to the front of the church house. The lid was usually open for people to line up, typically ushered row by row, approach the casket, quietly view the body and then make a quiet U-turn back toward their pews, as the entire church remained silent except for occasional coughs or sniffles.

One set of my grandparents and all of their relatives lived on farms in western Kentucky and Tennessee. My memories of those boyhood funeral services remain vivid. The mourners who filed in the country meetinghouse to attend the service and view the body might at first seem quaint to those accustomed to brief, carefully orchestrated funeral rites in an air-conditioned mortuary

chapel. The former lived in a different time and place—a rural, often impoverished, racially segregated region where little was known but hard work and rest
from these labors. They toiled on farms, many of them, with an almost reverent
attachment to the land. Others found hourly jobs in small factories and mills
where hourly wages were low and labor union organization frowned upon. Time
was measured less by the month and day than by the season and task—planting,
tilling, harvesting, and storing.

Only for the funeral of some brother or sister in Christ, and some occasional
weddings, did these hard-working brothers and sisters don their "Sunday best"
on some other day besides Sunday. And quite often that "Sunday best" might be
a plain, modest dress for the women and a pair of new jeans or khaki slacks and
a freshly-ironed sport shirt for the men. Truth is, many of these rural families
did not own dress apparel that could be considered business attire.

Funeral services began and ended with those nostalgic hymns about human loss
and eternal destiny, such as "Precious Memories," "Paradise Valley," "The Sweet By
and By," and "An Empty Mansion." The eulogist, often the farmer-preacher who
served the congregation as pulpit minister, would walk slowly to the podium with
the casket stationed between him and the audience, and begin reading solemnly a
collection of Scriptures from the KJV, which usually began with familiar words:
"Let not your heart be troubled … I go to prepare a place for you," and/or "It is
appointed unto man once to die," and/or "The Lord is my shepherd."

Eulogies in a rural church house could last from thirty to forty-five minutes,
even longer on occasion. The reason is simple: The eulogist felt free to become an
evangelist urging his audience members to repent and turn from their evil ways.
I shall never forget as a college freshman attending a rural church funeral service
for a man who obstinately resisted all appeals for his baptism. The preacher made
bluntly clear that the deceased, with his widow and other relatives seated near the
casket, was now headed for the flames of hell and that the rest of us better "heed
the warning before it is everlastingly too late." This preacher all but "offered the
invitation" near the end of his message and no one, not even his family members,
seemed offended by this lack of diplomatic delicacy.

The death of children, through illness or farm accident or some other sad tragedy, understandably created much grief and perplexity. In previous generations, few, indeed, were the families who were not touched by such special loss. One of my grandmothers, a farm wife and mother, died during childbirth. Herein, the church family huddled together, at the church house or in front of an open grave, and listened to words of consolation and sang "Rock of Ages," "Safe in the Arms of Jesus," and "Farther Along" ("We'll understand it all by and by").

Interment took place in the church graveyard on the grounds behind or to the side of the church house. This old custom placed the church building and all that it symbolized at the center of life's most important passages. The church graveyard enabled impoverished families' needs to be served at considerable financial savings as well as providing convenience in visiting the gravesite.

MINISTERIAL PROTOCOL FOR THE FUNERAL SERVICE

A veteran minister knows this experience: A funeral director calls him and identifies himself, and during that momentary pause the preacher knows instantaneously there has been a death of someone he knows and he will be asked about availability to officiate at a service. The funeral director will report the time that the family prefers, given the options the director has given the family, then asks the minister if he is available at that hour.

In many instances the director may tell the minister that members of the family are in the office with him and then say, "Would you like to say a few words of comfort to the spouse (or the adult child or other family members)? At that point, one can only say, "Yes, I'll be glad to express my sympathy over the phone." (In recent times there is a speaker phone in the director's office.) In that brief conversation, the minister expresses condolences and will likely say he wants to sit down with the family and inquire about preferences for the service, Scriptures to be used, kind of music or hymn selection, and other arrangements.

Realistically and sadly, the minister will have reports of death experiences that come totally by surprise and perhaps by tragic circumstances such as an automobile accident. He can be stunned as much as anyone else even though not as grief-stricken as immediate family members and close friends. There are two highly sensitive and painful death situations, at least from my experience: One is the death of a young child and the other is death by suicide. Those death experiences are occasions when words seem woefully inadequate and consolation elusive. Nonetheless, last rites must be performed. Importantly, the minister must acknowledge the raw and tough emotions of survivors as well as the basic unfairness of many personal events in our lives.

Before the service, the minister will want to arrive at the venue of the service at least several minutes early. I always feel a need to retreat to a private room in the funeral home or church house, take off my suit coat, and sit down for a few moments in quietness for prayer and meditation before beginning my expected role. In my experience, all funerals are stressful and almost always require a great deal of preparation, both emotionally and in message construction.

I recall an occasion of running late in a drive from the Nashville area to McMinnville, about eighty-five miles via I-24, and the funeral director and family members had already lapsed into a panic mode. The director and some family members were already standing on the curb anxiously awaiting my arrival as well as saving me the closest possible parking slot.

On another occasion, in my mind I had entertained the start time for a service being an hour later than what was scheduled. Once realizing my inexcusable mistake almost at the last minute, I broke every speed limit between Nashville and Dickson, Tennessee, to get to the service where people were seated in the chapel and quietly waiting my arrival. In the latter case, a cell phone was available for informing family and friends as to why I was late. Those are occasions the preacher cannot crack a joke about his delay—he can only sincerely apologize and beg forgiveness!

THE RITUAL OF LAST RITES

Ritual pervades funeral services and last rites. Typically, the minister will be in the visitation room as time approaches for the service to begin. Then, within five minutes of "start time," the director will politely ask the visitors to exit the room and the family to remain. The minister is directed to stand at the head of the casket, typically standing there with Bible in hand and a respectful, somber countenance.

The director will then state that family members may now approach the deceased for one last "visit," beginning with distant relatives and ending with the closest of kin—a spouse (if surviving) and children. The way some funeral directors, perhaps with less polished linguistic skills, offer the last directive to the family in that visitation parlor is almost cringeworthy: "If you want to come on up here and look at the body one more time, then this is the time to do it."

Invariably, before we all exit the visitation parlor for the chapel, the director will call on the minister or pastor to lead a prayer. I never felt totally at ease with that prayer situation; if there were any other minister co-officiating, then I would ask him to lead that prayer. The family would then be ushered out to their reserved pews at the front of the mourners, who had been asked to stand, and there they take their seats. The minister then walks ahead of the closed casket and takes his seat on the pulpit or platform, holding his Bible in hand, resting it on his lap, anticipating his time to speak.

The service typically begins with music. In good Southern tradition, there will be songs about heaven. There may be recorded music that sounds scratchy and uninspiring when played over an antiquated and inadequate sound system. I have officiated where there was a small group of singers who were standing in the "amen corner" or out of sight. Congregational singing is now considered a good option, the fact that many mourners are in no mood to sing notwithstanding. If attendance is sparse and mourners are spread out to the extent of many pews being empty, congregational singing is likely to be a bust.

When the service is over, the congregation stands for the last musical selection and the minister is directed to the head of the casket. The pallbearers are then summoned to roll the casket to the edge of the chapel or church and then carry it to the hearse. The family then comes out and various family members shake hands with the preacher and quietly thank him and inform him of "what a good job" he did in the service. At that point, quite often, a male family member may slip him an envelope that has a check or cash remuneration for his services.

The gravesite provides setting for another ritual. The minister is expected to walk slowly in front of the casket as the pallbearers lay it over the broad belts that hold it until lowered into the vault and grave. The director then gives the signal for the minister to stand at the head of the casket and make any comments, read a Scripture, and lead a prayer. In addition to comments and Scripture, I typically quote some poetry such as lines from Henry Wadsworth Longfellow's "Psalm of Life," believing some literary touches add a sense of class and dignity.

When the prayer is ended the minister is expected to slowly "walk the line" of the immediate family under the tent, squatting or stooping over and very softly making additional consoling remarks to each family member personally. To me, this final ritual seemed so artificial. At that point, after numerous family visits and funeral remarks, what more needs to be said? I always found it particularly difficult when the grieving family was composed of my very close friends, or even of my own family, because anything I might say at that point seemed a contrived bow to tradition and perfectly useless. Plus, it's cumbersome to reach and speak to family members on the second and third rows under the tent as the rows of folding chairs allow no walking space.

Then there is a kind of ritual in filling the grave. Those who sit under the tent or stand around that tent will observe complete silence as cemetery workers go through their work routine as quietly as possible: placing casket in vault, sealing the vault, lowering the vault into the grave, then sometimes doing a ritual shovel full of dirt tossed on top the vault, then backing a trailer with a lift lever and a loose tail gate that rapidly dumps all remaining dirt. I have wondered how the grave workers must feel when so many are silently watching their every move. The workers smoothen the dirt covering the grave and then place the larger flower arrangements around the site. At some point, the funeral director will somberly announce, "At this point, our service is completed." Some of us have a sigh of relief when that announcement is stated.

FINANCIAL COMPENSATION

Most full-time ministers serving churches of size will soon learn a paradox regarding financial compensation. A minister may devote an immense amount of time to a family when one of their loved ones is gravely ill. He may invest a great deal of emotion in preparation of the funeral eulogy as well as the time to travel to the funeral site and cemetery (indeed, it may be away from his home-town). And, then, he may receive nothing financially, or a mere pittance, for all his emotion, preparation time, and services.

On the other hand, a minister may be called to assist a family in time of loss wherein very little time or emotion is necessary to conduct the services, and then he discovers the family he has served rewards him with incredible generosity, graciousness, and gratitude. I have had both these experiences. For example, some twenty or more years ago a neighbor whom I liked and respected called and almost apologetically asked if I could do him a favor. "Sure, of course," I said.

"My dad has died," my neighbor friend said. "He was not in any way active with a church. My family wants just a brief and simple graveside service and for him to be buried next to my mom. Can you do that for us?" I replied that I would be honored to do so. I prepared only about ten minutes of remarks, complete with Scripture and prayer. There may have been fifteen to twenty present at graveside.

My friend thanked me graciously and he slipped something in my suit pocket, so I thanked him. I did not even look in my suit pocket till hours later, almost an after-thought, then I discovered he had slipped three or four "one hundred dollar" bills in that pocket. This neighbor seldom "darkened the church doors" himself, yet I called him immediately to thank him for his gracious generosity.

At a Nashville church I had served, a husband and wife worked as a close team in building a successful business. The wife became ill, I had visited her in the hospital, and her death came soon. The husband apologetically asked for my services as though he were imposing on my schedule. I was honored to deliver her eulogy and it was easy to share many good observations and reflections about her professionalism, character, and spiritual commitment.

After the service the family and visitors were standing on the sidewalk leading to the main entrance of the church house. The husband approached me. "It's a two hour drive up to the old family burial plot in east Tennessee, and I know you have a busy schedule, so I don't expect you to make the drive," he explained. "We have already made arrangements with the local Church of

Christ preacher in Celina to handle the graveside service there." He then placed something in my pocket and said, "This is for you. I will gladly give you more if this is not sufficient." I usually reply something to the effect, "Thank you very much. Just knowing your loved one is an honor sufficient enough, and I don't need anything." I knew this Christian businessman was incredibly thoughtful and considerate. Hours later, after making some pastoral visits, I returned home, routinely reached into my suit pocket, and pulled out the check he gave me—it was for a thousand dollars!

Bottom line: The minister does not conduct weddings and funerals for extra cash anyway. The preacher must surely feel gratified that he is asked to stand beside family members during their times of greatest need. He does serve, ideally, because it is true ministry (servanthood) to people he cares about during the most important rites of passages in their lives. The people he serves in these rites of passage, both young and old, in most (though not all) cases, are not likely to forget his name or how he served them on that important family day.

FUNERAL SERVICES—CONSIDERATIONS AND COUNSEL

For younger and less experienced preachers, I offer this reminder: the funeral service is not about you. Your primary concern is not how good you look or how great you sound or how eloquent you can become or how important you may be.

Occasionally, one can listen to a funeral speaker and, judging by the way that speaker tells personal stories of events in which the deceased was involved, seemingly the attention and honor are more intended for the speaker than the one being eulogized. I don't think preachers are as guilty of such egregious self-centeredness as family members or friends who have been invited to speak and share. Some family members and friends of the deceased almost seem to approach the occasion as one to look important and to entertain, maybe telling stories in which the speaker is the main character and the departed one's role in the narrative is minor.

Sometimes too much personal and private information is given. One funeral speaker, who shared a country music entertainment career with the deceased friend, told stories of his friend's frolicking adventures with his first wife before they were married. Turns out that the first wife, known well by the speaker but hardly by anyone else present at the service, was not in attendance, but the newly-widowed second wife was sitting on the front row of the chapel—another major lapse in judgment! In the utter silence one could almost sense the listeners gasping in shock.

The funeral is not a time for a sermon. Some preachers in the True Church have debated as to whether a funeral is a worship service as it seems to have three of "the five acts of worship." A few years ago, I was asked to officiate at the service for an elderly Church of Christ lady. She had been a widow for many years and died either right before or right after her one hundredth birthday. However, I did not know the lady and there was only her niece and a few friends for me to inquire about her personal life, values, legacy, and any memorable stories. After all, longevity per se is not so commendable in a funeral, else ole Methuselah would have merited the world's most impressive final rites.

In interviewing this lady's niece and asking questions so that I could craft my funeral message, I gained little helpful information other than she was a "long-time member of the Lord's church." I shall never forget what the niece then asked me: "You are going to review the plan of salvation in your message, aren't you?"

Reflexively, I laughed heartily. "Oh sure, I am. You never know who might be sitting out there who may be lost eternally in their sins." I continued to smile for a couple of moments, but her countenance was seriously pained. There was a long pause. "You're not serious about this, are you?" I inquired, and the niece assured me she was serious. She took offense at my laughter, for which I immediately apologized, and then she declared: "This is what my Aunt Bessie [not her actual name] would have wanted."

Such a sobering moment for me! However, I delivered the eulogy at Franklin Memorial Chapel and did my best to honor the request. The attendance was somewhat smaller, perhaps fifty to sixty, most were older except for a few friends of the niece. I shared what biographical information I had been given, then I pulled from my knowledge of twentieth century American history and reviewed some historical events, such as world wars, etc., this aunt Bessie would have lived through, having been born in Woodrow Wilson's presidential administration. (The history references were simply filler material.)

Then, time came for the conclusion. "Aunt Bessie was a faithful member of the church. She loved God. God wants everyone to be saved, but only according to the plan laid out in the New Testament," I declared, drawing from my Church of Christ roots. "There are five steps all sinners much complete to be saved: you must hear the Word, then believe in Jesus as God's Son, then repent of your sins, then confess the name of Jesus as God's Son, and finally be immersed in the waters of baptism." Incidentally, after each "step" in the "plan of salvation," I quoted the appropriate Scriptures I had been taught as a child and that my mom had written in the opening of my childhood KJV Bible.

My eulogy ended. Aunt Bessie's niece politely shook my hand offered what seemed an approving smile and a "thank you." We got in our cars, formed the line behind the hearse, and drove in slow pace with police escort to the cemetery.

FOR WHAT GREAT CAUSES MIGHT A PERSON RISK ONE'S LIFE?

The eulogist must be super-cautious in drawing moral lessons from the life of the deceased. One of the strangest services that I can recall involved a young single man who, as I was told, had fallen off a two-story roof, presumably in a roofing accident. I did not know the young man, but knew his lovely sister-in-law quite well as one of my former "parishioners" and felt gratified to offer comfort to her and others in her family.

Before the graveside service, with the casket open and the deceased young man wearing U. T. Vols orange regalia along with overalls, I whispered a question to this sister-in-law, calling her by name: "So, as I understand, your brother-in-law died in a roofing accident?"

"Well, not exactly that way," she whispered, telling me she could explain later. But there were a few more minutes till start time so she continued softly: "He had been out drinking a lot that night. It was late when he got in bed. His bed is on the second floor his parents' house and it has a door leading off the bedroom onto the balcony. It's always been a space to sit out late at night and enjoy the breeze."

At that point I was confused but it was quiet and surely about time for the graveside service to begin, and she softly continued: "And there was no reason he had 'go' out there on the balcony, because there is a bathroom right down the hall from his bedroom. But he did, and apparently he just lost his balance and tumbled over the balcony railing and landed on his head and did not survive the fall."

When the light came on in my brain, I thought, "Wow, this fellow risked death to save himself a walk down the hallway to urinate in his own bathroom after drinking too much beer. The balcony off his bedroom was much more convenient." I could not allow myself to dwell on this scenario for the next few minutes. After returning to the church office, I reflectively pondered this entire scenario. I could only juxtapose this unlikely fatal accident with some stories of the great martyrs of history, beginning with Jesus and then moving to religious and reform pioneers as well as political patriots and martyrs and our courageous military servants who put themselves in harm's way, and I reflected on the causes for which these courageous souls were willing to die. What a contrast with the young man who tumbled over the balcony railing at his parents' residence!

HOW LONG SHOULD FUNERAL SERVICES BE?

Because local resident church members will have listened to sermons under the tenure of various preachers, a family that selects a preacher to officiate will have some choices. Quite often a former preacher at a congregation will share speaking time with the current preacher. When I preached at Westwood, I so often shared funeral officiating and eulogies with James Vandiver, who had served that church ten years before going to Hendersonville and then Harpeth Hills in the Nashville area. At Franklin's Fourth Avenue, I often shared officiating duties with Myron Keith.

Some preachers are long-winded and rambling. When there are two or more speakers there may be an agreement as to how long each presentation should be. The odds of each speaker honoring that time limit, however, are not always so good.

Myron Keith could be the most unpredictable funeral speaker I ever heard. He usually began his eulogies as though they were starting in the middle of a paragraph: "She was baking bread for the upcoming street festival booth …" And when you hear such an "out of context" opening statement like that, one wondered, "What on earth is Myron talking about?"

A number of years ago, Myron and I were co-officiants for the memorial service for Frances Harris, long-time Fourth Avenue member and sweet and loving elderly sister. I had already officiated at her graveside in West Tennessee earlier in the week and the memorial service was conducted in our large audi-torium where hundreds could gather. When there is more than one officiant, there is usually a quick huddle and agreement on who speaks first, what songs are interspersed, and other cues to heed. I always liked to speak first so I could sit down and enjoy the speaker who followed and just maybe I could be the first to make certain points.

After a hymn or two then I rose, went to the podium, and delivered my pre-pared remarks, then sat down, and another hymn followed. Then Myron rose to speak. His first words blew me away: "Doesn't Perry look great? I remember him as a senior at Lipscomb and he preached here every Sunday as interim preacher." At that moment I thought to myself, "Wow, where is this going?" Then Myron reported, "I thought Perry had gained a bunch of pounds after he got married and a few years ago I challenged him to get his body back in shape the way it was when he was a student preacher."

I was incredulous. True enough, I had lost some weight through disciplined eating and more exercise. "I didn't think Perry could do it, but look at him now—he has got himself in shape and looks great," Myron added. I do not remember how Myron segued to the legacy of Frances Harris, but I shall never, ever, forget how he began his remarks. (I think Frances' adult children knew Myron well enough not to be shocked.)

Myron had the briefest funeral eulogies of any minister I have listened to and that even includes the times he did not share duties with another speaker. His eulogies typically could be eight to ten minutes. He spoke in a soft, preachery tone and posture that imitated the voice and visible style of Batsell Baxter. He became something of a legend in Franklin when, at the start of a twenty-eight year pulpit ministry at Fourth Avenue, it was little more than a sleepy town south of Nashville and Williamson County was largely rural landscape. I always maintained the highest regard for Myron and he gave so much pastoral tutoring, even took me golfing (his favorite pastime) when I was a student preacher.

In the fall of 1992, as a full time minister at Fourth Avenue, one Friday morning I attended a funeral service for one of our members that was conducted at Williamson Memorial. Start time was 10:00 A.M. Myron was asked to be the only eulogist and I felt that was appropriate. Jim Taylor, former Church of Christ youth minister who had taken a position at the funeral home, made an opening statement in the service.

Then Myron rose to speak at around 10:03. He spoke for about five or six minutes so that he had wrapped up the service at around 10:08-10:10. At the time I thought, "Wow, that's the shortest funeral service I have ever attended. I wonder if the grieving family feels cheated." Then we walked our way up the path to the cemetery which is behind the chapel. Under the tent at gravesite, Myron is not to be seen; I had planned to tease him privately about the brevity of his funeral remarks. Instead, Jim Taylor handled the graveside remarks and, as I recall, took as much or more time as Myron had taken with the main eulogy in the chapel.

After graveside services and the family and friends dispersed, Jim and I greeted each other. Jim is a life-time member at Fourth Avenue and a truly good and helpful servant to hundreds of families. Even today I am quite sure he conducts scores of funeral services each year, especially for families who have no church affiliation. I complimented Jim for his remarks and then said, "By the way, I didn't see Myron up here at the graveside."

"Oh, he had to slip out for some very important appointment. I'm not sure where he had to be. He just asked me if I could cover for him at graveside," Jim replied. I then simply dismissed the topic from my mind.

Fast forward to later that Friday evening. Glenda and I had been invited to the spacious home of Jim and Mary Ann Crowell for a delicious supper and a fun visit. Eddie Miller and Richard Ellis, two other staff ministers, and wives Debbie and Denise were also present. The women moved into the kitchen to visit while preparing the meal and the men stayed in the den where we discussed a range of topics: farming, Franklin city history, Fourth Avenue church history, U. T. Vols football, and other topics.

The discussion topic came around to golfing. "Aren't you and Myron and two other fellows in a long-time foursome, been playing for many years?" I asked Jim.

"Oh, yes, we are. We like to play on that course down at Montgomery Bell State Park one day every week that the weather is nice enough. In fact, we've been playing as a foursome for many years," Jim explained. "As a matter of fact, we played today," he offered. Calculating the drive from Franklin to Montgomery Bell is about 30 to 35 miles, the wheels of my mind began to turn. "We usually start at 10:00, but we delayed tee time today until 11:00 because Myron had some funeral he had to do at 10:00, but he arrived on time just like he promised he could do and we had a good outing."

"Aha," I thought to myself. That explains the ultra-brevity in the eulogy and waiving even a graveside cameo appearance. I could only smile inside at Myron's pastoral ingenuity. I should not have been surprised. I remember as a student preacher on the Fourth Avenue staff that on Wednesday nights during the winter months, in the five minutes between the Bible class in the chapel and on the way to the auditorium for the final devotional and closing of the service, Myron would open his office, shut the door, turn on his transistor radio, and check the score of the Vanderbilt Commodores basketball game. He would then emerge, make announcements, and "offer the invitation" as the service closed.

Others were in the church corridor at that time. They may have inferred Myron was going into his office, shutting the door, and spending a few moments in prayer, or maybe even grabbing his Bible and some notes for the closing devotional thoughts or the announcements.

Sometimes we just do what we have to do! (By the way, Myron would whisper the Vandy score to me as he walked out from his office into the auditorium on his way to the microphone to make announcements and deliver a brief message.)

CREMATION MAKES A DIFFERENCE

Some traditional customs continue in small towns and rural communities. The introduction of a modern element, however, may produce discomfort in a presiding preacher. A friend of mine told of attending a Tennessee country church funeral service for another friend whose body had been cremated. An urn with the deceased friend's ashes had been placed where a coffin would have been stationed. The preacher struggled through his prepared remarks, obviously distracted by the presence of mere ashes. In contemporary times, most ministers have officiated at memorial services where an urn with "cremains," the term now in vogue, is placed front and center.

The increasing popularity of the cremation option provides interesting options for disposal of the "remains." "Cremains" can be scattered nearly anywhere. George Spain tells of a terminally ill friend whose last request was for his body to be cremated and his ashes to be scattered above the Great Smoky Mountains. His friend had often hiked some of those trails and enjoyed the beauty of those scenic mountains.

When the time came to carry out this friend's last request, a private plane was chartered for a brief flight above some of those majestic mountains. The plane with George and his deceased friend's closest family members took flight. At what seemed to be the appropriate time above the mountain tops, George quietly opened a cockpit window and tightly gripped the urn as he moved it outside the plane's window, and then respectfully and slowly turned it upside down. A special moment for a departed friend was in the making, yet, according to George, such poignancy immediately became tainted by what seemed half or more of the ashes blowing back into the cockpit and into his face and the faces of his deceased friend's spouse and children.

After the plane landed and was returned to the cockpit, George exited the craft with his empty urn. He and his friends quietly and soberly walked toward the small flight office and parking lot. He had carried out that request as best he could. Before exiting the air strip, however, George turned back to where the small plane was positioned. There he saw the pilot sweeping the remaining ashes from his plane with a whisk broom. How realistic it is that our most solemn thoughts and sentimental actions become enmeshed with mundane indignities and unavoidable realities!

Just as wedding ceremonies can be customized, so also may be funeral rites. To cite one bizarre story: A lifelong minor league baseball fan, Larry Riddle, had attended so many baseball games over his lifetime. When he died in Elizabethtown, Tennessee, a few years ago, a memorial service was conducted at the team's home field. Riddle was eulogized as the team's most dedicated fan, the team being an affiliate of the Minnesota Twins. The deceased was dressed in the Twins baseball uniform and mourners were asked to sign the casket. Then four team members and coaches, dressed in their full baseball uniforms, caps, and cleats, rolled Riddle's casket around all four bases pulling it on a small wagon. When the casket crossed home plate, the team's general manager shouted "safe" with appropriate umpire gestures at the home plate. The fans cheered. The story, along with a color photo, was published in the *Tennessean*. I was glad not to be invited to participate in this service.

By contrast, the quietest funeral audience I have ever witnessed was an assembly left standing in shock at the conclusion of a Middle Tennessee service in which I officiated. At the conclusion of a funeral service for a long-time personal friend, a man who sadly died around fifty years of age, one of the deceased man's sons (a mid-adolescent) exploded in understandable grief and anger as the casket was being rolled from the front of the chapel down the center aisle to the front doors. The older brother ran after his younger brother, grabbing and restraining him in the open doorway and holding him in restraint and attempting to quieten him. The younger brother angrily resisted. The two brothers broke out into a physical fight and shouting match.

The entire audience remained standing, yet shocked and speechless, perhaps no one knowing quite what to do. There was a brief delay before all emotions were under control and we loaded into our vehicles drove to the cemetery. This son's grandfather, a venerated and kind Christian gentleman, had placed loving arms around the troubled youth and effected a quieting, loving, and consoling comfort. From that moment and at graveside and a dinner following, everyone seemed to speak in subdued tones. The younger son was given understanding hugs and support. A few years later I preached the funeral service for that wonderful grandfather and gentleman.

"SON, WE BURIED YOU TWO WEEKS AGO!"

A final story might put us on a happier track. The story comes from my dad and it combines the elements of both funeral and wedding.

In 1937 an explosion occurred in New London, Texas, that involved oil field workers. A mother lost one or two sons in the explosion and her sister had lost one or two, my dad recollected. The mangled body of a third young man was found. Identification of the third body as another son was made by the initials on a belt worn by the third victim. The families lived in Shawnee, Oklahoma, and there was much grief felt by all members of the local congregation as well as the entire community. This was such a shocking tragedy that evoked deep sadness in the entire community!

My dad preached the funeral for this third son. The family had experienced a terrible tragedy. A few days later this very son made a routine call to his parents from Salt Lake City to find out how they were doing.

"Son, we buried you two weeks ago! Brother Cotham preached your funeral," the incredulous and stunned mother declared.

The young man insisted that he was very much alive, that he was not an imposter, and that he had traveled to another work assignment in Utah. He was calling to report on the explosion and tell about his new assignment.

"Please come home immediately," his mother urged.

As it turned out, the young man had met a panhandler (of which there were many in those depression years) and had given him some clothing, including the belt with the personal initials. Bodies were so mangled in the explosion and fire that the belt was the only item for identification of that body. Thus my dad had preached the funeral for the wrong man.

A few weeks later the same young man, now with a young woman at his side and holding his arm, knocked at my parents' door at the parsonage in Shawnee. "Brother Cotham, you buried me," he stated; "now I want you to marry me."

And thus my dad conducted the wedding ceremony for a man whose funeral he had already preached.

The story, reported and narrated in the *Shawnee Evening Star*, came to the attention of producers for Ripley's "Believe It or Not" network radio show. The young man received an expense-paid trip to travel by train to New York City to appear on the show and tell his most unusual and unlikely story.

Surely in those moments of deepest joy or deepest sadness we learn some of life's greatest blessings—as well as experience some of life's little serendipities!

16

How Blessed Is the "Tie That Binds"?—Life Among Some of the More Interesting of God's Children

The South Harpeth Church of Christ is located along Tennessee's Davidson-Williamson County line and has been composed of a mix of college-educated young adults and older, rural citizens. When the members arrived at the meeting house for worship on the first Sunday in September 1991, they soon made an interesting discovery.

Seems that all the new hymnals, the third edition of *Great Songs of the Church* from Abilene Christian University Press, had been spirited away after only a few months of use. In their place in the racks was a much older song book that had been used previously. No one in this 200-member congregation, nor Minister Doug Varnado, had authorized or requested the switch, knew who made the switch, or knew the location of the heisted hymnals. Was this whole caper little more than a practical joke? Days passed before this little mystery was explained.

Turns out, one of the elders had used his "authority" and acted alone in removing and hiding the new "modern" hymnals. He had gone to the church house late at night and hastily boxed up the new hymnals and then returned the old song books to the book racks bracketed to the back of pews. This was no small task to be completed alone and may have taken several hours to complete.

Did this elder object to the inclusion of newer hymns in the collection? To the use of shaped notes? To the exclusion of some old and favorite standards?

Answer: None of the above. Seems that this elder was adamantly opposed to the inclusion of Scriptural readings amidst the hymns because it meant women, in clear violation of the Pauline prescription for the distaff gender to "keep silent in the churches," would be reading aloud in the assembly with the men.

Alas, women's voices may be heard *singing* words of Scripture in great hymns in the general assembly, but must not be heard in *reading* aloud those same words of Scripture.

THE BEST KNOWN "CLOSING HYMN"

The best known hymn that typically closes out a Sunday worship assembly in the True Church has been around for almost two and a half centuries: John Fawcett's classic "Blessed Be the Tie That Binds," the four stanzas having been written in 1782. The hymn is sung so frequently that likely most saints switch to "auto pilot" at the moment the song is begun and, from the standing position, put the hymnals in the rack, collect their coats or other belongings, and prepare to exit the HOW (House of Worship).

Any lack of attention to the lyrics is unfortunate, for the song indeed expresses simply and beautifully what Christian fellowship should involve: a common mind, a common love, a kindred spirit, an empathetic heart, a helping hand, a sadness at departure from one another's presence, and a longing to be reunited once again. We speak here of the "ideal."

The reality is, of course, that ideal is attainable but all too often not reached. Thus, safe to say "the tie that binds" is not always a blessing. Not that the tie is a curse, but the personality clashes among God's brothers and sisters and the church disputes and fights can be so hurtful and wounding that the B. Q. (Blessing Quotient) dips real low.

Originally, this chapter was conceived as a discussion of a wide variety of the topics and issues that have divided "the Lord's people" in the hope of realizing the utter irrelevance and impertinence of many of those issues. For example, one "issue" is how many communion cups should be used in the worship assembly. Our current Christian youth groups, if told that congregations once divided over that issue, would likely laugh and say "no way" or "you've got to be kidding." As a boy I recall attending with my family some rural congregations that were "one-cuppers," though invariably there were two cups in each communion serving—one for each section of pews to the right and left of the center aisle.

The list of divisive issues became too long for a detailed discussion of each. A century or so ago, True Church leaders argued about a millennial period based on certain scriptures in the book of Revelation. Subsequently, three positions emerged: premillenialism, post-millenialism, and amillenialism. Though the controversy was infused with high importance, most of the Lord's people could not even spell these words, much less understand the doctrines, and even less could understand the relevance of the issue to their daily lives. As a boy I often heard about the heresy of the "anti's," a sect that basically contended that when a few dollars were dropped into the church collection plate then suddenly limitations were imposed on how the local congregation could scripturally disperse those funds.

ALWAYS NASTY—CHURCH FIGHTS CAN INVOLVE THE FEW OR THE MANY

While rare, there have been occasions in "men's business meetings" wherein Christian brothers erupted in near physical altercations. I recall the shock and dismay I felt as a young minister for a Michigan congregation when, in a "men's business meeting," one of the brothers took issue with something said. He rose rapidly from his folding chair, throwing it back in anger, said some angry words, and then announced he was immediately leaving the meeting. He quickly moved to the exit door, opened it, walked out and slammed it mightily and noisily. While the rest of us sat in silent shock, the angry man's best friend in the congregation then rose from his chair, said he concurred with his indignant friend, and that he, too, was leaving. He stood up and exited the room also by a mighty slamming of the same door. The rest of us stayed in the room. We were all stunned and silent for a few moments. The meeting resumed and ensuing discussion was conducted in somber and subdued tones.

Sometimes a church fight seems to involve the entire assembled congregation. I have seen this happen on two unfortunate occasions. One was a sizable
congregation in the suburb of Roseville on the northeast side of the Metropolitan
Detroit area. An elder was reading a letter of resignation from their beloved and
respected pulpit minister (who was out of town on that Sunday morning and had
accepted an offer to serve another congregation). The letter was a gracious and
kind message to the entire church, and it expressed gratitude for the opportunity
to serve this congregation. Rather than leaving the proverbial "well enough"
alone, the elder put the letter down and began to add personal negative comments, such as: "I know a lot of you are now sad and disappointed, but Brother
John Doe [manifestly not the actual name] and his wife were never happy here.
He did not think his salary was high enough and his wife did not like the church
home we provided—it just wasn't good enough." There was immediate reaction
with widespread discussion in the pews and a sense of disorder, so much that
it seemed the eventual closing prayer was farcical and irrelevant. The elder's
comments offended me as I knew the preacher personally and considered him a
close friend, so a strong urge welled up in me to walk to the front microphone
and politely say a few kind and respectful words in my preacher-friend's defense.

A similar incident happened in a sizable congregation in Brentwood (Nashville
area) in 1976 at the conclusion of a Sunday worship service. The spokesman for
the elders announced the current minister's services were being discontinued and
a new, full-time pulpit minister would be hired. Before the assembly could be
ended, one man rose from his pew and made an emotional accusation, then another emotional statement was loudly uttered in support of the current minister,
then soon it seemed an ugly shouting match that continued for several minutes.
Again, nothing seemed holy or spiritual about the experience of worship that
Sunday. Worshipers went home both saddened and amazed that such a verbal dispute could follow a time of sacred worship among Christian brothers and sisters.
The elders' decision did not change, and a few weeks later some eighty or ninety
members left that congregation to begin a new one just two or three miles down
the same boulevard, hiring the dismissed pulpit minister as their own preacher.
Time can be a great healer. The original home congregation has become one of the

largest, most active, and most progressive ones in the Nashville area. The history of the dissenting congregation was short-lived.

Clearly there was no tie of blessedness between some of those brothers (and often sisters, too). Church fights and brotherhood "wars" have been around since the inception of organized religion. Outsiders to the faith have often used such fights and wars as the reason for non-acceptance of the faith and non-affiliation with any religious group. Perhaps, one might contend, disputes and fights are inherent within organized religion. Any institution that claims to be caretaker of absolute truth and that also asks for sacrificial contributions of financial and other resources becomes an institution whom members value and take seriously—they believe the institution's messages must be true and its actions right.

Church fights are almost always rooted in the non-critical acceptance of an unspoken premise—"my doctrine and my way are always right and your doctrine and your way are always wrong." And the issues being argued may be profound, such as the nature of God or the divinity of Christ, or may be a matter of preference and expedience, such as which ministerial candidate should be hired or whether a new church facility should be constructed or the old one renovated. Of course, what's important to one saint may be inconsequential to another. All too often the fight can largely be a personal one that involves a clash of personalities and preferences, but somehow the conflict get "transformed" into a moral battle for "truth and righteousness."

In this closing chapter I will discuss only two issues that have been divisive within my own generation, noting the "blessing quotient" is diminished when internecine fighting over those issues has occurred. Actually, in some ways these two issues are related. Then, I will seek to illustrate what true blessing might look like among "the Lord's people."

WORSHIP WARS

"Now don't go tampering with our church service." "There's absolutely nothing wrong with the way we've been doing things around here." "I don't mind change, but I'm not in favor of making change for the sake of change."

Those of us in the True Church who have sought to make worship assemblies more meaningful and relevant have heard these and similar statements. And many would have agreed with Maxie Boren, Ft. Worth-area minister and friend of my family for many years, that "clapping, choruses, praise teams and other human innovations is adding to God's word. If worship services are dull and embarrassing to some, may I suggest that this is actually a heart problem in the worshiper."

In church life perhaps nothing gets the brothers and sisters more stirred than changes in the corporate worship assembly or even proposals for change. Churchgoers see the evening news or read their newspapers and learn about one change after another—changes in the workplace, in politics and government, in education, in lifestyle, in entertainment, and in social behavior. And the Trump era has been a polarizing time of conflicting and confusing statements, both from political spokespersons and national media. Sure, much of this toxic rhetoric and many of these changes are perplexing. Some seem threatening. So Christians can "go to church" and be reassured that at least some things remain the same. Or do they? And should they?

The intense conflict over styles in worship gave rise to the expression "worship wars" of the 80s and 90s. Sometimes these wars got pretty ugly and rather petty. For example, in a larger Nashville congregation of several hundred members, the elders announced that there would be no more applause permitted during the Sunday assemblies and that the proper manner to observe the completion of a baptism was silence. Jesus informed us that when one sinner returns to the fold, then "the angels in heaven rejoice." I always wondered if angels rejoice by passively sitting on some long pew in heaven, keeping their heads down and wings quietly folded.

Jack Reese, a professor of Bible at Abilene Christian University, tells of a member of a congregation, a male in his 70s, who went to the HOW late one Saturday night and cut the electrical cords which ran to the microphones held by members of the church's praise team. Reese also tells of a brother who brought a decibel meter to the worship assembly and made the determination that contemporary songs were sung with much more volume. Occasionally, many of us have witnessed a person walking out of an assembly in a quiet but visible protest of something said or done which deviated from the standard, prescribed agenda or the worshiper's comfort zone.

A NEW GENERATION/A CONTEMPORARY STYLE

Christians take worship seriously. Even Christians who do not seem enthusiastically involved in corporate worship would say they take worship seriously. That part is good. Too many consider their own worship acts and styles as "right," and consider different worship acts and styles of others as "wrong." Nan Gurley attended a worship assembly one Sunday evening when a visiting U. S. missionary working in an African nation was giving a progress report on his family's establishing a Church of Christ among the natives in a village. (As an aside, I have found missionary reports can be highly interesting and "to the point" with colorful visuals, or they can be as boring as watching paint dry.) Nan reports that this missionary claimed he had "sought to teach the natives proper New Testament worship" and he was "proud to say" that he had "successfully shown them how to tone their worship down and make it less enthusiastic." "When I heard that statement in the mission report," Nan recalls, "I nearly fell off my pew!"

Readers supposing the opening story for this chapter is total fabrication must reflect on the fact that traditions about public worship and assembly are taken seriously in the True Church. Few issues stir Christians more deeply than controversy over corporate worship. A worship assembly tradition, especially its "order of worship," is a sacred cow. Like all sacred cows, it may be milked for the financial and emotional security of those who profit by its presence but it is never to be despised, taken lightly, criticized, or tinkered with in any way. A major factor intensifying worship wars in the True Church fellowship is that many members have been convinced that getting worship "right" down to the smallest detail is a matter of eternal salvation. That is, proper worship is a "salvation issue."

My last ten years with Franklin's Fourth Avenue church provided the context for involvement in worship wars. As in other congregations I served in ministry, I attempted incremental, creative changes in the style of worship. In 1999 Phil Williams, an elder, and I, along with our wives (Nancy and Glenda), traveled to Seattle to spend time visiting with Milton Jones, pulpit minister at the Northwest Church of Christ. This congregation successfully innovated in worship styles; we "picked Milt's brain" on matters of strategy for change. Upon returning to Franklin, the elders eventually though reluctantly granted me permission to present a series of lessons on worship for the Sunday evening services and implement some changes.

Every sermon delivered in this new series was on some aspect of worship. I was able to use PowerPoint in our assembly for the first time (seems so commonplace now, but a "major innovation" for some churches in 1999 and 2000). We organized a praise team to lead singing with each of eight "lead singers" holding a microphone. However, presumably because half the singers were women, the elders mandated the entire praise team sit on the front pew rather than stand and face the audience. For one lesson I had written a brief play which dramatized in a humorous way what worship in a first century congregation might have been like if an assembly were conducted in same style of True Church worship in mid to late-twentieth century. Most felt the comedic drama was instructive and hilarious—but not everyone! After the play and our service had ended, the elders met in my office and informed me of immediate complaints filed and deep offense taken. Apparently, drama exposing our traditions as simply traditions and therefore amenable to change was deemed inappropriate for a Sunday evening assembly.

The sixth lesson in the series was entitled "The Posture of Praise." I developed the idea that we are commanded to "love the Lord your God with all your heart and with all your soul and with all your mind and with all your strength" (Mark. 12:30), and that we cannot fulfill this command with a purely cerebral/rational approach—emotional states and physical responses demonstrate awareness of the presence of the holy God! I then granted permission for the whole assembly to express worship in some appropriate and sincere vocal and/or bodily form, possibly by kneeling during prayer songs, lifting up hands, clapping of hands (during upbeat hymns), proclaiming an affirmation of faith or spiritual truth (as in saying "Amen"), or any other sincere and spontaneous expressions.

The Monday following this lesson presented opportunity to learn a lesson. A written message delivered to me from one of our deacons was brief and to the point: "If last night's sermon is the kind of lesson you plan to present again, you need to resign from your position immediately." This deacon seemed to have more influence with our elders than any other deacon. The good news, of course, is that he signed his name and I could respond to the letter with a phone call. Later in the day, an elder came to my office, sat down on the sofa, and stated he represented all the elders. His countenance told me it would be a serious and not-so-happy conversation.

"There is good news and there is bad news," this elder began. "The good news is that you are not going to be fired, at least not as yet," he said somberly. "The bad news is that your worship series and your time preaching on certain topics is now officially over." I responded that I had more lessons lined up for the series. To no avail. "The series is over. Period," the elder declared. I realized the last lesson on "posture of praise" was more than some traditionalists could handle. I was informed the church was highly divided and some members might leave if the series continued. "Good grief," I thought to myself. "You'd think I had asked every female between eighteen and thirty-five years of age to jump out of her pew and move into the aisle and do high-kicking, Rockette-style, liturgical dances to an upbeat hymn."

Worship wars are not new, of course. They have been around as long as organized religion. Often they have been ugly. Usually there are victims who are left bleeding—emotionally and spiritually, of course, but Abel may have bled literally from the fratricidal act of brother Cain's jealous rage in biblical history's first worship war.

Consider first-century churches, especially when preferences of Jewish-based congregations clashed with preferences of the newer Gentile-based congregations. If there were worship wars in the first century congregations, what might have been the issues? Might we have heard, "Well, Paul, you're no John the Baptist or Elijah, so stop trying to be like Elijah and just preach in a normal tone"? Or, "I don't like these simple songs from the epistle writings of Paul. If singing the psalms of David was good enough for my parents and my grandparents, they're good enough for this generation as well." Or, "Most of us are Gentiles around here. Why on earth, pray tell, do we hear so much talk about Passover around here? Why, you'd think we were sitting in a Jerusalem synagogue right now!" It's almost amusing to imagine the concerns and issues of some first century worship wars.

In many quarters, "contemporary worship" became a catchall label to apply to anything in worship that critics do not like. In reality, its meaning could vary from denomination to denomination and from individual to individual. What is "contemporary" to one person may be old and traditional to another person.

The goal of contemporary worship seeks to more meaningfully and more fully engage the minds and hearts of people in Christian assembly. This goal is sought through experiments in balancing both freedom and order in worship.

In the True Church fellowship, geography may have played some role in affecting the profile of worship conflict. Congregations west of the Mississippi as a general rule seemed more open to contemporary worship than congregations in the Bible Belt. In my view, the factors were more cultural (or sub-cultural) than geographical. The education level, especially of the leaders, the heterogeneity of the congregation, the length of time the members have held membership in their respective congregations, the numerical strength and stature of the church in the local city—all seemed to constitute more important factors relevant to the nature and resolution of worship conflict.

Worship renewal seemed more likely and worship wars less likely in congregations with the following traits: leadership is strong; leaders are well educated; congregations are younger; membership is well educated and has been exposed to other traditions and styles; many new converts not raised in our tradition hold membership; and members possess mature understanding of God's grace.

WOMEN'S ROLE IN THE TRUE CHURCH

Many issues that Christian sisters and brothers have fought over, even divided over, possess precious little consequence on their spiritual growth and development. The "point of view" that wins out and is implemented bears no real relevance or consequence to anyone except those who harbor ego-investment in the controversy.

Thousands upon thousands of Church of Christ young people have been socialized into a religious system of doctrine and practice that discounted females—their intelligence, their giftedness, their talents, and their potential for service. Of course, plenty of Scriptures could be adduced in support of women's subordination to male leadership and discrimination in the assembly, the main one being the Apostle Paul's mandate for women to "remain silent in the churches" (I Cor. 14: 34).

My experience growing up in the True Church: While women could teach young children in Bible classes, prepare meals for the church fellowship dinners, serve as attendants in the church nursery, do clerical work and other behind-the-scenes tasks, they were not allowed to "usurp" male authority in worship services or church business. Even certain service roles were denied, such as passing communion in the assembly (admittedly, a woman could pass communion trays horizontally so long as her derriere or upper leg made contact with the edge of the pew, but she could not stand and pass trays vertically). A woman would not be considered as a song director, even if she knew music better or possessed a better singing voice than any male in the congregation. She certainly could not lead a prayer or even read a Scripture in the service. And God forbid a woman ever be considered for the role of serving either as a preacher or an elder in "the Lord's church"!

Of course, there were some compensating positives: A woman could teach a women's Bible class. She might be named in charge of the primary Sunday School department or the church nursery. A woman might write out an announcement for a male to read in the assembly, but never even considered making the announcement herself even if it concerned women's church activities. Women were certainly not invited to the "men's business meetings," but a Christian wife can exert her influence at home if married to a Christian man who would be attending the business meeting. She might even write out a statement that her husband can read in the meeting though, of course, he would never disclaim the statement as his own nor divulge its authorship.

Other gender role-rulings developed in *ad hoc* situations "on the fly." Charles Mickey, theologian-librarian and minister, as well as my much respected relative via marriage into our family, narrated an incident occurring in a large congregation located in a large urban area in the Bible Belt. The setting, in the mid-1980s, involved team teaching by two couples who were highly trained and licensed in marital therapy and counseling. The women were as knowledgeable, experienced, spiritual, and capable as their husbands. They shared speaking and teaching time in the church auditorium for all adults in a special VBS class. And, in that church setting, they integrated Scripture and biblical concepts with contemporary perspectives and illustrations.

Visitors attended these well planned sessions. One visitor, sad to say, was greatly offended and alarmed. After all, here were two women, alternating with their husbands, standing before the congregation, teaching and reading from the Bible. This appallingly violated the clear teaching of the Apostle Paul. The offended visitor sought out the elders to express righteous indignation. An "emergency elders meeting" was called. The minister, supporting the marital therapists, was also present. One elder was ultra-conservative, but, being a man of wealth who attended all the worship services, wielded much influence. This elder wanted the two women to cease teaching an adult class wherein men were in attendance. (Of course, it just requires one elder's objection to veto a positive ministry.)

Resolution was struck by compromise. Seeming unwise simply to end the class when adults needed and were blessed by the presentation of all four Christian therapists, especially in the middle of the program, the objecting elder agreed to a revised *modus operandi*. The female therapists were allowed to face the congregation and teach all adults only if two stipulations were met: (1) Each female therapist was required to sit on a stool, essentially a bar stool, with her husband standing beside her while she addressed the class, and (2) Neither female was permitted to read or expound a single verse of Holy Scripture while addressing the class. Manifestly, then, there was no reason even for either woman to hold a Bible in hand while teaching. At least the class continued and good was accomplished.

Sometimes an offended church member cannot wait to call an elders meeting, but simply must act courageously according to conscience. I recall the first few Sundays at Nashville's Woodmont Hills Family of God, around 2003 or 2004, when women were first allowed to line up around the front communion table and walk up the rows in serving the emblems. A Christian brother sitting on the end of a row (there were folding chairs, not pews, in the "great hall") was adamantly opposed to women serving communion. When a serving woman approached his row he made a silent demonstration of keeping his hands below the seat of his chair or tucked under his upper legs, indignantly nodding his lowered head. He adamantly refused to accept the tray that the silent, respectful female server was attempting to hand him. Then his wife, sitting next to him, quietly reached out her hand and accepted the tray from the server, placed the tray in front of her husband, and then the husband "partook" of the bread, then later "partook" of the cup in the same manner. The wife then handed each tray back to the female server. He never touched either tray. So a woman who is seated can hand a man a communion tray, but a woman who is standing cannot perform the same service.

Indeed, entrenched legalism can be an abomination unto the Lord, and a very present aid and comfort in the times our pet prejudices and human traditions are being assaulted!

A DIVISIVE ISSUE THAT COULD NOT BE DISMISSED

A funny thing happened after earning my B. A. in Bible and Preaching and in beginning graduate education at a state university and thinking for myself: I began to realize that such discrimination against females was inherently and spiritually wrong. Human reason and common sense informed me that women can do anything that men can do in areas requiring emotional strength, high intelligence, and spiritual leadership. Human reason and common sense also informed me that the gifts of the Holy Spirit intended to encourage and build up the body are not diced up according to gender. Then why on earth or why in heaven God would cordon off certain roles (*e.g.,* teaching adults, pulpit speaking, shepherding leadership, and handling church business) and declare that women may do everything except for those roles?

I realized this one issue could be dismissed as too controversial and divisive except for the fact that it directly impacted at least fifty percent of a church family and indirectly effected the entire church family. As a young minister I concluded that how we consider fellow human beings and the liberty we either grant them or deny them are both "heady" matters and vital concerns, the significance of which would be impossible to overstate.

Realizing I could not change the entire "brotherhood," I hoped to employ what little influence I possessed to make a positive difference in the True Church. I have both "enjoyed" and been "injured" by so many experiences in all churches I have served full-time on what is commonly called "the women's issue." A small volume could be written on these experiences.

In teaching adult classes I have invited various women in the congregation to assist me, perhaps by standing or sitting beside me as co-teacher or taking the floor for the entire period. At other times I have invited a woman to be moderator for the class. I have often asked women to write the lead article for the church bulletin or some other publication. Strange, isn't it, how tame and non-controversial these small assignments would seem to the current generation? Thus, just a few of my own stories might reinforce this regrettable reality for women in the True Church in the twentieth century.

CAN A WOMAN EXPRESS GRATITUDE IN A WORSHIP SERVICE?

One Thanksgiving weekend at Westwood in the late 70s presented an opportunity for me to involve any willing participants in the main worship assembly. Appropriately, my sermon was on the topic of gratitude. I made the lesson personal by reporting blessings in my life for which I was especially grateful. Then I announced I was somewhat tired from a round-trip automobile journey to Texas, so I invited any willing volunteers to stand at their pews and share a personal blessing or two.

This was a risky homiletical strategy, but I knew there were at least three or four fellows who would stand in the midst of 350 to 400 people and talk for two or three minutes. And indeed they did. I could tell that the strategy was proceeding nicely and that it was likely a totally new venture for a Sunday AM worship service. Then, after a few men had stood and recounted personal blessings, a woman stood and spoke up in sharing blessings for which she was especially grateful. My recollection was that this sincere sister was not raised in the True Church. I was taken a little by surprise, but indeed grateful in the moment and silently hoped another woman or two would stand and speak up.

After the Sunday dinner, our house phone rang. I was summoned to the phone. On the other end of the line our "lead elder" had a very serious tone of voice. "Ever since my family got home from church, my phone has been ringing off the wall," he began. "So many people have been offended that you allowed a woman to stand up and talk in church. That kind of thing can't happen again!"

"Well, I did not ask her to stand up and speak, but even if I had," I replied, "there would have been nothing wrong with it. In fact, I thought her standing and addressing the entire church was both surprising and refreshing and I wish other women felt as free to share their blessings." Despite my conciliatory and empathetic tone, the rest of the conversation with this elder did not continue so well.

"WHAT'S THIS BIG BROUHAHA ALL ABOUT?"

In the fall of 1982, my first year as minister at Nashville's Otter Creek Church, I was conducting a Wednesday evening devotional. I spoke a few minutes about prayer and then opted for a "season of prayer"—a period of a few minutes for people spontaneously to pray aloud or silently. That's a time the minister hopes there will be several who will speak up and pray aloud. I have learned the "season of prayer" can be a time of effective bonding or it can seem a pointless waste of time.

On this Wednesday night several men prayed aloud—just brief petitions or statements of thanksgiving, each bracketed by moments of silence. Then, apparently to almost everyone's surprise, Nan Gurley prayed aloud. She asked the

Lord for blessing upon her husband Wayne's mother in Irving, Texas, who was facing major surgery. Among Nan's gifts is the art of eloquence and emotional expression, not to mention her deep spiritual commitment. I felt so pleased she was uninhibited in prayerfully and publicly voicing her deepest concerns that evening.

Not everyone was so pleased with Nan. A day or so later the elders called a special meeting to deal with this incident. We met in the elders' conference room on the following Saturday morning. The room has a long table with about ten chairs. The elders had already met for early conference before the time Nan and I were requested to appear. Once we arrived, I recall Nan and I sitting together at the west end of the table.

Somber quietness filled the room as we sat down. Seemed as though we were facing the Sanhedrin Court. At first, no elder spoke. Then I recall the vivid way that Nan burst the tense silence with her strong and dramatic voice: "My brothers in Christ, what's this big brouhaha all about?" On any other occasion I would have laughed at her vocabulary, confidence, and assertiveness.

The elders seemed at a loss for words. After an uncomfortable pause they began to discuss the complaints from various members against both Nan and me regarding the "season of prayer." (As an aside, I have often learned the lesson that when an elder says he has heard "complaints," the complaint might primarily be coming from his wife or another family member.)

While the elders buttressed their point that Nan's public praying in the church assembly had shocked and offended some, and thus, in their view, was inappropriate, interestingly enough not a one of them contended she had sinned. In fact, several elders said, "Nan, we are not saying that you sinned. We are not judging your motive or spirituality. It's just that you and Perry created a problem for people here that we don't want to happen again."

Nan was the only female in the meeting. As I recall, she offered a respectful explanation that she was emotionally distraught over her mother-in-law's health and need for scheduled surgery and, at my invitation to anyone to pray, naturally lifted her voice in prayer. The elders then gave me an order I shall never forget: "Perry, the next time you conduct a season of prayer, then make it clear you are inviting only the males to pray aloud." I recall my immediate reply: "Well, then, in all due respect, with this restriction, I will no longer be conducting a season of prayer in the gathered assembly of this church."

WHAT IF THE *MISSION* EDITOR-IN-CHIEF IS FEMALE?

Two years later the board for *Mission Journal* conducted its annual meeting at the Disciples of Christ library in Nashville. The board, chaired by Robert Randolph, met over a weekend and wanted to worship at a more progressive Church of Christ while in our urban area. I felt it a compliment the board chose Otter Creek as the congregation to visit. The board also wanted to tell the story of *Mission Journal* to the entire Otter Creek family. Having several articles published in *Mission*, I was a huge supporter of their ministry in reaching out to a segment of our fellowship that cared especially about academic study of Scripture and social justice issues.

Mission Journal's editor at the time was Bobbie Lee Holley, English professor and author. I received the elders' permission for her to report on the journal, describe its founding and mission, perhaps even make an appeal for new subscriptions or financial contributions to support the ministry. The elders agreed to merge all adult classes in the auditorium and allow Bobbie Lee to do the report, but they stated clearly they wanted nothing more than the report—she was not to teach a traditional Bible lesson! I clearly and emphatically communicated these stipulations and expectations from our elders to Dr. Randolph and Dr. Holley.

Our Sunday School period followed our "regular worship service," to use True Church parlance. Announcement was made that all adult class members and their instructors should remain in the auditorium for a special presentation. I introduced Dr. Randolph and Dr. Holley and then stated our study time would be spent in learning about the *Mission Journal* ministry, its history, its outreach, and its current status.

After my opening remarks and introductions, I took a seat on a nearby pew. Bobbie Lee walked the three steps up to the pulpit, opened a big Bible and laid it on the podium, and then declared: "My original assignment was reporting on *Mission Journal* and giving a status report and financial update. But you can get that information on my printed handout. This is a rare honor, to stand before some two-or three hundred of you adults during your regular Bible study time, thus I cannot squander the opportunity to preach a lesson to you from God's Word." At that very moment, one of the deacon's wives rose from her pew with a most unhappy countenance and exited through the front entrance of the church house. A few squirmed and glanced at each other momentarily, but no one else abruptly departed.

Bobbie Lee then invited all of us to turn in our New Testaments to John's gospel (chapter 12) and follow as she read the narrative of the woman who washed Jesus' feet with expensive perfume and dried them with her hair. She informed the large class that this was one of her favorite stories in the life of Jesus, then eloquently expounded the story and drew some meaningful applications. Personally, I felt she presented such a powerful lesson. A good number of others agreed. On the other hand, I sat in the pew with some sense of discomfort and just wondering how much the elders would hold me accountable for her dramatic deviation from clear expectations.

At the next elders' meeting, the topic of the *Mission Journal* board's visit to Otter Creek was discussed. Some stated they felt discomfort during the class session. They all concurred, however, I had communicated expectations and the *Mission* board and editor were the ones responsible for disregarding those stipulations. I recall saying to the elders with a chuckle, "Thank you for not blaming me. We all agree Bobbie Lee gave an excellent exposition. As for women speaking in the churches, well, this is an issue that's not going away!"

As an aside, currently the Otter Creek church, now located in a much larger facility on Franklin Road in Brentwood, has become one of the most progressive congregations in our fellowship in terms of involving women in public worship assemblies. Women's intelligence is honored and their gifts are exercised for building up the body. Their faces are often seen and voices often publicly heard in every public worship assembly and classroom.

SHOWERS OF BLESSING

The tie that binds Christian brothers and sisters in deep, abiding love and unconditional acceptance is indeed a blessing. Many of us have experienced God's grace and brotherly/sisterly love at the point of our deepest spiritual and emotional need. The moment when this blessedness is felt deepest would be at the point where each individual sister or brother in Christ is confronting one's deepest tragedy or biggest need. Yet there are lighter moments where we see and hear the pitter-patter of those "showers of blessing" often sung about in the True Church.

The church's shared meal can become one of those blessings. In the True Church these shared meals may be called "pot luck" or "covered dish" meals. At Fourth Avenue Church I originated the idea of a "Super Bowl Sunday Dinner" that was held after morning services once a year on the Sunday of the NFL Super Bowl—everyone was requested to bring their food offerings in a big bowl!

Thus the long table was laden with all kinds of soups and chili. True enough, there were some food items that seemed a bit out of place in a bowl, but the general theme was deemed clever. Some brought decorations or logos of their favorite football team on their dish or bowl. And just after the dinner I conducted a brief devotional which met the legalistic requirement for an "evening service," and the church then dismissed for the day (some lucky ones ducked out prior to my devotional thoughts, thus technically they "forsook the [evening] assembly").

My own hidden agenda: I did not want to return to the HOW for a Sunday evening service right in the middle of the first half of the Super Bowl game. No one complained about this schedule change, and I was given special gratitude by the avid pro football fans in the congregation. Some elders pondered how those "providentially hindered" from attending the morning assembly could somehow "partake" of "make-up communion" in the evening; a volunteer elder agreed to re-open the building before 6:00 p.m. and have communion ready to serve at the top of the hour.

ESTABLISHED CHURCH TRADITION—POT LUCK DINNERS

"Pot luck" dinners typically become church tradition. Such "pot luck" affairs, now more likely to be labeled as "covered dish" dinners, must be embedded within congregational DNA. I could only "guesstimate" how many hundreds of these dinners my family and I have attended in our lifetime. From my experience, seven personal observations:

1. There is quite a range of taste-quality and nutritional value in the prepared dishes. Thus, "pot luck" is an appropriate name and a little easier to say than "pot providence." After a few dinners, most members know which sister in the congregation is the best cook and which dessert is not to be missed. True, on rare occasions a man might cook some dish to contribute to the shared meal. Some dishes might get a special name. One family often brought a delicious, rich, creamy chicken casserole with a golden brown crust topping that their teenagers facetiously called "the sick and dying casserole"—so named because their mom consistently made that same casserole whenever she delivered a dish to a private residence wherein a family member was seriously ill or the entire family was grieving a loss.

2. There is always a prayer of thanksgiving and blessing prior to the line proceeding down the table(s), a prayer that many pay no heed other than perfunctorily bowing a head (with eyes possibly half-opened) while waiting to grab a plate and plastic-ware and, in fact, it's a prayer that some may not even hear when there is no sound system.

3. Younger children and teenagers like to plunge into line first and have their choice of the favorite foods; occasionally and thankfully, parents of younger children attempt to restrain their little ones' greediness.

4. Preachers are often spoiled by preferential treatment, especially when the good sisters encourage them to be first in line. Preachers are also the ones who brag the most frequently and vocally about the delightful tastiness of certain dishes, thus they are encouraged to sample as wide a range of culinary offerings so as not to offend some saintly cook. Since they are considered experts in taste quality, a compliment from the preacher

on some covered dish is typically valued more than a compliment from another diner. Little wonder some preachers struggle with weight control and hardly a one would venture mentioning the word "gluttony" in a sermon or Bible class, much less condemn gluttony as a deadly sin.

5.   At times one might think there is competition as to who can load the most food on a plate. There can be creative stacking of servings. And there are some, especially the younger ones, who selfishly return to the table for "seconds" before a few polite, unassuming people have opportunity to prepare their first plate.

6.   There are far more willing to fill their plates, enjoy their meal, and then slip out for home or another engagement than there are people willing to stay later to clean tables, wash dishes, and fold and stack chairs and tables.

7.   There can be wide disparity in culinary contributions. For example, one might often see an elderly single woman who, admittedly enjoys cooking, bringing a box or big sack with several special dishes. She may have spent all of Saturday cooking and baking in her kitchen for this Sunday event, and may request help unloading the dishes from her car. Going along the service line after most others, she herself will prepare only one plate with small servings. For the same church dinner, a young married couple with several kids may arrive late with one sack from Kroger that unapologetically contains only a two-liter coke and a large bag of Lay's potato chips. And each member of that family prepares a plate with huge servings, shamelessly making two or more return visits to the table for extra servings.

The shared meal has always been conducive to ties of kinship and fellowship. These church dinners may be akin to the "Agape feasts" of the first century Christians. And there are variations on the theme of fellowship dinners. A congregation may establish certain fellowship traditions. At Westwood, the church enjoyed a "chili supper" on the Wednesday evening before Thanksgiving and an "ice cream supper" after the evening service on the Sunday closest to July Fourth. Families that possessed an ice cream freezer were encouraged to make a freezer of their favorite recipe of ice cream, and there could be recognition of what family brought the best-tasting cream or the most unusual flavor of ice cream.

While at Westwood we were blessed by having Carl and Reita Stanley as next door neighbors. Carl was a Christian businessman and a natural community leader who could do anything quite well in the church assembly or adult classroom other than lead singing. Most of all, Carl had a sense of humor and a repertoire of stories as to how that sense of humor had been deployed over the years.

In preparation for the Westwood ice cream supper, Carl would shop at some grocery store that carried exotic flavors of ice cream. He would buy three half-gallon containers of one special flavor, allowing the ice cream to soften just enough to pack it down into the canister of his ice cream machine. He would then place crushed ice between the canister and the bucket, put a covering on it, and bring it to the supper. I could only smile when hearing various people compliment Carl on such delicious "home-made" ice cream and, being some unusual flavor, would ask either Reita or him for his special recipe. Reita would answer, "You'll have to ask Carl," and, when he was asked, Carl would simply answer, "It's a secret family recipe."

HOPEFUL SIGNS THE "TRUE CHURCH" MOVES TOWARD BEING THE TRUE CHURCH

Fights and divisions, we have acknowledged, have been part and parcel of any significant religious movement, and the Campbell-Stone Restoration Movement clearly has been no exception. Only with the passage of time might we gain some perspective on the sources of division and then be able to chuckle at some of the folly and waste of it all—or maybe we laugh to keep from crying!

There are already hopeful signs for the future of the Church of Christ when spiritual renewal moves in the following directions (briefly stated):

1. The stewardship of the Christian mind is taken seriously. Jesus commands that we love God with our mind (Mt. 22:37). In our mental and intellectual nature, not our physical, we are created to reflect the *imago Dei*, "the image of God." Admittedly, there is a blind security

and comfort in believing that everything we have ever been taught and continue to believe is unassailably true. Mature Christians seek truth, keep an open mind, engage critical thinking, and seek points of agreement with people in different faith traditions. The mature Christian is not afraid of ideas. To be afraid of ideas renders one unfit for authentic discipleship. A mature disciple acknowledges other expressions and understandings of Christianity than the Western/Protestant/Evangelical/Fundamentalist/Bible Belt version that so many have been spoon-fed since toddler days. One example of honoring the "gifts of the mind" is the annual Thomas H. Olbricht Christian Scholars Conference, a convening of "people of faith" from many traditions for advancing interdisciplinary studies, sharing scholarly manuscripts and dialogue, and enhancing spiritual fellowship. Lipscomb University Professor David Fleer has taken the lead in planning, organizing, and administering this enriching and diversified event. The blessings of the intellect from such a conference and fellowship can only trickle down to bless the entire fellowship.

2. A True Church is real community, a place of true love and acceptance, not judgment, of one another. The by-product of the loving community is connection. We acknowledge we need one another and that we all need a sense of being valued and loved, thus we are in relationship with each other. This means getting rid of any narrow-minded and judgmental posture that makes people who are different feel second-class. We affirm people for who they are, love and accept them, and shun and denounce the use of biblical passages to clobber people for differences they did not choose, including sexual orientation. I concur with a simple quote from author Bob Goff: "I used to want to fix people, but now I just want to be with them."

3. A True Church rejects sectarianism and tribalism that says "I am right/better and you are wrong/not as good" and emphasizes the unity of all those who accept Jesus as Savior and attempt to follow in his steps. When there are disagreements, then discussion and dialogue follow but always

with loving respect and civility among parties. The church must model respect and civility in the midst of a political society that seems lacking respect for others with different values and priorities and lacking civility in discourse. The True Church should no longer be identified first and foremost as a religious group with some eccentric doctrinal position, such as adamant opposition to instrumental music in the worship assembly, but for positive and loving activism within the community and willingness to join hearts and hands with other believers.

4. A True Church assembles for worship that is truly *theocentric* (God-centered) with an openness to accepting any creative arts and acts of worship that bring honor and praise to God. The assemblies should be fulfilling and exciting wherein Christian brothers and sisters attend because of joyful expectation rather than out of dreaded duty. Preachers must delve deeply into the Word and explain the meaning of a text, but then make applications as relevant, clear, understandable, and challenging as possible. And while preachers are not called to be entertainers, there's no sin for speakers and teachers to be compelling and interesting. "We preachers cannot just phone it in," Jeff Walling once told me; "making Jesus boring is the greatest sin in the world." The public reading of the Scripture should be seen as an art to be performed effectively, renouncing the idea that any baptized, literate male of any age is automatically qualified for this important assignment. Biblical narratives and spiritual truth can be dramatized by gifted Christian actors. Finally, the True Church does well to study the theology of worship and, consequently, will dispense with absurd and ridiculous rules such as "a closing prayer ends formal worship, therefore a choral group or soloist may now perform or a woman can speak to adults or the church can applaud and God will not be deeply offended."

5. A True Church is filled with Christian brothers and sisters who maintain a sense of humor about all of life. If readers have gotten this far in my book, then surely they concur already. Back in the 80s, a small group of gifted young Christian actors (composed of Wayne and Nan Gurley and

Dan and Bonnie Kean) formed a drama group. Named Ariel, the troupe staged productions with a series of skits that hilariously highlighted the zaniness and, at times, absurdity of contemporary church life. In the 90s, with Steve Pippin replacing Dan Kean, the Glory Bugles emerged with skits and musical lyrics that winked an irreverent eye at self-righteousness and bad theology as those who only know it first-hand can perform. In 2008 Professor Lee Camp of Lipscomb University produced and hosted a "staged" radio show named "Tokens" with presentations to a live audience. Each show combined excellent music, both vocal and instrumental, special guest artist appearances (poets, philosophers, theologians, musicians, and humorists), humorous monologues, interviews with Christian activists, and humorous skits. The end result: People had a sense of "enjoying" their faith and their spiritual commitment, but were also challenged to think and understand faith commitments "outside the box" in which they were raised. "Tokens" is presented four times a year in different venues (and at least once each year at Lipscomb's Collins-Alumni Auditorium and Nashville's historic Ryman Auditorium) and has gained a loyal, passionate following.

The above traits render that "tie that binds" a true blessing, for sure. Perhaps readers have been stirred to recall ways in which that "tie that binds" has been a blessing to them over the years.

COUNSEL AND CAMARADERIE IN A MALIBU HOT TUB

In April 1981 I traveled from McMinnville, Tennessee, to Malibu, California, at the joint invitation of the University Church leaders and the Pepperdine University administration to audition and interview for a position that entailed half-time ministerial work with the campus church and half-time professorship in communication and/or political science. My first thought was what an awesome opportunity might lie ahead. Follow-up thoughts stirred some stress and anxiety. Succeeding Jerry Rushford as pulpit minister with all his knowledge of church history and his preaching skills, and then having University faculty and families in the audience each Sunday, were not calming thoughts. A deeper concern for me was moving so far away from Middle Tennessee which had been home for so many years.

Jerry was so helpful in providing background information on the campus church and passing along advice for my visit and delivering two "try out" sermons. On a Saturday evening I took the flight from Nashville to LAX, leased a Dodge Omni (a model likely unheard of today, but the cheapest auto available at the time), drove to the Malibu campus, and searched for the President's mansion in which I was assured accommodations for the next few days. There I met President Howard A. White, a widowed single man in his late 60s, as well as two sons and some of their family. Though there was a full generation of difference in our ages, Howard and I shared a Lipscomb connection.

The next morning I preached a sermon in Smothers Theater on campus. I was treated to Sunday dinner by President White, went back to my room for rest and study for the evening service which was conducted in beautiful Stauffer Chapel. I felt my Sunday evening message to be a little more "cutting edge" as I discussed challenges and hopes for the Church of Christ fellowship in the upcoming century. I made the point that some well-meaning yet greatly-mistaken individual had conveniently over-estimated the membership in the mainstream Church of Christ at two and a half million members for a national encyclopedia. In the middle of my lesson, I silently observed that M. Norvel Young, well-known preacher and former Pepperdine president, quietly slipped out of the chapel assembly.

After the service while still visiting in the chapel, one of the Pepperdine professors in attendance stated to me, "By the way, did you know that the academic person who actually submitted that inflated membership total to the encyclopedia was Norvel Young?"

"Oh, no!" I declared with great surprise. My pulse rate quickened a bit. "What a colossal, unwitting tactical mistake on my part! No wonder he got up and left during my sermon."

"Not a problem at all," the professor explained. "Norvel just made a general estimate at the time. Others have told him years ago that his numbers were too high and he concedes that now. He is one of our elders and he wanted to hear you speak again, but had to slip out early to catch a 'red-eye' flight to Nashville." I then felt major relief.

There were two or three additional days of just visiting campus, sharing lunch with department chairs, talking to professors, and visiting facilities, especially the library. And yet, every day ended later at night in the same routine. President White would invite me to meet him between 9:00 and 10:00 in the hot tub that was just outside the guest bedroom where I studied and slept. In those heated, relaxing, and pulsating waters, the President and I would have our own conference which began with reviewing the day and his seeking my observations and reflections. I could also ask him any question. He sometimes passed along advice. I had the sense that he really wanted me to come to Pepperdine.

The late night hot tub conversation could cover any variety of topics: the study of American history (Howard had been an inspiring history professor at Lipscomb in the 50s and was highly respected there as professor and historian); church news and developments; athletic events; life in the greater Los Angeles area; and family news and personal concerns. Never in my life have I ever experienced conferences as relaxing and free from the slightest pressure and stress than in those late night sessions—simply unforgettable!

SUNDAY DINNER ALONG MALIBU BEACH AND PERHAPS A HEAVENLY CALL

The Sunday morning service was over. I was relieved to have completed that first sermon. President White had planned to treat just the two of us to a quiet lunch and our first real visit as I had arrived on campus somewhat late the previous night.

Only a short drive from campus down the mountain brought us to an enchanting restaurant along the beach named Sand Castle. President White and I sat comfortably across a table from each other, then could glance westward and watch the blue Pacific Ocean waves roll in. Though dressed in our Sunday suits, glancing out the windows brought glimpses of bikini-clad folks of all ages who were enjoying sun and scenery even in April. The two of us may have been the only Sand Castle diners wearing suits, dress shirts, and neck ties.

In the middle of our dinner, the *maître de* came to our table, then looked at Dr. White directly and asked, "You are President White of Pepperdine, aren't you?"

"Yes, I am," he replied.

"Then you have a phone call. The phone is at the entrance desk and you can take the call right there. It's from a female and she speaks as though it is urgent," the *maître de* informed him. She paused a second or so and then said to him, "I think it's your wife." She then left to return to her post.

To my surprise, President White did not hastily rise and move right to the entry foyer. He sat there pensively for a few seconds with an ironic look on his face. Then he leaned in to speak softly: "You know, if she is right about this call being from my wife, I expect this will be one very interesting conversation."

He then rose and walked to the entry way and received the call.

I had to smile at the President's sense of humor. I knew then I could relate to his sense of humor and his self-confidence throughout my visit on campus. When he returned from handling that call, which did not last too long, I felt free to pick up the line of conversation and take it to a more serious level.

"Well, Dr. White, suppose that had actually been your wife calling from heaven. What do you think she might be asking you?" I felt confident he would not be offended by my question. "She surely would ask about the children and grandchildren you share together. Would she ask how you are enjoying presidency at Pepperdine? Would she ask about your biggest headaches in university administration? Might she ask when you plan finally to retire? After all, you are retirement age."

"Well, I think she would be asking all those questions and a whole lot more," he replied. "She can be pretty curious. But the big thing, I would be having a whole lot more questions for her, mainly so I might get a little preview on what to expect once I cross to the other side."

IMAGINING A PHONE CALL FROM DEPARTED SOULS WHO WIELDED THE GREATEST INFLUENCE IN OUR LIVES

As I updated this book from its first draft thirty years ago, how humbling to reflect on the many preachers, evangelists, professors, chairpersons, and just friends in general that I referenced in my first draft years ago who have passed beyond this mortal life.

Quite often in reflecting on people who influenced me—people such as Batsell Baxter, Willard Collins, Mack Craig, Carroll Ellis, or even two influential faculty advisors in my doctoral program, George V. Bohman and Rupert Cortright—what might a phone conversation from one of them on "the other side" (call it "the golden shore," "the sweet by and by," "land fairer than day" or whatever imagery one might prefer) actually be like?

There are times I think of how great it could have been to have enjoyed just one more final conversation with at least one or a select few important persons in my life. Such a fun "mind game" to speculate on how the conversation would go if we had a phone call from one or two of the significant and influential persons in our earlier lives! We might want to inform them, just in case they didn't know, of our latest and most significant professional achievements. Or maybe report some artistic achievement or academic accomplishment. Or maybe just share a personal achievement or milestone.

We want to believe they would be proud, perhaps even pleasantly surprised, of what we have achieved. Or is there some chance that this special person or persons in our earlier life might express disappointment that we did not measure up to the full potential of our gifts and opportunities that they had seen in us?

Perhaps we most would seek to thank this one or select few special persons for all the positive influence in laying a foundation for the building of personal character, critical thinking, and a worthwhile career. Or might one of them even seek our own understanding and forgiveness for some of his or her failures to set the right example, give the best counsel, or point us in the right direction? After all, we are all human—including our best and most revered instructors, advisers, mentors, and coaches. All of us live within a unique cultural context. Christians living in earnestness will walk and act in conformity with all the knowledge and insights available in their own generation.

Most of all, we would want to assure those influential professors, instructors, best friends, and family members that we have taken the light and energy they instilled in us and have ventured further down the path they set before us. Our hearts grow older as the years pass, but they can still be softened and warmed by the vivid memories of the unforgettably vital roles these special people played in our lives.

Indeed, we bear witness to those who have gone before us. We honor them in our memories and in our words, giving thanks for all God accomplished through them. And we can truly assert that tie that bound our hearts together in Christian love was truly a blessing for time and eternity!

2/21/20

About the Author

Perry C. Cotham retired in 2018 after more than fifty years of service in two fields: church ministry and university professorship. His last full-time position was Professor and Senior Lecturer in Communication Studies at Middle Tennessee State University. Previously, he held full-time teaching positions at David Lipscomb College (now Lipscomb University), Tennessee State University, and Nashville State Community College. He has taught part-time at these institutions as well as at Belmont University and University of Phoenix.

Cotham earned the B.A. in Bible and Preaching at Lipscomb, then the M.A. and Ph.D. at Wayne State University. He has completed post-doctoral studies in religion at Vanderbilt University Divinity School and in psychology at Middle Tennessee State University. His Master's thesis, "An Analysis of the Nature and Values of Expository Preaching," and his doctoral dissertation on the rhetoric of Franklin D. Roosevelt and Harry Hopkins of the New Deal and World War II era, show something of his diversified interests. At the college and university level, Cotham has taught courses in communication, religion, philosophy, Bible, history and political science, and ethics.

In church ministry, Cotham has served churches of various sizes in rural, small town, and large urban areas. He has appeared in a few conference and lectureship programs, including Pepperdine Bible Lectureship. He has written religious articles and book reviews for several church periodicals.

Cotham has written some twenty published books and numerous published articles in the fields of Bible, religion, worldviews, state and national history, political science, ethics, rhetoric and public address. He has been occasional contributor to the *Tennessean* editorial/opinion page.

An early book, *Politics, Americanism, and Christianity* (Baker Books, 1976), was honored by *Christianity Today* as one of the "best books of 1976." His study of the Tennessee Labor movement won the prestigious "Best Book Award" in 1995 from the Tennessee Historical Society and Tennessee Library Association. His recent major book, *American Rhetorical Excellence: 101 Public Addresses That Shaped the Nation's History and Culture* (Archway Publishers, 2017) received critical acclaim in the *Southern Communication Journal*; this book is the most up-to-date and fulsome single volume on American public address, one of Cotham's major interests. Another recent study explores all kinds of religious communication in the U. S. culture: *From Pilgrim Pulpit to the Electronic Era: The Varieties of American Religious Communication* (Westbow Press, 2014). One of his favorite religious book publications has been *One World/Many Neighbors: A Christian Perspective on Worldviews* (ACU Press, 2008).

Cotham and wife, Glenda, enjoy three children and nine grandchildren and four great grandchildren. He has an avid interest in all kinds of collegiate and professional sports and his hobbies include hiking, biking, and tennis.